The aim of the **Overcoming** series is to e̶........
common problems and disorders to take control of their own reco̶...
program. Each title, with its specially tailored program, is devised by a
practicing clinician using the latest techniques of cognitive behavioral
therapy – techniques which have been shown to be highly effective in
changing the way patients think about themselves and their problems.

The series was initiated in 1993 by Peter Cooper, Professor of
Psychology at Reading University and Research Fellow at the
University of Cambridge in the UK, whose original volume on
overcoming bulimia nervosa and binge-eating continues to help
many people in the USA, the UK and Europe.

Titles in the series include:

OVERCOMING DEPRESSION

*A self-help guide using
Cognitive Behavioral Techniques*

PAUL GILBERT

BASIC

BOOKS

A member of the Perseus Books Group
New York

Copyright © 1977, 2000, 2009 by Paul Gilbert

Published by Basic Books,
A Member of the Perseus Books Group
All rights reserved. Printed in Great Britain.
No part of this book may be reproduced in any manner
whatsoever without written permission except in the case of brief
quotations embodied in critical articles and reviews.
For information, address
Basic Books, 387 Park Avenue South,
New York, NY 10016-8810

Books published by Basic Books are available at special discounts
for bulk purchases in the United States by corporations, institutions
and other organizations. For more information, please contact
the Special Markets Department at the Perseus Books Group,
2300 Chestnut Street, Suite 200, Philadelphia, PA 19103,
or call (800) 255-1514, or e-mail special.markets@perseusbooks.com

First published in the UK in 2009 by Constable & Robinson Ltd.

A CIP catalog record for this book is available from the Library of Congress.

ISBN 978-0-465-01508-5

Important Note
This book is not intended as a substitute for medical advice or treatment.
Any person with a condition requiring medical attention should consult a
qualified medical practitioner or suitable therapist.

10 9 8 7 6 5 4 3 2 1

Table of contents

Acknowledgments

The Mental Health Research Unit was set up in 1996 as a joint project between the University of Derby and what is now the Derbyshire Mental Health Services NHS Trust. I am extremely grateful for their vision and support in our work. The Mental Health Research Unit continues to seek research funds and engage in research into mental health difficulties. There are many people in my unit I would like to thank. Special thanks go to Corinne Gale (research psychologist and research coordinator) and Kirsten McEwan (research psychologist and statistician) for their extraordinary dedication, hard work and wonderfully friendly dispositions. Special thanks also go to Lesley Futter for her hard work with this manuscript and with the Mental Health Research Unit. Thanks also to our super-efficient Kelly Sims who has just joined us. We are deeply indebted to Keith Wilshere for his skilful management of our unit, encouragement on the compassion projects, and keeping us all afloat, as well as his brilliant bass playing and technical skills for Still Minds.

Thanks to Sue Procter for her help in our first study of compassion-focused group therapy. Thanks also to psychologists Sharon Pallant, Michelle Cree and Andrew Rayner for their compassion-focused in-patient work. Two years ago some colleagues and I also set up a charity which has the mission statement 'To promote well-being through the scientific understanding and application of compassion'. If you go to the website at *www.compassionatemind.co.uk*, you will find lots of information, and you can download several of our publications. Key people have been fundamental to the development and support of this project, and special thanks go to my friend of over 30 years, Chris Gillespie. I would also like to thank the other board members: Chris Irons, Ken Goss, Mary Welford, Ian Lowens, Deborah Lee, Thomas Schroder and Jean Gilbert. Thanks to Diane Woollands for her skilful management of the website and board.

The University of Derby Psychology Department has been supportive, and thanks go to James Elander and in particular Frances Maratos for her support and expertise in fMRI, and enthusiasm for further studies on compassion with the universities of Aston and Glasgow. We are very excited about these studies; find out more on our website. Thanks also to Michael Townend for his enthusiasm and support for compassion-focused therapy. I would also like to thank Bob Leahy of the International Association of Cognitive Behavioral Therapists for his friendship and scholarship. I am also delighted to be able to thank the British Association for Behavioural and Cognitive Psychotherapies for their openness, support, friendliness and putting up with a quirky, evolutionary, archetype- and compassion-focused dude like me.

Nick Robinson and his staff at Constable & Robinson have been tireless in working to advance this series. They have been lovely to work with and special thanks go to Nick himself, Fritha Saunders for her soothing, and Eryl Humphrey Jones.

Last but of course not least, many thanks to my supportive family, Jean, Hannah and James, perhaps the biggest antidote to depression.

I would like to dedicate this book to all depressed people: may compassion help you light a candle in your darkness. I offer my immense gratitude to all those depressed people who have been honest and open and have educated and guided me in my therapeutic efforts.

Foreword

Many, perhaps the majority, of those who go to see their family doctor have some type of psychological problem which makes them anxious or unhappy. There may be a fairly obvious reason for this – the loneliness of widowhood or the stresses of bringing up a family – or it may be that their mental state is part of their personality, something they were born with or a reaction to traumatic experiences in their lives. Despite being so common, I soon discovered after starting in general practice over ten years ago that this type of mental disturbance (usually described as a *neurosis* to distinguish it from the *psychosis* of those with a serious mental illness like schizophrenia) is particularly difficult to deal with. What are the options? Well, there are always drugs – minor tranquillizers, antidepressants and sleeping pills. It is certainly easy enough to write a prescription and more often than not the patient feels a lot better as a result, but there is no getting away from the fact that drugs are a chemical fix. Sometimes this is all that is necessary to tide someone over a difficult period, but more usually the same old problems recur when the drugs are discontinued.

The alternatives to drugs are the 'talking therapies' ranging from psychoanalysis to counselling that seek to sort out the underlying cause of anxiety or unhappiness. Psychoanalysis is out of the question for many, being too prolonged – often lasting for years – and too expensive. Counselling certainly can be helpful for no other reason than that unburdening one's soul to a sympathetic listener is invariably therapeutic. But once the counselling sessions were over, I got the impression it was only a matter of time before the psychological distress reappeared.

Here, then, is one of the great paradoxes of modern medicine. Doctors can now transplant hearts, replace arthritic hips and cure meningitis but, confronted by the commonest reason why people seek their advice, they have remarkably little to offer. And then a couple of years ago I started to hear about a new type of psychological treatment – cognitive therapy – which, it was claimed, was not only straightforward but demonstrably effective. I was initially sceptical as I found it difficult to imagine what sort of breakthrough insight into human psychology should lie behind such remarkable claims. The human brain is, after all, the most complex entity in existence, so it would seem unlikely that someone had suddenly now at the end of the twentieth century found the key that unlocked the mysteries of neuroses – a key that had eluded human understanding for hundreds of years.

The central insight of cognitive therapy is not, it emerges, a new discovery, but rather is based on the profound observation originally formulated by the French philosopher Descartes that the essential feature of human consciousness was 'cogito ergo sum' – 'I think therefore I am.' We *are* our thoughts and the contents of our thoughts have a major influence on our emotions. Cognitive therapy is based on the principle that certain types of thought that we have about ourselves – whether, at its simplest, we are loved or wanted or despised or boring – have a major effect on the way we perceive the world. If we feel unloved, the world will appear unloving, and then every moment of every day our sense of being unloved is confirmed. That, after all, is what depression is all about. These types of thoughts are called 'automatic thoughts' because they operate on the margins of our consciousness as a continual sort of internal monologue. If these thoughts are identified and brought out into the open then the state of mind that they sustain, whether anxiety or depression or any of the other neuroses, can begin to be resolved.

So this type of therapy is called 'cognitive' because it is primarily about changing our thoughts about ourselves, the world and the future. The proof of the pudding, as they say, is in the eating and the very fact that this type of therapy has been shown to work so well, in countless well-controlled studies, is powerful confirmation that the underlying insight that our thoughts lie behind, and sustain, neurotic illnesses is in essence correct.

Nonetheless, some may be forgiven for having misgivings. The concept of cognitive therapy takes some getting used to and it is certainly hard to credit that complex psychological problems can be explained by such an apparently simple concept. There is perhaps an understandable impression that it all sounds a bit oversimplified or trite, that it fails to get to the root cause of the source of anxiety or depression.

So it is necessary to dig a bit deeper to examine the origins of cognitive therapy and perhaps the easiest way of doing this is to compare it with what for many is the archetype of all forms of psychotherapy – psychoanalysis. Psychoanalysis claims to identify the source of neuroses in the long-forgotten and repressed traumas of early childhood, so it is less concerned with thoughts themselves than with the hidden meaning which (it claims) underlies them. The important question, though, is whether psychoanalysis does make people better, or at least less unhappy. Many people certainly believe they have been helped, but when Professor Gavin Andrews of the University of New

South Wales reviewed all the studies in which the outcome of psychoanalysis had been objectively measured in the *British Journal of Psychiatry* in 1994, he was unable to show that it worked any better than 'just talking'.

In cognitive therapy, the importance of human thoughts lies precisely in their content and how that influences the way a person feels about themselves, a point well illustrated by one of its early pioneers, Aaron Beck. Back in the sixties, while practising as a psychoanalyst in Philadelphia, Beck was treating a young woman with an anxiety state which he initially interpreted in true psychoanalytic fashion as being due to a failure to resolve sexual conflict arising from problems in childhood. During one session he noticed that his patient seemed particularly uneasy and, on enquiring why, it emerged she felt embarrassed because she thought she was expressing herself badly and that she sounded trite and foolish. 'These self-evaluative thoughts were very striking,' Beck recalled, 'because she was actually very articulate.' Probing further he found that this false pattern of thinking – that she was dull and uninteresting – permeated all her relationships. He concluded that her chronic anxiety had little to do with her sex life but rather arose from a constant state of dread that her lover might desert her because he found her as uninteresting as she thought herself to be.

Over the next few years, Beck found that he was able to identify similar and quite predictable patterns of thinking in nearly all his patients. For the first time he realized that he was getting inside his patients' minds and beginning to see the world as they experienced it, something he had been unable to do in all his years as a psychoanalyst. From that perspective he went on to develop the principles of cognitive therapy.

Compared to psychoanalysis, cognitive therapy certainly does appear much simpler, but we should not take this to mean that it is less profound. The central failure of the founders of psycho-analysis was that they did not recognize the true significance of thoughts in human neurosis. Once that significance was grasped by those like Aaron Beck then human psychological disorders became more readily understandable and therefore simpler, but it is the simplicity of an elegant scientific hypothesis that more fully explains the facts. It can't be emphasized too strongly the enormous difference that cognitive therapy has made. Now it is possible to explain quite straightforwardly what is wrong in such a way that people are reassured, while allowing them to be optimistic that their problems can be resolved. Here, at last, is a talking therapy that works.

Professor Gavin Andrews in his review in the *British Journal of Psychiatry* identified cognitive therapy as 'the treatment of choice' in generalized anxiety, obsessive compulsive disorders and depression. It has in addition been shown to be effective in the treatment of eating disorders, panic attacks and even in the management of marital and sexual difficulties, in chronic pain syndromes and many emotional disorders of childhood. Its contribution to the alleviation of human suffering is remarkable.

James Le Fanu, GP

Introduction

Why a cognitive behavioral approach?

The approach this book takes in attempting to help you over-come depression is a 'cognitive-behavioral' one. A brief account of the history of this form of intervention might be useful and encouraging. In the 1950s and 1960s a set of therapeutic tech-niques was developed, collectively termed 'behavior therapy'. These techniques shared two basic features. First, they aimed to remove symptoms (such as anxiety) by dealing with those symptoms themselves, rather than their deep-seated under-lying historical causes (traditionally the focus of psychoanalysis, the approach developed by Sigmund Freud and his associates). Second, they were scientifically based, in the sense that they used techniques derived from what laboratory psychologists were finding out about the mechanisms of learning, and they put these techniques to scientific test. The area where behavior therapy initially proved to be of most value was in the treat-ment of anxiety disorders, especially specific phobias (such as extreme fear of animals or heights) and agoraphobia, both noto-riously difficult to treat using conventional psychotherapies.

After an initial flush of enthusiasm, discontent with behavior therapy grew. There were a number of reasons for this, an impor-tant one of which was the fact that behavior therapy did not deal with the internal thoughts which were so obviously central to the distress that many patients were experiencing. In particular, behavior therapy proved inadequate when it came to the treatment of depression. In the late 1960s and early 1970s a treatment for depression was developed called 'cognitive therapy'. The pioneer in this enterprise was an American psychiatrist, Professor Aaron T. Beck. He developed a theory of depression which emphasized the importance of people's depressed styles of thinking, and, on the basis of this theory, he specified a new form of therapy. It would not be an exaggeration to say that Beck's work has changed the nature of psychotherapy, not just for depression but for a range of psychological problems.

The techniques introduced by Beck have been merged with the techniques developed earlier by the behavior therapists to produce a therapeutic approach which has come to be known as 'cognitive behavioral therapy' (or CBT). This therapy has been subjected to the strictest scientific testing and has been found to be highly successful for a significant proportion of cases of depression. In recent years, one variation on CBT for depression has been the introduction of 'mindfulness' techniques. Another has been the appreciation of the importance of compassion in overcoming depression. Both of these innovations are dealt with extensively within this new edition of *Overcoming Depression*.

It has now become clear that specific patterns of disturbed thinking are associated with a wide range of psychological problems, not just depression, and that the treatments which deal with these are highly effective. So, effective cognitive behavioral treatments have been developed for a range of anxiety disorders, such as panic disorder, generalized anxiety disorder, specific phobias, social phobia, obsessive compulsive disorders, health anxiety, as well as for other conditions such as drug addictions, and eating disorders like bulimia nervosa. Indeed, cognitive behavioral techniques have been found to have an application beyond the narrow categories of psychological disorders. They have been applied effectively, for example, to helping people with weight problems, couples with marital difficulties, as well as those who wish to give up smoking or deal with drinking problems. They have also been effectively applied to dealing with low self-esteem.

The starting-point for CBT is the realization that the way we think, feel and behave are all intimately linked, and changing the way we think about ourselves, our experiences, and the world around us changes the way we feel and what we are able to do. So, for example, by helping a depressed person identify and challenge their automatic depressive thoughts, a route out of the cycle of depressive thoughts and feelings can be found. Similarly, habitual behavioral responses are driven by a complex set of thoughts and feelings, and CBT, as you will discover from this book, by providing a means for the behavior, thoughts and feelings to be brought under control, enables these responses to be undermined and a different kind of life to be possible.

Although effective CBT treatments have been developed for a wide range of disorders and problems, these treatments are not currently widely available; and, when people try on their own to help themselves, they often, inadvertently, do things which make matters worse. In recent years, experts in a wider range of areas have taken the principles and techniques of specific cognitive behavioral therapies for particular problems and presented them in manuals (the *Overcoming* series) which people can read and apply themselves. These manuals specify a systematic program of treatment which the person works through to overcome their difficulties. In this way, cognitive behavioral therapeutic techniques of proven value are being made available on the widest possible basis.

The use of self-help manuals is never going to replace the need for therapists, and many people with emotional and behavioral problems will need the help of a qualified professional. It is also the case that, despite the widespread success of cognitive behavioral therapy, some people will not respond to it and will need one of the other treatments available. Nevertheless, although research on the use of these self-help manuals is at an early stage, the work done to date indicates that for a large number of people, such a manual is sufficient for them to overcome their problems without professional help. Sadly, many people suffer on their own for years. Sometimes they feel reluctant to seek help without first making a serious effort to manage on their own. Often they feel too awkward or even ashamed to ask for help. It may be that appropriate help is not forthcoming, despite their best efforts to find it. For many of these people, the cognitive behavioral self-help manual will provide a lifeline to a better future.

Peter J Cooper
The University of Reading, 2009

Preface to the third edition

Bringing compassion to our practice

When Nick Robinson invited me to prepare a third edition of *Overcoming Depression* I was both delighted and daunted. I was delighted because it is over 10 years since the second edition was written and so much has happened in that time in regard to working with depression. I was daunted because I knew there would have to be a fairly substantial rewriting. So, over a year and many five o'clock in the mornings later, here we are.

What is so new that we should get excited? One thing is that the past 10 years has seen a major focus on what is called *mindfulness*. Mindfulness was originally developed within ancient spiritual traditions in the East. Like many other traditions, it proposes that our attention and thoughts contribute to our well-being or distress. It teaches ways to attend to the thoughts and feelings in our minds by becoming more observant and non-judgemental. It also provides various 'exercises' we can practise, which help to balance our state of mind. There is increasing research evidence that this can be extremely helpful to us when we are depressed (and throughout our lives). It is particularly helpful when we tend to avoid our feelings or ruminate on them or judge them to be bad or overwhelming. Chapter 7 is dedicated to this approach.

The second major excitement is the way that our understanding of *compassion* has developed in the past 10 years. We are learning how we can develop it as a major antidote to depression. There is increasing evidence that training ourselves in compassion and kindness, with regular practice, can actually change our brains. Researchers are now exploring this in detail.

This is exciting, because humans have evolved to be very responsive to kindness. For example, babies don't survive or grow without care and support. If we think about times when we're distressed, it is easy to recognize that the kindness of others helps to soothe us and pull us through. We have also discovered that individuals who are kind and supportive to themselves are also more resilient to life's difficulties than those who are critical and self-condemning. Our brain does not respond very well to self-criticism.

In the preface to the first edition, written 15 years ago, I wrote that 'I see depression as a state of mind that we have a potential for, just as we have a potential to feel grief, fear, sexual arousal and so forth. And like any state of mind, depression is associated with very real changes in the brain.' I went on to say that depression is a brain state and a brain pattern that can affect any of us to differing degrees. Once we know this, then all efforts can be aimed at changing this brain pattern, trying to shift brain states (discussed on my CD *Overcoming Depression*). This is where kindness comes in again, because in Chapter 2 I outline in detail how our emotional systems work to create different patterns and states of mind. I also describe how a combination of mindfulness and compassion can help balance them.

The key message is that there are many ideas to help us when depression grabs hold of our feelings, thoughts and behaviors. We can however learn to act against the desire to withdraw that operates within depression. We can stand back and view our thoughts from the balcony, as it were, and develop a balanced perspective rather than an overly hostile, critical or pessimistic one. We can learn to develop and seek out helpful and supportive relationships.

Whatever we choose to do to bring more balance to our minds, if we learn to do it with the feelings and intentions of kindness, support and encouragement, recognizing how painful and hard depression is, we are more likely to be successful. When we allow ourselves to feel compassionate – and for some people that is quite a big step – we open ourselves up to being helped and to healing things we may be ashamed of.

Many of the original ideas are still core to this book, but they are now more linked to the importance of compassion for oneself and others, and how to develop it. If you like this approach you may want to pursue it further in other writings, or perhaps further your own explorations into its healing properties.

You will see that as in the previous editions I use a lot of case material. For confidentiality reasons I can only include stories that people have agreed I can use; elsewhere I have combined themes and created fictional characters. To protect confidentiality they are designed to be non-identifiable, and are used primarily to create a narrative that helps the reader's understanding.

I know this a long book but we cover a lot of ground, and you can easily dip in and out of it. Good luck.

Preface to the first edition

Sadly, some people seem at risk of certain types of depression, and we now know that genes appear to play a role. However, while I do not want to underplay the biological dimension of depression, some forms are surprisingly common and genes probably play a major role only in a minority of cases. Life events and early childhood experiences seem by far the more common sources. I suspect this was true for me. My early years were spent in West Africa. It was a place of tremendous freedoms and I would roam happily in the outback. For nearly a year we lived in the 'bush' with no running water or electricity – and no school! My memories are still vivid of that time and when the skies are dull and cold I remember with great fondness the excitements, the blue skies and expansiveness of Africa. When I came home to England to go to boarding school I found the confinement and harshness of it difficult. I also found that I was behind in my education and had serious problems with the English language. To this day I do not like confinements and can easily feel trapped in places. The life events that triggered my depression were all related to feeling trapped and failing.

I see depression as a state of mind that we have a potential for, just as we have the potential to feel grief, fear, sexual arousal and so forth. And like any state of mind, depression is associated with very real changes in the brain. In my own work I have explored the reasons for this by thinking about the typical things that tend to trigger depression. This led to a consideration of whether the capacity for depression might be something that evolved along with us as we plodded the conflict-ridden trail from reptiles to monkey to humans. I won't go into the details of that except to say that depression probably affects animals. As with humans, depression seems to strike mostly when an animal loses status (is defeated), loses control and/or is trapped in adverse environments. When these things happen the brain seems to switch into depressed-like states. In humans, signals of being valued as a person have evolved as important mediators of mood states.

The other thing to consider, if we stay with an evolutionary view for a moment, is that although the brain is a highly complex organ it is also something of a 'contraption'. Deep in our brains are structures that evolved with the reptiles. Neuropsychologists even called this part of the brain 'the reptilian brain'. Evolution does not create totally new designs. Rather, old designs are adapted, added to or altered as a species evolves. It is rather like developing a car, but each new design must include the old – you can't go back to the drawing board and start afresh. So the brain has various structures within it that stretch way back many millions of years. This is why we can see the brain as a cobbling together of different bits that do different things. We have the potential for great violence, terror, lust, love and compassion. We are a mosaic of possibilities arising out of this jerry-built brain of ours.

Provided these various parts of the brain work together then it functions reasonably well, but if they get out of balance then it functions less well. Due perhaps to childhood trauma or difficulties and later stressful life events, we sometimes find it difficult to keep this mixed array of possibilities under control. They start pulling in different directions. The brain may tell us that there is far more danger than there is, and we panic; it may tell us that we are inferior, worthless and to give in, and we feel depressed; it may tell us that we need to get our own back, and so we seethe with the desire for revenge. Each of these parts has its own job to do, but they must work in harmony. In depression we lose this harmony and have thoughts and ideas that lead us to feel more defeated, inferior and worthless, and thus more depressed.

What we find in depression is that people experience all kinds of thoughts and feelings coming from different systems within the brain, and these can be difficult to control or make sense of. Another way to think of this is that we have different parts to ourselves and can play different roles, e.g. child, hero, lover, parent, friend, enemy, helper and so on. Evolution has provided many brain systems that enable us to enact different roles. Each part tends to see the world in its own way. For example, the hero part strides out and risks all. The coward part says, 'You must be joking. I'm not going out there.' Now if the two work together then they will make a sensible compromise and evaluation of risk. But if the hero does not listen to the coward then the hero puts the self in danger. On the other hand, if the coward does not listen to the hero, the coward just hides in the corner. In reality, of course, there are no actual 'parts' as such; what we experience is the activation, to a greater or lesser degree, of different brain systems. When we pay attention to our thoughts and feelings we can actually recognize which brain systems are turned on. Our thoughts and feelings are windows on these different systems in us.

So what to do if you feel depressed? The first thing to say is that the thoughts we have when we are depressed tell us that the depression system is switched on. That may not seem very helpful, until we realize that there may be ways to turn it off again and bring ourselves back into balance. For example, when we are depressed we may think in ways that seem right 'to the depression', but which may seem very wrong to other parts of ourselves. The rational and compassionate parts of ourselves may have a very different view of things. The more we can say, 'OK, my depression is a part of me; one of my many brain systems, but it can't be relied on to be accurate or helpful', the more we can step in to try to take control of it.

Second, as we get depressed the depression system tends to throw other systems out of balance. For example, we may become more irritable or anxious. And as a result we may judge ourselves and/or others more harshly, which feeds the depression. Typical of depression is to devalue things, usually ourselves and accomplishments, but we may also devalue others. We may start to believe that things are darker than they are.

Third, depression is about how the brain is operating at any particular time. So depression is very much felt 'in the body' and is about feelings. Depression was designed (evolved) to slow us down, to weaken self-confidence and make us more sensitive to possible social losses and threats. It does this by changing the way our bodies work. However, if we can get other systems to challenge the depression, by learning how to think differently about ourselves and events, then we have an opportunity to get things back into balance. This book will discuss how to recognize important depressing thoughts to work with and how to challenge them.

This book is for people who would like to know more about depression – what it is and how to help oneself. It is not a cure-all, nor a substitute for therapies like drugs or psychotherapy, nor can a book like this change the painful realities of living.

It is simply one approach. Each person's depression is, in part, similar to other people's and in part unique to that person. What understanding can do is to offer a way to move out of depression rather than plunge further into it. There are many ways to challenge some of the negative thinking of depression. I will try to point out some pitfalls to watch out for and suggest some methods that will enable you to develop a more rational and compassionate approach to yourself.

The book is divided into three parts. The first is the most technical. I have included this because many of the depressed people I see say that they would like to know more about depression itself. If it seems too technical, you can skip those bits you find difficult to follow; in fact, you can skip the whole of Part I if you like. Part II outlines some basic approaches to self-help. Here we will explore the role of thoughts and feelings, and how to challenge some of the thoughts and feelings that lead to a downward slide. There is a chapter devoted to how depressed people treat themselves (which is often very badly) and how to treat yourself more kindly. The more you learn to value yourself (or at least to stop devaluing yourself), the greater the chances of turning the depression system off. Each chapter in Part II is followed by a series of exercises you can try. In Part III the basic approaches covered in Part II are applied to special problems. These include the need for approval, anger, shame, lack of assertiveness, disappointment and perfectionism.

You will read of many other people's depression. All names have, of course, been changed. Also, to avoid any chance of identification, the details of all the stories have been altered. Sometimes two or three cases have been rolled into one, again to avoid identification. The focus of each problem is on the specific themes that reveal the dilemmas and complexities of depression.

Our journey together may be a long one, but I hope it will equip you with some ideas of how to move out of depression. Recovering from depression usually requires time, effort and patience, but if you know what you are trying to achieve, and have a way forward, you are likely to be more successful in your efforts. So let's begin.

PART ONE

Understanding Depression

1

What is depression?

If you suffer from depression, you are, sadly, far from being alone. In fact, it has been estimated that there may be over 350 million people in the world today who have it. Depression has afflicted humans for as long as records have been kept. Indeed, it was first named as a condition about 2,400 years ago by the famous ancient Greek doctor Hippocrates, who called it 'melancholia'. It is also worth noting that although we cannot ask animals how they feel, it is likely that they also have the capacity to feel depressed: they can certainly behave as if they do. To a greater or lesser degree, we all have the potential to become depressed, just as we all have the potential to become anxious, to grieve or to fall in love.

Depression is no respecter of status or fortune. Indeed, many famous people throughout history have had it. King Solomon, Abraham Lincoln, Winston Churchill and the Finnish composer Jean Sibelius are well-known examples from history. What is important to remember is that depression is not about human weakness.

What do we mean by 'depression'?

This is a difficult question to answer, because a lot depends on who you ask. The word itself can be used to describe a type of weather, a fall in the stock market, a hollow in the ground and, of course, our moods. It comes from the Latin *deprimere*, meaning to 'press down'. The term was first applied to a mood state in the seventeenth century.

If you suffer from depression, one thing you will know is that it is far more than just feeling 'down'. In fact, depression affects not only how we feel, but how we think about things, our energy levels, our concentration, our sleep, even our interest in sex. Depression has an effect on many aspects of our lives. Let's look at some of these.

- **Motivation**. Depression affects our motivation to do things. We can feel apathetic and experience a loss of energy and interest, nothing seems worth doing. If we have children, we can lose interest in them and then feel guilty. Each day can be a struggle of having to force ourselves to perform even the smallest of activities. Some depressed people lose interest in things. Others keep their interest but don't enjoy things when they do them, or are just very tired and lack the energy to do the things they would like to do.

- **Emotions**. People often think that depression is only about low mood or feeling fed-up – and this is certainly part of it. Indeed, the central symptom of depression is called 'anhedonia'– derived from the ancient Greek meaning 'without pleasure'– and means the **loss of the capacity to experience any pleasure**. Life seems empty; we are joyless. But – and this is an important 'but' – although the ability to have positive feelings and emotions is reduced, we can experience an increase in negative emotions, especially anger. We may be churning inside with anger and resentment that we can't express. We might become extremely irritable, snap at our children and relatives and sometimes even lash out at them. We may then feel guilty about this, and this makes us more depressed. Other very common symptoms are anxiety and fear. When we are depressed, we can feel extremely vulnerable. Things that we may have done easily before seem frightening, and at times it is difficult to know why. We can suddenly feel anxious at a bus or shop queue or even meeting friends. Anger and anxiety are very much part of depression. Other negative feelings that can increase in depression are sadness, guilt, shame, envy and jealousy.

- **Thinking**. Depression interferes with the way we think in two ways. First, it affects concentration and memory. We find that we can't get our minds to settle on anything. Reading a book or watching television becomes impossible. We don't remember things too well, and we are prone to forget things. However, it is easier to remember negative things than positive things. The second way that depression affects our thoughts is **in the way we think** about ourselves, our future and the world. Very few people who are depressed feel good about themselves. Generally, they tend to see themselves as inferior, flawed, bad or worthless. If you ask a depressed person about their future, they are likely to respond with: 'What future?' The future seems dark, a blank or a never-ending cycle of defeat and losses. Like many strong emotions, depression pushes us to more extreme forms of thinking. Our thoughts become 'all or nothing' – we are either a complete success or an abject failure.

- **Images**. When we are depressed, the imagery we use to describe it tends to be dark. We may talk about being under a dark cloud, in a deep hole or pit, or a dark room. Winston Churchill called his depression his 'black dog'. The imagery of depression is always about darkness, being stuck somewhere and not able to get out. If you were to paint a picture of your depression, it would probably involve dark or harsh colours rather than light, soft ones. Darkness and entrapment are key internal images.

- **Behaviors**. Our behavior changes when we become depressed. We engage in much less positive activity and may withdraw socially and want to hide away. Many of the things we might have enjoyed doing before becoming depressed now seem like an ordeal. Because everything seems to take so much effort, we do much less than we used to. Our behavior towards other people can change, too. We tend to do fewer positive things with others and are more likely to find ourselves in conflict with them. If we become very anxious, we might also start to avoid meeting people or lose our social confidence. Depressed people sometimes become agitated and find it difficult to relax. They feel like trapped animals, restless, pace about and can't sit still, wanting to do something but not knowing what. Sometimes, the desire to escape and run away can be very strong. However, where to go and what to do is unclear. On the other hand, some depressed people become very slowed down. They walk slowly, with a stoop, their thoughts seem stuck, and everything feels 'heavy'.

- **Physiology**. When we are depressed there are many changes in our bodies and brains. There is nothing sinister about this. To say that our brains work differently when we are depressed is really to state the obvious. Indeed, any mental state, be it a happy, sexual, excited, anxious or depressed one, will be associated with physical changes in our brains. Recent research has shown that some of these are related to stress hormones such as cortisol, which indicates that depression involves the body's stress system. Certain brain chemicals, called neurotransmitters, are also affected. Generally, there are fewer of these chemicals in the brain when we are depressed, and this is why some people find benefit from drugs that allow them to build up. The next chapters will explore these more fully. Probably as a result of the physical changes that occur in depression, we can experience a host of other unwanted symptoms. Not only are energy levels affected, so is sleep. You may wake up early, sometimes in the middle of the night or early morning, or you may find it difficult to get to sleep, although some depressed people sleep more. In addition, losing your appetite is quite common and food may start to taste like cardboard, so some depressed people lose weight. Others may eat more and put on weight.

- **Social relationships**. Even though we may try to hide our depression, it almost always affects other people. We are less fun to be with. We can be irritable and find ourselves continually saying no. The key thing here is that this is quite common and has been since humans first felt depressed. We need to acknowledge these feelings and not feel ashamed about them. Feeling ashamed can make us more depressed. There are various reasons why our relationships might suffer. There may be conflicts that we feel unable to sort out. There may be unvoiced resentments. We may feel out of control. Our friends and partners may not understand what has happened to us. Remember the old saying, 'Laugh and the world laughs with you. Cry and you cry alone'? Depression is difficult for others to comprehend at times.

- **Brain states**. A useful way to think of depression, then, is that it is a change in 'brain states'. In this altered state, many thing are happening to your energy levels, feelings, thoughts and body rhythms. There are many reasons for this change in brain state that we call depression, and there are many different patterns that are linked to depression, as we will see. But the key thing is to recognize there has been a change in brain state, and your thoughts and feelings are linked to that. It is very important **not to blame yourself** for the difficulties that this depressed brain state makes for you, but rather **work out what will help you shift it** – and that is what we will be exploring in this book.

Are all depressions the same?

The short answer to this is no. There are a number of different types. One that researchers and professionals commonly refer to is called 'major depression'. According to the American Psychiatric Association, one can be said to have major depression if one has at least five of the possible symptoms listed in Table 1.1, which have to be present for at least two weeks.

I have included this list of symptoms here to give you an idea of how some professionals tend to think about depression. Although a list like the one in Table 1.1 is important to professionals, it does not really capture the variety and complexity of the experience of depression. For example, I would include feelings of being trapped as a common depressed symptom, and many psychologists feel that hopelessness, irritability, and anxiety are also very central to depression.

TABLE 1.1 SYMPTOMS OF DEPRESSION

You must have one of these symptoms:	Low mood
	Marked loss of pleasure
You must have at least four of of these symptoms:	Significant change in appetite and a loss of at least 5 per cent normal body weight
	Sleep disturbance
	Agitation or feelings of being slowed down
	Loss of energy or feeling fatigued virtually every day
	Feelings of worthlessness, low self-esteem, tendency to feel guilty
	Loss of the ability to concentrate
	Thoughts of death and suicide

Researchers distinguish between those mental conditions that involve only depression and those that also involve swings into mania. In the manic state, a person can feel enormously energetic, confident and full of their own self-importance, and may have great interest in sex. If the mania is not too severe, they can accomplish a lot. People who have swings into depression and (hypo)mania are often diagnosed as suffering from *bipolar illness* (meaning that they can swing to both poles of mood, high and low). The old term was manic depression. Those who only suffer depression are diagnosed as having *unipolar depression*.

Another distinction that some researchers and professionals make is between *psychotic* and *neurotic* depression. In psychotic depression, the person has various false beliefs called *delusions*. For example, a person without any physical illness might come to believe that he or she has a serious cancer and will shortly die. Some years ago, one of my patients was admitted to hospital because she had been contacting lawyers and undertakers to arrange her will and her funeral as she was sure that she would die before Christmas. She believed that the hospital staff were keeping this important information from her to avoid upsetting her, and she tried to advise her young children on how they should cope without her (causing great distress to the family, of course). Sometimes people with a psychotic illness can develop extreme feelings of guilt. For example, they may be certain in their minds they have caused the Iraq war, or done something terrible. Psychotic depression is obviously a very serious disorder, requiring expert help but, compared with the non-psychotic depressions, it is quite rare.

Another distinction that is sometimes made is between those depressions that seem to come out of the blue and those that are related to life events, e.g., when people become depressed after losing a job, the death of a loved one or the ending of an important relationship. However, in psychotherapy, we often find that, as we get to know a person in depth, what looks like a depression that came out of the blue actually may have its seeds in childhood.

Clearly some depressions are more serious, deep and debilitating than others. In many cases, depressed people manage to keep going until the depression eventually passes. In more serious depression this is extremely difficult, and getting professional help is important. Depressions can vary in terms of onset, severity, duration and frequency.

- **Onset**. Depression can have an acute onset (i.e. within days or weeks) or come on gradually (over months or years). It can begin at any time, but late adolescence, early adulthood and later life are particularly vulnerable times.
- **Severity**. Symptoms may be mild, moderate or severe.
- **Duration**. Some people will come out of their depression within weeks or months, whereas for others it may last in a fluctuating, chronic form for many years. 'Chronic

depression' is said to last longer than two years, and 10–20 per cent of depressed people have it.

- **Frequency**. Some people may only have one episode of depression, whereas others may have many. About 50 per cent of people who have been depressed will have a recurrence.

The fact that depression can recur may seem alarming, but this should really come as no surprise. Suppose, for example, that since a young age you have always felt inferior and worthless. One day this sense of inferiority seems to get the better of you and you feel a complete failure in every aspect of your life. Perhaps a drug will help you to recover from that episode, but even if you become better, you may still retain, deep down, those feelings of failure and inferiority. Drugs do not retrain us or enable us to mature and throw off these underlying beliefs. Therapies are now being developed to help prevent relapses.

How common is depression?

As indicated, depression is, sadly, very common. If we look at what is called major depression, the figures are:

	Women	Men
	(per cent)	
Having depression at any one time	4–10	2–3.5
Lifetime risk	10–26	5–12

The figures are even higher in some communities (e.g., with poverty). Moreover problems such as eating disorders, drug and alcohol problems and aggressiveness can also be linked to depression, and recede as depression is treated. New research also indicates that rates of and risks for depression have been steadily increasing throughout the twentieth century, but the reasons for this are unclear. Socio-economic changes, the fragmentation of families and communities, the loss of hope in the younger generation – especially the unemployed – and increasing levels of expectations may all be implicated.

In general, then, there are many forms of depression – in fact, so many that the term itself is not so helpful. But it is important to recognize that not all depressions are the same and they can vary greatly in severity and duration.

KEY POINTS

- Depression is very common and has been for thousands of years.
- Depression involves many different symptoms. Emotions such as anger and anxiety are common and at times more troubling than the low mood itself. People who are depressed may also have a strong desire to escape, for which they may feel guilty.
- There are many different types of depression.
- Some depressions are quite severe, while others are less so but still deeply disturbing and life-crippling.

If you suffer from depression, my key message to you is that if you feel a failure, if you have a lot of anger inside, feel on a short fuse; if you are terrified out of your wits, if you think life is not worth living, if you feel trapped and desperate to escape – whatever your feelings – these reflect your brain state, are not your fault, and millions of others have these feelings too. Of course, knowing this does not make your depression any less painful, but it does mean that there is **nothing bad about you because you are in this state of mind**. It is a shift in brain state that is painful – depression pulls us into thinking and feeling like this, so these feelings are sadly part of being depressed. True, some people who have not been depressed may not understand it, or may tell you to pull yourself together, but this does not mean that there is anything bad about you. It just means that they find it difficult to understand.

Importantly, there are many things that can be done to help us when we get depressed so a key message is: 'please talk to your family doctor.' There are some helpful (for some people) drugs (anti-depressants) available and many effective psychological treatments. We can learn to train our minds to shift us out of depressed brain states. This is covered in Parts II and III.

2

Causes of depression:
How and why it happens

As we saw in Chapter 1, when we are depressed our brains, bodies and minds shift to different patterns of thinking, feeling and behaving. We can call this *a depressed brain or mind state*. A key question, then, is how and why this happens. After all, these depressed states are very unpleasant and don't seem very helpful in our lives. Understanding why our brains can go into depressed patterns is a key research question. In the next few chapters we are going to explore this.

If you're feeling depressed, you may find these chapters tough going at times because they contain *technical* information, and it can be difficult to concentrate when you are depressed. Please don't worry about that. You don't need to read these sections if you don't want to, and even if you do read them it is quite likely that you may only remember one or two key ideas, so there is a summary at the end of each chapter. If you wish, just note those key points and go straight on to Part II, 'Learning How to Cope'. When you feel better, you could return to these chapters, or dip into them. I have expanded them from the first and second editions because depressed people and their relatives often ask to know more about what causes depression. I have also expanded them to explain a new focus on compassion.

Being gentle with ourselves will be helpful in our journey out of depression.

How our minds got to be the way they are: old brains and new minds

Old brain and mind – what we share with other animals

It is very easy for us humans to see ourselves as special and different from other animals because we have a certain self-awareness and recently evolved abilities to think, reflect, plan and ruminate – with a kind of 'new mind'. But even though this is true we also have many motives, emotions and social needs in common because of how our brains have evolved and are constructed. For example, animals (e.g., chimpanzees) can become anxious, angry, lustful, vengeful, sad, distressed, agitated or excited, happy, playful, and affectionate. Like us, too, they seek out certain positive things such as food and comforts, and create certain types of relationships. They can fight with each other over status or territory; they can seek each other out for protection, support and friendships; they can form close bonds; they can develop sexual relationships, and can be very attached to their offspring, protecting them, nurturing them and providing for them. Like us, too, they appear to become stressed and depressed if they are socially rejected, defeated or threatened. Indeed, we see these desires, encounters and relationships going on in their billions in many life forms on this planet every day.

We too are constantly engaging in these behaviors. From the day we are born we seek a loving and caring attachment with our parents. We can struggle for status, recognition and acceptance from other human beings. We want to form relationships with others who care about us and help us. We feel good when relationships go our way. We don't want to be criticized or rejected: then we can get sad, upset or angry. When things go wrong and we feel unable to achieve these desired goals, and/or we feel unloved, or rejected and inferior, our mood can go down, as it can for any other animal.

We can call all these forms of behavior, with their various desires and efforts, *archetypes* because they are forms of feeling and thinking that ripple through many life forms, including us. They give rise to our feelings and desires. Look at this carefully:

We did not create these desires for certain types of relationship and feelings – rather, they are created within us, from our genes and our evolutionary history and are shaped by our life experience.

The point is that we all just find ourselves with this body, with this mind with its varieties of emotions, born into particular families in particular places at particular times – none of which we choose. We sort of 'wake up' through our childhood to the fact of us 'being here' and then try to make the best we can of this strange mind of ours. So, much of what goes on in our minds is not our fault – evolution put these abilities there but, by understanding how our minds work, we can learn how better to cope with unpleasant feelings that can ripple through us, and train our minds to cope. We can influence how our brains are working and steer them towards feelings of well-being and away from depression.

The three emotion systems and their influence on our minds

Let's now look a little closer at how the brain helps us navigate through life, noticing and trying to avoid threats, seeking out things we want, and influencing our feelings in our relationships. The way the brain does this is very complex but we can simplify it in a very useful way. We have special brain systems (networks) that regulate three different types of emotion and action:

- a system that helps detect, track and respond to things that threaten us
- a system that gives rise to desires and feelings of motivation
- a system that helps us feel content, at peace, safe and happy. This system is especially important in social relationships when we feel cared for.[1]

These systems are constantly interacting and it is from their interactions that we get 'states of mind'. Figure 2.1 is a diagram of these interacting systems.

Types of Affect Regulation Systems

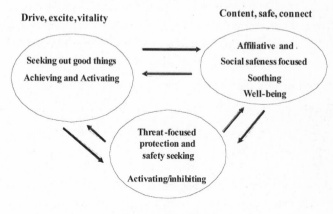

Figure 2.1 The interaction between our three major emotion regulation systems.

As we become depressed *the balance between these systems changes* and we have far *more* threat-linked feelings of anxiety, irritability, pessimism, shame and anger, far *fewer* feelings of motivation, energy and optimism, and also far *fewer* feelings of contentment, peacefulness and sense of connectedness to other people. It is helpful to understand this in terms of a shift in the balance of feeling and thinking systems. Then we can stand back from the depression and recognize that it is a particular pattern in our brains that we are having to deal with. The reasons these brain systems have become out of balance, or have taken up a new pattern, will be the subject of later chapters.

Thinking about depression in this way gives us an opportunity to think about how we can rebalance the three emotion systems. If you like, we can think about working on ourselves as a kind of *physiotherapy* for our minds. In the second half of this book we will explore how we can rebalance our systems by working on our behaviors, thoughts and feelings. Exercise, diet and medication may also help, but they are not the main focus of this book (see the appendices for some thoughts on these). Next we explore these three emotion regulation systems in more detail.

The threat-protection and safety-seeking system

Life on our planet faces a variety of dangers, from other life forms that want to eat them, fights with others of their own kind, lack of food or shelter, to viruses, bacteria and so on. Because life forms face so many threats, they need to have systems in their brains that can detect them and respond.[2]

We can call this the *threat-protection and safety-seeking system*, or *threat-protection system* for short. It is designed to detect threats, activate protective emotions such as anxiety and start behaviors that will help us to keep safe, such as running away or avoiding things. In humans and other animals this system can be activated very quickly, giving rise to feelings of anxiety, anger or disgust, with their associated behaviors for fighting, running away, and trying to get rid of things. Note too that we can have these feelings if we see others – especially those we love – in danger or distress: we want to rush in to protect them.

Although this system was developed for our protection, many of the emotions, feelings and thoughts associated with it can cause us problems and indeed underpin many mental health difficulties. For example, our anxiety or anger can become too easily triggered or too intense, or difficult to turn off. We might become anxious about situations we don't want to be anxious about – such as standing in a queue, going to a party or job interview. Our emotional brain and our logical (new) brain seem to be saying rather different things. When we experience our emotions getting in the way of what we can logically want to do or feel, we tend to see such feelings as 'bad' and 'to be got rid of', but in fact they are only designed as self-protection. It is often because we don't understand that they are part of our alarm and self-protection system that we can have such a negative approach to these emotions. When this happens we tend to fight with them, avoid them or even come to hate them rather than *work with them*.

Our new brains may focus thinking and rumination on threat and losses. The last time I had to take an important exam I found it difficult not to think about it, or to sleep well the night before. That can be useful, of course, because I prepared well (I hope). After the exam I started going back in my mind over what I had written and wondering if I had answered questions correctly or sufficiently, oscillating between confidence and doubt. That is how our minds are, worrying about the future and reflecting on the past. Sometimes focusing on threat and preparing for it is very helpful. However, feeling one's mind constantly pulled to focus on a threat or loss can be very unhelpful. Then we worry and fret about things, and at times we give up trying altogether, anticipating that it will go badly – so we feel there is no point.

Depression as a threat-protection response

Many researchers are now looking at depression from an evolutionary point of view.[3] Research has shown that when we are depressed, an area of the brain (called the amygdala) that is associated with detecting and responding to threats seems to become more sensitive.[4] Indeed, some depressed people can have greatly increased anxiety and/or anger and irritability because the threat system has become 'inflamed', if you like. This may be linked to threat in our current situation, genetic sensitivity, unresolved anger or anxiety issues from the past, or other reasons, but it is useful to think about some aspects of a depression being linked to this *physiological sensitivity* in our threat-protection system. We can then consider how to work on reducing this sensitivity and help to settle it down.

The situations that can trigger depressive changes in our brains are linked to particular difficulties, and we will be looking at these in the next two chapters. Situations that are important to us but where we feel we have lost control, or we feel no matter how much we try we can't reach our goals, or we feel overwhelmed by demands on us, or we find ourselves trapped in situations we don't want to be in (e.g., isolated, or with critical or unkind others), or feeling defeated or exhausted – can all contribute to depression. Feeling isolated, alone, misunderstood, or unlovable and cut off from others is also strongly linked to depression. Depression is a kind of shutdown, a 'go to the back of the cave and stay there until things improve' response.

The feel-good emotions

Depression is not just about having more anxiety and irritability. A key element of depression is that positive emotion systems seemed to be toned down too. We are not able to enjoy things or look forward to things. Things we used to enjoy, such as talking to people, going to parties, planning a holiday or even having sex can become things that are actually unpleasant to do; they fill us with dread and we can see nothing but problems and difficulties in doing them. In fact, although feeling accepted and connected to others is associated with feelings of well-being, when we are depressed we often feel disconnected from other people, as if there is a barrier between us and others, almost as if we are an outsider or an alien. *This tells us that positive emotion systems in our brain are toned down.* So to help us out of depression we have to practise stimulating our positive emotion systems, to get them active in our brains again.

Recent research has shown that there are in fact *two very different types* of positive feeling and emotion systems (see page 17).[1] One type is linked to a system that is activating and energizing; it is the system that gives rise to desires, and the buzz of excitement if something good happens to us or to people we care about, or even if our football team wins. It energizes us. This emotion system helps us to become active, to seek out good things, and to try to achieve and acquire things in life – it gives us certain feelings and drive.

The other positive emotion system is almost the opposite; it's not about achieving but about being safe and at peace. It is soothing and calming and gives feelings of contentment and well-being. It is the system that people who meditate try to stimulate.

These two systems evolved over millions of years. Let's look at them a little more closely.

The activating system

This system motivates us to achieve things and do things. It gives rise to our wants, and our desires to satisfy these. When good things happen, we can also get a buzz from this system. For example, if you win the lottery tonight and become a million-aire you may have bursts of excitement and become agitated; your mind will be churning with thoughts of your future; you'll find it difficult to stop smiling and you may also find it difficult to sleep because your mind will be racing. This is the system that can become overactive in people who have bipolar disorder. But if you are very depressed, even winning the lottery might wash over you because your positive emotion system only gives a slight splutter and you quickly get pulled back into the threat system, dwelling on all the problems having money will bring – how much to give to Uncle Tom and Aunty Betty and what happens if you upset cousin Alfred – what's the point of money anyway if it makes you feel this bad?

Of course, usually the drive system is not nearly as highly acti-vated as this but it gives us our little bursts of energy and excitement. If we are overstressed or push ourselves too hard, this system can get exhausted, and we can start to lose feelings of motivation and interest in things. We start to feel that we can't be bothered; even deciding what to have for lunch is boring and we can't think of anything we fancy. We find, as the Rolling Stones once wrote, that we 'can't get no satisfaction'.

There are many ways in which the drive system can become exhausted. If we overwork and become very tired the system can start to struggle; it runs out of fuel because we've been overusing it. If we are under a lot of stress for a long time, this again can affect our positive emotion system and we lose energy and moti-vation. Feeling helpless and out of control can cause the system to become exhausted. If we are being bullied or criticized at home or work, or if we are in a conflict relationship, or if we are very divided on what to do, whether to stay in this job or relation-ship or leave – these stressors can gradually tone down the drive system.

So when we are depressed it is useful to think about whether this system has become exhausted and, if so, how we can start to heal it, exploring what it needs to get up and running again. If you are self-critical for being depressed or tired, then this is only going to exhaust the drive system even more. Self-criticism does not – under any circumstances – increase enthusiasm, motivation or pleasure. It motivates through threatening and a fear of failure – that is, through your threat system. Sometimes we have to work hard to become more active and put positive things in our lives as best we can. This can mean deliberately training our attention to focus on positive things – things we appreciate, no matter how small – such as the taste of your first cup of tea in the morning, or the smile of a friend. If we recognize that we have a particular problem in a particular system in our brain then we can design a program to get it going again. Taking exercise can help stimulate this system too.

Useful and important as the drive system is, there are signs that Western society is rather overstimulating it and leading us to believe that we can only be happy if we have and achieve things. This leads people to constantly compare themselves with others, to reflect negatively on themselves – and that's pretty depressing, because it takes away enthusiasm and hope of success. We are also overworking and getting exhausted in the drive for the 'competitive edge' or proving ourselves competent.

Contentment, soothing and kindness

How does kindness fit into feelings of depression and a lack of well-being? Well, it does so in some very interesting ways. First, we should note that in our brains we have a system that regulates the experience of 'having sufficient, enough, and contentment'. When animals are not dealing with threats, and are not having to pursue things like food or other resources, they can be quiet, resting, quiescent and peaceful. We now know that this state is not just about low activity in the threat system. There is a system in our brain that gives us feelings of contentment where we are not seeking or feeling driven to achieve things – we are happy as we are, *right now, in this moment*. Think back to times you might have had feelings of contentment, being satisfied with where you were. People who meditate and become mindful (see Chapter 7) and spend time trying to develop calm states of mind often describe positive feelings of contentment, well-being and peacefulness.

But what has this got to do with kindness? To understand this you need to know that the evolution of our brains and bodies always uses systems that already exist. It is very difficult for evolution to design something totally new. The system that gives us our feelings of peacefulness, calmness and soothing is also linked to affection and being cared for. How did that happen? Simply put, millions of years ago the young of our mammal ancestors that were fed and protected survived and so passed on the genes for care and protection. Over millions of years these spread throughout the world. Today, whether you look at birds looking after their chicks in the nest, your family dog looking after her pups, monkeys caring for their infants or humans loving their babies, we see the enormous importance of love and affection in the process of protecting and caring. If you look carefully at these interactions you will also see something very interesting. When in close contact with its mother, the young infant is often peaceful and quiet.[5] An extreme example is the emperor penguin, where the baby chick has to sit on the parent's feet and *not move* or it will freeze.

What do caring relationships do to and for the child? First, they turn off the child's threat system. Indeed, think how a mother is often able to calm and soothe a distressed infant. Through the mother's tone of voice, or cuddling and gentle soothing, the child's brain registers that it is being looked after and this calms the threat system. *This ability to soothe distress with kindness is fundamental to how our brains work.* It is part of our evolutionary design. Our brains are designed to want kindness, and can respond to kindness. And it's not only in child–parent relationships that kindness is powerful. Kindness is one of the most important qualities that people look for in a long-term partner; it's one of the most important qualities people look for in friendship and (along with technical ability of course) one of the most important qualities we look for in our doctors, nurses, teachers and psychotherapists. We may not always be good at giving it, and sometimes we can be grumpy toads – but humans value and look for kindness because their brains are organized to feel more secure and safe in the context of kindness.

To help you think about how kindness operates in the body, consider the following scenario. You are upset about something: maybe a project you were planning hasn't worked out, or you are very disappointed over something, or someone you spoke to was unkind. Imagine you go to a friend, but they are very dismissive or they quickly switch the conversation around to their own difficulties, or are even critical of you and tell you to stop making mountains out of molehills. How will you feel. How will you feel in your body? Think about that. Now imagine you go to a friend who listens very carefully to your story. They sympathize and empathize with your upset, they say how they can understand why you are upset. Maybe they put an arm on your shoulder. How do you feel? You see, you already know in your heart that kindness will have a very different impact on your body. *You have inner wisdom on the value of kindness* and can learn to tune into it rather than getting caught up in the angers, frustrations, disappointment and fears of your threat system. As we will see in a moment, this is also the case for our own self-focused thoughts and attitudes to ourselves – these too can be rather bullying, but we can train them to be kind and supportive.

Kindness is important, too, because it underpins trust. When we trust people we are no longer orientated by threat, nor are we striving to impress them. We can turn to them if we need to. In a way kindness and trust can also tone down aspects of our drive and threat-protection systems and bring them more into balance. This is important to understand, because sometimes people who are vulnerable to depression feel they have to drive themselves hard, to impress others or to be liked and accepted. The drive system gets out of balance because of feeling insecure with other people, which means that the soothing system requires some development. We will be looking at exercises to help you with this later.

Without going into too much detail, these kinds of emotions use different chemicals in our brains, in different patterns to those of excitement and achievements.[1] These calm, good feelings of well-being are linked to endorphins (the body's natural opiates) and a hormone called oxytocin. This hormone has generated a lot of interest recently because it is linked to feelings of close-ness and trust with other people, and the warm feelings we get from affiliation and affection.[5]

Problems with our new minds

Our thoughts can also affect how these systems work and balance each other. Over the past two million years or so the human brain has been evolving abilities to think, to imagine, to predict, to ruminate and plan. We can form mental images in our minds. We can imagine the future, and think about how we can create a future that we want (or feel trapped in one we don't want). Much of our life is spent thinking about and planning for our wants; generating hopes, planning for our future, developing goals and worrying about obstacles and setbacks. Animals simply live out their lives, but humans are life planners and try to live according to their plans. This thinking gets pretty sophisticated. Indeed, it is because we can think like this that we have an intelligence that underpins science and technology. Our ability to imagine, think and plan with some complexity is central to the *human* mind.

As we will see later though, *what* we focus and think about, and how we focus our attention and thinking, can seriously affect our moods. Monkeys don't worry about being able to pay the mortgage, or failing a job interview, nor how to get out of a marriage; nor do they ruminate about feeling depressed in the future. Humans clearly do, though, and this can be one reason for low mood.

We also have a complex language, can talk to each other and can share wonderful ideas and feelings. We can share and build our plans and goals together. We can use symbols that help us to think. We have also evolved *a sense of self-awareness*. We have an awareness of being 'alive', being a self with a consciousness. These are wonderful abilities and give rise to our science, art and culture. We create and follow fashion because we have a sense of ourselves and how we wish to appear to others. We can create a sense of self-identity and this varies according to where we live. Think how different our self-identity would be if we grew up in a Buddhist monastery, in the backwoods of Alaska, in glitzy Hollywood or in a poor inner-city area.

However, there is a *downside* to these wonderful new mind abilities, because if our thinking about ourselves or future becomes overly threat- or loss-focused then we can lock ourselves into threat-process thinking and some very unpleasant feelings indeed.

How our thoughts and imaginations affect our brains

To help you explore how thoughts, images and memories can have powerful effects on systems in our brains, look at the brain depicted in Figure 2.2. It demonstrates how external things and *our imagination* of external things can work in a very similar way. Let's start by using examples that I commonly use and have discussed on my CD *Overcoming Depression: Talks With Your Therapist*.

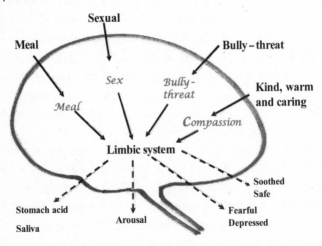

Figure 2.2 The way our thoughts and images affect our brains and bodies.

Imagine that you are very hungry and you see a lovely meal set out on a table. What happens in your body? The sight of the meal stimulates an area of your brain that sends messages to your body so that your mouth starts to water and your stomach acids get going. Spend a moment really thinking about that. Now suppose that you're very hungry but there isn't any food in the house, so you close your eyes and *imagine* a wonderful meal.

What happens in your body then? Again, spend a moment really thinking about that. Well, those images *that you deliberately create in your mind* can also send messages to parts of your brain that send messages to your body, so again your mouth will water and your stomach acids will get going. Remember though, this time there is no meal: it's only an image that you've created in your mind, yet that image is capable of stimulating those physiological systems in your body that make your saliva flow. Take a moment to think about that.

Here's another example, something that some of us have come across: you see something sexy on TV. This may stimulate an area of your brain that affects your body, leading to arousal. But equally, of course, we know that even if you're alone in the house you can imagine something sexy and that can affect your body. The reason for this is that the image alone can stimulate physiological systems in your brain in an area called the *pituitary*, which will release hormones into your body.

The point is that thoughts and images are very powerful ways of stimulating reactions in our brain and our body. Take a moment and really think about that, because this insight will link to other ideas to come. Images that you deliberately create in your mind and your thinking will stimulate your physiology and body systems.

Let's consider a more depression-linked example. Suppose someone is bullying you. They are always pointing out your mistakes or dwelling on things you are unhappy with, or telling you that you are no good and there is no point in you trying anything, or being angry with you. This will affect your threat-protection and stress systems. How do you feel if people criticize you? How does it feel in your body? Spend a moment thinking about this. Their unpleasantness will make you feel anxious, upset and unhappy because the threat emotion systems in your brain have been triggered. If the criticism is harsh and constant, it may make you feel depressed. You probably would not be surprised by that. However, as we have suggested, and here is the point – *our own thoughts and images can do the same*. If you are constantly putting yourself down this can also activate your stress systems and trigger the emotional systems in your brain that lead to feeling anxious, angry and down. That's right – our own thoughts can affect parts of our brain that give rise to more *stressful and unpleasant feelings*. They can certainly tone down positive feelings. Who ever had a feeling of joy, happiness, contentment or well-being from being criticized? If we develop a self-critical style then we are constantly stimulating our threat system and will understandably feel constantly under threat. Self-criticism then stimulates the threat system. This is no different from saying that sexual thoughts and feelings will stimulate your sexual system, and the thoughts of a lovely meal will stimulate your digestive system.

There are many reasons for becoming self-critical. One common reason is that others have been critical of us in the past and we simply accept their views as accurate. We don't stop to think whether they were genuinely interested in our welfare and really cared and wanted to help us – in fact they may just have been rather stressed and irritable people who were critical of everyone. We have gone along with their criticisms of us – as one often does as a child – and never stopped to think if they are accurate or reasonable. Or it may be that we are trying very hard to reach a certain standard, or to achieve something, or present ourselves in a certain way. When it doesn't work out as we would like, this can frighten us because we may think we have let ourselves down or *other people will reject us*. In our frustration we then criticize ourselves and take our frustration out on ourselves. All very understandable, but not helpful, because we are giving ourselves negative signals that *affect our brains*. Research on what happens in people's brains when they are self-critical confirms that it really is the case that we stimulate threat systems in our brain. The more self-critical we are, the more those systems are stimulated. Learning to spot self-criticism and what to do about it is a key issue in later chapters.

The power of self-kindness

We have spent some time looking at the three emotion regulation systems and we explored a system in the brain that helps to soothe and calm us when things are hard or we are frightened. We feel soothed when other people are kind and understanding, supportive and encouraging. We have a system in our brains that can respond to those behaviors from others. Suppose that when you are struggling there is someone who cares about you, understands how hard it is, and encourages you with warmth and genuine care – how does that feel? Maybe you could spend some time thinking about this right now. Or imagine that you are learning a new skill and finding it hard; maybe other people seem to be getting the hang of it more easily than you. However, you have a teacher who is very gentle and warm, pays careful attention to where your difficulties are, helps you see what you are doing right and how you can build on those good things. Compare this with a teacher who is clearly irritated by you, makes you feel you're holding up the class, and focuses on your deficits. Most of us are going to prefer the first type of teacher, and indeed will do much better.

So using exactly the same idea as imagining how a meal can stimulate sensations and feelings in our bodies linked to eating, we can think about how our own thoughts and images might be able to stimulate the kindness and soothing system. If we can learn to be kind and supportive – to send ourselves helpful messages when things are hard for us – we are more likely to stimulate those parts of our brain that respond to kindness. This will help us cope with stress and setbacks. As this book unfolds, you will learn how to engage with compassionate attending, thinking, behavior, imagery and feeling (see Chapter 9). Bear in mind all the time that this is about helping you to re-balance systems in your brain.

What happens in our brains when we focus on self-critical or self-reassuring and self-compassionate feelings? Self-criticism stimulates parts of our brain linked to threat, whereas self-compassion and reassurance stimulates parts of our brain linked to empathy and soothing. However, there is an added complication. For some people who are very self-critical, starting to become self-compassionate can seem like a threat. Some people feel that wanting kindness, or even making an effort to be kind and gentle to oneself, is a weakness or an indulgence. They believe that either they or others simply don't deserve it. Our research indicates that when people first start to be kind to themselves, they can feel it as rather strange or threatening. They have to work through these 'fears' to start training their minds in self-kindness.

Nonetheless, there is now a lot of evidence that being compassionate or kind to yourself is associated with well-being and being able to cope with life stresses. You can read more about this from a leading researcher at *www.self-compassion.org*.

There are important differences between self-compassion and self-esteem. For example, self-compassion is important when things are difficult or going wrong, and you are having a hard time. Self-esteem, on the other hand, tends to be associated with doing well and achieving. Self-esteem is more linked to our drive-achievement system. It often focuses on how well we are doing in comparison with others, and this is why low self-esteem is often linked to feeling inferior – as we are judging ourselves in comparison with others. Self-compassion, on the other hand, is about focusing on our similarity and shared humanity with others, who also struggle as we do.

Our brains have been designed by evolution to need and to respond positively to kindness, so it is not a question of 'what we deserve'. It is not self-indulgence, any more than training your body to be fit and healthy is a self-indulgence. It is simple a question of treating our brain wisely and feeding it appropriately. This is really no different from (say) understanding that our body needs certain vitamins and a balanced diet. It's not a question of whether you deserve to give your body vitamins or not, you simply do it because it's sensible. It's the same with kindness. It's not an issue of deserving, it's an issue of understanding how our mind works and then practising how to feed it things to help it work optimally. We will be looking at this as we go through the book because some people find this a bit tricky; they can even be frightened to give up their sense of being inadequate or bad in some way. However, they can practise switching to self-kindness each day and see how things go.

Not our fault

I'm sorry if I seem a bit repetitive here, but this is an important idea to convey: 'depression is not our fault and there is nothing bad about us'. Indeed, evolution may have designed depression (with its reduced positive feelings and increased negative feelings) as a kind of protection when we are in a high-stress environment – like a safety switch or fuse on an electrical circuit that trips out if it is overloaded. The reason for hammering away at this idea is because some depressed people struggle terribly, feeling responsible, inferior or inadequate in some way for being exhausted or depressed. That's why so many depressed people don't seek help – because they are ashamed of depression. They may not even recognize it themselves.

If you can take the approach outlined here, you can see that our depressions need our compassionate understanding – to be worked with, worked on and healed as best we can. We did not design any of the mechanisms in our brain that give rise to depression – nor any of the desires that may be thwarted, and cause depression – nor the genes that might make us vulnerable to depression – nor the early life experiences that also make us vulnerable to depression. If we see this, then we also see that depression cannot possibly be our fault.

However, because the depression is happening inside our heads the question is, how can we take responsibility or be *'response able'* – that is, come up with healing and balancing responses to our depressed brain states? Can we learn to settle down our threat-protection systems? The moment we give up self-blaming and shaming, refuse to see depression as a personal weakness or even be frightened of it (but instead see it as a brain state pattern that has been created in us), we can turn around and face it and do what we can to overcome it. Seeing that the basis of our depression is not our fault is not to say that we aren't doing things that are making the situation worse, or that we couldn't help ourselves more than we are. Indeed, we may need to take *more responsibility* for changing our behaviors, our thoughts or even styles of relating, and work our way out of depression.

The need for kindness

We are going to be looking at many ways that we can tackle depression throughout this book, but there is a key message that I want to convey: whether you work with your thoughts or feelings or your behaviors, if you learn to do it in the spirit of support, encouragement and kindness, this will give you an extra boost to your efforts. Indeed, kindness to yourself may be one of the things that you haven't been too good at, and one of the skills that require practice. Some of you will be frightened of that idea; you may see self-kindness as an indulgence or weakness or letting yourself off the hook, or you don't deserve it, or you might feel that if you're kind to yourself and enjoy life something bad will happen tomorrow; you've always got to pay for the good times. Or it may touch sadness in you because it reminds you that you've been yearning for kindness and connectedness for a long time. If you are feeling or thinking this, you are certainly not alone! Many depressed people have these types of beliefs and fears. So we are going to work a step at a time. But as I have suggested, think about self-kindness in a different way. Take a physiotherapy approach to your brain and think about exercising/training it – a kind of emotional fitness training. Self-kindness is a way to restart that soothing system and bring balance to your mind.

KEY POINTS

- Our brain has been built and designed over many millions of years through a process of evolution.
- In our brains today are actually two types of mind. One is the emotional mind, which we share with other animals, that can spring into action quickly with (for example) anxiety and anger. The other is the thinking, imagining, fantasizing mind that can increase or dampen our emotions.
- To help guide us through life we have three different types of emotion system in our brain:
  - a threat-protection system that helps detect, track and respond to things that threaten us
  - a drive system that gives rise to desire and feelings of motivation

- – a soothing system that helps us feel content, at peace, safe and happy. This system is especially important in social relationships when we feel cared for.
- Our thinking and imagining can stimulate any of these three emotion systems. When we focus on threats, interpret situations as threatening or loss-filled or ruminate on threats and losses, we tend to stimulate the threat-protection system. When we focus on achieving and attending to our efforts we are more likely to stimulate the drive system. When we focus on contentment and kindness we tend to stimulate our soothing system.
- This knowledge allows us to take more control of which systems we will stimulate through our thinking, imagination and rumination. We can learn to how to adjust our thinking and behavior, and engage in various exercises for our minds, which can bring these emotion systems more into balance and counteract depressed brain states.

How to do this is the subject of Parts II–IV of this book.

3

How evolution may have shaped our minds for depression

In this chapter we're going to look at the possible *functions* of depression, or the purpose behind it. By doing this we can understand that depression is not (just) about an illness or some pathology, but evolution has actually made it possible for our brain to create these states, and we can think about why that is the case.

Emotions and their uses

Let's start by thinking about the functions of our emotions in general. Different emotions evolved because they help us to see and react to the environment in different ways.[1] Emotions *guide* us (and other animals) towards certain important goals, such as developing relationships, or avoiding harm, or overcoming obstacles. Our emotions make things matter to us. If you didn't have feelings about things, would anything really matter to you? Let's look at some emotions related to our threat-protection system. As we look at each emotion think carefully about how they are part of self-protection. They are not designed to give us a hard time but actually to help us.

- **Anger** can be triggered when we are frustrated, or something we want is blocked, or we see an injustice, or if someone puts us down. Anger makes us want to approach the problem, do something about it, 'sort it out'. Anger can also make us want to retaliate against another person who has upset us or someone we love. When anger gets going, our bodies 'feel' a certain kind of way, our minds focus on things that annoy us. We have certain types of thoughts that go with anger; think about your own thoughts when you become angry. There will probably be particular things in your life that trigger anger for you; we all have our buttons that can be pushed. Notice how anger pulls your thinking in certain ways – almost like a whirlpool.

- **Anxiety** is focused on threats; it gives us a sense of urgency, prompting us to do something. Anxiety can make us want to run away and keep ourselves safe and out of harm's way. When anxiety gets going, it pulls our thinking to focus on dangers and threats. Again, like anger, there will probably be certain things in your life that tend to make you anxious.

- **Disgust** makes us want to expel noxious substances or turn away from them. Disgust feels different from anxiety and anger. It was originally designed to keep us away from poisonous substances, and is commonly believed to be linked to bodily things. When disgust blends with anger, we can have **contempt**.

- **Shame** is usually a blend of other emotions of anger, anxiety, and disgust. It is an emotion that is specifically linked to a sense of ourselves. Typically, shame makes us want to run away, or close down and be submissive, to avoid rejection. We can have a sense of shame if we think others look down on us.

- **Guilt** makes us wary of exploiting or harming others, and prompts us to try to repair the relationship if we do. We will be looking at shame and guilt in later chapters.

What about positive emotions? What functions do they have?[2]

- **Excitement** is an emotion that is energizing and directs us towards certain things. We generally feel excited about something we want to do or achieve. We can also have a buzz of pleasure when we do achieve. Positive emotions direct us to things that are helpful to us. We can also get small feelings of pleasure from simple things such as enjoying a meal, or the sun of a warm day, or going for a walk, or talking to a friend.

- **Contentment** is a very different positive emotion to that of excitement. It gives us a sense of being at peace and of well-being. Contentment helps us to stop driving ourselves and 'wanting' all the time. This allows us to rest. Interestingly, it's not an emotion that Western societies focus on very much, but it is key to well-being.

- **Love and affection** are emotions that indicate positive relationships between people and tell our brain that we are safe and tone down the threat system. The feelings help us build bonds, and think about each other when we are not currently in sight. As we noted in the last chapter, affection can have very soothing qualities.

Think of each emotion in this list and ask yourself: 'What does my body want to do if this emotion is aroused in me? How does emotion direct my thinking? How does my thinking differ if I'm angry or anxious or in love?' The $64,000 question here is: are you thinking about your emotions, or are your emotions thinking for you? The honest answer can be both, but note that we often get caught up in an emotion and the emotion directs our thinking. Sometimes we haven't learned how to stand back and not get caught up in the whirlpool and dragged into the emotion. The emotion says 'think this', 'dwell on this', 'fret about that' – and we simply do. But of course it is a two-way street. How we think about things, the interpretations and meanings we put on things that happen to us, can also stir our emotions.

Emotions, then, have certain functions, even if they are unpleasant and painful to us. We sometimes call threat self-protective emotions (of anxiety or anger) *negative* or *bad*. However, this puts us in the wrong frame of mind for dealing with them. They are not negative emotions simply because they feel bad: they are part of our self-protection system and once we start to befriend them we will find they are easier to deal with. Or put it this way – *there are many good reasons for feeling bad*. Imagine what a person would be like who did not have the capacity to feel anger, fear, disgust or guilt. These emotions are part of our being; they have evolved as part of our human nature. We can suffer various painful states of mind because we have normal, innate potentials to switch into them.

We live in a world that stresses the importance of happiness and feeling good. The problem is, you can be led astray by some of these claims because they don't also tell you that feeling bad is at times a normal, indeed important, part of life – and can be good for you in the long term. Anxiety about failing your exam may make you study hard, or anxiety about certain areas of the town you live in will keep you away from there.

Consider too that if someone we love dies, we can find ourselves in a deep state of grief. And very unpleasant it is too, with its associated sleep problems, crying, pining, anger and feelings of emptiness. We may have learned to share these feelings or to keep a stiff upper lip, but there is, in most of us, a potential grief state of mind. As another example, we all have the potential for aggressive, vengeful fantasies and attitudes: if someone harmed your child, your inner desire for revenge could be intense. Also, of course, we all have the potential for feeling anxious. All these possible feeling states are in our genetic blueprint. There are genetic and developmental differences among us that affect how easily or intensely these emotions can be triggered in each one of us.

Our potentials need to be triggered

We can have innate potentials for many negative (and positive) emotions but never (fully) activate them. Suppose nobody you love dies before you do? In that case you might never have an occasion for profound grief, and even though you almost certainly have the innate capacity to experience grief, you may never actually feel it. If no one does you or your family serious wrong, you may never experience the urgent and repetitive nature of vengeful thoughts and feelings. The fact that many people don't suffer certain states of mind (e.g., grief, sadistic vengefulness, depression) does not mean they do not have some capacity for them.

We can look at the helpfulness of emotions in terms of four aspects: what *triggers* the emotion, how *intense* the emotion is, how *long it lasts* and how *frequently* we experience it. There are many factors that can influence each of these four domains, so we can train our mind to work on each aspect of a difficult emotion.

One of the most important aspects of our compassionate, evolutionary approach is therefore to recognize when emotions are helpful, and when they have taken a life of their own, or when our thoughts or style of interpreting things keep us living in the shadows. Emotional systems themselves can rather overpower and 'take control' of our thoughts and sense of self. I'm sure we have all had the experience of being anxious or angry, and knowing in our hearts that we are probably letting our emotions run away with us, but without practice it's sometimes difficult to rein them back.

So what's the point of depression?

However, you may well ask, what is the point of depression?[3] The adaptive value of anger, anxiety and love is easy to see, but depression seems so unhelpful. Well, to be frank, it often is. Now one way to think about this is in terms of balance. For example, a certain level of anger can be helpful but intense anger and aggression often aren't. Anxiety can be helpful, but intense panics usually aren't. Although we have a basic anxiety and anger system, for a whole number of reasons these emotions can get out of balance and become too intense, too easily triggered, and last too long.

The first thing to recognize is that depression is partly linked to old brain systems. This is why animals can go into depression-like states, and scientists study those states in animals to understand depression better. We know depression is about toning down positive emotions and toning up threat-focused ones. Our key question is: *under what conditions might it have been useful for animals to lose confidence, be less positive, become more threat sensitive, and become less active in their environments? When might it have been useful to have a 'go to the back of the cave and stay there until it's safe' brain state?*

When we pose the question in this way we search for answers quite differently than if we assume depression is simply 'a disease'. You may already have some answers forming in your mind about when it is useful to tone down positive emotions and tone up negative ones. In fact it turns out that there are a number of conditions that can trigger these brain state patterns in animals.[3] One is loss of close attachments, particularly in the young, another is social isolation, another is conflict, bullying and defeat, another is helplessness over major stressors, and another is entrapment. When you think about it, there are many situations where we can see a toning down of positive emotions and a toning up of negative ones. In all these situations, the brain will automatically shift into patterns of toning down positive emotions and toning up negative ones.

We can get further insight into this by looking at what the new brain's abilities for thinking and self-awareness makes of our depression. How do depressed people see our world – what do our minds focus on when we are depressed? Is it love or the loss/lack of love? Is it winning or losing and feeling defeated? Is it harmony or conflict? Is it freedom or entrapment? Is it control or feeling out of control? Well, of course, it is usually the latter in each case. We know that depressed people often lose energy and give up on things; they see themselves as inferior, even worthless; they lose confidence and behave submissively rather than assertively. Just as we can ask, 'When was it useful to get anxious or angry?' we can ask, 'When might it have been useful for our ancestors to give up on things, to see themselves as inferior and to behave submissively?' There are a few answers.

Stopping us from chasing rainbows

Many people believe it is important for us to follow our dreams; to have clear goals and go after them. There is a lot of wisdom in this. Indeed, being able to decide on goals, the kinds of things you want in life, and committing yourself to try and achieve them is helpful. However, we all know that on this path we will have to cope with disappointments and setbacks, losses and failures. Sometimes we might even need to recognize that the thing we so dearly want is actually out of our reach and we have to change direction. We come to realize that our expectations are too high, we have been chasing rainbows and running to the horizon. This can be hard to acknowledge, and sometimes it's very difficult to let go.

One view of the value of mild depression, for us and other animals (and keep in mind throughout this section that by depression, we are talking about 'toned down positive emotions and toned up threat-focused emotions'), is that it helps us to give up aspirations that we are unlikely to fulfil or achieve.[4] Supposing you want a bigger house or a better car. You work hard for the money, but you just can't get enough. At some point your energy and enthusiasm begin to wane and eventually you give up and switch to another possibility; you have to tone down your aspiration. Without any internal signal that could prompt us to give up pursuing the unobtainable, we could well continue to pursue it and so waste a lot of time and energy and end up with nothing. Low mood is a 'give it up' signal from old brain systems. Feelings of frustration and low mood can be automatic. At times we have to learn when to override them and keep going or listen to them and make changes in our lives.

Whether the mood is a mild dip or a more serious depression may depend on whether we are able to accept giving up and come to terms with our loss, or whether we keep pursuing the unobtainable and failing. It may also depend on how our new brain, with its thinking, ruminative and self-aware abilities, deals with this loss. If we see having to give up as due to a personal failure, or rejection in some way, this will tone positive emotion systems down even further. You have probably seen this yourself.

People who are able to come to terms quickly with having to give up on things and losses, and are able to move on, are less vulnerable to depression than those who struggle to let go, who ruminate, remain frustrated or angry, self-blame, and so forth.

Consider David, who is trying to date Helen. He has strong feelings and desires for her. Over a few months, he builds fantasies and dreams about how great it will be if they can get the relationship working and he tries various things to woo her. Then she agrees to a first date, but at the end of the first date, Helen says, 'Thank you, I've had a lovely time but I don't want to make it a long-term relationship; so it's a one-off for me.'

It is normal and natural for David to have a dip in mood in response to this disappointment and setback, because it's the end of his striving, plans, fantasies (that gave good feelings) and hopes. He must now live in a world where those fantasies and desires are not going to happen. Not only has he lost the possibility of the future he wanted with Helen, but also it is the end of the fantasies that gave him good feelings and stimulated his excitement system. Consider what David would need to do to get depressed about this. What would he think about and dwell on? And now, in contrast, consider what he could do to get over this sad but not uncommon event as soon as possible and move on.

Interestingly, we know that some depressed people don't know how to tolerate and accept painful feelings, how to think and behave, to move on from major life setbacks. They can get stuck, in various ways. They tell themselves that feeling the pain of setbacks and disappointments is awful and unbearable, and are desperate to escape from those feelings, rather than learn how to 'be with them and work through them'. Or they may be angry and demand that life shouldn't be like this – when clearly life is often unfair and harsh. Sometimes people go in for self-blame or ruminating, hoping this will help them find a way to control things in the future. For some a loss might bring back painful memories of previous rejections, perhaps from childhood, and feeling unlovable. David might even make this sad situation worse. He might start to phone Helen up, trying to change her mind; or he might become unhappy and try to woo her by making her feel guilty. He might tell her he is drinking, or even that he is now depressed. There are many ways he could behave that will actually turn Helen's positive feelings for him quite negative. She would then reject him more harshly, which will then hurt him more, which would then feed into his feelings that he is unlovable, or other people are uncaring. David probably won't recognize that his own behavior is part of the problem here.

The point is that we can't avoid the pain of life, and dips in mood are normal reactions to major setbacks. Learning tolerance and acceptance of life's pain is at times the way forward. What we can do is learn how to treat ourselves kindly and compassionately to get through these difficult waters. We can also learn how to let go gently, and this means coming to terms with grief as part of life.

Reactions to loss: depression and grief

Coming to terms with not being able to be as we wish, or have what we want, or the relationships we want, is about grieving and our ability to allow ourselves to grieve. It has been suggested that some forms of depression are like grief. Grief can have a social and a non-social aspect. For example, think of the footballer with a promising international career who damages his knee and can no longer play. Sickness, illness (including mental illness) and injury are common reasons for changing the course of one's life and can require a lot of adjustment and grief work. We are confronted with grief for the loss of the person we wanted to be or hoped to become. As for David above, these losses also involve the loss of a fantasy life, the loss of how we would enjoy imagining, planning and thinking about how we were *going to be*, how life was going to be, what we would be part of.

Loss of feelings of connectedness

Responding to the loss of a loved one with pining, anger, anxiety, sadness, loss of positive feelings and motivation is the way our threat-protection systems respond to important losses. Many young animals, including rat pups, baby monkeys and human infants, can show what we call a 'protest–despair' response to separation from, or loss of, the mother or those they have affectionate bonds with. Commonly, at first the infant *protests* and becomes more active (restless, angry and anxious, and in humans tearful) but if the mother does not return the infant becomes quiet and withdrawn. This condition has been called a *despair state*. What on earth could be the value of such a display or state? Keep in mind that this is toning down of positive emotions and toning up threat-protection. For juveniles in the wild, who are unprotected by a parent, it is important that they don't move around too much, get lost, get dehydrated in the sun, or that their crying and obvious distress attract the attention of predators. The way evolution designed this was to create a potential brain pattern that would tone down positive emotion and tone up negative emotion. The infant will go into a very anxious and vigilant state, which urges it to hide away.

We think that something like this brain state and pattern can be triggered in depression, because the depressed person often feels as if they are disconnected from others, alone and lonely, cut off, and, without a sense of connectedness, the world feels dangerous to them. The 'go to the back of the cave strategy' switches in and they lose energy, confidence and motivation to go into the world.

The mechanisms for coping with loss, which have evolved over millions of years, seem to be the rough blueprint for many of our human responses to serious personal losses. We too can go through a protest stage of feeling angry and looking for the loved one, followed by numbness and despair. Of course, most grief in humans is complex, and people can move back and forth through several phases, so I do not mean to oversimplify it, only to indicate that there are evolved mechanisms at work. 'Attachment losses' are painful and stressful because we are biologically set up for them to be so. Having these feelings arise in us is not our fault – but we need to think how we can help and heal them.

In some depressions the protest–despair mechanism works in very subtle ways. It is as if there is a continuous background sense of not really feeling close enough or connected enough to others, and yet desperately wanting to. Sometimes depressed people will say they have a background feeling of always 'feeling alone and disconnected from others'. Sometimes people become depressed even though they have not *recently* experienced any actual major loss, but in the course of therapy it may turn out that they have never felt loved or wanted by their parents or partners, and are in a kind of grieving–yearning state for the closeness they lack.

Loss of our ideal other

There are always two types of parent in our heads: the one that we had, and the one that we wanted. If these are too far apart, people can experience conflicts over the one they actually had (warts and all) – and desires for the one they wanted (protecting, affectionate and understanding). If we had difficult relationships with parents, it is easy to forget that sometimes we may need to grieve for the parent we so wanted and never had, and work out how to deal with those feelings. One depressed woman, when considering this, acknowledged that she had never really allowed herself to think about the kind of mother she had wanted, because she had felt disloyal to her own (angry and depressed) mother. However, giving herself permission to think about this allowed her to grieve for the mother she had wanted. This helped her to 'feel more at peace within myself and give up trying to pretend or hope that my mother could be anything other than she is. She can never be as I want her to be.'

Some people want to be close to others, but in their early family life have experienced closeness as associated with punishments or threats, or as something withheld or not available. Thus we can have a deep yearning for closeness with others (it's part of our nature) but also a basic belief that we are unlovable and/or that other people are unreliable and will severely disappoint or hurt us. The depression has to do with our being in a state of wanting closeness but being unable or frightened to get it.

How we relate to others in close relationships

Relationships are major arenas for depression because so many of our desires and wants focus on them. Relationships can stimulate excitement-drive and pleasure centres and also soothing, contentment and well-being centres in our brains. This does not mean you can't be happy without a relationship – many people are, and in fact many people today are choosing not to engage in intimate relationships but enjoy the single lifestyle.

Some people experience what is called *anxious attachment*. They are frightened of being rejected or abandoned; they become anxious if left on their own and angry at separations. In contrast, other people may decide that attachments to others are too painful and difficult, and so they *avoid* closeness. Others move between anxious and avoidance styles: sometimes they seem to want a lot of closeness and reassurance that they are loved (and lovable), but at other times they are aloof and distant. This style can be difficult for partners, who can't always make sense of the person who needs closeness today but wants to escape tomorrow, so (stressful) conflicts can arise. All of us can have these various relating styles to varying degrees, and stress can affect them. For example, when we are under stress, we may want more reassurance and closeness from our loved ones; but when our jobs and lives are going well, and we feel good, we may want less closeness and more freedom to come and go. Lonely, 'despair-type' depressions can arise when it seems that we cannot get close enough to others; we feel cut off from others. When people are depressed they often feel emotionally alone and isolated; *this is commonly part of the depressive experience*. It can feel as if there is a barrier between oneself and others.

However, depression can also arise from *too much closeness*. We may feel trapped and weighed down in relationships and can't get away, or don't have enough space or distance from others. Relationships can feel suffocating. We might feel guilty about even wanting to get more space. Too much *and* too little closeness can cause stress linked to depression.

Helping us cope with defeats and hostile places

Another evolutionary approach looks at why some depressed states are associated with feeling *inferior to others*, *subordinated* and *defeated*. The 'stop pursuing rainbows' and grief models described above do not really tell us why depressed people would feel inferior or defeated. We need to consider the fact that depression can make us give up attempting all sorts of challenges and reduces our aspirations; it knocks out our optimism and 'go for it' attitude; it can leave us with feelings of inferiority and shame. How could this have been adaptive?

According to this approach, there are biological differences between animals who have high rank and those who have low rank. It is now known that animals that have been subordinated or have suffered a lot of attacks from others show behavioral and biological changes similar to those in depressed humans. In some very subordinate animals the stress systems are in overdrive. Some of this stress is caused by the harassment of subordinates by higher-ranking animals, but there is another aspect to it. It might not be a good idea for a very subordinate animal to stroll around as if it were powerful, competent and dominant; to do so will only invite fights that it will lose, probably being injured in the process. It is in the subordinate's interest to keep a low profile, not be ambitious, and to look out for trouble. Toning down positive systems and toning up threat-focused ones is one way the brain enables a subordinate animal to protect itself, stay out of trouble and be socially on guard.

Some depressions, then, may be related to potential states of mind that can be triggered by certain no-win situations and/or where there is *enforced subordination* (feeling you have to do things you don't want to, often because of fear; feeling that others have some power or control over you). This is a kind of 'stay low' mechanism. This may be a reason why depressed people often feel inferior, worthless, and at the bottom of the pile (like a low-ranking animal) and find it difficult to be assertive.

Subordinate thinking

'Subordinate thinking' or 'thinking of oneself as inferior and subordinate' is very much a part of how many depressed people think about themselves. Depressed people may label or judge themselves and/or feel judged by others in ways that are not only negative but also suggest they have been allocated a low rank or status. In extreme cases, they might actually feel ostracized and excluded by other people. Judgements such as 'inferior', 'unlovable', 'worthless', 'bad', 'inadequate', 'useless' and so on are, in effect, assignments of status that give the individual a low rank in the social order.

Mood, then, is partly an energy control system that signals status and confidence. The better our (drive-linked) mood, the more confident we feel and the more we seek out those things that are important: friends, sexual partners, good employment, and so on.[2] Like our primate cousins, the more confidence we feel the more we stand tall and display that confidence. As our mood goes down, our confidence slips away as if we are becoming subordinate in a potentially hostile or rejecting world, and we take a low profile. Indeed, depressed people often don't stand tall but tend to slouch with head down and eyes averted. We may put on a front, but as our mood drops further this deception is harder to keep up; we lose enthusiasm for trying to 'go for it' and want more and more to get out of the way and hide.

Of course, if we are happy being subordinate (and in fact we often are, so long as those above us are nice to us, and we feel the 'higher ranks' will help us rather than look down on us) then being subordinate is not stressful at all. Letting others take the strain can be a good choice. The kind of subordination that is stressful and is related to depression is the kind that is forced and/or unwanted. Many kinds of unwanted subordinacy are easy to see: being bullied, for example, and/or criticized and unsupported, being treated by others like inferior subordinates. Other cases are more subtle. Darren's wife Anne had an affair with another man. Darren concluded this was because she preferred this other man; therefore, in Anne's eyes, he was inferior to her lover and as an inferior would lose any 'battle' to win her love. He became depressed, with an acute sense of being in a subordinate position (to the other man) and not able to do anything about it except be angry (and risk driving his wife away) or leave someone he loved.

To show you how, for humans, our 'new brain thoughts' are often involved in our sense of (stressful) inferiority, consider two overweight women. One says, 'Well, I would like to be thinner for health reasons but hey, "big is beautiful" and I am a really nice person. I just have to keep trying.' For this person her weight may be a disappointment, but is not related to feeling inferior 'as a person'. But the other woman thinks, 'Oh God, I am so fat nobody will love me. When I look at the magazines I see how thin those women are. I can't let others see me like this. I will hide away and not go out to nightclubs or parties.' This woman has an acute sense of inferiority and of being subordinate to other (less weighty) women. And because she hides away, she reduces input to her positive feeling systems, which then get toned down further, making her more depressed and maybe eat more – it's a sad, vicious circle. Subordinate animals also lurk at the edges of their groups and, when we feel like this ourselves, we too might try to hide away, not going out much, which makes us more lonely and isolated. We also give up doing things that stimulate positive feelings.

You have probably noticed yourself how your moods can seem to make you behave more or less like a fearful, unconfident subordinate. One day you might just feel down. The confidence that was previously there feels as if it has suddenly gone, and you don't feel like facing the world. Or think of the extrovert man who loves parties but then gets depressed. An invitation for a party drops through his door: he feels anxious about it, and thinks it is all too much effort. He does not go. So you can see that mood seems to be strongly linked to feeling subordinate in some way, and prompts us to keep a low profile and stay on the edge of things even when we don't really want to be like this.

If we can learn to recognize compassionately that these inferiority thoughts are linked to this subordinate system that has been triggered, step back and decide to be gentle, kind and supportive and (as best we can) resist hiding away, this can move us forward. Whatever our source of stress, when we experience kindness, support and encouragement, we are stimulating systems in our brain that soothe the stress system. This is the story I will come back to time and again.

Feeling defeated

Feelings of *exhaustion and defeat* often pervade our experience of depression. The key feature of defeat is having engaged in some kind of struggle to do or achieve something, and feeling one has lost. Defeat states are designed by evolution to make those who lose a contest tone down their efforts and pleasure. Think of how losers in competitive sports behave, in contrast to winners. The winners go out on the town to celebrate; the losers may prefer to slink off home, not wanting to socialize much. Although some losers are more graceful and resigned to the outcome than others, these are pretty universal reactions, though of course they vary from very mild to severe.

Exhaustion and defeat states can be extremely painful and there are ways of thinking that make the acceptance of defeats even tougher. Some people take defeats as evidence of some personal inadequacy. This eats away at the inner sense of oneself. We may set ourselves up for this by thinking that being an 'okay person' depends on being successful. If so, what happens if you try for something and fail? Then, by definition, you are not an okay person. By thinking in certain ways, we can allow a defeat to make us feel like failures – subordinate and inferior. If feeling overwhelmed with exhaustion and a sense of defeat (maybe you failed an important exam or broke up with someone, or are struggling with children) then this can trigger suicidal feelings of escaping. If possible, try to recognize this as a brain state, be kind to these feelings but do not try to act on them – give yourself time to let things settle and recuperate. Remind yourself of other times you have come through; consider how others have also had these setbacks rather than feeling ashamed. If possible, talk to your family doctor.

Unrealistic standards

We are often told, 'whenever things don't work out, try, try and try again'; or, 'you can do anything if you really want to and try hard enough'; or, 'if X can do it, so can you'. Sometimes this is encouraging, but at other times it is very silly advice. Sure, these slogans can inspire us to put in effort; but they can also set us up for impossible dreams and expectations which cannot be met and so will end in defeat. We need to have realistic expectations. We can set ourselves up for feelings of defeat when we aim too high, trying to be perfect and/or never to make mistakes. Since this is impossible to achieve, we will feel constantly defeated and depressed.

Others are better than me

We can feel defeated when we look around us and compare ourselves with other people. They seem to be coping better, seem less tired or angry, or are dieting better or succeeding more than we are. Try as we might we feel inferior – and with help from the media we can get a sense that we are 'not making it' while other people are – leaving us feeling defeated. This is also a theme of shame, a subject we shall consider in detail in Chapter 17. Our research has shown that people who feel they need to strive to prove themselves worthy, with the fear of not keeping up, and feeling inferior, are vulnerable to depressions.

Self-criticism on top of a sense of defeat

Our anger at the disappointment of a defeat can turn into an attack on the self. Depressed states of mind often focus on feeling worthless, inferior, not up to it and inadequate compared with others. The messages that others, or we ourselves, are giving us are not messages of love, acceptance and value, when we need these things most, but of criticism and put-downs. The more hostile the criticism, the more the stress system is activated. In many depressions there is a connection between feeling defeated, feeling subordinate and inferior, and continually knocking ourselves further down.

Chronic conflicts

Feelings of defeat can come from chronic conflicts in our relationships that we never seem able to resolve. Often these involve much (usually unexpressed) anger, accentuated by a feeling that we always lose these battles, or 'can't afford' to say what we 'really feel'. For Fran, the conflict was with her mother. Whatever she did, her mother would always find fault and tell her how she should have done it. Fran never felt able to tell her mother what she felt about this, and developed a deep sense of being no good, and that whatever she tried to do it would never be good enough. If they did have arguments, it always felt to Fran that her mother was by far the stronger person, and exerted a hold over her. Fran often felt like a defeated subordinate in many of her relationships.

Entrapment

The 'defeated depressed brain state' is particularly likely to be activated in situations of enforced subordination and entrapment. Someone in an unhappy marriage or a terrible job, or living in a place they hate but can't get away from, can easily come to feel stuck, with no way out. This kind of perceived entrapment is a chronic stressor. Here are two examples.

- When David, a highly paid executive, had to put in increasingly long hours at work, he came to hate his job. The situation was made worse when a new, overly critical boss arrived. However, David had a big mortgage, had got used to a certain lifestyle, and could see no way of getting another job. He felt trapped in a position where he was being constantly pressured and criticized. Stress built up and depression set in – as it can when we are overloading our stress system.
- Cathy lived in a poor area with high unemployment. With an abusive husband and little money of her own, she felt totally responsible for her two children. She felt trapped, put down and unsupported.

My colleagues and I have been exploring feelings of entrapment in depression, and we have found that many depressed people feel trapped. This is often associated with wanting to run away or get away. Sometimes people are simply not able to do this because they don't have the resources or there is nowhere to go; or they may stay because they feel guilty about leaving or moving away from others. Sometimes actually getting away is helpful, but at other times exerting more control or becoming more assertive reduces the desire to escape. The key point is that strong desires to escape means that the threat self-protection (in this case) fight/flight system is constantly active. The more people want to get away, the more they are likely to be in a state of high and long-acting stress. And, of course, the more they brood on their entrapment, the more stressed and depressed they will be. This state will gradually tone down positive emotions and systems. If these feelings and brain states are getting too much and you are thinking of self-harming then do talk to your family doctor, as there are many things that may help you.

Overview

It is clear, then, that certain states of mind and brain patterns can be turned on by certain situations. There are two particular reasons for exploring these ideas with you here. First, it will help you to make sense of some of your experiences of depression. It is not just *any* stress that can trigger depression, but *certain kinds* of stress. It is stress that is related to (perceived or actual) losses and defeats, which often cause people to feel 'separate' from others, inferior, worthless and trapped. These seem the most crucial aspects of the stress–depression linkage. Second, if you think of depression as being a brain pattern, which exists in our brains because of evolution, and which has been triggered in you, you'll see that depression is one of many potential states of mind; it is no more the 'real' you than any other state of mind one might be in. By recognizing that depression is not our fault, but is linked to how our brains work (that is why it feels so horrible), we can learn to stand back and heal this brain state. We can feel terrible pain if we break a leg because of how our pain systems evolved and work – however, that feeling of pain is not our fault – but doing all we can to get the leg fixed is our responsibility, of course.

When and why depression is not adaptive

Although life has got much easier in many ways for a lot of us (we in the West suffer less disease, famine and war than our ancestors) there are also many stresses and strains on us now that were not present as we evolved – and these, frankly, can over-tax our systems. Culprits might include overworking and generally competitive lives (e.g., working long hours to keep our jobs; women competing to be thin with computer-enhanced images in the media); segregating systems (e.g., women on their own trying to cope with young children); and exclusive tendencies (e.g., poorer people being unable to gain access to the benefits that wealthier others can afford, while being only too aware through the media how much others have). Although marriage works well for many, we are not monogamous by nature. When relationships go wrong, we can feel trapped in them. Even the concrete jungles we have built that starve us of green and open spaces can be linked to depression.

In the past few years a number of books have appeared that explore this issue of how troublesome our innate needs (e.g., for love, status and approval, friendships, a sense of belonging and community) can be in modern societies – which do not always respect them.[5] One consequence of this discrepancy is that our stress systems have become too easily triggered, are too intense for the level of actual threat, and stay turned on for too long. A mixture of the circumstances in which we are now living and our self-aware and self-judging thoughts contribute to this. Training our minds to move away from depression and develop more compassion and sense of connectedness is very urgently needed these days.

KEY POINTS

- Depression is a powerful state of mind that is related to biological processes. Your brain is in a different physical state when you are depressed from when you are not. This is important, and helps us to acknowledge the inner felt sense and bodily feelings of depression. On the other hand, all states of mind, be they happy ones, telling jokes, or concentrating on a mathematical problem, are associated with different brain states – so there is nothing special about this idea.

- Sometimes depression results from something that has been 'turned on' in us. Just as a painful state of grief can be turned on by the loss of a loved one, so too 'depressed brain states' can be turned on by the problems we have in our lives and how we come to view them.

- There are aspects of depression that seem to relate to mechanisms in the brain that evolved long ago (e.g., for coping with loss of loved ones and/or coping with being subordinated and/or defeated and/or trapped).

- Depression therefore tends to focus our minds on certain kinds of thoughts, e.g., unlovability, inferiority, defeat or entrapment.

- Once depression starts, our thoughts can play a powerful role in whether the depressed state remains 'turned on' or comes back under our control.

- Self-attacking may activate more stress, whilst being self-supporting and kind to ourselves may reduce it.

4

Bodies, genes, stress and coping: More on the mind–body link

When we feel depressed we can feel tired and aimless; we may not be sleeping well and so feel exhausted. We can also feel physically unwell and 'heavy in the body' compared with our normal selves. One patient said, 'My whole system seems stuffed with black cotton wool.' This is because when we become depressed there are very real changes in our bodies and brains. The fact is that our brains work differently when we are depressed. Depression is as much a *physical problem* as a psychological one. Although we sometimes still tend to think of the mind and body as separate, they are not. The mind and body are one. Over 2000 years ago, the Greeks thought that depression was caused by too much 'black bile' in the body. Indeed, 'melancholia', another word for depression, means 'black bile'. Although, as they were well aware, this raises another question: What causes the black bile to increase? The Greeks had rather good ideas about this. They thought that there were people who 'by their nature' had more black bile – melancholic types. But they also believed that stress, diet and seasonal changes could affect the amounts of black bile in the body. The Greeks recognized that we can be upset by things that happen to us and that these upsets can affect our bodily processes – that is, affect the black bile. Their approach to depression was the first truly *holistic* one, taking body, mind and social living into account. Today, we call this holistic approach the *biopsychosocial* one. This simply means that we need to understand not only the bodily and mental aspects of depression but also the interactions between our biology and bodily processes, our psychology (how we think and cope) and the kinds of social circumstances in which we live.

Today we no longer think in terms of 'black bile' but in terms of chemical changes in the brain and other bodily processes. However, the idea that some people are, sadly, 'by their nature' more prone than others to certain types of depression has been confirmed by research.[1] Research has also shown that most depressions arise from combinations of early life experiences, current life events, lifestyles and the way we cope with them. Our central task in this chapter is to understand how these interact to produce the bodily and mental states of depression. The more we understand these interactions, the more sense it will make to help ourselves by using some of the methods outlined later in this book.

Biological aspects

The brain is affected by depression in many ways. The sleep system is disrupted; the areas of the brain controlling positive feelings and emotions (joy, love, pleasure, fun) are toned down; and the areas controlling negative emotions (anger, anxiety, jealousy, shame) are toned up. In other words, when we are depressed, not only does life stop being enjoyable, but we are also more anxious, sad, irritable and bad-tempered. These changes in our feelings happen because there are changes in the way messages are relayed between one nerve cell and another in the brain.

Chemicals that operate as messengers between nerve cells are called *neurotransmitters*. There are very many different types of neurotransmitters in the brain. One type is called *monoamines*. These include dopamine, noradrenaline (norepinephrine) and serotonin. These three neurotransmitters control many functions in the brain, including appetite, sleep and motivation and are especially involved in moods and emotions. In depression these mood neurotransmitters are believed to be depleted and not working efficiently. The same may be true for transmitters that influence the soothing system and give rise to feelings of calm, safeness and peaceful-contentment feelings, such as the endorphins (natural opiates) and the hormone oxytocin.[2] These are important chemicals in our brain, which are responsive to feeling cared for. A key question is: why have these changes occurred in the brain, and what can we do to help us to recover?

In fact, there are various ways in which our mood chemicals can be affected to make us vulnerable to depression. The three most important are our *genes*, our *history* and *current stress*. Let's look at each of these in turn.

Genetic influence

Genes are segments of DNA that control a vast number of chemical processes in our bodies and brains. The genes we inherit from our parents are the blueprints from which we were created. The first possibility, then, is that there is an *inherited* biological sensitivity to depression. On the basis of current evidence, it does seem that there is a genetic or inherited risk for some forms of depression; vulnerabilities to depression can run in families. Genes may affect the ease with which depressed brain states are activated by life events. They can also affect how we cope with life events and how we cope once we become depressed.[1]

We must be careful though not to draw over-simplistic conclusions from these findings, such as 'all depressions are inherited diseases'. In the first place, much depends on the type of depression. Some depressions (especially bipolar or manic depression) do have a high 'genetic loading'. In addition, some people have an increased risk of certain types of depression if some of their close (genetic) relatives have certain disorders, including anxiety and alcoholism. Over the years there have been studies on thousands of twins, and genes seem to affect many behaviors and personality traits right down to preferences in clothes and food! In fact recent research shows that there are a number of *different* genetic vulnerabilities to depression. Most of these interact with life events and early life experiences to influence whether depression occurs or not.[1] However what is also very important is that research shows that even if we carry a genetic risk for certain depressions, the kind of early life we have may do much to change or even remove this risk – and the kindness we experience is key.

Early life and how the brain develops

Although genes give us a blueprint, pathways in our brains (and our mood chemicals) develop from the experiences we have. We now know that the brain is very flexible or 'plastic' in this regard: it's called *neuroplasticity*.[3] The brain of a child who is loved and wanted will mature differently from that of a child who is abused and constantly threatened. Indeed, research has shown very clearly that love and affection, in contrast to coldness and abuse, affect the way areas of the brain that control moods and emotions develop. For instance, there is increasing evidence that many people who are susceptible to chronic forms of depression have histories of abuse, and that the stress systems of some of these people have an increased sensitivity.

As we come to recognize our own personal sensitivities, psychological understanding and training can do much to help us cope better and change our sensitivities. However, prevention is of course better than cure, and the more we understand about the role of our early relationships in how our brains mature, the more seriously, as a society, we must take childcare.

Stress and depression

Many depressions are triggered and maintained by stress. Stress can be a source of many different psychological problems, including anxiety, irritability, fatigue – and depression.[4] The way we cope with stress, too, can give rise to different psychological problems. Some people under stress are able to recognize it and back off from what is stressful to them. Others, however, are not able to escape from things that are stressful; for example, if we are in a job or a relationship that is 'stressful', it may not be easy just to walk away. Other ways of coping with stress may cause problems of their own: for example, drinking too much alcohol. Before we look at how our thoughts and coping efforts can make stress worse, let's explore what happens in the body when we are stressed.

Stress and our bodies

In recent years there has been growing interest in how stress (arising from the threat-protection system) works in depression. For example, one effect of stress is for adrenal glands to produce more cortisol. Cortisol is an important hormone that circulates in the body all the time, increasing and decreasing over each 24-hour period. This hormone does some useful things. It mobilizes fat for use as energy; it has anti-inflammatory properties; it is involved in the functioning of the liver; and it may also increase the sensitivity to and detection of threats. This all seems very positive and useful. When we are under chronic stress, however, the amount of cortisol circulating in the blood is increased, and it turns out that a *prolonged* high level of cortisol is bad for us. It is bad for the immune system (indeed, the effects of cortisol may be one of the problems in those who suffer from chronic fatigue syndrome), and it can cause undesirable changes in various areas of the brain that are involved with memory. Problems with memory and concentration may well be symptoms of excessively high cortisol levels. Cortisol also affects our mood chemicals. It can also make us hypersensitive to threats, which is not necessarily useful if it makes us focus too strongly on the threatening and negative aspects of situations and events. Research has revealed that many depressed people have highly stressed-out bodies with increased cortisol levels.

Let's think about another important aspect of stress: control. Can we control the effect of stress on us, and what happens if we can't?

Uncontrollable stress

Over 40 years ago, the American psychologist Martin Seligman found that, if animals were put under stresses that they could not control, they would become very passive and behave like depressed people. This did not happen if the animals could control the stress. These extremely important findings were later taken up by other researchers who wanted to see what changes took place in the brains of animals subjected to uncontrollable stress. It was found that some of the changes were similar to those associated with depression. For example, activity in areas of the brain that control positive emotions and behavior was reduced, stress systems went into overdrive and the mood chemicals – dopamine, noradrenaline and serotonin – were depleted. However, if other animals were subjected to the same stress *but had the means to control that stress*, different changes took place: the areas of the brain that control positive emotions and active (rather than passive) behavior were toned up and the mood chemicals were enhanced. This tells us something very important. The same stress, but with different levels of control, can produce quite different changes in our bodies and brains. If you are stressed and can do something about it, your brain will react in one way; but if you think you can't do anything about it, it will react in a different way. The way you cope with stress is a key issue. Although taking control is not always easy, as we will see, there are many things that we can do to help us have more control over our lives and depression and thus influence our mood chemicals.

The straw that breaks the camel's back

We often talk about 'the last straw' because we know that stress can be cumulative – it builds up. Take Nicky. Her firm was experiencing financial difficulties and she believed she was likely to lose her job, leaving her with a very uncertain future. The threat of redundancies had been hanging over the office for a couple of months and the atmosphere at work was very gloomy. Then, driving home late one evening, she was involved in a car crash. Responsibility for the accident was unclear, but she felt that it was partly due to a lapse in concentration on her part. She wasn't seriously injured, but her car was damaged and she was shaken up for quite a while. As she was recovering from this, her mother had a heart attack. Nicky had not been sleeping well for a month or so, and shortly after her mother became ill her sleeping became even worse. She began to brood more and more on the car accident and her responsibility. She also thought that maybe the worry of all that had contributed to her mother's heart attack, through stress. She felt she should do more to help her mother, but found that visiting her took up a lot of time and energy. She began to feel very low in mood, increasingly anxious and irritable, and personally inadequate; she found it difficult to get out of bed in the morning, and was prone to thinking 'There is not much point because things just happen out of my control.' Not being able to 'get her old energy back' was itself depressing.

In many cases of depression there is a combination of stresses and setbacks. There may be financial worries, worries over a job (or lack of one), conflicts at home or at work, children having problems, health worries and so forth. Over time the cumulative effect of these difficulties increases stress and edges us closer to maladaptive feedback, where we begin to ruminate on all the problems and spiral down into depression.

The small things get more difficult

One of the things that many people notice as they become depressed is that small things, or things they used to do easily, like calling the garage to have the car fixed, or having friends over for dinner, or queuing in the supermarket, become filled with anxiety or are hard to do. They start putting them off, and at the same time worrying because they have not been done. Suddenly, small things become big things. If this happens, then recognize your anxiety is a normal (if unpleasant) effect of your over-stressed brain state and will settle as you get better. Try as best you can to do those small things and not let them build up and get on top of you. You will feel better for it, even though it may take a lot of effort; whereas if you do put them off, you may start to brood on them and that will increase your stress. Recognize that your experience is a common one, and doesn't mean that you are 'personally useless'.

Stress spirals

A lot of what we try to do when helping people cope with depression is to stop spirals of stress. All kinds of events can happen to us at any time. Our plans and aspirations may not be working out; our relationships may be falling apart; we may be involved in car accidents, financial reverses and health changes. Or we may simply be overworking, trying to cope with the demands of a job, children or both, caught up in the 'hurry, hurry' society. All these experiences can be stressful to the extent that they tax our stress systems, raise cortisol levels and deplete mood chemicals. As the amount of cortisol in our system goes up, we become more focused on the negative, more fatigued and more stressed (see Figure 4.1).

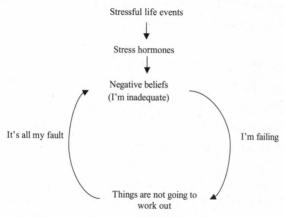

Figure 4.1 Relation between stress and thinking.

Stress and built-in irrationality

There are many times in life where our decisions are not based on rationality. Falling in love, choosing this career over that one, wanting children, liking this movie but not that one, are all based on how we *feel* about things. Our feelings can be automatically triggered and affect how we think about things and what we do. So there is another reason why we can become more focused on the threats and losses and become locked into the kind of loops described above. *Our brains are built to be irrational at times!*

Consider an animal peacefully grazing in an open field. Suddenly its attention is drawn to a movement in the grass. What should it do? Should it ignore it? Wait to find out what it is? Or get the hell out of there? In many cases in the wild, the best thing to do is 'get the hell out of there', because the movement could be a predator. In fact, the grazing animal only has to make the wrong decision (underestimate the danger) once, and it's dead. It would be far better to run away when there was no need to than stay and take the risk. If the animal runs away it has lost some time feeding, but it is still alive.

When we are under threat, our brains have been designed to work on a 'better safe than sorry' principle. That is, our brains were designed *not* to think rationally in all situations, but at times to jump to conclusions and assume the worst, which allows a rapid response if needed. It does not matter that this jumping to conclusions could be wrong, only that it works and protects us. The strange thing about this is that it means that *the brain is designed to make mistakes*, especially when we are under stress: to lead us to assume the worst and take defensive action unnecessarily. It helps to recognize that when we find ourselves being irrational and assuming the worst, this is not because we are stupid but because the brain has a natural tendency to do just that – to *catastrophize*. Today, jumping to conclusions and assuming the worst can lead us to feel pretty miserable and lock us into stress loops (see Figure 4.1), so we need to train our minds to help us gain more control over our feelings. This is the focus of Parts II and III of this book.

It is important to note though that even though this is not our fault (because we did not design our brains like this) our thoughts can amplify the bodily stress response and affect how our brains are working. Remember the examples we used on pages 28–29. This capacity for our thoughts, images, memories and coping efforts to stimulate our emotional and physiological responses is profoundly important. When people start to work on their depression, it is not uncommon for them to say: 'But surely my thoughts can't make me *feel* so bad?' or: 'Surely changing my thoughts can't make that much difference and affect my body?' The answer is yes, they can. Of course, there is much more to depression than depressive thinking; but imagine walking around in the world thinking that you are unlovable and worthless, or focusing on how depressed you feel, or ruminating on your anger and loneliness. Very understandable, of course, but what do you think will happen to your stress and mood systems? Unfortunately, if those things go over and over in your mind, your stress system will release stress hormones. Noticing and then trying to interrupt this feedback is one of the things this book will help you with.

Of course, breaking out of the loop may not be easy. People who are vulnerable to depression may not have anyone they can ask for emotional support, or they may feel ashamed to ask. We will discuss this later; but you can see that at some point we need to break this loop that will lead into a downward spiral. If you are so exhausted that you can't sleep and life has become very black, you may need to try some medication. But we also need to stand back and look at how we think and how we cope, and recognize how our threat-focused thoughts (natural though some of them might be) are too much in control of our minds.

So depression is not just psychological, or 'all in the mind', and certainly not a sign of a weak character or anything like that. Depression is about how our bodies and brains respond to stress, and about our genetic and developmental sensitivities.

Being depressed and tired can itself be stressful and depressing. If you feel ashamed of being depressed, remember that you did not design your body to respond in the way it does – you'd much rather not be stressed and depressed. If you don't like the term 'depression' then tell yourself you are exhausted or burnt out or in cortisol overdrive, and seek help – but recognize that there are things you can do to help you regain some balance in your three systems (see page 17) and bring your stress spirals under control.

KEY POINTS

- Depression involves changes in body and mind.
- Some people have a genetic risk of depression, but biological sensitivity can also arise from early life experiences.
- As we become stressed, biological changes take place in the brain, and these can lead us into downward spirals.
- Some of our negative ways of thinking are due to the way stress works, making us focus on the negative and assume the worst.
- Learning to exert more control over our lives and our thoughts can help us in many ways, not least by giving our brain chemistry a chance to recover.

5

Early life and the psychological and social aspects of depression

When psychologists explore depression they focus on two key areas. The first is how we *give meaning* to events and feelings. To one person, a divorce is a tragedy; to another, a relief. To one person, feeling angry is empowering; to another, it's frightening. The second area is how we *cope* with life's difficulties. Some people are able to break problems down into manageable tasks, seek out help from others and plan ways to overcome the difficulty, whereas others feel overwhelmed; they don't share their problems, but hope they will just go away.

These two processes, how we give meaning to events and how we cope, are key to an approach to therapy called *cognitive behavior therapy*[1] or CBT for short. As we'll see as we go on, learning compassionate thinking and behavior uses a lot of CBT ideas and ways of working and is key to helping us work with our depressions. Of course what is happening in your life is important to your feelings. If someone is threatening or assaulting you then you are likely to be experiencing the world in a certain way; our thoughts, feelings and mood states are linked to the *contexts* of our lives. It is not that our thoughts 'cause' depression, but rather that they contribute to depression.

Giving meaning

There are many ways we *give meaning* to feelings and events, and some meanings are more likely to increase depression than others. The cognitive approach suggests that particular kinds of thinking go with particular kinds of problems (see Table 5.1)

TABLE 5.1 THOUGHTS ASSOCIATED WITH PROBLEMS

Problem	Thoughts
Panic	I am going to die from these symptoms of anxiety.
Social anxiety	I will do something that will make me look foolish/stupid and I'll be rejected or shamed.
Depression	I am a bad/weak/inadequate person and the future is hopeless.
Paranoia	People are out to get me.
Anger	Other people are bad/unkind, are treating me unfairly, or taking advantage, and deserve to be punished.

By focusing on the *thoughts* that are associated with certain types of problem, we can learn to see how much our depressed moods push and pull us to see things as major threats, stimulating the threat self-protection system. CBT then helps us to test the evidence *and usefulness* for our thoughts and learn to generate alternatives – to balance our thinking. Being depressed often goes with feeling and thinking in certain ways (e.g., feeling defeated, subordinate, inferior). However, this suggests another question. How did we get into thinking negatively in the first place?

Early life and core feelings and beliefs

There is now a lot of evidence that early life experiences can *biologically* sensitize people to certain forms of stress and overstimulate their threat-protection systems.[2] We know that the types of love and affection children receive have an impact on their brains and how those brains grow and mature.[3] We also now know that children with different genetic profiles can be more vulnerable and at risk of mental health problems in the context of difficult early life experiences.[4] According to CBT, when we are young – and throughout our lives too – a variety of influences (including genetic) and events create within us emotional dispositions and *basic* or *core beliefs* about ourselves, others and the world. Let's look at how these are formed.

Core beliefs about oneself are fused with emotions

We all have core beliefs about the world – that the Earth goes around the Sun, or the Earth is round and not flat. These are linked to our fundamental ideas and knowledge about how the world is.

We also have another set of core beliefs based on our sense of self and other people. These core beliefs are very different from simple knowledge-based ones because they are fused with emotion. A self-focused *core belief* is something that you feel is basic to you. You might say, for example, 'When all is said and done I feel *this* about me,' or 'At heart I feel …', or 'Right in the centre of me I feel …'. Suppose a parent is angry with a child and calls her stupid. The child not only hears this label being used to describe her, but also has a fear. She *feels* stupid and has a sense of shame. The feeling of fear, shame and the label of 'stupid', *are fused together* in that moment. You can imagine what feelings might come back to her if she makes another mistake. Over time these feelings about herself may become part of her 'felt sense of self', the kind of person she feels herself to be.

When something unpleasant happens it is usually the emotions and feelings that strike us first; only later do we recognize that these feelings are associated with core beliefs, memories and ideas about ourselves. Let's work through an example to explore this. Sally had a fairly neglectful upbringing. When she was still relatively young, her mother told her that she had got married when she became pregnant with Sally. Unfortunately, the marriage was unhappy and her mother would ponder on how things might have been different for her had she not got pregnant. She would often say, 'If it hadn't been for you, I would have done such and such.' Sally felt that her mother saw her as the reason she had not done more with her life. Generally, these comments were not said in anger but with regret and sadness. At times, Sally's mother had strongly hinted that she felt like leaving home. Sally had taken these 'hints' as serious threats of abandonment, and gradually developed certain beliefs and ideas: 'I am a nuisance to others. I stop people doing what they want to do. People don't really want me around. I must not do anything that might push them away. Others might leave me at any moment.' Remember, these beliefs will be *glued in place with emotion*.

Sally carried these basic beliefs inside her throughout her life. Whenever there were conflicts, she would feel anxious and think/feel, 'Maybe I'm being a nuisance' or 'I must let others do what they want to do.' If she ever felt that she was putting others out, or letting them down, she would feel very guilty. A major unintended consequence of this way of being was that in trying to *protect herself* from others not wanting her around, she found it difficult to assert herself. She was constantly on the look-out for clues that she was being a burden to others. When an important long-term relationship with a boyfriend broke up, her automatic thoughts were: 'Well, I guess nobody really wants me. I am just a nuisance. I will never be loved for myself.' So her self-protection system quite understandably made her rather submissive, but the safety strategy had unwanted consequences.

As you might guess, underneath Sally's surface set of beliefs was another set. Here there was a high *degree of anger*. Having to give in to others all the time (in effect, subordinating herself to the needs of others) had led to feelings that this was unfair. After all, Sally hadn't asked to be born. Why should she have to keep doing what others wanted? Why was she so unlovable? But, of course, she thought that if she asserted herself, this would expose her to threats of abandonment and feeling a nuisance. If anyone made her very angry these inner rage feelings would be very frightening to her, because then she would feel others *really* wouldn't like her. These feelings had to be 'repressed' and avoided. She also felt, since her mother had done her best for her, that she had no right to be angry with her mother. Even thinking about her anger towards her mother for her threats of abandonment made Sally feel bad, like a traitor, and more stressed.

As you can see, and we will go over this many times, our thoughts are complex and can take us on a downward spiral into depression: as we become stressed and depressed, we have more negative thoughts; emotions of shame or fear of abandonment come back, we become more depressed with more negative thoughts and feelings.

Here is an overview of Sally's beliefs and feelings and how they affected her:

EARLY CHILDHOOD EXPERIENCES

- Mother said that had it not been for me she would have done more with her life.
- Worried that mother might leave one day.

BASIC BELIEFS FUSED WITH EMOTIONS

- I am a nuisance to others.
- I stop people doing what they want to do.
- People don't really want me around.
- I must not do anything that could push them away.
- I must be to others what they want me to be.
- Expressing anger and/or asserting my needs could lead to rejection.
- I am a bad/ungrateful person if I express my dissatisfactions.

BASIC SOCIAL BEHAVIORS AND SAFETY STRATEGIES

- I am not assertive.
- I avoid conflicts.
- I don't initiate things I want to do.

DEPRESSION-TRIGGERING EVENT

- Break-up of a relationship; loss of a valued person who blamed me for being rather boring.

TYPICAL THOUGHTS

- I am a nuisance to others.
- It would be better if I weren't here.
- Relationships are too difficult.
- I can't bear to be alone.

SYMPTOMS

- Poor sleep and exhaustion.
- Constant thinking about loss and self-blame.
- Feelings of worthlessness.
- Loss of pleasure and capacity to enjoy things.

- Feeling that the future seems hopeless.
- Weight loss.
- Inner feelings of emptiness.
- Increased fear and general feelings of disorientation.

You may have noticed two things about Sally. First she was very anxious about forming close relationships, and felt vulnerable to being left and abandoned. That anxiety and fear fuelled the underlying stress. Second, the way she behaved and coped with this – her self-protection strategy – was to act like a subordinate or even a servant. Her relationships did not boost her self-esteem very much. Indeed, apart from making herself 'fit in with others', she felt that she had no power to hold on to good relationships. When it came to asserting her own needs and opinions, she felt that she had neither the right to do so, nor any justification for doing so. Without a lot of reassurance, she felt empty and vulnerable, and often felt inferior and subordinate to others.

Sally's threat self-protection strategy was designed to help and protect her as best it could when she *was a child*. Being subordinate and trying to make Mum love and want her was very sensible for a vulnerable child, but through no fault of her own this strategy got her into serious problems later in life and stunted her growth. This is one example where we can see that depression is not our fault and neither is it the fault of the threat-protection strategies – it is an unintended effect of early efforts to get safe. The same is true for children who learn to be aggressive to defend themselves; this attitude may well get them into serious trouble later in life. These early self-protection strategies can be tricky to spot and to change. That is why training our minds becomes so important to understand.

Try this: Sit quietly for a moment and then focus on as much kindness as you can within you and reflect if there is anything about Sally's story that resonates for you. If there is, be gentle and kind about that. If you feel upset, go back to focusing on your inner kindness. If that is difficult – notice this and return to reading.

The role of early traumas

One powerful way in which some individuals learn how to judge and rate themselves is through having very painful experiences in childhood. For example, if they have been sexually abused, they might come to feel that sex is bad, disgusting, dirty or dangerous, and that they themselves are in some way bad or dirty and their sexual feelings are dangerous. In effect, the trauma robs them of their sexual lives and feelings of goodness.[5]

Sometimes parents are unable to cope, and when things get tense, they lash out at their children or call them names. This is intensely painful for the children, who find it difficult to recognize that their parents have a low tolerance for frustration. The children on the receiving end of this rage may blame themselves and think that they really are very bad. Sometimes parents are unable to give their children physical affection, perhaps because they don't know how or because they feel very awkward about it. One of the saddest things is that some parents still think that being physically affectionate towards their children, especially their sons, will turn the boys into sissies. As we have seen, affection is in fact very good for our brains (see pages 23–26).

AFFECTIONLESS CONTROL

Research has suggested that many depressed people can look back and see that their early life was often rather barren of affection, and sometimes even very harsh. Parents may have demanded high standards or have been very controlling. This is called *affectionless-control parenting*. Because most of us, as children, are unable to see our parents as flawed individuals with problems of their own, we tend to think that the way they treated us was our own fault; there was something about us that made them behave in the way they did. If they were very critical of us, we tend to carry on the tradition and be critical of ourselves. However, with understanding, insight and hard work, we can change these habits and learn to be compassionate towards ourselves.

UNPREDICTABILITY

Another very common pattern we see in the lives of depressed people is that their parents were unpredictable. These are parents who can be very loving and kind, but then are not available, leaving the child with yearning; or they can become aggressive, say hurtful things and even be physically abusive. It is very difficult for the child's threat self-protection systems to sort out what is safe and what is not. A parent can be seen as a source of comfort, but also a great threat. This kind of conflict is known to cause difficulties in how our brains deal with relationships. Sometimes people find it very difficult to sort out the feelings of both love and also fear, at times even hatred, of the parent. Moreover, because the child (and later the adult) wants to be loving, they can have a negative view of their own anger towards the parents, or even be in denial about that.

UNRELIABILITY

Unreliable parents can also be problematic for our emotional development. These are parents who talk a lot about love and being in a loving family but don't always behave like that. For example, Kay's mother was so preoccupied with her career and marital problems that she did not really attend to her daughter's mood changes just before adolescence. Kay was being bullied at school and abused by the next-door neighbour, but felt unable to tell her mother. She found her mother was never really there to get close to, although she was constantly saying 'what a loving family we are'. Children who experience their parents as unavailable for protection or support, or for forming a bond with them, can be left with ongoing desires and searching for closeness. They often anticipate that people will be superficially nice but with no real depth to their affections.

RESCUER CHILDREN

Some children grow up in circumstances – maybe with both parents working or in single-parent homes – where they have to take on responsibilities (e.g., looking after siblings). Gradually they see themselves as needing to achieve things, to help or rescue the family. Their expectations of themselves and the demands they put on themselves get out of proportion and they end up feeling overwhelmed and fearful of failure and being unable to live up to the expectations they have set themselves – becoming very perfectionistic (see Chapter 21). They can have dark feelings of defeat and inner collapse.

These are some of the relational backgrounds that a depressed person may experience early in life. There are many others. The key thing is the way in which people experience a sense of connectedness and safeness in the world because they know they can turn to and rely on others.[6] Our early relationships help us to experience the world as safe or dangerous, and this influences the balance of the threat and positive emotions systems we saw in Chapter 2.

Relationships and social needs

A lack of positive experiences (e.g., love, affection, support and care) in human relationships can be depressing. One reason for this is that the brain needs certain levels of positive inputs to maintain reasonable levels of mood chemicals and low levels of stress. On the whole, human beings throughout the world tend to be happier in some situations and unhappy in others (see Table 5.2).

TABLE 5.2 HAPPY AND UNHAPPY SITUATIONS

Happy situations	Unhappy situations
Loved and wanted	Unloved and unwanted
Close to others	Abandoned
Accepted and belonging	Not accepted/rejected
Have friends	Do not have friends
Accepted member of a group	An outsider or ostracized
Have value to others	Have little value for others
Appreciated	Taken for granted
Attractive to self and others	Unattractive to self and others
Have status and respect	Losing status or forced into low status

The situations in the left-hand column are associated with low levels of stress hormone and tend to boost our mood chemicals. They are 'feel-good' things. Those on the right-hand side are associated with increased stress and dips in our mood chemicals. The reason for this is that the brain is wired up to want the 'feel-good' things. Individuals who were able to have these needs met, who were 'socially successful', did better in evolutionary terms than those who did not – they survived better and left more offspring. We are biologically inclined to try to achieve the things in the left-hand column and avoid the things in the right-hand column. Desires for social success are wired into our emotions. The more our beliefs begin to shift towards the things in the right-hand column, the more threatened and unhappy we are likely to become.

Core beliefs, caring and relating

As described above, we can develop core beliefs about ourselves that 'at my core I am *this* or *that*'. Given how important relationships are to our feelings and moods, our feelings and beliefs about relationship can be important to how we create them, maintain them and cope with ending them. Depressed people can have very negative ideas about their ability to gain support, help, affection and approval from others. These beliefs might include:

BELIEFS ABOUT BEING A BURDEN TO OTHERS

- Nobody could care for me.
- My needs often seem a nuisance.
- It is pathetic for me to need love and reassurance.
- A needy person is a weak person.
- A needy person is a greedy person.
- My needs are far too much for anyone to cope with.

These beliefs can make it difficult for us to reach out to others. As you can imagine, they will also increase stress and make developing positive relationships with others more difficult. Talking to friends about these feelings can be helpful, because in this way we are making attempts to reach out to others and 'owning' our needs. Indeed, knowing what our needs are, and being able to express them, is important for mental health, especially if we are successful in eliciting supportive signals from others.

We can, of course, also have beliefs *about others*. These cover two broad concerns: the refusal or inability of others to care, and views that we are entitled to be cared for but others aren't doing enough.

BELIEFS THAT OTHERS ARE NOT AVAILABLE OR WILL BE ANGRY

- Others are too busy to bother with me.
- They are not up to caring for me.
- They don't understand.
- They will like me less for needing.
- They have too many problems of their own.

Exploitation and distrust

We are born with a sensitivity to cheating, because being cheated is a threat. Think how common it is for humans to feel angry at being cheated. Finding that your lover has been unfaithful, or that your friends have let you down, or that an important promise has not been kept – all these tend to activate strong negative feelings and low mood.

However, when we become depressed we can see deceptions almost everywhere because, under threat, the brain jumps to conclusions. When Jane returned to work after being off sick, her colleagues asked her how she was. But Jane thought, 'They are only asking this to make themselves feel better, not because they really care about me.' In effect, Jane was saying that her colleagues were actively trying to deceive her. When we are depressed, we become far more sensitive to the possibility that others are only pretending to be nice, that they are cheating us. And if we receive mild put-downs or people ignore us for whatever reason, we can read all kinds of things into that. This is because, when we are depressed, we are on the look-out for various kinds of social threat. Our basic beliefs can lead us to let these fears get out of hand.

BELIEFS ABOUT EXPLOITATION

- People really only care about themselves.
- If people are nice to me it's because they want something.
- People act nice to make themselves feel or look good.
- People will use me until I am no further use to them.
- Others will exploit me if they know my weaknesses.

Status

As we saw in the last chapter, some of the issues in depression are about our social standing in the world. Do we see ourselves as equal to others or inferior? Do we feel defeated and losers, or winners? Do we feel we have the 'power' to exert some influence over our relationships, or do we feel other people have more power? Recent research has found that depressed people often feel that others have more power than they do. The following are examples of basic beliefs about our status.

BELIEFS ABOUT INFERIORITY AND DEFEATS

- Compared with others, I am not so good, I'm inadequate, useless, worthless.
- I lack confidence to get what I want.
- I must achieve great things to help others, or to prove myself, or to feel life is worth living.

When Mary lost her lover to another woman, it was not so much the loss that upset her (she had had doubts about the relationship and had wondered whether she wanted it to continue). Instead, her distress was focused on the 'status thought': 'What does she have that I don't? Maybe I wasn't so good in bed. Maybe I'm less attractive than I thought.' It was these concerns with *why* she had lost out to another woman that made her feel most depressed.

Inferiority beliefs show themselves in our feelings of shame and inadequacy. When John got depressed and lost an important argument at work, he thought, 'I didn't put my point of view well enough. I'm inadequate. I'll never be able to win when it matters to me.' As he said later when he felt better, normally, although he would have been disappointed by the loss, he had always lived by the motto: 'You win some, you lose some.' In this case, however, the disappointment and stress of losing had led him to start jumping to conclusions. Interestingly, at the time, his love relationship was not going well. This background stress could have elevated his stress hormone level and made it much easier for his brain to switch to feelings of defeat and inadequacy.

The different sides of ourselves and their conflicts

We have different sides to our personalities, don't we? We say things like 'part of me wants to do this but another part of me wants to do that'. The problem is that different parts of ourselves can be in conflict. Having inner conflicts is actually common and normal. If we think in terms of balancing our minds, then sometimes we need to think about what part of ourselves is *missing* just as much as what we express. For instance, if you look at the example of Sally, what do you think she is avoiding – anger and assertiveness, maybe? When we hear Sally's story we might feel angry at her mother for saying those things to her. We might feel the anger that Sally struggles with because she is frightened of it. Sally wants to be loved and accepted and is therefore frightened of anger and about how stirring things up in conflict might make people reject her. In our own lives we might avoid asserting ourselves to avoid feeling guilt or shame.

Our brains are actually designed to have conflicting emotions. For example, if someone criticizes, you might feel the anger *and* anxiety, but you can't express both at the same time. You might become anxious about expressing anger if it's towards your boss, or you might be angry with yourself at being too anxious. Sometimes we can behave very submissively and then later, when we are alone perhaps, we ask ourselves, 'Why didn't I say that?'

As we go through this book we will keep this in mind, understanding that our brains can go *into conflict* over things: 'Should I or shouldn't I?'. Research shows us that our conflicts over what to do, say or think can be very stressing and – over time – depressing.

The social environment

It is also *very important* to recognize that the social environment has a major influence on our beliefs, feelings about ourselves, behaviors and moods. For example:

- Poverty is clearly linked to depression.
- In some parts of the world women are not allowed out without covering their faces with a veil. In other places women can dress and behave as they please – go skateboarding in bikinis if they like.
- Some of us grew up believing that there is a God who can send us to hell if we're too sinful, but others think this is sadistic nonsense.
- In some parts of the world children are likely to die before

the age of five, while in other places, infant mortality is relatively low.

- In some of our inner cities crime, drug problems, intimidation, pollution and poverty are the rule, but in the leafy suburbs these are rare.
- Some of us grow up with happy, doting parents; others with violent, abusive and alcoholic ones.

Many writers and commentators worry that we're creating mentally unhealthy environments – be this through the increasing selfishness of Western capitalism or our entertainments becoming more sadistic. Teachers are not able to hug distressed children for fear of prosecution. Constant school tests play children off against each other and focus on them being constantly judged and evaluated. To attract ever-shrinking audiences, TV programmers make programs where people are thrown out and shamed (*The Weakest Link, The Apprentice*), soap operas focus more and more on conflicts presenting people as highly self-centred and with low emotional control or kindness, and so on. All around us we are dissolving feelings of belonging, acceptance and tolerance. These social aspects will also be influencing our brains and moods. There is no question that some social environments are breeding grounds of stress and depression. In our rush for economic prosperity we don't focus nearly enough attention on building societies that promote psychological health.

Life events and depression

Not surprisingly, then, depressed people often have a mixture of problems, internal (styles of thinking, negative feelings) and external. Poverty is strongly linked to depression, as are poor and conflictual relationships. Social researchers George Brown and Tirrel Harris have found that, in women, external, social factors play a large role in the onset of some depressions and in the recovery from them. They found that there are things that make us vulnerable to depression (*vulnerability* factors *and chronic difficulties* such as low self-esteem, low social support, and having to look after young children) and things that push us into depression (*provoking agents* such as a major event that can overwhelm us).[7]

Social roles

Social psychologists recognize that much of our self-esteem and stress comes from our roles as mother, father, worker, boss, lover, student, spouse, etc.; in other words, from what we do. Psychologists Lorna Champion and Mick Power,[8] for example, have pointed out that our roles also give us a sense of self-esteem, status and some rank in society. Sadly, today, bringing up children and being a 'home-maker' or 'housewife' are not seen as roles conferring much status, despite these being some of the most important and emotionally taxing activities that people can tackle.

A major concern with depression in young people is that they may lack clear roles, especially if there are few jobs available, and they don't feel *part of integrated communities*. Feeling that we have something *to offer to others,* and that we are appreciated and valued for what we do, are important sources of self-esteem and social status. Jobs also give us some direct control over our lives, as well as allowing us to plan for the future and providing opportunities to interact with other people. Without jobs, we can feel unwanted by society, feel deprived of an identity, and find it difficult to make plans. We can also feel socially isolated. In my view a reason for the increasing rates of unhappiness, especially in our younger people, is that we are not providing important social roles where they can contribute *and feel included, needed and valued*.

Sometimes we invest a lot in a certain role, and then if that fails we go under with it. Consider Kath. She had always wanted to get married but had never met the right person. However, she had dedicated herself to nursing and this had become her life. Then, at the age of 54, she developed a serious illness, which meant that she had to take early retirement. Grieving for the one thing in her life that had given her meaning, she slipped into depression and gradually lost contact with her friends, especially those who were still working.

Social isolation

Some Western ways of life are rather isolating, but humans evolved to live in close-knit communities where children were not enclosed in small homes, but were mostly active out in the open, where friends and relatives could keep an eye on them. Young mothers and older people were certainly not separated from the working of the group, as they can be today. Some of the high rates of depression are due to *our abnormal social patterns and lifestyles*.

Depression can arise from real economic and social hardships. There may be things in your life that make depression more likely. Once you give up blaming yourself and feeling inadequate, you might begin to see how to make changes. It is also important to note, for example, that a life looking after children on your own does not necessarily lead to happiness. On the contrary, it has been shown that the arrival of children can lead to a reduction in happiness in the relationship of the parents. This is not to say, however, that children can't bring great pleasures. Indeed, some people become depressed when they lose this parenting role, as children 'fly the nest'.

Why are women more at risk from depression?

As noted women are around two to three times more likely to suffer from depression than men. There are various theories about why this should be so.

Biology

This view is that the higher rates of depression in women are due to differences in reproductive biology (e.g., the levels of certain hormones). Recent research suggests that emotional information may be processed slightly differently in the brains of men and women, although whether this increases the risk of depression is unknown.

Psychology

This view is that the higher rates of depression in women are due to differences in the way we are 'socialized' as we grow up. Women are brought up to be more accepting of subordinate positions, are schooled to be carers and, compared with men, encouraged to be less assertive or competitive. The incidence of sexual abuse is higher in women than in men.

The ways in which men and women recognize and cope with distressing life events may be different (e.g., women are more likely to focus on feelings and blame themselves). Women, then, are more in touch with and able to express sad and unhappy feelings; and they may be more vulnerable to 'lonely-based' depression. Women may dwell more on unhappiness, although this can be because they can be more socially isolated.

Social factors

This view is that variations in the incidence of depression between the sexes are due to differences in social opportunities and gender roles. Women are more likely to occupy subordinate positions in society and the family, to be restricted to the home and to be subjected to male dominance, even abuse. Marriage in particular may not always be helpful for women if it maintains them in subordinate positions with reduced opportunities to socialize with others and to engage in meaningful social roles outside the home. Spending time alone with children each day may be linked to some depressions.

My own view is that the differences in rates of depression between the sexes and also between different communities are, on the whole, due to a mixture of these factors but are mostly social ones.

Overview

There is, then, no single cause of depression. Although some of us are more genetically susceptible than others, part of the problem lies in how our brains were designed by evolution – and of course the social worlds in which we grew up and live. However, once we become depressed there are some typical things that happen, such as a shift in the balance of our inner systems towards more threat-processing (increased anger and anxiety and pessimistic thoughts) and a toning down of positive feeling (loss of drive and feeling of closeness to others and hopeful thoughts). If we work on these, in the various ways outlined in the next sections of this book, we might be able to shift the depressed brain state patterns into a new pattern.

KEY POINTS

- Depression is associated with increased threat- and loss-focused thoughts and reduced positive thinking and behavior.
- Many of the things that make us feel good in life are associated with the quality of our relationships and, when we are depressed, we often experience some of our relationships (e.g., with parents, friends, work colleagues or bosses) as unhelpful – being too distant or too critical.
- Vulnerability to depression might arise because we carry a number of latent negative beliefs/ideas/views/memories about ourselves (e.g., as unlovable or a failure). We often develop these in childhood.
- These basic beliefs can become reactivated when threatening or loss events happen to us. As a result, we tend to explain or interpret the reasons for the negative events with our negative beliefs e.g., 'This relationship broke up because of me. I am unlovable.'
- Many things that depress us can relate to conflicts we are having within ourselves, with others or over what to think, say or do. We can get stuck not knowing what to do and recognize there are benefits and losses in whichever way one moves.
- It is often our social roles that give us a sense of self-esteem, and not having a valued social role can be depressing.
- Social environments can do much to help or hinder our goals and pursuit of meaningful social roles.
- Depression is never about personal weakness or inadequacy, although we might think so. It is about how our systems have become overstressed and exhausted, leaving us feeling defeated. It is the brain state and pattern in us.

6

The relationship between our thoughts and feelings in depression

This chapter explores how our thoughts and feelings are often linked together, and how together they can push and pull us down into depression. Cognitive behavioral therapists argue that when events happen to us, or some feelings and thoughts arise in our minds, we also decide what they mean. The meanings we give to things and dwell upon can deeply affect our well-being. One way of looking at this is to distinguish the event that might stir feelings in us from the meanings we give to them. We can explore this by setting it out in three columns:

Event	Meanings	Consequences
Triggering event	Beliefs and key thoughts	Emotions
	Interpretations	Behavior
		Physical reactions

Suppose a good friend promises to phone you at 11 p.m. and asks you to wait in for the call, but then the time comes and goes and there is no phone call. What are the various possibilities for the consequences – what might you feel? Well, you could feel many things: anxiety, anger, sadness or even relief, and you would be absolutely right to say that it all depends on what you think the reason is for the person not phoning. That's the point.

We can see this below using the three columns again.

Event	Meanings	Consequences
No phone call	Something has happened to him/her – maybe an accident.	Anxiety
	S/he went to a party and forgot about me.	Anger
	S/he doesn't care enough to remember.	Sad
	S/he will phone tomorrow so I can go to bed now.	Calm/relief

Automatic thoughts and feelings

In the above example, the negative emotions of anger, anxiety or sadness indicate that the lack of the phone call is taken as some kind of threat. Jumping to the conclusion that, for example, your friend has had an accident is called an 'automatic thought' or 'automatic reaction'. You can't know what has happened, or the reasons why she didn't phone, until you have the *evidence*. At this point our thoughts are guesses or theories. Nonetheless, you may feel anxious or worried. As the term implies, automatic thoughts are those interpretations or ideas that seem to come automatically to mind; they are our 'pop-up' thoughts. They are immediate, consciously available thoughts that require little or no effort and can seem plausible. They are not arrived at through much in the way of reflective reasoning. They will often flush through our bodies with feelings; as if we are riding on a wave of feeling.[1]

Let's consider these thoughts a little more, this time using the example of anger over the missing phone call. The first thing to note is that you probably don't often think in *words* like, 'Oh, I think my friend has gone to a party and has forgotten to ring and left me waiting in for the call.' More likely, you have flashes of pictures in your mind. If your first flush was anger, how would you answer these questions: Is she having a good time? Is she talking with other people? Is there music playing? Is it classical or disco music? I would imagine that you can answer these questions fairly easily.

Sometimes automatic thoughts are difficult to catch because they happen quickly or are not in full consciousness. Had I not asked you about the party, those thoughts might have gone relatively unnoticed or been only semi-conscious, but when I drew your attention to them, you may have become aware that you had had them. *Sometimes, when we feel a change of emotion, we have to focus on our thoughts and what is actually going through our minds.*

It is common for automatic thoughts to occur in images, daydreams and fantasies. As in the example above, we may construct scenarios of seeing the friend in some particular place (e.g., the party) and imagine her having a good time, laughing, drinking and so on. We may also enter into a kind of discussion with ourselves as a result of our automatic thoughts and fantasies. For example, having decided that the friend is out having a good time while you are waiting for her call, you may start to rehearse in your mind an argument or what you intend to say the next time your friend does phone. You might even rehearse something that you know, in reality, you would not do because of fear of being rejected/disliked, or because of moral concerns.

Sometimes we may not be fully aware that we are constructing such scenes in our heads. For example, when the phone doesn't ring, you may find yourself becoming more sad or irritated, but your awareness of your thinking processes may be hazy. Sometimes we let the scenes in our minds run on, as if there is some 'inner director' in our heads feeding our minds various ideas and pictures that are full of meaning. Hence, we may need to train ourselves to sharpen the focus of our automatic thoughts and make them more easily known, recognized and challenged. We may need to use active imagination – that is, to allow ourselves to tune into the thoughts so that we can examine and deal with them more easily.

Here is a question for you. If you focus on those thoughts and play those kinds of scenarios in your mind, which brain systems are you stimulating? Is that helpful for you?

One thought leads to another

You may have noticed something important in the examples given above – one thought leads to another. Humans are highly creative in their thinking, and we are usually not happy with just one or two thoughts. At times, especially when we are heading into a depressive spiral, our thoughts spin down into catastrophes. Our threat system is in the driving seat. For example, let's consider how someone heading into a depressive spiral might think about the friend who didn't phone. The sequence of thoughts might go like this:

> *He hasn't phoned.*
>
> *This is because he has forgotten about me.*
>
> *Maybe he had better or more fun things to do.*
>
> *If he cared about me, he would have phoned.*
>
> *Therefore, he doesn't really care.*
>
> *I don't ever seem to be able to find someone who cares about me.*
>
> *What's wrong with me?*

Maybe I am just too boring and unattractive.

I'll never have a good, long-lasting relationship.

I'll always end up abandoned.

Life is completely pointless and empty.

This cascade can be so rapid that we hardly notice it. Rather than just being disappointed or slightly irritated by the phone not ringing, we end up feeling much more depressed because we become focused on being boring, not cared for, are going to be abandoned or are being used by others. When we enter into depression brain patterns, we often experience rapid cascades of thoughts like those above. One reason for this is because *our threat-protection system is hypersensitive and always goes for 'assume the worst' and 'it is better to be safe than sorry' while our rational and soothing-reassuring systems struggle to keep a perspective or help us calm down* – and we will explore what to do about it shortly.

Sometimes it is what we feel within our bodies that generates negative thoughts. For example, people who have panic attacks may notice that their heart rate goes up when they become anxious. This leads to the thought: 'There must be something wrong with my heart for it to beat like this.' They then focus attention on their heart rate, and because they are thinking that there is something wrong with their heart, they become more anxious. And, of course, as they become more anxious, their heart rate goes up even further. Even though the heart is basically a pump and is designed to increase and decrease its beating as circumstances require, the idea that an increased heart rate signals an oncoming heart attack produces an intense anxiety spiral (Figure 6.1).

Hence we can see that we can have negative thoughts about ourselves, others and the future, all of which can increase our depression, and that these can be sparked off by events, our inner feelings, things we notice in our bodies or past actions.

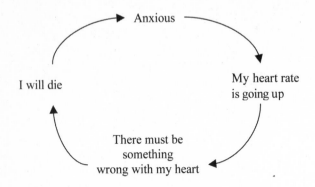

Figure 6.1 How thoughts and feelings interact.

Downward spirals and emotional amplifiers

Usually thoughts like these provide feedback for each other. For example, when we are depressed we often don't feel like doing much; when we don't achieve much, we may tell ourselves how useless we are or feel unlovable or defeated because we are depressed and ratty, which increases depression; we feel depressed about being depressed (Figure 6.2).

You can probably see that if we are caught up in understandable spirals, it can be difficult to get out of it, unless we take steps to stop them. These thoughts might be called *emotional amplifiers* because, as they go around and around, they become more intense. There is nothing in the spiral that damps them down. You need to build in *emotional dampeners* – ways to break the cycle. You may also see that there are some key links in this spiral that you could challenge. You might 'mindfully' accept your depression as your current state of mind (see Chapter 7),

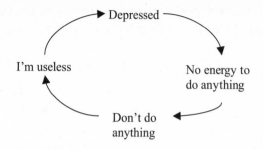

Figure 6.2 How thoughts and behaviors interact.

which is not your fault, and be kind to yourself. You could do a little bit of some activity and then give yourself a lot of praise for doing something even though you're depressed (see Chapter 12). You know praise will stimulate your positive emotion systems, so you can learn to praise your efforts rather than the results. Think about how you would speak to a friend in the same situation and treat yourself the same way (see Chapter 9).

If you are depressed, don't be surprised if these suggestions don't impress you. You can be expected to discount them – after all, you feel depressed, and that's what we tend to do when we are depressed. We stick rigidly to what we think and the way we see things. A thought to keep in mind for later is to consider whether your feelings of being useless or unlovable are related to frustration and anger about being tired, and you then direct these feelings at yourself, or whether you might actually be frightened to see that you are better than you think you are.

Thoughts about feelings

Although it is often situations and events that spark off threat-related thoughts, this is not always so. Our moods can set us up for certain types of thought – we think differently when in a depressed, anxious, angry or happy mood. Sometimes our feelings can be triggered by things of which we are not fully conscious.[2] Importantly too, we can have inner feelings such as anger or feeling trapped and then have thoughts about those inner feelings. For example, you might think it is bad to have intense feelings of anger. Or you might have sexual feelings about someone and feel very guilty because you tell yourself that such feelings and fantasies are bad. Or you might feel anxious about something and then think that you are stupid or weak for feeling anxious. You may wake up *feeling* tired and think, 'Oh, God, another bloody day! How am I going to get through it?'

When depressed we can have all kinds of beliefs about some of our own inner feelings. For example, we may believe we have fantasies or feelings that other people don't have. These may be related to frightening, escaping, sexual or aggressive fantasies. We feel we can't talk about them because people will regard us as odd.[3] But of course humans have had these thoughts and fantasies for millions of years, and when it comes to frightening, defeatist, sexual or aggressive ones some people write books about them and make a lot of money! They may be pretty horrible fantasies, but they are not abnormal. People may believe that their feelings will overwhelm them. Of course feelings can be very powerful at times, and we need to learn how to tolerate them without acting them out. Stories and films like *The Hulk* appeal to us because we have all had the experience of feeling high levels of rage, which can frighten us. Sometimes it is sadness, tearfulness and grief that depressed people feel they are overwhelmed by, and sometimes they try to avoid feeling. Sometimes depressed people can have conflicts with those they love, and they may believe that this means there is something wrong with their relationship. They may believe that if you love somebody you should never feel very angry or want to leave them.

So it is not just things that happen in the outside world that can worry or upset us. It can also be thoughts and feelings that come into our minds, which we think indicate something bad about us, that can also be distressing. Learning how to cope with our own minds, and realizing that a lot of what goes on in them is because of how our brains evolved, and is not our fault, is important. You have the capacity for intense anxiety, rage or grief because your brain has been built to have those capacities; and you can read about them in novels and see them acted out in films. We have to learn how to cope with strong feelings, what they mean and how they can blend together; but not blame ourselves for having them.

So you see we can have feelings about feelings. We can become anxious about being depressed, depressed about being anxious, angry about being anxious, anxious about being angry – and round and round we go.

Thoughts and behaviors

We may also have negative thoughts about what we have done or failed to do. For example, because we are anxious, we might not go to a party or some other function to which we have been invited. We might then think that we have behaved badly and let other people down. We become preoccupied with guilt. For example, because he suffered from social anxiety, Colin did not go to a friend's leaving party at work. He had the following thoughts:

I should have gone.

I've let my friend down.

He will be angry that I didn't go and will lose interest in me.

Others will wonder what's the matter with me.

I have missed out on a good time again.

I'm useless in social situations.

I'm pathetic to get anxious.

The more these thoughts took hold, the more anxious and depressed he became.

When Richard looked back at his life he picked out things he felt bad about and dwelt on them. This of course kept him depressed, and stopped him doing anything about them. He recognized that when he was not depressed, he could see his life as complicated and that like all human beings he had made helpful and unhelpful decisions. It is very easy for us to fall into focusing on regrets – 'if only I had or if only I hadn't.' Acknowledging but coming to terms with, maybe grieving for, and moving on from regrets can be helpful to us. We cannot change a single second that has passed, but the future is yet to be written.

Some of the decisions we feel bad about can be major things such as getting drunk and sleeping with somebody we didn't want to, or staying in or pulling out of a relationship and then regretting it. As we will see later in this book, it is important to learn to become kind to ourselves and balanced in our thinking about things in our lives we are not comfortable with, or are disappointed in ourselves about. Very few of us get through life without making mistakes and having regrets. It is how we think about and deal with those things that is important for either learning from them or getting lost in depression over them. Depressed people often are not just unhappy with their behaviors but tend to judge *themselves as a person* rather negatively. We will address these issues in Chapter 13 on self-bullying and Chapter 17 on shame.

Writing down your thoughts

In Appendices 1 and 5 you will find a form where you can write down automatic thoughts, similar to the one we used with the phone call example on page 96. Turn to the appendix quickly and have a look. In this form you will see that, in the first column, various things can spark off negative thoughts and lead to various negative evaluations and conclusions. You can include events such as people criticizing you or things not working out as you would like (such as not receiving the phone call). We can also make negative evaluations of our *feelings* (e.g., I am a bad person for feeling angry; it is wrong to feel sexual attraction towards someone else who is not my partner), our *behavior* (I should not have acted like that; I am a bad person for losing control) or our *bodies* (when my heart rate goes up, this means there is something wrong with it and I might die). Then you can fill in the other two columns as before, that is, the beliefs and key thoughts of the 'triggering' event and its consequences.

The key thing is to choose what you want to focus on, then write down the thoughts that go through your mind. If you habitually write these down, you will get better at identifying them. Writing thoughts down helps to clarify them and allows you to concentrate on them, thus avoiding having them slip in and out of your mind in a rather chaotic fashion. A good way to start is to notice how your moods and feelings change. Try to remember what might have been happening to you at the time your mood dipped or you had a flush of unwanted feelings, or unwanted thoughts popped into your mind – for instance, a criticism, or something that did not work out as you wanted it to, or something you hadn't done or thought you ought to do. Next, write down the thoughts associated with these situations. Sometimes you will not be able to identify specific things, so just write down thoughts that seem associated with difficult feelings.

Stop reading for a moment and see if you can think of a situation that made you upset recently. Try to identify your thoughts and interpretations that went along with those feelings. Practise this on a few events that you can remember happening to you recently. Gradually you'll get the hang of noticing that when something happens that makes you feel upset, the upset feeling goes with a set of thoughts about yourself, others, and the world or your future. You are learning that you can have thoughts but you can also stand to the side of them, look at them, understand what they are, and coolly write them down. Over time you can learn to monitor these thoughts as they occur. You can even make a judgement about them that says 'Although they may be understandable, they may be too influenced by the emotions I am in right now so I need to stand back and give myself some space' or 'Dwelling on those thoughts is unhelpful to me so I need to work on this'.

Another useful way to begin is, if you notice a change in your feelings, or even if you notice that you are feeling something that you can identify as anxiety, depression or sadness, ask the question: 'If my feelings could speak, what would they say to me?'

You will notice that there is a fourth column for writing down alternative helpful thoughts. Some worked examples are given for you. As you go through this book, you'll get better at identifying what goes through your mind and noting your own depressive spirals (and emotional amplifiers). You'll also be able to stand back from your upsetting thoughts and not let that 'better safe than sorry' and 'assume the worst' type of thinking run away with you. It takes time and practice. The way we stand back and learn to generate alternatives, and learn to generate a kind voice in our head when we are suffering (instead of the harsh, frightening or critical one), is what we will explore in later chapters. The first steps, however, are about learning that our feelings and moods come with ways of thinking about ourselves and the world, and our ways of thinking bring up feelings and moods.

How to identify your thoughts

Sometimes it is difficult to know what are the main worries from our threat and self-protection system. Well, one way is to ask ourselves some questions. For example, let's suppose that you tried to do something and it did not turn out right. You feel disappointed and your mood takes a dip. You could then ask yourself:

Question	Possible fears and threats
What do I think are the implications of this event?	*I won't be able to achieve what I want to achieve.*
What conclusions am I drawing from this situation?	*I am not going to succeed in what I want to achieve.*

You can also ask questions about what you think others will think or how they will react.

What do I think they will think about my failure?	*They will think I'm not capable of much – rejection.*

Another set of questions asks you to think about the conclusions that you might be drawing about yourself as a person. Ask yourself:

What does this say about me?   *If I fail at this, it means I am inadequate.*

What do I think this means for my future?   *I will never get anything right.*

In general, there are three basic types of question to ask yourself. These are:

1 **Questions about how you think others see or think about you and how they will be with you as a result**. These questions are focused on the *external world* and on other people in it. Notice here your attention is outside of you – on thinking about other people – trying to work them out or what you need to do to make them like you.

2 **Questions about how you see yourself as a person**. These questions are focused on your *internal world* – on yourself. Notice your attention is turned inward on you this time – on your sense of yourself and on your feelings.

3 **Questions about implications, including for the future**. These questions are focused on your *goals and things you want to happen* and possible blocks to them.

So then, if we take our example of 'trying to do something that does not go well', we might have a set of thoughts that are something like this:

EXTERNALLY FOCUSED THOUGHTS

- Other people will think I am not capable of much.
- They will be critical.
- They will distance themselves from me, not want to include me or even reject me.

INTERNALLY FOCUSED THOUGHTS

- I don't have what it takes to succeed – may be inadequate – not the 'right stuff'.
- I will lose my confidence and be anxious.
- I feel depressed / angry / fed up – life is a pain.

FUTURE-FOCUSED THOUGHTS

- I am not going to succeed in what I want to achieve.
- I will be stuck and not go forward as I want to.
- Life will be miserable or pointless.

If these seem like your thoughts, then see that they are the thoughts of depressed minds – all over the world. This can help us stand back and realize this is *depression thinking in us* and these thoughts can change when our mood changes. I am not saying your thoughts 'cause your bad feelings', because it's a little more complex than that. However, by looking at our thoughts *we have a window* on what's going on in our minds. We can see that the frustration of not succeeding doesn't stay at that level of a mild annoyance but (in this example) has rippled out to be more intense and create a sense of an inadequate self, a self we don't like and that isn't going to be able to do much in the future! It is these ripple effects in our thinking that contribute more depression. When we are stressed our threat systems are super-sensitive and these ripple effects are very common. Therefore we must take steps to work with them. These thoughts might not have been obvious before we asked ourselves the questions. Moreover, taking the time to consider these questions allowed us to focus on our thoughts. By asking certain questions, we can get some insight into what we think about certain situations and events.

Basic beliefs and attitudes

You may well ask: where do these negative feelings and thoughts come from? One answer is that they are generated by the state of depression itself. However it is also often the case that automatic thoughts are generated from the various attitudes and basic beliefs we have about ourselves, others and life in general, and these often predate the depression (see pages 74–83).[1] They include such beliefs as:

- If people make mistakes, they are inadequate.
- People who show strong anger are unlovable.
- You can never be happy if you do not have a conflict-free, close relationship.
- If you have strong arguments with someone close to you, they don't love you.
- If your parents did not love you or treated you badly, you are unlovable.

There are many types of attitudes and basic negative beliefs like these that tend to lead to negative conclusions. In my own case, I was bad at English and I developed the negative belief: 'Being poor at English equals being stupid.' When I was depressed, this belief seemed very true to me – and I therefore felt not very bright or able. When I noticed poor spelling in my work, or I was criticized for my poor English, I would have a particularly uncomfortable 'sinking feeling'. It was only later that I realized that this belief ('I am stupid') was untrue and that I only applied it to myself and not to others, but that's the way with basic beliefs – we often don't realize that we have them. It is how our feelings react to certain situations that tells us that we should be alert to the possibility that we may have some basic negative beliefs that need identifying and changing.

Let's take this back to our three circles that we saw on page 17. Why does being bad at English, or even being not that bright, feel important? Because it is associated with other experiences such as rejection or criticism. As I have mentioned before, humans have evolved to want approval from others (the pats on the head and smiling faces) because if we feel accepted and wanted we feel safe. It's all about threat and safeness! It is the association of an element of ourselves with the threat of criticism or put-down and thus rejection, or inability to reach our valued goals, that causes the problem. If you are overweight, or struggling at any activity, you're going to feel a lot better if you know people will not judge you negatively but will accept or love you, and help you. Indeed, in some societies women *put on* weight because that is deemed attractive! So if we do not do so well, somewhere in our minds can be feelings of shame or of being seen as different from others in some way, that gives us a sense of aloneness. This is the basis of a sense of threat in these situations. And it is because this threat underlies many of our negative thoughts and beliefs that learning to be kind and compassionate is so important. It will help us settle our threat systems.

Let's get back to basics. As a rule of thumb, threat-focused automatic thoughts are triggered by situations or things that arise in our minds at specific points in time. They may often include basic threat-focused beliefs, some of which are like our basic views about life. They too can be internally focused on the self or externally focused on others, and some will be focused on life goals. We had a look at some of Sally's beliefs in Chapter 5 – now let's look at them again in a more complete way, in Table 6.1.

TABLE 6.1 INTERNALLY FOCUSED BELIEFS

About the self	About others	Future and goal-focused beliefs
I am a nuisance to others	Other people are easily upset and become critical	I am unlikely to get the confidence to do what I want in life
I stop people doing what they want to do	Other people are more powerful than me and can hurt me	My future is really dependent on how I get on with others
I must not do anything that could push them away	People don't really want me around	
I must be to others what they want me to be	Other people won't tolerate or try to understand my feelings	
Expressing anger and/or asserting my needs could lead to rejection	Other people may act nice but they think different things underneath	
I must be grateful for love	Other people think I am deficient in some way	
I am a bad/ungrateful person if I express my dissatisfactions		

Although these thoughts and beliefs were not active all the time, it did not take much to trigger them. Keep in mind too that it is not just beliefs that are triggered, but emotional memories associated with where Sally learned those beliefs. For example, the idea that expressing anger leads to rejection will be associated with emotional feelings and memories of rejection. The beliefs and the feelings that come with them together form a tight tapestry of experience. The beliefs are the verbal descriptors that shape meaning. Can you see how Sally's threat system and feelings of insecurity might be at the root of these difficulties? Can you see how her beliefs are like warnings and things that are frightening to her – they are sort of 'better safe than sorry'. If you assume that other people see you as deficient, then you can try to protect yourself – so better safe than sorry.

Dwelling on thoughts

When we dwell on something, we turn an idea or set of beliefs over and over in our minds. This is called *rumination*. A common situation is to lie in bed and worry, your mind focusing on a particular train of thoughts. This is not the same as having an immediate reaction to something and then pulling back and seeking out the evidence. When we dwell on things, we are allowing ourselves to think along a certain path for many minutes or even hours. Depression involves not only automatic thoughts and immediate reactions to situations, but also ruminating, dwelling on the same negative thoughts. This type of thinking is important to recognize and interrupt.

Remind yourself about the three circles in Figure 2.1 on page 17, and also remind yourself about the way the thoughts and scenes we run, and go over in our minds, stimulate our emotion systems as discussed on page 28. Dwelling and ruminating is very easy, it's like letting the wind blow you along. The problem is although the wind is strong, you might be sailing in the wrong direction! Think about what dwelling on negative things does to your brain; think about the systems you are stimulating when you dwell on the threat and loss. This is not a criticism, because our threat system will hold you in the negative, because it's focusing on threat and protection – which is what it is designed to do. It is not bad, or your enemy, but we can appreciate it's actually taking us in the wrong direction. Our goal is to stimulate the positive emotion systems – to work towards our well-being. We want to calm the threat system, not keep it turned up. That's why we need to learn how to refocus on kindness, getting a wider perspective and standing to the side of these distressing or angry thoughts. The practice of mindfulness, of (just) observing our thoughts without engaging with them and/or of deliberately shifting to compassionate imagery and thinking can be helpful, and we explore that in our next chapter. We *need to make efforts* to create a warm and kind voice that is understanding about our pain when we find ourselves ruminating.

By now, you will probably be aware of the kinds of things you dwell on. These may be thoughts of inadequacy, injustice and unfairness, revenge, loss, and/or negative predictions of the future – in fact, just the kinds of thoughts that everyone has from time to time. Become more aware of any common 'themes' in your thoughts. If you find it difficult to recognize when your mind is dwelling on things, you can leave notes to yourself around the house that remind you to check on what you are thinking. Or you could carry a small object such as a stone in your pocket so that, each time you feel it there, this will be a signal to check on your thoughts. If you have been dwelling on certain things, gently remind yourself that you can break off from these thoughts. Indeed, do whatever works for you to help yourself from dwelling on negative thoughts and indoctrinating yourself with them.

KEY POINTS

- When something happens to us, we often have various thoughts about what the event means to us. These are our interpretations and they are personal to us.
- These thoughts can be automatic and just pop into the mind.
- One automatic thought can lead to another and spiral us down into deeper, more depressed feelings.
- We can have negative thoughts not only about particular situations but also about our inner feelings, fantasies and past actions.

- Our thoughts can be difficult to pin down, but if we ask ourselves certain types of questions, they might become clearer.
- We may ruminate and dwell on unpleasant feelings, thoughts and ideas, and so spiral down into deeper, more depressed feelings.
- We often need to train ourselves to become more aware of our automatic thoughts and the themes we tend to dwell on.
- One way to begin to gain more awareness of your thinking is to make a habit of writing down your thoughts.
- Some of our negative automatic thoughts are triggered because we have underlying basic negative beliefs. Until we recognize our automatic thoughts, we may not be aware of these basic beliefs that could be guiding our lives.

EXERCISES

Exercise 1

At first, you might use a notebook that you keep handy. Draw up three columns that allow you to separate out triggering events, beliefs and key thoughts, and feelings, and then stand back and refocus on helpful, compassionate thoughts and feelings.

- Write down whatever comes into your mind – even if, at first, it does not make much sense.

- Start to consider your thoughts when your mood changes. Learn to 'catch' your thoughts. Give yourself time and space to focus on them.

Exercise 2

To gain more insight into your thoughts, ask yourself some questions. These can include:

- Questions about how you see yourself as a person.
- Questions about how you think others see you.
- Questions about implications, including for the future.

Exercise 3

Use or make copies of the thought monitoring form (see Appendices 1 and 5), familiarize yourself with it, and try using it. As you become better at catching and noting your thoughts, work on the fourth column – creating and generating compassionate, helpful alternatives to your thoughts. We will be exploring how to do this in a lot of detail in the chapters to come, but you already have some ideas such as trying to create a compassionate point of view in your mind.

• Watch out for threat-focused thoughts that are frightened to try or that always focus on the 'can't do' rather than "Maybe this won't help, but what have I got to lose from trying?'

PART TWO
Learning How to Cope: First Steps

7

Mindful preparations for working with depression

Your journey journal

We have now arrived at the *work* and *practice* part of our exploration together. You might find it helpful to have a folder or a journal that you keep to write in reflections on different exercises, or thoughts you've had during the day, or ways in which you might respond to things differently, or even note changes in your dreams. It's like a personal log. You can also gather things along the way – pictures, poems or articles – to stick in it. We know that writing about our thoughts and feelings reflectively can be very helpful to clarify them and can also provide insights. You will find there will be some days when you may want to write in your journal and other times you may not. Having a journey journal is, of course, only a suggestion, although I will be inviting you to use it in different ways as we go along.

First steps: mindfulness

On the road ahead we are going to explore how to work on thoughts, feelings and behaviors, to change depressed brain states. One of the most useful skills to help us in all these efforts is called *mindfulness*.[1]

In recent years researchers all over the world have dedicated a lot of attention to mindfulness and how it can help depressed people, and indeed all of us.[2] The idea of mindfulness itself goes back thousands of years. Here we focus on mindfulness as *a way of learning to pay attention, and hold attention in the present moment with a specific focus and with judgement*. This it can bring new balance to our minds and awareness.[3]

Many of the great teachers of meditation point out that we only exist in *this moment* – we are a 'point of consciousness' passing through or in time. Our consciousness does not exist in the moment just gone nor in the moment yet to arrive – we only exist *now*. Mindfulness is learning how to bring us to be fully alive to the *now* of our conscious existence, the only place we actually exist. We can be so lost in the hopes or fears of tomorrow, or the regrets of yesterday, that we miss the moment *now* – we live in a remembered or imagined world, not in the world of 'right now'. Of course, sometimes it is very important to reflect back and project forward, but when we do this we want to do it purposely rather than being automatically dragged there by depressed states, fears, angers or strong desires.

The word *meditation* actually means *becoming familiar*. For us becoming more mindful is to become familiar with the contents of our minds and how our minds work. Mindfulness also means becoming more aware and more 'in' one's experience; to pay open or curious attention to the details of one's inner feelings and thoughts as they emerge in one's mind. How many of us, for example, when anxious or angry, actually stop and pay attention to where this feeling is in our bodies, what our voice sounds like, what part of our mind is now issuing the instructions to our thoughts and bodies; what are our key thoughts and fears? How often do we stand back and practise *observing* what is actually happening in our minds? Mostly we don't, and our brain patterns and emotions are just 'doing their own thing'. Mindfulness is learning how to change this 'being caught in the automatic-ness' of the unpleasant emotions and moods.

Yourself and consciousness

Let's think about ourselves as existing as *a point of consciousness* 'in this moment of time'. Consciousness of this type can be regarded like water. Water can contain a poison or a medicine, can be clear or muddy – but water is water – it is pure *and is not what it contains*. So too with our consciousness – it can be filled with joy, anxiety, anger or depression but consciousness itself is not those things. Learning to recognize yourself as a point of consciousness and distinguish this from the content (your moods, feelings and thoughts) can be helpful. A key to help us is learning about our attention.

Learning to attend

Mindfulness is a way of understanding our attention. The attention can be located as an act of choice. For example, if I ask you to concentrate and attend to the big toe on your left foot, you will suddenly *notice* sensations from that part of the body. If you now switch your attention to the top of your head, you will experience different sensations. Our conscious attention can be thought of as a spotlight that moves around. It is learning how to direct that spotlight, via our attention, which is key to mindfulness.

Mindfulness is therefore about the clarity of observation. Let's try an example of eating an apple mindfully. First, you would look at the apple, and note all of its colours and textures. Hold the apple in your hand and feel the quality of its skin. Don't rush, spend time observing. When your mind wanders from your focus on the apple (as it very easily can), gently bring your focus back to it. In this exploration, you are not judging the apple, you are simply exploring its properties. Then you take a knife, and maybe peel the apple, or cut into it. Once again, notice the effect that you have on the apple, the colour and texture of the fruit beneath the skin. Take time to really observe. Next, you may take a bite of the apple, and now you are going to focus on the senses of taste and what the apple feels like in your mouth. Chew slowly, feeling the texture in your mouth, noticing how the juice might stimulate your saliva and how it feels in your mouth. As you chew, notice how it becomes more mushy. As you swallow, pay attention to the sensations of swallowing. All focus is on the apple.

So we have explored the apple visually, by touch and feel, by smell, texture, and by taste. If we had dropped the apple, we would have been able to hear what it sounded like. In this interaction, there is *no judgement*, there is *only your experience of your interaction with the apple*. This is mindful attention, being in the activity, rather than distracted from it by other thoughts, and exploring all aspects of the activity to the full.

Notice how your mind can wander: 'These are not good apples, where did I buy them from; I ought to eat more fruit; actually I don't like apples! Oh damn, I cut my finger!' If you are depressed you might have thoughts like, 'What is the point of this, it doesn't solve my problems' – thoughts that will put you back into stimulating depressed patterns in your mind. One reason for doing these exercises is to practise shifting out of patterns of thinking and focusing that increase rather than diminish depression in our minds. The mind can 'rest' in this moment.

Mindfulness is important because most of our lives are spent doing one thing and thinking about something else, and we are never fully 'in this moment'. Our minds are constantly distracted. Take driving, for example. We can get home and realize we can't really remember how we got there, because our minds were full of a hundred and one other things. If something unexpected happened, such as a group of naked motorcyclists zooming past us, our attention would have been alerted, or if the driver in front of us suddenly put on their brakes, our attention would be focused again. But this is not *savouring* the moment; this is being brought to alertness for a specific reason. Mindfulness is about being in the moment.

Soothing rhythm and mindful breathing

We are now going to use the same idea as mindfully peeling and eating the apple, but this time focusing on our breathing. Our breathing will become a central focus around which we will do some compassion-focused exercises later. Learning how to breathe mindfully will be useful when we come to do these exercises. The key here is simply to practise without worrying if you are doing it right, correctly, adequately and so forth. These thoughts are common and understandable but they are distractions. If they arise in your mind, simply notice them and call them 'your judging and evaluative thoughts', *smile* kindly to yourself and bring your attention back on task.

To start with, find somewhere you can sit comfortably and won't be disturbed. Place both feet flat on the floor about a shoulder's width apart and rest your hands on your knees. Keep your back straight. Look down at about 45 degrees – or if you prefer close your eyes – whatever you find best for you. You may prefer to sit on the floor, or cross-legged on a small meditation stool. Find postures that are comfortable for you but not slouched. Sometimes lying flat on the floor can be helpful, if that is the most comfortable position for you to start your work. In my CD, which covers aspects of this book, there are ideas that you can listen to.[4] The idea is not to become sleepy but to develop a certain type of alertness, focus and awareness. I will, however, explore a set of relaxation exercises with you later in this chapter.

Gently focus on your breathing. Breathe through your nose. As you breathe in, let the air come down into your diaphragm – that's at the bottom of your ribcage in the upside down V. Place a hand on your diaphragm and notice your hand lift and fall with your breath. Feel your diaphragm – the area underneath your ribs – move as you breathe in and out. Do this for a few breaths until you feel comfortable with it and it seems natural and easy for you. Next place your hands on each side of your rib cage, as low as you can. This is slightly more awkward because your elbows will be pointing outwards. Now breathe gently. Notice how your rib cage expands against your hands outwards, your lungs acting like bellows. This is the movement of the breath you're interested in; you feel your lungs expanding. You want a breath to come in and down but also expand you out at the sides. Your breathing should feel comfortable and not forced. As a rough guide, it's about three seconds on the in-breath, a slight pause and three seconds on the out-breath. But you must find the rhythm *that suits you*. As you practise, replenish most of the air in your lungs but not in a forced way.

Notice your breathing, and play around and experiment with it. Breathe a little faster, or a little slower, until you find a breathing pattern that, for you, seems to be your own *soothing, comforting rhythm*. There will be a breathing rhythm that feels natural to you, and as you engage with it feel your body *slowing down*. It is as if you are checking in, linking up, with a rhythm within your body that is soothing and calming to you. You are letting your body set the rhythm and breathe for you, and you are paying attention to it. Rest your eyes so that they are looking down at about 45 degrees. You may wish to close your eyes, but notice that sometimes if we do that we can become very sleepy. Spend 30 seconds or so focusing on breathing, noticing the breath coming through your nose, down into the diaphragm, your diaphragm lifting, your chest gently expanding sideways, and then the air moving out, through your nose. Notice the sensations in your body as the air flows in and out. Stop reading this book, and focus on that for 30 seconds (longer if you like) and sense a slight slowing with your breathing. Some people find that focusing their attention on just the inside of their nose, where the air comes in, can offer a helpful attention focus. Try it and see.

You might notice how your body responds to this breathing, with feelings of slowing and feeling slightly heavier in your chair. If you've done the exercise you may notice how the chair is holding you up. However, some people can find these first stages quite anxiety provoking, and don't actually like them. For those who do not like the breathing bit, you can practise mindfulness by holding your attention on something in the way we did above with the apple; choose something like a flower, a tree or the sky. Hold your attention there and if you mind wanders, gently and kindly bring it back. Don't worry at all if you find the breathing tricky (many people do) and we can do the compassion exercises in later chapters without doing the mindfulness breathing. Nonetheless, it could be useful to practise, so that even if you can only do a few seconds and gradually expand over the days that would be helpful too. The sensations in the body can be difficult for some people – so practising and coming to feel comfortable with the sensations can help.

Wandering and grasshopper mind

Assuming all went well, you may have noticed that actually, although it was only 30 seconds or so, your mind may have wandered off. You may have had thoughts like 'What's this about? Will this help me? Did I do my job correctly yesterday? Where did that pain in my leg come from?' If you practise for any length of time, distracting discomforts are very common. You may have heard various things outside the room; your attention may have been drawn to the postman pushing letters through the letterbox, the traffic outside or whatever. The point about this is that our minds are indeed very unruly and the more you practise this short breathing exercise and the longer you extend it, the more you will notice how much your mind simply hops about all over the place. When you first do this kind of mindful focusing, it can be quite surprising how much your mind does shift from thing to thing. This is all very normal, natural and to be expected. We need to train the mind, and the only thing that is important in this training is *not to try to create anything*. You are *not* trying to create a state of relaxation. You are *not* trying to force your mind to clear itself of thoughts – which is impossible. All you are doing is *allowing* yourself to playfully and gently notice when your mind wanders and then with kindness and gentleness bring your attention back to focus on your breathing. That's it. Notice and return. Notice the distractions, and return your attention to your breathing. Notice how often your judging mind tries to get in on the act with thoughts like 'Am I doing this right; is this helping me; am I relaxed now?' Just notice these thoughts and return your attention to the breath. The act of noticing and returning your mind to the task at hand (in this case the breath) *are the first steps to becoming mindful!* In other words, the exercise is simply an exercise where we learn to focus attention. *You are not trying to achieve anything*. If you have a hundred thoughts, or a thousand thoughts, that doesn't matter. All that matters is that you notice and then, to the best of your ability, gently and kindly bring your attention back to the breathing.

If you practise that 'attention and return', 'attention and return', with gentleness and kindness you may find that your mind will bounce around less and less. It may become easier. Remember, *you are not trying to relax* as such. All you are doing in this exercise is noticing that your mind wanders and then return it to focus on your breathing. Notice and return, and each time it wanders, that's fine; don't get angry with it, kindly bring it back to the focus of your breathing. It can also help if you *allow yourself to smile* when you notice the wandering mind. Develop an attitude of gentleness and kindness to your wandering mind.

This exercise of mindfulness is allowing yourself some time where you focus on your breathing and for your mind to come back to that single focus. You may take an interest in how much of a grasshopper (or kangaroo) mind you have, but at all times try not to condemn your wandering mind, always be gentle, always kind. Notice and return. If you have thoughts that you are not doing it right or that it cannot work for you, then note these thoughts as typical intrusions and return your attention to your breathing.

Some people like to go on and have a focus for their attention, such as a candle or a flower (concentrative meditations). Again the issue here is learning how to enable one's attention to focus, without it being cluttered with various thoughts, reflections, concerns, worries and so forth; or if it is, to notice this as 'thoughts arising'. Another variation is to have a mantra, which is a word or phrase to focus on in one's mind. Some people think you need to be given your mantra whereas others believe you can choose one for yourself such as 'om', 'peace', 'calm' or 'love'. The key word should have meaning for you, and 'feel calming'.

Applying the principles of mindfulness

You can use mindfulness in many different ways. Another aspect of mindfulness is to become more fully aware of each moment we are in. For example, while eating, you may practise really focusing your attention on the taste and texture of the food, chewing and eating slowly. Waiting for a bus or lying in the bath or while out walking, really focus on where you are. If walking, focus on the movement of your body. Notice how your feet lift and fall in coordinated action; how the foot comes down from heel to toe as it hits the ground; how your arms move and your breathing flows with the action. In mindfulness we can focus on the thought, 'I am walking.' Or focus you attention on what is around you. The idea is to help your conscious mind focus on where you are 'right now' – using all your senses – noticing the colours, the sounds and the textures.

A pleasant place to practise mindfulness is in the bath. Often when we relax in the bath we allow our mind to wander all over the place. However, practise breathing your soothing rhythm and breath and attend to the experience of being in the warm water. Feel how your weight is different, explore from the tips of your toes to the top of your head the warmth of the water caressing your body. 'Be' in every detail of the sensory experience. These exercises can be enhanced if you allow yourself a gentle compassionate smile and facial expression.

Noticing where we are

You may wish to be in the moment in different ways by paying attention to your senses. While out walking, direct your attention and notice the sky – keep the focus there – notice the changing textures of the sky from the horizon to overhead, or the rushing of the clouds, or their shapes or how the light catches different aspects of the clouds; or on the trees with their different shapes, textures and leaf colours, the feel and taste of the air. Again, if the mind wanders, gently bring it back. The very act of seeing colour and hearing sounds, and sensing the air we are enmeshed and live in, can become like new experiences to us, focused on what is around us in-this-moment.

When we get depressed or worried or preoccupied we can withdraw from the world of the senses and being fully in this moment, and become focused on our thoughts about tomorrow or yesterday, or on feelings or feeling states – the heaviness in the body or the butterflies and anxiety of dread. We do not live in the present moment, but somewhere else. When we are on automatic pilot we are lost to our thoughts and we may hardly notice the outside world. There is evidence that learning to be mindful can help depression because it lifts us away from over-focusing on the negative; gives our brain a chance to rest without being bombarded by negative thoughts.[2]

Developing Emotional Tolerance

We know our minds will give us a range of thoughts, feelings and moods. Mindfulness can help us to become aware of them without forcing them away, being frightened of or fighting with them, avoiding them, or getting caught up in them. We learn to stand back and observe; to take a 'view from the balcony', if you like. If you are feeling sad, be with that sad feeling rather than pushing it away. If you're fretting or worrying over something, notice how your mind pulls you this way and that. In mindfulness we are not trying to change thoughts but *change our relationship* to our thoughts and our feelings.

Jack's suicidal feelings and thoughts had previously worried him, and he would try to put them out of his mind. This of course made them come back even harder. He learned to acknowledge them and recognize that they came and went from time to time; but it was possible for him to acknowledge them, to stand back from them and become less frightened of them; he noted that he shared these experiences and thoughts with many millions of other people; and he could be compassionate to them. Of course, different people find different things helpful in coping with these thoughts. Some people find distraction works, or talking to others, or reminding themselves that they have had such thoughts before and they passed. And of course if you feel unable to control them, then contact your family doctor.

Karen was, in her own words, a 'fretter'. She learned to pay attention to her thoughts and noticed that they were often full of 'What would happen if . . .?' 'What would happen if I didn't do . . .?' Gradually she learned to stand back from them, became more observant of her fretting thoughts, 'let them be' and found that 'by themselves' they became less intense.

Mindful relaxing

So now we can let be, we can move to another exercise using 'notice and return', but this time we are going to focus on allowing ourselves to relax. I am going to talk about letting tension go, and by this I mean trying not to see tension as a bad thing or your enemy that you have to get rid of, but rather as an understandable way your body has tried to protect you by becoming tense and ready for action. We need to be gentle and help the body understand that it does not need to be like this right now. As we let go of our tension, it is like giving the body permission to relax – for which it is grateful.

You can hear this guided exercise on my CD.[4] So now once again focus on your breathing until you click into, find, sense, or feel the rhythm that feels most comfortable and soothing to you. If that seems hard, not to worry, just breathe in as comfortable a way as you are able. Spend about 30 seconds finding your rhythm – longer if you wish. When you have done that, focus on your legs. Notice how they feel for a moment. Imagine that all the tension in your legs is flowing down through your legs and down into the floor and away. Let it go on its way. As you breathe in, note any tension and then, as you breathe out, imagine the tension flowing down through your legs and out through the floor. Imagine your legs *feeling pleased and grateful* that they can let go. Imagine your legs smiling back at you. Sometimes people find if they slightly tense their muscles as they breathe in and then relax as they breathe out this can be helpful. Spend 30 seconds (longer if you like) letting that tension go with kindness.

Let's focus on our bodies and imagine the tension in our bodies from our shoulders down to our trunk and again, as you breathe out, imagine the tension leaving this part of your body, going down through your legs, down through the floor and away. Again if it helps, gently tense your stomach and back muscles as you breathe in and then relax as you breathe out. In a way it can be like imagining emptying a vessel of the tension that's now running through your legs and down through the floor. Your body *is grateful* and you feel kind to it.

Focus on the tips of your fingers, through your wrists, arms, elbows and shoulders. Imagine that the tension that was there can be released – can be let go of. Gently let the tension go so that it can run off down through your body, down through your legs and out through the floor and away – free.

Imagine the tension that sits in your head and neck area and forehead. The tension has been your alert system in action, and it would like to be released now – to take a rest. Again, as you breathe out, imagine it running down through your body, down through your legs and out through the floor.

So now you can focus on your whole body. Each time you breathe out, focus on the keyword RELAX. Imagine your body becoming more relaxed. Spend a minute or so doing this (longer if you like). Create a 'calm' facial expression.

Ending

You can end this exercise by taking a deeper breath, moving the body around a little and stretching your arms out. Note how your body feels and how gently grateful it is to you for spending time to let go of the tension. Take a moment to experience the idea of your body being grateful to you for spending time with it. When you are ready, get up and carry on with your day. You can practise this exercise as often as you find helpful. It can help with sleep too. Remember that if your mind wanders when you do it, you can gently bring it back to the task at hand – with a slight, kind smile. And of course practice will help it to become easier for you.

Variations

There are many variations on this basic exercise. It's up to you how you go about exploring different relaxation exercises and finding ones that works for you, or that you like. The one that I've given you is one with a mindful and compassionate focus, and helps some people. The idea is to do the practice and then see what happens for you. When you are trying to relax, 'notice and return' when your mind wanders from the focus on relaxing. Remember, it's a bit like sleep: we create the conditions to aid sleep, but if we focus too much on sleep it slips away. The idea is that as you sit there, allowing yourself to focus on your breathing, you may become more relaxed as you become more familiar with your body and the feelings of relaxation; you may become more aware of where tension sits in your body.

Gradually, you can come to think of your body as a friend, and you can become a friend to your body and take an interest in your body and how you can nurture it, care for it and help it relax. Tension is not your enemy to be 'got rid of', because it only came as a form of protection and preparing your body for action – so it is grateful for its release from your body. It's like telling the army 'the battles are over and you can all go home now'. Focus on the feeling of *gratitude* in your body for doing these exercises. Each time you finish an exercise feel your body's gratitude for a moment. Developing this attitude to relaxing counteracts tendencies to force yourself to relax, getting irritated if it is difficult, or seeing tension as 'bad' and 'to be got rid of'.

Relaxing in activity

Sometimes people can notice certain feelings in their bodies that are unpleasant and are associated with emotions. Sometimes people find relaxing actually makes them feel more anxious. This is not uncommon. When we are in different mind and brain states, relaxing might be a bit tough. If I am very uptight or agitated about something I find focusing on soothing breathing with *some physical activity* works for me. I might focus my mind on the here and now and engage in soothing breathing but along with physical activity such as cycling, digging the garden, taking a walk, doing the dishes (okay, emptying the dishwasher) or playing guitar.

Sensory focusing

When Sue Procter and I ran a group for people with mental health difficulties, they found mindfulness and relaxation hard at first.[5]

We brainstormed the issue together and they felt that if they had something they could focus their attention on, other than their breathing and bodies, this might help to get them started. Together we came up with tennis balls to focus on. They would do their soothing rhythm breathing and mindful attention, but focus on holding a tennis ball, exploring its textures and feel in the hand – and yes, it made for some very amusing comments – 'Hold on to your balls, we are going mindful!'

Grounding

In many parts of the world people have a focus on things like worry beads that are smooth to the touch and can be run through the fingers. When I lived in Dubai in the late 1960s I was struck by how many people used worry beads, with the very clear understanding that these were to help them with attention and staying calm. These beads help to 'ground' them, keep their attention focused.

Sometimes people like to ground their meditations or relaxation exercises. You can do this in a number of ways. One is to find a stone you like the look and feel of. As you do your relaxation exercises, hold the stone gently in your hand. Feel it as you breathe. This will help link the feeling of your stone to your state of relaxation. We are going to use the same idea when we look at compassionate imagery in the next chapter. Then later, if you're feeling tense you can breathe the soothing rhythm and hold your stone, to help ground you slightly.

Another grounding aid can be to use smell. Some people like to associate relaxation and calm with a scent of some kind. Aromatherapists can provide all kinds of smells/scents that are associated with relaxing. If (with or without their help) you find one that suits you, you can carry it with you so that if you want to relax you can engage your breathing and also use your smell/scent. Psychologists suggest that we can prime states if we use multiple senses, such as attention, smell and/or touch.

Another common grounding experience is to gently touch your index finger and thumb together while you're doing your relaxation exercises. Then when you relax once again, bring your index finger and thumb together. For example, if you were practising your relaxation at work, you can sit with your fingers in that position. Sometimes if we are upset and we want to ground ourselves we can just engage in the soothing rhythm breathing, with index finger and thumb touching.

As with all the exercises in this book, once you understand the principles of what we are trying to achieve (that is to bring some balance to our emotion systems and activate the soothing system in our brains), then look to your own feelings and experience to guide you – try out different things and see what works for you. You have intuitive wisdom; you just need to listen to it.

Keep in mind also that these ways for being with our bodies can also be used when we are engaging in activities. Suppose we have to do the washing up or the ironing: we can practise doing them by working through our relaxing training, rather than being on automatic pilot and ruminating on our difficulties. Developing a relaxed body is a way of being kind and gentle with it and nurturing it. Sometimes we have to be reminded to do it, so it can be useful to put notes about the place – perhaps behind the sink, or near the bath.

Bring relaxation into everyday life: the chill-out

Being alone

It is often useful to recognize that although caring relationships are very important for us, at times it is important to be alone.

Of course some people live alone and feel lonely, but for others it can be hard to find personal space and time in modern houses that are designed as small boxes. And of course the British weather can trap us inside. However, for millions of years we would not have needed to wander far to get away from others. Aloneness as choice is of course very different from loneliness which we do not choose. If possible, get some time alone. I have known some women who feel guilty about this, or for telling the family they need chill-out time alone. One woman noted that even when she went to take a bath it wasn't long before voices would call at her, 'Where are you; where did you put my shirt; Mum, have you seen my homework?' Explain to people that we all need time for ourselves, to chill out, and this is not a reflection at all of not wanting to be with people. The point is to put time aside to be alone and think about how to use that time to *nurture and nourish* yourself.

Chill out in your mind

If you are busy, small chill-outs can be helpful. Keep in mind all the time that what you're trying to do is to stimulate and regulate brain patterns. For example, you get a phone call and someone upsets you. Stop for moment and focus on your breathing. Notice the feelings rippling through your body. Try putting them into words, as research shows that this helps with regulating our feelings. For example, 'Right now my body is feeling tense. I have this tension and butterflies in my stomach, my face is tense, my mind is leaping from one angry or upset thought to another. Okay, let's find the soothing rhythm and reside there for a while. My old brain will be rushing along as it does, but I am going to be with my soothing rhythm for a moment and *watch* my thoughts and feelings go by.' Perhaps you have seen those colourful spiralling patterns that are created on the computer when we play music – it can be something like that. This learning and practice, to stand back and observe our minds, can be very helpful. Shortly we will be looking at compassionate imagery and how it can be added into this work.

In Chapter 4 we noted that we can have many mixed and conflicting emotions all at the same time. If we are rushing we don't take time to pull back from the many feelings swirling around in us. For example, in addition to being angry about something, we might feel sad and anxious. We can engage in soothing rhythm breathing, and pull back from our emotions, become more observant and aware of their mixed and varied textures. As we become more emotionally aware we can learn to recognize these feelings, and even to spot them as they arise. This can be very helpful because it means we can take steps to help ourselves have more control with feelings.

Mindfulness can be a way of engaging in *all aspects of our lives*. Although it is extremely helpful to have time aside which you can dedicate to mindful practice, it is also useful to bring it to key activities in *all facets* of your life. Mindfulness can help us to enjoy the small things more, to savour our pleasures.

Becoming an alien for a day

There is a rather nice playful exercise that you can try to see if this creates a type of mindfulness for you and new feelings about being alive – this is to imagine becoming an alien for a day. Imagine that you come from a very different planet, maybe one where there is little light and the sky is dark, and you're visiting here. You are fascinated by everything that you see and sense; by the sky and its ever-changing colour patterns, the smell and feel of the air, the sounds around you, the colours of the cars, the trees and the grass. Allow yourself to be amazed and fascinated by the greenness in the living plants and the shapes of leaves. The idea is to playfully begin to experience the world anew; to bring a freshness to our perceptions and senses. I once read about some funny graffiti. Someone had written 'Is there any intelligent life on this planet?', clearly bemoaning some of the silly things we humans do. Underneath someone had written, 'Yes, but I'm only visiting'.

The art of appreciation

If we can direct our attention to where we want to direct it, to the top of our head or to a big toe or to the plants sitting on the sideboard, why not use this ability to stimulate some of our positive emotions? There is an old saying that 'The glass can either be seen as half full or half empty'. When we feel good the glass is half full; when we're feeling depressed we see it as half empty (if we are a bit paranoid, we might wonder who has been drinking our water!). We know that our moods shift our attention. The glass is the same whatever – it does not change – only our feelings and perceptions of it do. But we can also practise learning to shift our attention to the things that we appreciate, things that stimulate pleasures and nice feelings in us; *we can practise directing* our attention to the half-full bit of the glass. Here's how to have a go.

Each day when you wake up, focus on the things that you like or that give you just a smidgen of pleasure. For example, you may have liked being in a warm bed. Rather than focus on how having to get out of bed is annoying, smile to yourself at the enjoyment you have had in being comfortable and warm and in just 16 hours or so you can come back here. Think about how you enjoy the shower or the taste and feel of your first cup of tea, or the taste of your breakfast, or reading the newspaper. When you make your tea and toast, try doing it mindfully. Pay attention to the water, that life-giving fluid, and how it gradually turns brown as the tea infuses in it; notice the toast has got lots of dark crumbs; if you were an ant crawling over your toast it would be a lunar landscape. When was the last time you really tasted fresh toast and butter; I mean took the time and attention and *really* tasted it? Do you know the smell of the air of a new spring day; do you take time to really breathe it, notice it and appreciate it?

Even doing something mundane such as the washing-up, do you notice the warm feeling of the water, do you notice the bubbles and the way in which you can see rainbows in the bubbles? We lose our fascination because we are a species that easily gets used to things, we get bored and want something new. We're also thinking about so many other things – one of which is that it is a drag to have to do the washing up when we are tired and want to do so many other things – like get back to that warm bed. But learning 'to notice', to feel and to see, can stimulate our brains in new ways.

Appreciating other people

Take time to appreciate what people do for you. Choose a day and spend time focusing only on the things that you like and appreciate in people. The things you don't like you will let go and not focus on. You can do that tomorrow if you want to, I guess. Think about how all of us are so dependent on each other. People have been up since 4 a.m. so we can have our fresh milk, bread and newspapers, and every day they do the same. What about the people you work with? What are their good points? How often do you really focus on those? How often do you make a point of telling people that you appreciate them? What you are doing in these exercises is practising overruling the threat system that will focus you on the glass being half empty.

It's what it's designed to do, and what we can so easily be pulled into. So let's start to take control over our feelings and *deliberately* use our attention to practice stimulating emotion systems that we want to stimulate because they will give rise to brain patterns that give good feelings; appreciation is one way of practising doing this.

Sadness

If we are depressed then in becoming mindful we can also become aware of unaddressed issues in ourselves. When people practise mindfulness, it is not uncommon for them to become sad and even tearful because they are now open to unaddressed issues. Once the mind stops rushing from thing to thing it can begin to experience the more subtle levels of itself. For example, Jennifer discovered that working with a compassionate form of mindfulness made her feel sad. Then she realized it touched a part of a memory of the death of her mother five years earlier. In her heart she knew she had been trying to avoid grieving – almost as if, if she didn't grieve, then maybe mum hadn't really died.

So if you have sad or anxious feelings arising in your work, stay with them – be mindful and observant of them, maybe write about them in your journal. If you have friends or a partner you may wish to discuss your feelings with them. If these feelings seem an important block to you, and you'd like to find a way to work with them, you may want to find a group to work with and share your experiences. Or you may want to find a mindfulness or meditation teacher, or a therapist who works with mindfulness, or offers you space and reflection for your feelings. The point is that there is nothing wrong with you or with your mindfulness if distressing feelings start to bubble up; this simply may be an indication that there are things you could address, and perhaps obtaining the help of others will be really useful to you at this time in your life.

Sometimes of course we focus our attention on certain things, or do certain things, to avoid certain feelings, thoughts or memories. Again, this is very understandable, and sometimes helpful. For example, Karen, a young doctor, tried not to think about the death of a close friend when she was at work as she didn't want to be tearful in front of her patients. Sonia did not want to think about her unhappy childhood experiences in class when she was teaching. The ability to control attention and emotions is of course very helpful. The point is though, do we give ourselves the opportunity to create space and time to explore these things and themes and heal them, or are we always on the run from them? If you are very busy you may skip lunch, but if you keep avoiding eating your body will become weak. As they say, there is a time and place for everything. However, depressed people are notorious for never creating space, or finding it very difficult create space, to actually deal with the things that are hurting them inside.

If you are very depressed you may find these exercises hard because our positive systems are toned right down, but do have a go and give it some time. You may find the exercises easier as your mood shifts.

Overview

Mindfulness is a way of learning to use our attention and train our minds. What I have written here are some basic ideas. If these appeal to you then do seek out trained practitioners who can take you further on your journey of exploring mindfulness, teaching the traditions and opening up new ideas for you. There is much more to mindfulness than we have space to explore here.

KEY POINTS

- Our minds are often easily pulled and controlled by our emotions, key worries or moods.
- We can learn to become more aware of this and exert more control.
- A key skill is that of mindfulness which is learning to pay attention in a particular non-judgemental way. Recent research has shown this can be very helpful to people.
- Mindfulness can also be used to direct attention in a particular way, on specific activity.
- Mindfulness can be used to bring you a new interest in the world and appreciation of aspects of it.
- Directing our attention so that we learn to focus on the half-full rather than the half-empty glass, and learn to focus on what we can appreciate and enjoy in ourselves and others, can be helpful to our minds.

EXERCISES

Throughout this book we will be exploring various exercises. The more effort you can put into these exercises the better, of course. But some exercises suit some people better than others, so do find what suits you. On the other hand, don't give up on things too easily if you find the exercises difficult, because they might still be very useful to you. Indeed, the very fact that they are difficult may suggest a need for practice. Be honest with yourself. Here are some exercises in regard to mindfulness.

Exercise 1. Putting time aside to practise

You may listen to some of the CDs mentioned in Appendix 3. Or just practise your soothing breathing relaxation. Or seek out a group in your area to practise with.

Exercise 2. Bringing mindfulness into your everyday life

Whether you are waiting for a bus, having lunch or a bath, talking to your friends over coffee, practise being fully in the moment; if your mind wanders on to different topics, fears or concerns then gently bring it back. When talking to people, listen to what they are saying, rather than getting caught up in thoughts about whether they are interested in you.

Exercise 3. Sometimes just sit

Practise the ability to sit or just be with your thoughts and feelings and simply observe. Notice that you will have easy and hard days for this.

Exercise 4. The journey journal

Keep notes in your journey journal to reflect on how your practice is unfolding.

8

Switching our minds to kindness and compassion

This chapter explores some ways in which we can direct our thinking and attention to activate a soothing part of our brain. We're going to be looking at developing *kindness for ourselves and for others*. Both these can really help our minds become more settled and cope better with life difficulties. However, some depressed people are actually resistant or frightened of the idea of being kind to themselves, even when this can help with depression. If this idea of self-kindness seems strange or threatening to you, just stay with it for a while and later we will explore your *fears* of becoming kind, understanding and compassionate to yourself. But it is always just a step at a time.

In this chapter we are going to use our *imagination*. Some of you might think, 'Oh, I am not very good at imagining things, I have no imagination.' Well, don't give up on the idea yet, let's have a go and see how far we can get. In fact, you don't have to be good at imagining things; it's the act of trying that is important. The key is trying to direct your attention and create things in your mind that are good for your brain.

What imagery isn't

It is important to recognize that when we 'imagine things' we usually don't see detailed pictures in our minds. Generally, images are fleeting and we get fragments and glimpses of things. For example, if I ask you to imagine your favourite meal, or the house you might like to live in, or what you will be doing tomorrow, you probably will not get a clear picture in your mind; more like fleeting impressions and feelings. When we talk about imagery we are really trying to create 'a sense of' as opposed to a 'clear picture of'. It is about how we direct our attention, the focus of our minds. For all of the exercises below it's really the effort to create things in your mind, in a certain way, that matters rather than the results, or having clear pictures in your mind.

Mindful imagery

When we do these exercises we do them mindfully (see Chapter 7), aware that our attention will wander. You might be able to focus for a few seconds and then your mind wanders off to various things you have done, think you should do, or want to do and so on. It does not matter if your mind wanders a hundred times, gently bring your attention back on to the task. The act of noticing and redirecting your attention is the important bit. If you find thoughts like 'I can't do this', 'I am not doing this right, I cannot feel anything', notice these thoughts, and then gently and with kindness bring your mind back to what you're trying to do. You will also notice that some days you will find it easier than others. In all these exercises there is no forcing or pushing oneself to do things. We simply put time aside to do the exercise, without judgement of whether it goes well or badly, because there is no well or badly (unless you make that judgement) – rather there is just 'the doing'. Practice on a regular basis helps, of course, as it does for any skill we want to learn, be it playing golf, the piano, or painting – practice will help us improve.

Safe place imagery

The first imagery exercise we'll do is about creating a place in our minds that we feel comfortable in. Let's deliberately practise creating in our minds places that we find soothing, calming and where we want to be. To begin with, it is useful to start by sitting or lying down comfortably and going through your soothing breathing rhythm and a short relaxation exercise (see pages 123–5). If you don't like the breathing exercise then sit quietly for a few moments. Then allow your mind to focus on *and create a place* that gives you the *feeling of safeness, calm and contentment*. The place may be a beautiful wood where the leaves of the trees dance gently in the breeze. Powerful shafts of light caress the ground with brightness. Imagine a wind gently on your face and a sense of the light dancing in front of you. Hear the rustle of the trees; imagine a smell of woodiness or sweetness in the air. Or your place may be a beautiful beach with a crystal blue sea stretching to the horizon where it meets the blue sky. Underfoot is soft, white fine sand that is silky to the touch. You can hear the gentle hushing of the waves on the sand. Imagine the sun on your face, sense the light dancing in diamond sparks on the water, imagine the soft sand under your feet as your toes dig into it and feel a light breeze gently touch your face. Or your safe place may be by a log fire and you can hear the crackle of the logs and the smell of wood smoke. These are examples of possible pleasant places that will bring a sense of pleasure to you, which is good – but the key focus is on feelings of *safeness* for you. They are only suggestions, and your safe place might be different.

When you bring your safe place to mind, allow your body to relax. Think about your facial expression; allow yourself to have a soft smile of pleasure at being here. It helps your attention if you practise focusing on each of your senses; what you can imagine seeing, feeling, hearing and any other sensory aspect.

It is also useful to imagine that as this is your own unique safe place, *the place itself feels joy in you being here*. Allow yourself to feel how your safe place has pleasure in your being here. Explore your feelings when you imagine this place is happy with you here.

When you become stressed or upset you can practise your soothing breathing rhythm for a few minutes and then imagine yourself in this place in your mind and allowing yourself to settle down, to give you some chill-out time. Keep in mind that we are using our imagery not to escape or avoid, but to help us practise bringing soothing to our minds. Keep in mind too that these are all what we call *behavioral experiments* for you to try out and see what happens inside you. You get your own evidence for what is helpful to you, and build on that.

Compassion-focused imagery

Compassionate colour

Sometimes depressed people like to start off with imagining a *compassionate colour*. Usually these colours are pastel rather than dark. Engage in your soothing breathing rhythm and imagine a colour that you associate with compassion, or a colour that conveys some sense of warmth and kindness. Spend a few moments on that. Imagine this colour surrounding you. Then imagine this entering through your heart area and slowly through your body. As this happens, focus on this colour as having wisdom, strength and warmth/kindness, with a key quality of kindness. It would help if you can create a facial expression of kindness as you do this exercise.

One patient noted when he used compassion to help him face up to difficult decisions, the colour he associated with it became stronger. He was good at experimenting and seeing what worked for him; listening to his own intuitive wisdom. He began to think about his compassionate colours as helping him with different things.

Compassion qualities

Compassion is 'being sensitive to distress with a desire and commitment to try to relieve it'. It is also an openness to the desires to see self and others *flourish*, and taking joy in that flourishing. Compassion and warmth are not just distress-focused – but a commitment for creating 'contented joyfulness' too. We can see compassion in lots of different ways, for example as simple and basic kindness, openness and generosity. We can add to these the idea that compassion is also related to *wisdom* (it can't be unwise), *strength* (it is not weak and indeed often helps us develop courage), *warmth* (linked to the feelings of kindness) and non-judgemental attitudes. In the next chapter we will look at these qualities and skills in more detail.

The flow of compassion

Compassion-focused exercises and imagery are designed to try and create feelings of openness, kindness, warmth and gentleness in you. You are trying to stimulate a particular kind of brain system through your imagery. We can do this in a number of ways, such as using our memory and also our imagination.

Compassion-focused exercises can be orientated in three main ways:

- **Compassion flowing out from you to others**. In these exercises we focus on the feelings when we fill our minds with kind thoughts and wishes for other people.
- **Compassion flowing into you from others**. In these exercises we focus our minds on opening to the kindness of others. This is to open the mind and stimulate areas of our brain that are responsive to the kindness of other people.
- **Compassion for yourself**. This is linked to developing feelings, thoughts and experiences that are focused on kindness to yourself. Life is often very difficult and learning how to generate self-compassion can be very helpful during these times and particularly to help us with our emotions.[1] The key is practising, developing and focusing your compassionate mind.

Now we are going to explore experiences for each of these three aspects. In all these exercises below it is your intentions and efforts that really matter. You may need to practise your feelings before they come naturally. So we can learn how to become compassionate because we try to practise thinking and acting compassionately, whereas the feelings may be harder to generate.

Becoming the compassionate self

The first set of exercises is focused on you practising generating feelings of compassion within yourself. Here we are going to work on your inner kindness and how to focus it, build on it, learn how to direct it and practise it. In a way we are going to use exercises that good actors use to create states of mind in themselves. For example, if actors want to convey anger or anxiety or sorrow, they try to create these feelings in themselves. Indeed when they 'get into role' it can actually change their bodies and physiology. If you get into an anger or anxiety role, your heart rate may go up. Imagining ourselves in a role, or as having certain feelings and thoughts, changes our physiology. We can use this well-known fact to create compassionate healing patterns in our bodies.

First, find a place where you can be alone and quiet. Now, gently, with your soothing rhythm breathing, if you can, imagine that *you are* a wise and compassionate person. Think about all the *ideal qualities* you would love to have as such a person. Imagine that you have them. It does not matter if you have these qualities or not in reality because we are simply imagining them. Research has shown that just imaging doing certain things changes our brains – and might actually make us better at that thing. Imagine that you have those qualities right now, in this moment. Imagine having great wisdom and understanding. Spend time imagining what that feels like.

Imagine having strength and fortitude. Spend time imagining what that feels like. Next imagine having great warmth and kindness and never being judgemental and again spend time imagining what that feels like. Think about what other qualities you'd like to have in your compassionate self. Imagine that you have them. Imagine your inner sense of calmness in your compassionate self that is based on wisdom. Try imagining each quality, noticing how that feels. Adopt a kind and gentle facial expression and spend time exploring that. Assume a body posture that feels compassionate to you, and spend some time exploring that too. You can also bring to mind 'you at your best', recalling a time you have felt calm, kind and wise. Breathe your soothing rhythm and focus on these memories and qualities.

Imagine the sound of your voice, your tone, pace and rhythm when you speak from this compassionate self. Imagine the emotion and feelings that are in you and are expressed in what and how you speak. You might imagine yourself as younger or older than you are now. Imagine yourself dressed in a certain way. I don't know why, but for me I imagine having longer hair – it's somehow associated with my image of a compassionate self. Maybe I am being kind to the fact that I am going bald!

Each day, put some time aside to 'play with' this role of being a 'calm compassionate self'. Sometimes depressed people tell me that they're like this already because they are kind to others. Indeed that might be so, but they can also be a bit submissive and do things they don't really want to do because they want to be polite or they want to see themselves as a nice person and worthy of being loved (people pleasers). And that is perfectly understandable. However, the compassionate self we are thinking about here is not worried about what other people think. We have to distinguish true compassion and kindness from submissiveness.

Compassion under the duvet

Many meditation guides will advise you to spend time on your practice, perhaps sitting for 10 or 20 minutes a day. Tibetan monks may spend hours each day on their meditations. When we are depressed, that's a bit tough! So let's begin with what I call 'compassion under the duvet'. When you wake up in the morning, or before you go to sleep, spend a moment or so with your soothing rhythm breathing, wearing a kindly expression and making a commitment to try as best you can, without judgement, to become a compassionate person. Focus on your kind facial expression. Imagine that you are a compassionate person and run through the exercise above.

Any time you have, such as waiting for a bus, or sitting on a train, or in a waiting room, or lying in the bath or walking – concentrate on your breathing and focus your attention on being a compassionate person inside yourself. These are times when our mind is often just idling along thinking all kinds of things, so why not use this time more productively to practise your exercises? You may find that if you practise *every day*, even if it's only for a minute or two, the sense of compassion will actually stay with you more and more and you will want to practise more. Little and often can be very helpful.

Using your compassionate self

Different people find that they prefer to do things in a different order to that which is given here. Try for yourself and see what works for you. Perhaps focusing on compassion for others or developing your compassionate image (see below) is best for you as a starting place.

Wanting to be free of depression

When you feel you have the basic idea of imagining yourself as a compassionate being, and can notice but don't engage (in fact smile at) all those thoughts that whisper in your mind, 'No you're not; you can't do this; it's not going to work you know,' you can focus on a few key statements such as:

- May I be well.
- May I be happy.
- May I be free from suffering.

Focus on the *desires* in the words and your kindly facial expression. Feelings may come slowly with practice.

If you feel this is a bit overwhelming, pull back to focusing on just being a compassionate person; focus on your breathing, your facial expression and the tone of your voice. If you feel uncomfortable – say you feel you do not deserve compassion or for some other reason – then stay with the exercise for as long as you are able. You are slowly desensitizing yourself to fears and concerns about being kind to yourself. Try not to engage with arguments for or against in your mind – just do the exercise as best you can. If you feel very little, do not worry as the practice itself can be helpful – simply give some time to the exercise. Again, go at your own pace and explore how these ideas work for you. If this is still tough for you then you might want to start your practice with compassion for others (see below). If this is still difficult then there are other exercises throughout this book that you might get on with. The point is to try not to force anything – just be as mindful and open to possibilities as you can. It's like sleeping – we can't force ourselves to go to sleep, and if we keep checking 'Am I nearly asleep now?' it doesn't help. We can only create the conditions where sleep may occur.

Developing self-compassion for the difficult parts of ourselves

We are now going to use this compassionate self and focus it on others and on ourselves. When you feel you have practised becoming *the compassionate self* a few times, and are beginning to get the hang of it, you can use this exercise to help you cope with difficult feelings or setbacks in your life. For example, imagine that you are angry but are also fighting with yourself about it. Sit comfortably for a moment and create your compassionate self. Remember to adopt suitable facial expressions. If you have been engaged in your soothing breathing, just have a sense of your body calming. Now imagine your angry self; see it a few metres in front of you. Look at the angry expression and note the feelings inside this angry part of you – the frustration or sense of injustice – feelings that are not very pleasant. Now feel compassion for the angry part of you that you can see in front of you. You are not trying to change anything, because you realize that anger is part of our human brain that can be powerful and unpleasant. To the best of your ability, send compassion to that anger you see in front of you. It can have as much compassion as it needs. Notice what happens if you just sit compassionately with your anger.

If you find your mind wandering, refocus it on your powerful compassionate qualities. If you feel you are getting pulled into the anger and starting to feel angry again, then break off, pull back and refocus on your breathing and becoming the compassionate self. See your compassionate self as the wiser, older, more rooted part of yourself – *you at your best*. When you feel back in that role then re-engage. Your sense of yourself should also stay in the compassionate position, so pull back and refocus if that slips. If you feel yourself become critical of yourself, then again pull back and refocus on being the compassionate self.

Notice how if you hold your compassionate position, somehow that can feel quite powerful because it comes from a position of wisdom, fortitude and strength. Explore that sense of powerfulness from this position. I chose anger as the emotion to focus on here because anger and frustration are often emotions depressed people struggle with. Another emotion you might wish to work with might be anxiety.

When you feel ready you can engage with 'the depressed self'. Once again see this (depressed) self in front of you, and in your wisdom recognize our brains have been designed to allow depression, and that is not our fault. Life can be very hard and painful. The depressed self is only one of many selves and brain patterns. The most important thing is to practise having compassionate kindness towards this self rather than anger, contempt or fear. And this is *not* self-pity or feeling sorry for yourself, because compassion asks you to develop wisdom, strength and courage as well as warmth and kindness.

When you first focus on the depressed self you might feel pulled into the depressed self, and tearful. Pull back, and refocus on the compassionate self so that compassion grows in you – feel yourself expanding and becoming stronger based on wisdom and understanding. This may take time.

People's experiences with this can be very different. One woman felt tearful and cried, but felt this connected her with important feelings. She felt better because she was able to end her sitting with a compassionate focus. Another woman started out okay, but then felt overwhelmed and could not hold the compassionate self position. She needed more practice. Another person become agitated and had to work slowly on the compassionate self. The key thing is not to be overwhelmed but to work at your own pace and explore what is helpful for you. Your goal is to become kind to yourself and understanding of your depression. In these exercises we are not trying to change the depressed self but take a compassionate stance towards it.

Happy self

Recall a time when you were happy. Looking through the eyes of your compassionate self, see yourself smiling, happy and feeling content. Let your compassionate self feel joy for the happy self. Notice what feelings come up when you focus on being 'happy' – strangely it might make you feel sad because happiness might seem a long way away! Or you might notice other resistances. If so, stay with these feelings as best you're able and always pull back to just *being the compassionate self* if it feels over-whelming. The important practice here is creating in your mind the potential for happiness and self and support from the compassionate self. We can learn to imagine ourselves as 'well', 'happy' and free of suffering. You can extend to any other posi-tive aspects of yourself that you wish.

Compassionate practice is not just with threat-based feelings but with positive ones too!

Compassion and kindness for others

In our next exercise we are going to imagine kindness flowing out. Some of you might find this an easier exercise than the one above, so might prefer to start here. There is now increasing evidence that if we practise trying to focus on compassion for others this stimulates key brain areas which are helpful in combating depression and anxiety.[2]

Recall a time when you felt very kind and caring towards someone (or if you prefer, an animal). Don't choose a time when that person was very distressed, because then you are likely to focus on that distress. As in the experience of remembering some-body being kind to you, ensure that you have space to practise without distraction, sit comfortably and engage in your soothing rhythm breathing. Remember to create a kindly facial expression with (say) a slight smile. Notice your feelings in your body and the sense of yourself that emerges from such memories.

Next, bring to mind a person or people whom you want to feel you can help to be free of suffering. This may be a partner, a friend or a child. The idea is to *practise filling your mind with compassion for another* – you can choose who the other will be. Proceed with the following steps.

- Imagine yourself expanding as if you are becoming more powerful and wise.
- Pay attention to your body as you remember your feelings of kindness and the compassionate self.
- Spend a few moments feeling this expansion and warmth in your body (but don't worry if these feelings do not seem to be there – it is the trying that is important). Note your real genuine desire for this other person to be free of suffering and to flourish.
- Spend one minute thinking about your voice tone and the kind of things you say or the kind of things you might do or want to do.
- Focus now on your real desire for the person to flourish and be free of suffering. See them in your mind as smiling back at you. Focus on three key ideas (and the feelings and desire within them):
  - May they be well.
  - May they be happy.
  - May they be free of suffering.
- Spend one minute (more if you can) thinking about your pleasure in being able to be kind.
- When you feel able, you may also focus on feelings of kindness in general, the feelings of warmth, the feelings of expansion, the voice tone, the wisdom in your voice and in your behavior. When you have finished the exercise you might want to make some notes about how this felt in your body.

If you want to take this practice further, you can gradually expand the circle of people to whom you send your compassion – to friends and acquaintances, then to strangers and even to people you don't like. They too have all found themselves here with a brain they did not choose and passions, desires and feelings they did not design, and are ignorant of the forces that operate within them. However, this is more advanced practice and if you are depressed you might want to start slowly and build up. The basis of the practice is to fill your mind with desires and feelings for all living things to be free from suffering and to flourish. If you can expand your practice time to, say, five and then ten minutes. Longer would be helpful, but any time you can give to practice is useful.

Being joyful in other people's flourishing

In this exercise we are going to focus on creating what is called *sympathetic joy*, which is joyfulness in the flourishing and well-being of others.

Find a place where you won't be distracted and can sit comfortably and engage in your soothing rhythm breathing. Do that for about one minute until you feel ready to engage in the imagery. Now try and remember a time when you were very pleased for someone else's success or happiness. Perhaps it's someone close to you in your family; seeing them do well made you very happy. Recall their facial expressions in your mind. Feel the joy and well-being in them. As you do this, focus on your own facial expressions and feel yourself expanding as you remember the joyfulness of that event.

Notice how this joyfulness feels in your body. Allow yourself to smile. Spend two or three minutes sitting with that memory. Then, when you're ready, let the image fade and maybe write some notes.

In the next stage you can focus on your feelings of joy for the successes or relief from suffering of others, eventually expanding this to all living things.

Compassion flowing in

Imagining your ideal compassionate image

We are going to change the flow a bit. So far we have focused on your internal feelings of the compassionate self and being compassionate to different parts of you. Then we directed this to others and tried to fill our minds with kindness and wisdom. In the next exercises we are going to practise exploring our feelings as a recipient of compassion, by imagining another mind – wiser, stronger and warmer than our own – wanting us to be free of suffering and to flourish. I call this 'imagining your ideal compassionate image'. Let's now focus specifically on the ideal compassionate image that brings compassion for you. You can work on this using the worksheet on page 174.

The usual way we experience compassion is, of course, through the kindness of others. This usually flows in and through relationships. We can practise stimulating our soothing system by imagining *relating* to 'compassionate others'. Just as we can imagine ideal meals or ideal sexual partners, that can stimulate our bodies and physiologies in specific ways (see page 28), so we can create inner images that can stimulate the soothing system. The idea here is to play with, create, discover, build and develop your compassionate imagery; experimenting with what works for you. In fact the idea of imagining a compassionate other, and practising and focusing our minds on that image, as a way to help ourselves develop emotionally and heal, is thousands of years old.[3]

Let's think about how we might create a compassionate image that we can relate to using *fantasy images*. When you think of compassion, what kinds of images come to mind? Close your eyes for a moment and allow the word *compassion* or *kindness* to sit gently in your mind. What colours are associated with it for you? What sounds and textures? There is no rush. Maybe a mixture of colours and sounds come to mind.

In the next step we are going to focus on creating a specific image that you can feel has great compassion for you – that is 'is sensitive to your suffering and has a deep wish to help you with it.' The image that might arise could be of a person, but some people prefer animals, or even a tree or a mountain. Remember you might only get a fleeting sense of something (see pages 145–146). What are the qualities that you see as central to compassion? Spend a moment and think about that. It might be kindness, patience, wisdom, and caring. The act of thinking about compassion and its qualities helps you start to focus your attention on it. When you have had some thoughts of your own you can consider giving your image four basic qualities. We met them earlier, but let's look at them in a bit more detail now. These qualities are:

1 **Wisdom**. Imagine that your compassionate image under-stands completely what it means to be a human being, to struggle, to suffer, to have rage, feel depressed, but also to have desires, to feel joy. It understands the evolved creation of our human minds with all their complex feelings, lusts, desires, happy and distressing thoughts, that can conflict inside us. It knows these are part of being human. Some people like the idea that their compassionate image has been through similar things to themselves but is now older and wiser; it understands you perfectly because it has been there itself. The image has a wise mind because it knows from expe-rience, but has reached the point of inner peacefulness. This sense that it will have had the same feelings, conflicts, fantasies and emotions as you can be important as a source

of kinship, and points (and can inspire us) to the ability to move on and develop.

In Buddhism certain images of compassionate others (called Bodhisattvas) are indeed like this. They have been fully human and subject to the same passions and desires, mistakes, aggressions, depressions and regrets as all of us, but through their training, study and practice have gained insight and developed compassion that has emerged from personal struggle and suffering.

2 **Strength and fortitude**. Give your image the ability to endure and tolerate painful things, but also the strength to defend and protect you if necessary. Imagine it as strong and courageous. As we will see later, sometimes compassion requires us to have courage. Sometimes, too, it requires us to be able to tolerate and not act on our more destructive thoughts and feelings, or learn to be assertive, or acknowledge we need to face things that we are perhaps frightened of facing.

3 **Warmth and kindness**. Imagine your compassionate image has warmth and kindness that radiates from and around it. This key quality is specifically there for you because this is your own unique image that you are creating and building.

4 **A non-judgemental/non-condemnatory approach**. Our compassionate image is never condemning, judging or critical. This does not mean it doesn't have desires or preferences. *Indeed, its main desire is for your well-being and flourishing.* Nor does being non-judgemental mean it is happy to go along with whatever feeling or action you decide; but it won't condemn you for it but rather invite you to understand your feelings and thoughts and choose a compassionate path – which at times can mean learning to be assertive.

So these are our key qualities that we are going to build into our compassionate image. The idea here is to create an image that is *unique and special for you*. The image is yours and yours alone. Keep in mind that it is *your ideal* and in that sense suffers from no human failings but is *fully and completely compassionate every time* because it embodies these qualities exactly. Note that the idea of it being 'an ideal' is that it is ideal *to you* (it may not be ideal to anyone else). You give it every quality that is important *to you*, just as if you thought about your ideal house, meal or car you would give it everything that you wanted and wouldn't hold back. So it is with your ideal image; you imagine it to have every aspect of compassion that is important to you. Deborah Lee has referred to this aspect as your 'perfect nurturer' – somewhat parental-like and protective – and some people really like that idea. Others see compassion in different ways, say as a friend or mentor – so you can decide exactly what qualities it has. Again, these kinds of exercises are used by various therapists to help people.[4]

Some people like to use religious images, for example of Buddha or Christ. If these images are helpful then by all means use them, of course, but for *the exercises we are doing here*, create *a new one just for you*, because it also represents a creation of your mind; it is your inner sense of compassion that you are learning to give a voice to. Sometimes religious images can have associations that are not helpful – such as the concern that Christ might disapprove of sin – whereas the compassionate image we are developing here is never judgemental or punitive in any way.

Find somewhere to sit comfortably where you will not be disturbed, and decide if you want to use a CD of chants or music, or have (say) a water fountain on, or a candle or some other sensory aspect in the room. Later you may not want these additions, but they can be helpful to start with to create the mood.

I know some pieces of music help me, but the choice of music can be very personal. Thinking about listening to and finding music that helps you and stimulates feelings of kindness and gentleness can itself be interesting and helpful.

Sit with eyes looking down or closed, and engage in your soothing rhythm breathing. When you feel that your body is now into the rhythm of breathing, start to imagine your ideal of compassion. Bring a slight, gentle smile to your face and consider the following questions.

- If you could design for yourself your ideal compassionate 'other' (that may or may not be a human person) – what qualities would it have? What would it look like?
  If you are struggling with this, try this exploration:
- If you could design the ideal compassionate other for a child, what qualities would it have – how would it change as the child grows into an adult and what would it be like when the child is an adult?'

On page 174 there is a worksheet you can use. If you want to do this exercise then go to the worksheet now, read through the instructions, then engage your soothing rhythm breathing for 30 seconds and see what (if any) image comes to you. The idea is to do it mindfully so that if your mind wanders off task, you just bring it back.

When you are doing this exercise, go into as much sensory detail as you can. For example, think about how old the image is (if it's a human one), the gender, type of eyes. Can you see it smiling? Do you have a sense of the hair style and colour? Do you have a sense of its clothes and postures? Next, focus on the sounds, the tone of the voice. If it communicates with you, what would it sound like to you? If there are any other sensory qualities that you would like your compassionate image to have, bring them into your exercise. One person I worked with saw a tall and bushy tree. It had been there for a long time and she felt she could snuggle into its branches and feel protected.

Think about how you would like your image to relate to you. Some people would like the image to seem older and wiser and very protective. For example, the person who thought of the tree for her compassionate image focused on its protective aspects, feeling surrounded by its branches. Other people like the idea of imagining being cared for, or cared about. One person wanted their image to truly understand how painful and difficult certain aspects of her life had been and still were. Sometimes our image may be parent-like – it can have all the qualities of the parent we always wanted, completely loving, forgiving and admiring; taking pleasure in our being. It is interesting to imagine that your compassionate image has 'pleasure in your being'. Notice those intrusive 'Yes, but.' thoughts when you do this. They are common and understandable but, in this exercise, bring your attention back on task.

Your image might be not so much parent-like but more mentor-like or friend-like. It might give you the feeling that you are a valued member of a team or part of a community. This can be useful to help you think about feelings of belonging, and the idea of being in some relationship to others pursuing similar goals. This is central in Buddhist practice – feeling on the same journey with all others, with some being ahead of you ready to help. Your compassionate image can help you feel that we are all part of the human race. Even if you are depressed, remember there are many millions of people who suffer depression. If you see yourself as inferior or bad in some way, or are filled with anger or worry, remember there are many millions of people who feel as you do because we all have the same kind of brain. It is so easy to feel isolated. When we feel depressed we can make an effort to open our hearts up to the fact that depression is sadly part of the human condition. Our depression puts us right at the heart of being human.

Relating to your image

You might also think about how you would like to relate to your image, how you would like to speak to it, the kinds of things you would want to communicate to it. Spend some time imagining talking to your image. After all, think how much time you spend imagining talking to other people, what you might like to say to them. Sometimes people can find it useful to talk out loud, explaining their feelings but, when you do this, imagine that you're not talking to thin air but to a very compassionate, understanding other.

Keep in mind that we are using imagery, and the only source of these qualities is your own mind, so we are tapping your own inner wisdom about the nature of compassion. Keep in mind that you are using this exercise to put you in contact with competencies and strengths within yourself. It is a way of contacting your own inner compassionate side; no one else can imagine it or create it like you can. This is for you – only you. Remember also that the images we have in our minds are not complete pictures; they are fleeting, impressionistic glimmers and glimpses. Do not worry if nothing clear comes to mind; just be aware that you are practising stimulating different systems.

Meeting your image

In some traditions of meditation imagery, such as Buddhist practices, there are a number of imagery exercises such as imagining a clear blue sky, and the emergence of a landscape with trees. One then imagines the Buddha under the tree and compassionately linking to the Buddha; imagining the Buddha sending compassion from his heart to your heart. At the end of the exercise the Buddha dissolves back into the landscape and the landscape dissolves back into a clear blue sky. This is to symbolize the emergence and dissolving of all things.[2,3]

A variation of this which can be helpful is to imagine meeting your image in your safe place (see pages 146–7). Occasionally people feel they don't want anyone else in their safe place, compassionate or otherwise. Others, however, like the idea of meeting their compassionate image in this way. For example, if your safe place is by the sea you could imagine your image coming along the beach to meet you, smiling and being delighted to see you. Sometimes seeing the image moving towards you, or the face breaking into a smile, is helpful. Sometimes people like to imagine sitting next to their compassionate image and the image having a very concerned, thoughtful and understanding expression; or, if it is a non-human image, to have a sense of concern, kindness and wisdom emanating from the image to the self. These are things to experiment with and see what helps you.

Difficulties with an image?

If, over a period of time, you are struggling to create any sense of a visual image then it may be that sounds would be an easier focus for you. You might think about the sound of a compassionate voice: is it male or female, softly spoken or powerful? One person I worked with had an image of a Buddha dressed as an earth goddess. She never *saw* this image clearly but she just had a sense of nurturing and great warmth. She could focus on this image or sense when she was distressed.

Another thing you can try, if you are struggling to generate an image or sound or sense, is to look through magazines or on the Internet for pictures of compassionate faces or people, and then use them as a template to get started on your imagery. Research has shown that if people practise focusing on looking for suitable pictures they are gradually training their brain to pick up on these cues, and this can have an impact on their self-esteem.[5]

Some people are not so keen on creating their own ideal, rather than of there being someone who wants to be compassionate to them. One person I worked with noted that, 'I guess in a thousand years we may be able to build robots that look, feel and sound like humans and can be extremely compassionate. However, I am not sure that would work for me.' This person wanted to experience compassion but from someone who wanted to relate to him, rather than someone whom he had created. However, we built into the imagery that his compassionate image wanted to relate to him but needed to be 'tuned into'. We can't communicate by e-mail unless we first turn on the computer and set it up to receive messages. Imagery practice means beginning to open up to hear these messages from within us. The point is that we want to stimulate our minds in certain ways. Clearly, if you feel that because these images are not real they are not helpful, then this may not be the exercise for you – at least, not yet. As with all these exercises, you have to find what works best for you.

Some people (often those who have been abused or have had difficult childhoods) can find human images too threatening. Sometimes they prefer to have a compassionate image such as a horse, an eagle, a mountain or a tree. These are fine, provided they are imagined as having human-like minds. The only slight problem with them is that it can be difficult to imagine a gently smiling or concerned compassionate face. Imagining this kind of expression on the face of another individual can be helpful, because there are areas in our brain that pick up on those signals and respond to facial expressions.

The exact relationship you have to your image can vary. For example, as I have noted, some people like to imagine their image as almost parental and they obtain a sense of being cared about and nurtured in a parental way. Other people like to think of their image more as a guide or a guru that is not nurturing them like a parent but guiding them. Yet others like to imagine their image as a companion. A variation on this imagery work can be to imagine that there are many individuals who are trying to bring compassion to our difficult feelings and relationships. It is hard, but imagine being part of such a community who are seeking compassion and healing. You imagine yourself linked into (a part of) the community of individuals who are seeking to bring kindness to the harshness of the flow of life.

Sometimes it can be very interesting to change the gender of our image. This is perhaps a more advanced approach that you might want to explore when you feel okay with earlier ideas. Keep in mind that you can have different images if you wish.

Some people like to imagine the kindness and warmth of the compassionate image being focused as a kind of energy. People who use this approach have developed a form of working with images that they call HeartMath.[6] This group of researchers has been studying various ways we can train ourselves to improve a physiological process called heart rate variability, and reduce our unpleasant emotions, by imaging compassion flowing into our heart region. You can find out more through the HeartMath website.

Grounding

We can use our compassionate imagery to stimulate certain patterns in our brain. As we will see in later chapters, we then want to use these patterns to help us. Sometimes this is to help us think things through in a kind and supportive way, or help us to engage in things that we find difficult. For example, supposing you have a difficult phone call to make. You can engage in the soothing rhythm breathing, spend a few moments imagining your safe place or compassionate image and it offering support for you. Then, from that state of mind, make your phone call. It's not magic, but it might give you a little helping hand to create these states of mind before the phone call.

If you do find this kind of imagery helpful then it can be useful to *ground* your imagery. This means that you practise your imagery while at the same time holding maybe a smooth stone or crystal or some other object in your hand. Then you can carry this object in your pocket so that when you hold it, it links you to the image and the feelings that you have been practising. You might like to find or buy a smooth stone or object that feels soothing in the hand and hold it while doing your imagination exercise. We call this grounding. Ideally, use something that can be replaced if lost, especially if you often have holes in your pockets!

In various spiritual traditions, imagery and invocation exercises are associated with other sensory triggers and processes called *mudras* and *mantras*. Mudras are gestures, body postures and hand movements that are associated with particular processes. For example, if you practise your compassionate imagery sitting in a traditional meditative style, i.e. sitting cross-legged or (what is more comfortable for many people) sitting in a chair, then you may want to rest your hands in your lap with index finger and thumb touching. This gesture can be used when doing the compassion imagery so that by breathing and holding the index finger and thumb together you can recreate the feelings generated in the imagery session. For example, you might have been practising your compassionate image at home in the morning. You then set off to work and are waiting for a train. What you do is engage your soothing rhythm breathing, hold your fingers in the same way and bring to mind your compassionate image or create within yourself the sense of being a compassionate self. Don't forget that relaxed posture, slight smile and facial expressions, of course. You can imagine radiating compassion to everyone around you on the station – those who are also caught up in the flow of life and the hustle and bustle even though they may not want to be there either. Which finger the thumb touches can have different meanings in Eastern traditions. You can look these up on the Internet and read all about them if you are interested. Have some fun!

Overview

In many ways these imagery exercises are doing what all authors and writers of fiction do – which is to create scenes and characters in our minds. The only difference here is that you are doing this mindfully and exploring the impact on you from a soothing, connecting, compassionate point of view. If you come across images that don't work for you, then drop them. If you know that your images change, for example with (say) your menstrual cycle or some other cycle, go with the flow, provided it seems to connect with your soothing system.

Ultimately some people may find that they are attracted into the more traditional spiritual traditions and want their images to be traditional. The point about all of this really is not to get lost in complexity but to recognize the spirit and the purpose of your work. It is to help you stimulate patterns of activity in your mind that give you access to and help to develop a compassionate mind and a soothing mind. This takes practice; it takes time to recognize and work with a mind that is like a grasshopper, but if you stick with it you may find it is useful to you; you may find that you do indeed train your mind for compassion.

Fear of compassion

Some people recognize that they are simply not used to this way of thinking and it seems odd to them, but they can understand its value and the importance of practice. However, other people can be much more resistant. For example, they may feel they do not deserve to be kind to themselves, they may see it as a weakness, or a self-indulgence or even selfishness. If these beliefs are strongly held they can get in the way of practice. One way around this is to simply note these beliefs as common, but to practise anyway. Think about it like physiotherapy. If you had a weak muscle in your leg, perhaps as a result of injury, you wouldn't tell yourself you don't deserve to have a stronger muscle. Let's build these qualities, and then if you decide you don't want to use them, that's up to you.

For some people kindness begins to touch them in a deep way and can make them sad and even tearful. This is because it touches an inner wisdom, a 'knowing' – which is that many of us wish to be cared for, cared about and feel connected to others, and depression is such an isolating experience that there is a yearning inside us for reconnection. Some people are unsure about kindness because their parents could be kind one day but horrible the next. For them feelings of kindness and horribleness are somehow mixed up together. As they begin to feel kindness, the feelings of horribleness come back as well. If you feel like this, keep your focus on the feelings of kindness, notice other feelings creeping in, smile gently and bring the attention back to exactly what it is *you want* to focus on. Only go with things you feel comfortable with.

Another major block to compassion can be anger. Depressed people can struggle with anger or even admitting they have anger (see Chapter 20). Others may have thoughts that it's not kindness they want to develop, but to find a way to fight back, to stand up for themselves or even get their own back on people who have hurt them! For people who feel like this, doing compassion exercises can actually make them feel a bit ashamed of their anger because they feel if they are compassionate they shouldn't feel angry. *This is a misunderstanding of compassion.* As we'll see in our chapters on anger, being able to be honest, and to acknowledge and express assertiveness are actually skills, but denying our anger or rage, sulking or telling ourselves we are wrong to feel it, or blindly acting it out – is not compassionate. Recognizing how painful rage is, is compassionate. Coming to terms with the fact that angry rumination is harmful to us is compassionate; learning how to work with anger is compassionate.

So there are many and various reasons why people can be wary of compassion and we will address these concerns as we go.

Overview and compassion practice

As in all things, practice will help you. To give you a plan and direction, try filling in the practice forms at the end of this chapter. These are really to focus you and give you an opportunity to reflect on your practice. Spend time with them if you can so that by the end of each week you can look back on what you've written on your practice imagery sheet.

As we go through this book we will be looking at your thoughts and behaviors. However, we will be doing this compassionately and you will often find that I suggest you create a gentle and kind position in your mind as you come to look at your thoughts and behaviors.

KEY POINTS

We have gone through some useful compassion-focusing exercises, derived from ancient wisdoms and practices and modern research, which focus on:

- compassion flowing out from you to others
- compassion flowing into you from others
- compassion for yourself.

Keep in mind these should be thought of as behavioral experiments, to see what happens if you put time and effort into practising. Each of these exercises may help stimulate part of your mind and brain that will help with bringing balance to your feelings and moods. Work through each one even if some are more difficult than others.

EXERCISES

Exercise 1: Building your compassionate image
This exercise is to help you build up a compassionate image for you to work with, and develop key areas of your mind. You can have more than one image if you wish, and they may well change over time. Whatever image comes to mind, or you choose to work with, note that it is your creation and therefore your own personal ideal – what you would really like from feeling cared for and cared about. In this practice it is important that you give your image certain qualities, including wisdom, strength, warmth, and a non-judgemental attitude.

For each box below think of these qualities and imagine what they would look, sound or feel like.

TABLE 8.1 BUILDING YOUR COMPASSIONATE IMAGE: WORKSHEET

How would you like your ideal compassionate image to look – visual qualities?

How would you like your ideal compassionate image to sound (e.g. voice tone)?

What other sensory qualities can you give to it?

How would you like your ideal compassionate image to relate to you?

How would you like to relate to your ideal compassionate image?

If possible, begin by focusing on your breathing, finding your calming rhythm and making a half smile. Then let images emerge in the mind as best you can – do not try too hard. If nothing comes to mind, or your mind wanders, gently bring it back to the breathing and practise compassionate acceptance.

Here are some questions that might help you build an image:

- Would you want your caring/nurturing image to feel/look/seem old or young; male or female, or non-human – an animal, sea or light?
- What colours and sounds are associated with the qualities of wisdom, strength, warmth and non-judgement?

Indeed, if you only have a sense of a compassionate colour surrounding you that feels warm and caring, that's a good start. Remember, your colour and image has compassion *for you*.

TABLE 8.2 COMPASSIONATE PRACTICE DIARY

	Mon	Tues	Wed	Thurs	Fri	Sat	Sun
Compassionate self (directed to self and/or others)							
Compassionate image							

In each box note the time and for how long you practised, what you found helpful and any other useful or interesting reflections.

Exercise 2: Experiments to try out

- See which you find easier: creating compassion by imagining being a compassionate self, and/or creating an ideal image that has compassion for you.
- What do you feel if you alter the gender of your compassionate image? This exercise is not helpful to everyone, so only practice what you feel is helpful.

These exercises can also be used as meditation practice, where you put time aside in a quiet space, but also wherever you can focus your mind, e.g., in a break at work or on the bus.

9

Changing unhelpful thoughts and feelings: Balance and compassion

In the last few chapters we noted that, when we become depressed and feel low and tired, our thoughts tend to take us downward. They rarely encourage us or offer uplifts when we most need them. If anything, our thoughts are rather bullying and critical. In this chapter, we are going to explore ways of breaking out of this downward spiral. Look at the fourth column of the 'Thought monitoring and creating helpful alternatives' form in Appendix 1. We are going to learn about how to use this – how to create and refocus on helpful thoughts that are more likely to stimulate soothing rather than threat emotions in us. In the last part of the chapter I will explore with you how to make your own thought forms to suit your needs.

Before we get started, a word of warning. Depressed people are constantly being told that they are too negative and to look on the bright side and focus on positives. Of course, this is very unhelpful because depressed people know this perfectly well for themselves! Moreover, they can get a bit annoyed and resistant. As one of my patients said to me 'I am fed up with being told I am too negative and to be more positive. The problem is I don't have a positive thought in my head and if I did I wouldn't be here.' It's a fair point. Everything that we outline below is an invitation to explore and try things out, become your own therapist, learning how to generate thoughts and behaviors that are genuinely helpful to you. It is absolutely not an instruction to 'Look on the bright side', 'Give up your faulty thinking' or other such unhelpful ideas. It is rather a journey into experimenting with new ideas and to discover helpful things.

Refocusing

Rational minds to the rescue

Our moods or fears colour and direct our thinking, so we have to help our thinking to stand back from them.[1] To help control the spiral downwards into depression, we need to stand back and encourage our *fair and rational* minds to do more work. As we noted in Chapter 3, high stress anxiety and anger can push this rational part of us to one side. Under stress, we automatically look at the negatives, so try to refocus those thoughts onto helpful ones.

One way of doing this is to be more rational, balanced and fair about them, so let's look at the functions and qualities of the rational mind, since we want to recruit it to help ourselves.

- The rational mind likes to look at the evidence. It is like a scientist or detective and treats ideas and thoughts as theories that can be proved incorrect. The rational mind does not settle for simple answers; like Sherlock Holmes, it observes carefully and wants to know as much as possible before coming to a decision.
- The rational mind likes to have several alternatives to choose from. It does not like to have too few choices, because it tends to assume that there is always more than one way of seeing things..

- The rational mind likes to test things and run experiments.
- The rational mind does not like being overly influenced by emotional appeal or hasty conclusions.
- The rational mind knows that knowledge develops slowly. Things become more complex as we know more, and this is a source of fascination and deepening understanding.
- The rational mind knows that sometimes we learn most from trial and error – that, in fact, we often learn more from our errors than we do from our successes.
- The rational mind will attempt (if given the chance) to weigh up the advantages and disadvantages of a particular view or course of action.
- The rational mind likes to take a long-term view of things and recognizes that we often get to where we are going step by step. It realizes that it is our long-term interests that are important, regardless of short-term setbacks or benefits.

So the 'rational and fair approach' is a side of ourselves that we need to cultivate. We do this by deliberately trying to focus on this part of ourselves and asking ourselves, 'What would my fair and rational mind (part of me) say about this?'

However, cognitive therapists point out that focusing on evidence and rationality alone is not always helpful and indeed can be positively unhelpful. Imagine that you are on the high-wire or climbing a steep rock face. You could look down and focus on the thought that if you slip you'll die. That's absolutely correct – no doubt about it – but it's not the best or most helpful thought to focus on. It's better if you look ahead, focus on one step at a time –

and keep going. We only use our rational thoughts *if they are going to be helpful*.

In fact our rational minds work best at combating depression when they are focused and in the service of *compassion and kindness*; and cultivate our *compassionate mind*. Thus, we need to develop a *compassionate and friendly rationality*, not a cold and impersonal one. In the last chapter we developed various exercises to help us engage our thoughts and feelings with compassion. We are now going to use compassion focusing to help us with our depressing thoughts and behaviors.

The compassionate mind

In the last chapter we considered compassion based on wisdom, strength, warmth and non-judging or condemning. Our compassionate minds are empathic, kind and understanding. Can we treat ourselves like this so that when we generate alternative thoughts (with our rational minds) we hear them in wise, kind, gentle and helpful tones?

When we get depressed, there are not so many of these positive caring signals. We become more self-critical and generally negative. When times are hard we *do not* take an understanding, warm and kind approach with thoughts like, 'Well, this has been hard for me and I am bound to feel sad and disappointed about it.' Instead, we are more likely to become angry or feel hopeless, rather than understanding and supportive. It is understandable, because that is how the brain works – so we have to make an effort to bring our soothing and gentle system back on line in our brain.

To heal ourselves, there are things we can learn to cultivate a compassionate mind. The compassionate mind, like the rational mind, has certain qualities:

- empathy and sympathy for those who are in pain and hurting
- concern with growth and helping people reach their potential
- concern with supporting, healing and listening to what we and others need
- listening and enquiring about problems in a kind and friendly way
- quick to forgive and never condemning because it understands how hard being a human being is, with our difficult minds and brains that evolution has given us
- not attacking but seeking to bring healing, repair and reunion
- recognizing that life can be painful and that we are all imperfect beings
- not treating ourselves or others simply as objects with a market value – we are points of consciousness travelling through time (see Chapter 7)
- filling our minds with warmth
- helping us to develop courage to face difficulties in life – things we are frightened to confront but which might block our lives and abilities to grow and flourish.

We can learn to train our thoughts to be warm and friendly and cultivate the qualities of the compassionate mind. For some of us, especially those who have not received much in the way of warmth and kindness when young, this can be a most difficult but helpful step.

Compassionate mind training: the key elements

The components of compassion can be broken down into basic *attributes and qualities* and the *skills* of compassion. You may feel there are a lot of aspects here, but don't worry if you only get a sense of what we're talking about – that's fine. If you think that *the main quality of compassion is kindness,* and that is all you can recall – no worries – just stick with that.

Attributes and qualities

Looking at compassion in a slightly more technical way, we can see that it is made up of different aspects of our minds.

- **The first attribute and quality of compassion involves making a decision to try to be compassionate**. In other words, we are to be motivated to (want to) have a go at becoming more compassionate, to see this as desirable. We recognize that the compassionate self (see pages 149–53) is a self worth feeding and working to develop.
- **Second, we make an effort to train our minds to become sensitive to our feelings and thoughts**. We also need to become sensitive to our genuine needs. It's difficult to be self-compassionate if we are completely insensitive to our pain, upset, wants or needs, so we learn to notice our thoughts and feelings as they arise (see Chapter 7).
- **Third, compassion requires us to be emotionally open to our own suffering and that of others**. This means that we are emotionally touched, moved and sympathetic to suffering. Sympathy is an emotional reaction to our own and other people's emotions and states – it is that immediate wince if we see someone fall heavily or cut themselves. Sympathy can also operate when we are

moved and take joy from the flourishing and well-being of others.

- **Fourth, we can only be open to feelings if we can tolerate them**. We have a variety of feelings, sometimes sad, angry or anxious and sometimes joyful. However, sometimes we are critical of our feelings, or try to run away from them, hide from or suppress them. But when we are compassionate we can learn to be open, tolerant and accepting of our feelings. A key aspect of compassion is learning how to tolerate and come to terms with, become familiar with our feelings, and less frightened of them. This doesn't mean, of course, that we don't wish to change our feelings – for things or for other people or even ourselves. Indeed, we may well do, but we are unlikely to change through criticism, running away or suppressing our feelings; rather we have to face them openly and kindly.

- **The fifth aspect is called empathy, and this is about how we come to understand and think about our feelings and our thoughts**. We become open-hearted, curious, explorative, wanting to know why we feel what we feel or why we think what we think – so that things can make sense to us. When we have empathy for others we make an effort to think about things from their point of view, to understand that they may think and feel differently from us. This requires some work. For example, if somebody hurts you but you realize that they were under enormous stress, so you forgive them and don't take it personally, you are showing kind empathy.

- **Sixth is the important attribute of giving up and not engaging in condemning and judging**. The depressed mind can be filled with condemnation of self or others.

Giving this up is linked to becoming mindful; we become more aware of thoughts and feelings but from an observing point of view. We don't judge them, nor suppress them or push them out of our minds, avoid or run away from them. Rather we learn to notice our feelings but not act on them.

Remember these abilities can be gained in small stages, step by step. All of them are engaged with a genuine desire to relieve suffering and increase our growth and flourishing. Although I try to develop my compassion, my beloved wife still tells me I am becoming a grumpy old man – so still much training required for me, I guess!

The skills of compassion

These involve learning to direct our *attention* in a compassionate and helpful way, learning to *think and reason* in a compassionate and helpful way and learning to *behave* in compassionate and helpful way – all of these with warmth, support and kindness. As we have said, is the glass half full or half empty? When something negative happens or you are unhappy with yourself, can you redirect your attention to something that is helpful? So the *attention* is very important. Mindfulness is about training our attention.

The next skill is compassionate *reasoning or thinking*. Can we train our minds to focus on reasoning and thinking about ourselves, our relationships and situations in a way that is compassionate and helpful? When we ruminate on our anxiety, disappointments, anger or aspects of depression this is only going to lock these feelings in. Can we practise deliberately choosing to refocus our reasoning helpfully – to really ask ourselves the question, 'What is a helpful way for me to think about this problem, situation or difficulty?' Imagine reasoning it through with a friend, or imagine having a dialogue with your compassionate image (see pages 159–166) and see what is helpful for you here, and what you need, to act on this. Do not become confused with the idea that compassionate thinking is simply 'being nice'. Thinking things through compassionately means being honest and at times thinking about difficult thoughts or painful, even aggressive, feelings and dilemmas.

The next skill is learning how to *behave compassionately*, in ways which you identify will be helpful to you and help you with your suffering and difficulties and move you forward in your life's journey. Sometimes compassionate behavior can mean being nice to yourself, recognizing if you need a holiday, if you need the support of others, or just treating yourself kindly. Maybe you really need chill-out time in a nice bath, or to back off from things for a while. You recognize that you can't continue to deplete your resources: like a bank account you can't keep taking money our without putting some back – because then it gets empty! But compassionate behavior can also require courage to do things that may be blocking us. Sometimes it is about acting against the depression or anxiety and doing things even though we don't want to (see Chapter 12). It's compassionate because although taking what might seem an easier short-term path (e.g., avoid doing anything) might give us temporary relief, it doesn't take us anywhere in the long run.

Finally, a key skill to cultivate is generating feelings of warmth and kindness while doing all of the things we have mentioned. This is where many of us struggle. Some say they can feel kindness for others but cannot feel it for themselves. Don't worry too much about that, as it is common. We know that when we are depressed our feeling systems may not be working quite so well, so it's only natural if we struggle with the feeling. We might have to wait for that system to get going a bit. We can help it, though, by doing the exercises outlined in Chapters 7 and 8. We can train ourselves to practise compassionate attention, thinking and behavior, and allow the feelings to come with time.

Really the key issue for everything is learning to work out, and then focus on, what is helpful for you – but not in a selfish 'me-just-me' way, because you will find that is not helpful and other people will lose interest in you. Genuine compassionate helpfulness thinks about other people as well as ourselves. It is never submissive, however, and does not simply mean giving in to what other people want, leaving us feeling resentful or very needy for their approval. Learning to be assertive can actually be very compassionate. Compassion has to be wise, thoughtful, curious and open.

Compassionate attributes and compassionate skills are used to counteract the feelings, styles of thinking and behavior that arise in depression (a summary is given in Table 9.1).

Different states of mind

You might want to consider how, if your threat system is active so that we have 'threat mind', this will influence your feelings and motives, what you attend to, what you think about and how you think about it, and your behavior. The kinds of images and fantasies that pop into your head and your dreams may also have threat themes – because the threat system is active. When we are in 'threat mind' all these will be quite different to when we are trying to generate a compassionate mind (see figure 9.1). This is why making a real effort to create this mind can help us stand back from 'threat and depressed mind' and create different patterns in our mind and brain. With practice we might strengthen compassionate mind patterns – tough, but worth having a go.

TABLE 9.1 COMPASSIONATE ATTRIBUTES AND SKILLS

Compassionate attributes	Compassionate skills
Developing a motivation to be helpful and caring of self and others	Learning to deliberately focus our attention on things that are helpful and bring a balanced perspective, developing mindful attention and using our attention to bring to mind helpful compassionate images and/or a sense of self (Chapters 7 and 8)
Developing sensitivity to the feelings and needs of self and others	Learning to think and reason, use our rational mind, look at the evidence and bring a balanced perspective, writing down and reflecting on our styles of thinking and reasoning (Chapters 9, 10 and 11)
Developing sympathy, being moved and emotionally in tune with our feelings, distress and needs	Learning to plan and engage in behavior that acts to relieve distress, against the depression and moves us (and others) forward to our (or their) life goals – to flourish (Chapter 12)
Developing abilities to tolerate rather than avoid difficult feelings, memories or situations Developing our understanding of how our mind works, why we feel what we feel; how our thoughts are as they are Developing an accepting, non-condemning, and non-submissive orientation to ourselves and others	Learning to slow down and focus on feelings of warmth and kindness

Don't worry if this seems a bit of a handful and too many things to think about, or it seems too tough. As we go through the book you will see how we can use compassionate attributes and skills to help ourselves. Don't try and learn it all or remember it all. Even if you only have a very vague idea about kindness, that's fine.

Figure 9.1 Comparing Compassionate Mind with Threatened Mind.

Questions that generate helpful alternatives

When we have depressing thoughts and feelings flooding in on us it can be helpful just to notice these and *push our pause button*. You could use your soothing breathing rhythm, for example – just take a breath or two. Then, when standing slightly back from the thoughts we can learn how to generate alternatives and not be so caught in the narrow focus of threat, loss and depression. Thinking like this can be tough, but it's important to try. Below is a short selection of useful ideas, divided into three groups to get you started: some are based on rationality and logic, some are based on compassion; and some are based on a problem-solving approach to thinking about life's problems and tackling them in potentially helpful ways. Some will appeal to you more than others.

RATIONAL AND LOGICAL QUESTIONS

- What is the evidence that may support my belief and what is the evidence that may not support it?
- How would I typically see this if I were not depressed? To what degree therefore is this way of thinking reflecting my mood state rather than some 'truth'?

- What alternatives might there be to this view?
- What other explanations might there be for this event?
- What kind of thoughts would help me cope with this at the moment?
- How might I see this event in three or six months' time?
- What are the advantages and disadvantages of thinking about this difficulty in this way?
- What are the advantages and disadvantages of changing the way I think?
- If I overcame my depression, how might I look at this situation?
- What might I learn from changing the focus of my thoughts?

COMPASSIONATE QUESTIONS

- If I had a friend who felt like this, how would I help them see this differently?
- How would a kindly person, who was helping me with this, sound?
- How would I like someone who cared about me to help me see this differently?
- If my thoughts were sympathetic, warm and compassionate, what would they be and how would I feel?
- How would I like a caring person to be with me? How can I be like that to myself?
- If I put myself into compassionate self mode (see pages 149–155) what thoughts and ideas come to me?
- If I imagine my compassionate image (see pages 159–166), how might it help me see this differently; what kinds of things might the image say, and in what tone?

PROBLEM SOLVING

- How could I break this problem down into smaller chunks?
- Is there one bit of this problem I can tackle?
- How could I generate a step-by-step approach to this problem?
- Can I think of anyone who might help me?
- Can I ask them for their help and support?

Generating warmth

To generate warmth using thought records, start by writing down some of the alternatives to your distressing thoughts that seem helpful to you (see Appendix 1 for examples). Suppose that you have the kind of thoughts noted above and you lie in bed a lot. You could say to yourself, 'Come on, get out of bed, you lazy sod. You'll only feel worse in there. For goodness' sake make yourself a plan and stop feeling sorry for yourself', and so on. Note that the tone is impatient and aggressive, even though you are trying to help yourself get up. Having thought or written out your alternative thoughts and got some plans to act against your depression, make sure they are not aggressive or bullying. Develop supportive thoughts, then read them through and express them in your mind *with as much warmth as you can*. If the words you have written down do not sound encouraging, but instead rather hectoring and harsh, try again to express them in less hostile terms. This may not be easy for you, but persevere: go over your alternative helpful thoughts a number of times, and each time you read them or rewrite them, *really feel* a certain warmth, understanding and encouragement coming through. If it helps, try going to your compassionate self first (see pages 149–53).

Looking for alternatives – balancing our thoughts

When we jump to conclusions, we usually don't do much in the way of gathering evidence. We'd make very poor scientists or detectives. We often need to encourage ourselves to do this, and train ourselves to take the time to collect evidence. When we have a negative idea about ourselves, others, our future or the world, we need to ask, 'Do I have enough evidence for this conclusion?'

Let's look at a simple example. Anne thought she had ruined a dinner party by overcooking the meal, ruminated on what people must've thought of her and felt angry with herself and down. Suppose it is you who is struggling with this kind of event. How might we help you *not to dwell* on the overcooked meal, but instead to focus on what was good about the evening? (It is the old 'glass half full or half empty' issue, and you can choose where to focus your attention.) One way is first to go into the emotions (frustration and disappointment) be understanding and kind and ask, 'What am I really thinking here?' Take a moment to become more aware and clarify your thoughts by standing back a bit. Now take a thought, such as, 'I've messed up the whole evening with my overcooked meal'.

- Recognize that (understandable) frustration and disappointment have taken hold of the way we think, and may be out of balance.
- Once we recognize that frustration and disappointment are running the show, we can learn to stand back and bring our rational and fair minds to our thoughts.
- We make a deliberate attempt to generate feelings of compassion and kindness towards the frustration by understanding it 'as only natural', but also gently take a wider, more balanced view because we don't want to

get stuck in those (understandable but unhelpful and depressing) feelings.

- Bringing a more balanced and wider view requires us to focus on four aspects:
  - our **attention** and what we focus on
  - the way we **think and reason**
  - how we focus on **helpful** and supportive behavior.
  - how we put **kind feelings** into efforts to help ourself

Using Anne and her dinner party as an example, let's spell this out by working on the feelings and thoughts that 'the whole evening was messed up.' Look at Table 9.2.

So we have taken a simple event and looked at how to re-focus our attention, thinking, behavior and feelings. These are going to be the basis of all that follows in the rest of this book.

If Anne focuses on going through her alternatives, trying to *feel* support and kindness in the words, this will help. Again, you can try this for yourself. Read Anne's alternatives through as if you're trying to convince yourself of an argument. Judge it on its logic, evidence and accuracy. *Now read them through again, but this time focus on the kindness, support and warmth in the words* – the real understanding of the upset and fear. Stop reading and try it. Can you see how the combination of taking a rational and fair approach, and then putting kind feelings into it, can be helpful? That's why we need our rational and compassionate minds to work in harmony with each other.

Conflicts and thinking about the minds of others

Conflicts with others are often a source of unhappiness, and some of our more extreme and black-and-white views emerge there. For example, Jane and Terry had an argument over money.

TABLE 9.2 USING OUR RATIONAL & COMPASSIONATE MIND

Rational mind	Compassionate/friendly mind (kind, warm tone)
Empathic understanding	
My thinking is understandably clouded by my frustration, and it's difficult to be objective. Also I am anxious about what they might think of me and then how they will behave towards me.	It is understandable I feel frustrated because I put a lot of effort into the party and really wanted people to enjoy themselves and to feel good about me as the host in putting on a great party.

Here Anne shows that she recognizes the problems as frustration and anxiety clouding her feelings and thoughts. She is compassionate because she recognizes (is sensitive and sympathetic to) her frustration/disappointment as understandable and reminds herself why she feels like this, so she doesn't dismiss her feelings but accepts her disappointment with understanding – it is unhelpful to tell ourselves we should not feel what we do – when we clearly do.

Rational mind	Compassionate/friendly mind (kind, warm tone)
Shifting attention	
Where is the evidence that the whole evening was messed up? Our guests seemed happy. If I am are unsure I could ask people.	It is understandable that my attention will be on the meal. Like the newspapers, humans tend to focus on the things that have gone wrong rather than the things that go right. Understandable, but not helpful – so to get more balance I need to refocus my attention on the good things and things I enjoyed about the evening. So I can close my eyes and bring to mind the memory of the party and now look around the room and remember people talking intently, laughing with and smiling at each other. Now I create that compassionate facial expression and see if I can feel any warmth for myself here – be in the pleasure of that shared enjoyment.

Here Anne is practising directing her attention in a different way and not letting her frustration dictate what she brings to mind. She is taking control and making choices about her attention and focus

Rational mind	Compassionate/friendly mind (kind, warm tone)
Reasoning	
Would you say the harsh things you are saying to yourself, to a friend or person you cared for? Do you think your friends will come again if asked? Yes, I am sure they would. So what does that mean? Well, I guess for them it was not so messed up.	With a friend I would help her to realize that it doesn't matter that much, we are all here having a good time, and we are very grateful for her efforts to put the party on so we can have a good time. Actually part of me would be relieved to know other people make errors too.

Here Anne is learning to reason and think about the issue rationally and fairly and then with warmth and kindness, thinking of how she would talk about this if it happened to a friend. She is recognizing that her compassionate, caring side sees things and thinks about things in a different way to her angry, frustrated vulnerable side or part of her.

Behavior

Work out what went wrong and develop a plan to learn from the experience. All life is about learning from our mistakes and moving on. As Paul says in Chapter 22 of this book the secret to success and happiness is the ability to know how to fail – ah well.	It is understandable why I might feel I don't want to be bothered in the future. This is my frustration and vulnerability talking. It would help to have another go and practise building my confidence. If necessary ask people to come and help me.

Here Anne is thinking about compassionate behavior – behavior that will help her move forward, develop, learn from mistakes, grow and develop confidence. Compassionate behavior then is about kindness but is also about encouraging and being supportive in changing our behavior, taking on the challenges of change and not avoiding difficulties.

To generate compassionate feeling, Anne can now look through her alternative thoughts, engage in soothing rhythm breathing and focus on the words but imagine a compassionate image, or a compassionate voice speaking the words; in this part it is not so much convincing herself through evidence but focusing on the kindness, support and understanding in these alternatives that is key.

Because the argument got rather heated, Jane concluded that Terry no longer loved her. You can imagine the difference between having a heated argument, where you know it will end and you will go back to feeling that you care for each other, in contrast to losing contact with those feelings and memories. Sometimes, therefore, it really helps us to recognize when an argument is no more than an argument and is not an indicator of being unloved (despite our feelings in that moment). Table 9.3 shows how Jane might develop a more balanced perspective.

In this example we see that Jane tries to switch perspective and think about it from *Terry's point of view*. She tries to imagine what is actually in Terry's mind rather than just focus on her feelings and fears of being unlovable. This is using empathy: she has

TABLE 9.3 REASONS WHY WE HAD THE ARGUMENT

Upsetting ideas	Compassionate alternatives
He doesn't care about me	*It is understandable to have those feelings when one has just had a difficult argument and given my background with my own family it is clear arguments like this are bound to stir things up in me (note how Jane is being sensitive and sympathetic to her distress here).*
	He is worried about money too, and is prone to say hurtful things when he's worried and loses his temper, and if I'm honest so do I. Well, I think them even if I didn't say them. He is stressed out at the moment because of his job and it is difficult to be understanding and calm under that sort of stress. We wouldn't have gone at each other had we not been so stressed.
	Here Jane is being sensitive and sympathetic to Terry. She brings to mind his coping style and that it is an issue with him, not about her — so her attention is not just on herself. She is also being honest about herself.
	When things calm down it might be useful for us to talk about what happened and reflect on our experience, learn from it. It would also be useful for us to revisit the good things we like about each other and to remember that all of us need to keep things in perspective and how we might pull through this together.
	Here Jane is thinking about what would be helpful behavior now. She recognizes that it would be helpful to learn to discuss and understand this difficulty in their relationship and then forgive and move on.

refocused her *attention from herself* to the mind of the other (Terry). If she then focuses on going through her alternatives trying to feel support and kindness in the words she has written down, this will help. The idea is not to 'excuse' Terry but to see how a shift of perspective can be helpful.

The idea of these examples is to give some thoughts and ideas that you can try for yourself. Note the importance of kindness in the alternatives. For example, read them through as if you're just trying to convince yourself of the reasonableness of the alternatives. Now read them through again but this time read them slowly and 'hear them in your mind' with as much kindness, support and warmth as you can. Look at them as wise ideas. Can you see the difference? This is why we need the rational mind to help us get a balanced perspective and the compassionate mind to generate the feelings for change and growth.

When Jane went through some alternative reasons for the hurtful things that had been said, she still felt unhappy about the conflicts in her relationship with Terry. However, she recognized that there were a number of factors related to the argument and not just the idea that she was not loved. When the heat had gone out of the situation, she decided to talk to Terry about this. At first, he said that he thought that she didn't really understand how he felt and how difficult things were for him – in other words, it was not that he did not love Jane but that he felt misunderstood by her. Although they then got into something of a competition over who was the less understanding, eventually they talked about the fact that the shortage of money was the common problem. They agreed that both were under stress because of that, and that they needed to join together against the common problem rather than venting their anger at each other. This would have been difficult to achieve if Jane had hung on to the idea that Terry's anger was evidence of his not loving her. In fact, both of them tended to interpret arguments as evidence of a lack of love.

Of course, it may well be that, when you are angry, the person you are arguing with is not your best-loved person *at that moment*; but this does not mean that you do not love them, nor does it mean that they don't love you. And we all need to watch out for the terrible 'must': 'I must be loved all the time', or 'In a love relationship we must never be angry with each other'. Many people in good, caring relationships have times when they wonder why they got married at all and why they are still there! But in the back of their minds they know that these feelings and thoughts are coming from the moment, the power of the emotion, and in a few days' time they will feel different again.

Time to break up

Sometimes, however, the evidence points in the other direction – that there may not be much caring in a relationship. Karen had been going out with Tim for about 18 months. He tended to be demanding and rough sexually. At times he would come to her flat drunk, and he often broke their dates. Increasingly depressed, Karen made excuse after excuse for him. It was her *positive* ideas that were the problem not her negative ones (see Table 9.4).

TABLE 9.4 THINKING OF ALTERNATIVES

Positive ideas	Alternatives
He'd change if we were married.	When I saw his last girlfriend she said that he was the same with her and that I was welcome to him. All accounts I have read suggest that, on the whole, people don't change that much after marriage.
This is typical of all men.	I know many other men who are not like this.
When he's down, he always likes to talk to me.	There is more to a relationship than just supporting people when they are down. I might be being used here.
He is often nice and takes me out sometimes.	Even Hitler was nice at times. It's really what I feel about it overall that counts.

Here Karen needed to focus primarily on the evidence that this is not such a loving relationship. Doing this was difficult for her, but when she began to look at alternatives to her idea that Tim did care for her, unfortunately the evidence was that he did not – or at least, not in the way that she wanted. 18 months was a reasonable time to get enough evidence!

Generating alternatives means that we get more than one point of view. Sometimes we don't want to think about the alternatives because they lead to painful decisions. In Karen's case, she had a deeper belief that if she gave up this relationship, she might not find another. It was this belief that had stopped her looking at alternative thoughts about whether Tim cared or not, and really focusing on the evidence that he did not. When she did look hard at the evidence, she realized that, on the whole, this was not a good or supportive relationship to be in. There was more pain than gain.

When she tried to use her compassionate mind by focusing on how she might talk to a friend, Karen came up with these ideas:

I know I'm worried about being on my own. But I can learn to face this possibility. I might be more miserable if I stay in than if I get out. Even if I get out of this relationship, this doesn't mean that I'll give up trying to find a better one. I can think about the qualities I could bring to a relationship and not just focus on my bad points. I'm honest and very loyal. I try to consider other people's feelings. Of course, no one's perfect but I deserve better. In my heart, I know this. It has just seemed too frightening to end it. But then again, I have survived on my own before, and rather than hoping that a relationship with a man will make my life great, I can start to work on relationships with other people who can give me some pleasure and closeness. Ending this relationship doesn't make me unlovable.

Karen wrote this down and recorded these ideas on tape when she wasn't feeling too depressed. She was then able to read and listen to them whenever she felt down. She was encouraged to feel kind and compassionate when she offered herself these alternative ideas and words of advice (today I would stress this aspect much more). This helped her to stop sinking into depression and face up to getting out of the relationship. Once again, we see compassion is about the *courage* to be honest and to act.

One typical response at this stage might be, 'Well, okay, I can generate alternative views; but I don't really believe them. I'm just trying to fool myself.' If this is what you think, consider that this is typical of depression – depression always thinks it knows what's real and accurate. At this stage, the act of generating alternatives and avoiding concentrating on single ideas is the important first step. Then bringing in the feelings of caring and kindness can help even more. Even if it is difficult to generate kindness in your alternatives, don't worry because it's the practice and the effort that count. Sometimes people like to start from the caring position or to imagine their compassionate images, or become the compassionate self and think of the alternatives once they have those feelings a bit – try it and see which you like.

Conflicts and dilemmas

Writing things down can also help you to clarify conflicts and dilemmas. In this case you can write down two columns: advantages (pros or gains) and disadvantages (cons or losses) of making a change. Kevin was in two minds about moving house, so he wrote out the advantages/pros and disadvantages/cons (Table 9.5)

TABLE 9.5 PROS AND CONS	
Advantages (pros)	Disadvantages (cons)
Nicer district	Further to travel to work
Bigger house with more space for the family	Unfamiliar; I like my present house
Bigger garden that I could enjoy and relax in	Might not have the time to maintain it
Good investment	More expensive

Kevin's next task was to weigh each pro and con. He did this with his family, with him and his wife putting arguments for and against. Through discussion, it became clear that it was the un-familiarity of a new house and district that was the biggest hurdle. Kevin realized that he did not like to leave the familiar. Once this was clarified in his mind, he was able to reconsider this view and accept that although it might take him time to adjust to a new home, in the long term it would be a good decision to move.

Sometimes we can feel very blocked in changing our basic views of ourselves or changing our ways of doing things. There always seems to be a cost or fear. In therapy, Karen realized that, if things went wrong in relationships, she tended to blame herself. Although she readily acknowledged that giving up doing this would be helpful, she found it difficult to do. She wrote down the pros and cons of giving up self-blame to discover why (Table 9.6).

TABLE 9.6 PROS AND CONS OF GIVING UP SELF-BLAME

Advantages		Disadvantages
I would feel better	but	I would become more angry with others I would become like my mother who always blamed others, and whom I disliked
I would take more risks	but	I would provoke others to be angry or reject me
I would not feel inferior	but	I might not see my faults, and might become arrogant

By writing these thoughts down, it became clear that, for Karen, there were a number of unrecognized disadvantages to changing – not least *the fear* of becoming the kind of person she did not like. Of course, no one would change if they saw that as the possible result. Karen needed to consider the evidence for the disadvantages that she had identified. What evidence was there that not taking the blame for everything would make her arrogant? Aren't there lots of people who do not blame themselves but are also not arrogant? See the responsibility circle on page 285.

Fear of change

In therapy, people often see many disadvantages to changing. Of course, they don't want to be depressed – but getting out of depression may appear to involve rather difficult things. We identify what these might be. What would change involve? What might be the fear in that? Not every advantage of change has a countering 'but' or problems associated with it; still, it is useful to think of such possibilities. We can continue to resist change if the perceived disadvantages and fears associated with change are not explored. Once we can see more clearly what is blocking us, we may be better placed to start (kindly but firmly) challenging some of those blocks.

Sometimes advantages and disadvantages are not seen. For example, someone who feels a need to be in an intimate relationship to be happy can become dependent and tend to stay in unsupportive relationships – as in Karen's case. Someone who, by contrast, feels a need to be strong and independent might suffer the disadvantage of being unable to ask others for help. They may keep others at arm's length and find it difficult to let other people become emotionally close.

You can do these written exercises on pros and cons many times, and can carry them out quite slowly, allowing time for self-reflection and/or discussion with others along the way.

KEY POINTS

- To help us shift depressed brain patterns it helps to have two types of focus: balanced thinking and a compassionate focus.

- Gaining balance requires us to generate alternatives and to think about an issue, belief, or problem from as many different angles as we can. This practice helps us to break out from the narrowed vision that depression can sometimes give us.

- Our compassionate mind is not irrational but focuses on wisdom with feelings of warmth, support and kindness.

- Important qualities of compassion include the desire and motivation to be compassionate, being sensitive and sympathetic, learning to tolerate painful feelings, being able to think about painful feelings in ourselves and in others so that we get a balanced and insightful perspective and understanding. Compassion can require that we develop courage. Compassion is not condemning or judgemental because it is based on the recognition that human minds and situations are complex, difficult and often harsh.

- Rational and compassionate skills involve us learning to pay attention to things that are helpful and trying to get a balanced approach by reasoning and thinking through things in as balanced and compassionate way as possible, orientating behavior towards helpful actions.

- Regaining balance can be helped by writing things down (see Chapter 11), considering the advantages and disadvantages of things, imagining oneself in the shoes of others.

EXERCISES

In these exercises we are going to combine some of the principles of mindfulness (Chapter 7) with using our rational and compassionate minds. The first exercise is learning to be mindful and accepting of our negative thoughts and feelings without worrying that we have to change them – this helps to take the pressure off ourselves.

Exercise 1

Write down your depression-linked thoughts about some situation, which will normally be something you feel threatened by or on which you are loss-focused. It usually helps if we start off with something that's not too major and gradually work up to more difficult things. Engage in your soothing breathing rhythm and allow your thoughts to be there as thoughts that have emerged in your mind. In this exercise you are not trying to change them but just be mindful and aware of them. The key here is learning that we can sit with them quietly, focusing on our breathing 'in and out', the rising and falling of the chest as we breathe, the point just inside the nose where the air comes in. In this moment we are simply breathing and noticing.

Exercise 2

In this exercise imagine your compassionate side (and this may be imagining yourself as a compassionate person or imagining your compassionate image) to be in a conversation with you. Imagine warmth, kindness and understanding for your depressing thoughts and feelings. Again we are not trying to change anything at this point; rather we are developing our compassion for our situation. Let your thoughts be there, with compassionate understanding for them. This can help you to stop fighting with yourself and condemning yourself for what you feel. Try to feel compassion for your situation and feelings – remember that you did not design your brain or choose to feel like this.

Exercise 3

Look at your thoughts and think about them with kindness but also from different points of view. Are there things that you can focus your attention on, that will be helpful to you? As a compassionate person, how would you like to talk to a friend in your situation? How would you like your compassionate image to talk to you and support you? Remember your compassionate side is wise and is not persuaded by negative feelings. It will help you to think about reasons to be more balanced in your thoughts. You could try writing this down, if that helps you.

These exercises are designed to begin the process of developing your rational balancing and compassion skills as guides on the road out of depression. All the time, remember you are the best judge of what works for you, so try out different things and don't be put off if something seems difficult as this may be exactly the thing you need to practise and to try out.

10

Styles of depressive thinking: How to develop helpful styles

This chapter looks in more detail at the kinds of ways our thoughts can become problematic for us when we get depressed and how to work with them in a compassionate way. Depression can often be linked to difficult life situations: conflicts and problems in relationships, or at work, or with finances, or physical health, or feeling stuck in places we don't want to be. Coping with these can be hard, but it can become even harder because as we become depressed, the way we think changes. Threat and loss-focused thoughts, interpretations and memories become much easier to bring to mind and dwell on. There is a shift to what is called a *threat and loss (negative thinking) bias*, and then we are on a downward spiral. [1] A typical spiral is outlined in Figure 10.1.

As our thinking follows a downward spiral, we start to look for evidence that confirms or fits our negative beliefs and feelings. We may start to remember other failures, and the feelings begin to spread out like a dark tide rolling in to cover the sands of our positive abilities. Such thoughts tend to lock in the depression, deepen it and make it more difficult to recover from (see page 101). They drive a vicious circle of feeling, thinking and behavior – and this gives us one route into disrupting the depressing spirals.

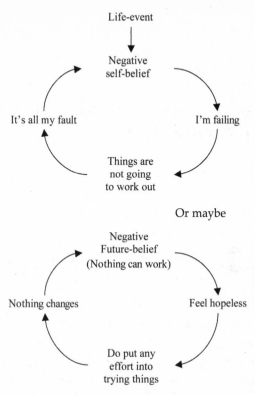

Figure 10.1. A typical downward spiral.

Certain *styles* of depressive thinking are fairly common. Professor Beck, who started cognitive therapy, noted about six or seven types of negative (or as I prefer to called them 'threat-focused') thinking biases.[2] We will explore some of them here. To work on our biases in a more balanced way, we have to (1) recognize them and (2) make an effort to bring our rational and compassionate minds to the problem. It is important to recognize that humans are often not that logical or rational – we can be, but we have to work at it. In fact a lot of research has shown that many of our ways of thinking about ourselves, other people, different groups, and our hopes for the future can become very biased and inaccurate – even at the best of times![2] So working for balance takes effort and training of our minds. Below we go though some typical biases that tend to appear with depression. We'll start with jumping to conclusions because this is absolutely typical of the threat-focused and 'better safe than sorry' mind.

Jumping to conclusions

If we feel vulnerable to abandonment, or have the basic belief, 'I can never be happy without a close relationship,' it is natural that, at times, we may jump to the conclusion that others are about to leave us. This will often impel us to cling on to these relationships, unable to face up to our fear of being abandoned.

The part of our mind that focuses us on threats will tell us that we could not possibly cope with being alone. We might worry about how we think we could cope with everyday life, or we might worry about being overwhelmed by grief, feelings of loss and emptiness. Sometimes these feelings go back to childhood. If you have a fear of rejection or of losing a relationship, one way of helping might be to write down that fear and see if you can think of ways of coping with a break-up – if it occurs. Of course, the break-up may be painful: you can't protect yourself from life's painful things, but you can work out how to be supportive and compassionate to yourself in this time of difficulty. It's hard but it can help us to actually shift our attention and think about how one *could* cope. For example, be understanding and kind to your distress: it is only natural to feel upset. We might consider how we could elicit help from friends, or remind ourselves that, before we had a relationship with this person, we had coped on our own; or that many people suffer the break-up of relationships and survive.

There might even be advantages in learning to live alone for a while.

Putting thoughts into the minds of others

Another form of jumping to conclusions is called 'mind reading' or sometimes projection. We make assumptions about their thoughts and feelings. For example, we may automatically assume that people do not like us because they do not give sufficient cues of approval or liking us. In 'mind reading' we believe that we can intuitively know what others think.

The key point here is mindfully examining your thoughts rather than automatically assuming that your thoughts about what other people are feeling and thinking are accurate. Research has shown that some people struggle here. For example, parents may believe the annoying behaviors of their children are to wind them up; they take it personally. Or that disobedient children are showing that they don't care about or respect the parent; again they take it personally. But they are reading intentions into their children that simply are not there. Young children are not thinking about 'the mind of the parent' at all. They are not thinking about how to 'wind the parent up' or cause them emotional upset – they are simply behaving in these ways to try to get what they want. It's about them – the child – not the parent.

So the way we attribute intentions and feelings to other people's behavior is important. When we get depressed we often think other people's withholding, avoiding or ignoring behaviors are directed at us. Some men think that if their wives do not want to sleep with them when they want to it's because they don't love them enough – in reality there may be differences in sex drive, or timing or desire. Women may feel that if men don't talk about feelings it's because they don't love them. In reality the man may have difficulties in talking about feelings in general. When people disappoint us it's important to think that maybe it's not really about 'us' or 'me' it's about 'them'. We have to find ways to be compassionately understanding and explore (take time to think about) the 'minds of others' in more detail.

Predicting the future

We often need to be able to predict the future, at least to a degree. We need to have some idea about what threats, opportunities and blocks lie ahead to know whether to put effort into things or not. How much energy and effort our brains devote to securing goals depends a great deal on whether we have an optimistic or a pessimistic view of the future. It may be highly disadvantageous to put in a lot of effort when the chances of success appear slim. The problem is that, as we become depressed, the brain veers too much to the conclusion that nothing will work, and continuously signals: 'times are hard'. Depression says, 'You can put a lot of effort into this but not get much in return. Close down and wait for better times' (see Chapter 3). Getting out of depression may involve patience and a preparedness to think that the brain is being overly pessimistic about the future.

Emotional tolerance versus avoidance

Our brains have evolved over many millions of years to be able to have very strong emotions. One of our greatest difficulties is learning how to tolerate and come to terms with strong emotion. We can certainly look to how our thoughts may be making them stronger than they need be, but it's also important to learn to tolerate the natural and normal power of our emotions; to recognize that there's nothing wrong with us in having strong emotions. Rather it's the way we deal with them, either by acting on them impulsively or by trying to get rid of them, avoid them, suppress them, or deny them that causes the difficulties.

A colleague told me a sad story he read in a local newspaper. A woman who was looking for her local Alcoholics Anonymous meeting got lost and couldn't find the way there. She became upset, frustrated and anxious, so she sat in her car and drank a bottle of wine. She was picked up by the police well over the limit. She had simply not been able to tolerate the upset without wanting to turn off those intense feelings.

Another type of avoidance is the person who feels angry with a parent (say), but is frightened to acknowledge it or work through it. When anger arises she distracts herself or binge eats. Or a person may be frightened of (say) homosexual thoughts and feelings and so drinks to avoid them; or might drink to avoid feelings of loneliness or shame. We can run from all kinds of emotions. Our emotions can also stop us from doing things. Consider a socially anxious person who would love to go to university but the anxiety dictates their actions and they don't go. Think about how often fears and worries stop you from doing things you really want to do. Sometimes we think about this in terms of confidence, but often it's about our ability to tolerate emotions and act against that emotion. Most addictions, forms of self-harm, anxiety disorders, reckless and impulsive behavior and some depressions are linked to problems in tolerating emotions.

Given the problems we have with strong emotions and our 'old brains', distress tolerance is key to well-being. Compassion can be very helpful in how we learn to work with and tolerate strong emotions. Here are some ideas to have a go at.

Step 1: seeing the point of having a go

- Make a commitment to learn to tolerate your emotions as something you want to learn to do.
- Recognize the value of doing this; see how it will strengthen you.
- Consider the value in giving up the short-term benefit of trying to avoid your emotions (e.g., by avoiding them, drinking or binge eating) in favour of the longer-term benefits of tolerance.

Step 2: what to do next

When you have agreed your motivation then these are some things to try:

- Develop an attitude of mindfulness, with two types of focus:
  - Sometimes distractions help – focus on something outside of yourself in the 'here and now' such as the colour of someone's clothes, or floor patterns. When I was anxious about giving talks I would try and see a face in the audience that looked friendly and focus on that person, or look just above people's heads.
  - The second form of focusing is to pay attention to how your emotions feel in your body; become curious about them, notice how they come with certain types of thinking and urgencies. You become the observer.
- Put your emotions into words as they're happening: 'I am beginning to feel frustrated and this is because . . . It is affecting my body by . . . and I am noting a certain urgency . . . There is nothing wrong with me for feeling

emotions like this because . . .' Our brains can give us strong emotions. Research is showing that putting 'emotions into words' helps to slow us down and stimulates certain areas of our brain that can help us.

- As you notice emotions arising, focus on your soothing breathing rhythm.
- Make a commitment not to act on your emotions immediately. Pull back and observe them as best you are able.
- Remind yourself there is nothing wrong with you for feeling strong emotion (look out for self-criticism).
- If you find yourself thinking, 'This is unbearable, intolerable, impossible' and so on, acknowledge these thoughts as notions and judgements that reflect a certain fear in you. However, remember you have made a commitment to try to hold the line – at least for a while.
- Keep in mind that these emotions will settle down in time: 'this too will pass'.
- Perhaps you might remember previous occasions when this has happened, so stay with your breathing and focus on 'This will pass. By tolerating this I am becoming stronger and stronger.'
- If you can give yourself some time where you tolerate your emotion, even if it's only a few moments, you are beginning to learn how to do it.
- Be aware of any threat-focused thoughts such as 'I will lose control,' 'this emotion will harm me', 'I'm a bad person for feeling this emotion.' Think through alternatives: 'I have had these emotions before and have not lost control or been harmed; these feelings are common throughout the world so it can't be me who is

bad. Even if I can only tolerate the emotion briefly it's a start.'

• Learn to acknowledge, value and praise your courage.

Step 3: compassion focusing

• With your soothing breathing rhythm, create a compassionate facial expression.
• Imagine that you are a compassionate person who *can* tolerate strong emotion. See an image of yourself tolerating the emotions and being pleased afterwards.
• Bring to mind your compassionate image and imagine talking out your emotion to your image.
• Write a compassionate letter in your mind about your emotions or what you are feeling this moment.

In these exercises you are practising buying time, being *with* your emotion, and tolerating it. These are just some ideas and you may find others once you have committed yourself to learning to tolerate strong emotion. It's not easy, but over time it will get easier for you. Regular practice of mindfulness and compassion work can actually help us become calmer inside. You may also have your own ways of working on this issue. For example although I am not religious myself, I know it can help some people. One woman thought about Jesus: 'If he can tolerate that, I can tolerate this'. She did not use this to shame herself about her emotion (there are no 'shoulds' and 'oughts' here), rather it helped her feel 'one with the suffering of Jesus' and was very helpful to her. A person who was trying to control her urges to eat when hungry thought about starving children in the world. If they can tolerate that, she could tolerate her urges. It's not unknown for actors to have severe nausea, even vomiting, on the first night of a play, but they work through it because they really want to act. The first step is really getting clear in your mind the advantage of learning toleration, of putting up with painful feelings.

Emotional reasoning

One of the reasons that we can have problems with emotion tolerance is because our emotions can be more powerful and long-lasting than they need to be. Strong feelings and emotions pull and push us into thinking in certain ways, and this can happen despite the fact that we know it is irrational. The problem is that, at times, we may not get our more rational and compassionate mind to help us. Given the strength of our emotions, we may take the view, 'I feel it, therefore it must be true.'

Feelings are very unreliable sources of truth. For example, at the times of the Crusades, many Europeans 'felt' that God wanted them to kill Muslims – and they did. Throughout the ages, humans have done some terrible things because their feelings dictated it. As a general rule, if you are depressed, don't trust your feelings – especially if they are highly critical and hostile to you. In Table 10.1 there are some typical 'I feel it therefore it must be true' ideas with some alternatives.

In their right place, feelings are enormously valuable, and indeed, they give meaning and vitality to life – we are not computers. But when we use feelings to do the work of our rational minds, we are liable to get into trouble. The strength of our feelings is not a good guide to reality or accuracy. See if you can come up with any other alternatives for the thoughts and ideas in Table 10.1.

TABLE 10.1 FEELINGS, NOT FACTS

Situation	I feel it, therefore it must be true	Alternative balancing ideas
Going to a party	I feel frightened, therefore this situation is dangerous and threatening	This is related to my shyness and confidence, not any actual danger – I can go a step at a time and be kind with my feelings.
Feeling anxious	I feel as if I will have a heart attack, therefore I will	This is understandable anxiety which can feel like this – but I have had these feelings many times before and it was anxiety not a heart attack.
Being accused of a minor fault	I feel guilty, therefore I am guilty and a bad person	It is understandable to be disappointed but there is so much more to me than that – feeling a bad person is maybe a reflection of my annoyance at being criticized. Learning to cope with criticism will strengthen me.
Losing my temper and shouting	I feel terrible when I get angry, therefore anger is terrible and I am bad and rejectable	Yep anger is not a nice feeling but it's very much part of human nature – I did not design these feelings – and I am trying to understand and work with my anger.
Wanting to cry	I feel that, if I start crying, the flood gates will open and I will never stop; therefore I must stop myself from crying	It is easy to feel overwhelmed especially if one is not used to crying and being in touch with one's pain – but crying does subside and I have shown myself to be effective in turning off my emotions if I really need to. Maybe a little at a time, and staying with my emotions might actually help me.
Feeling self-conscious when I cry	I feel ashamed when I cry, therefore crying is shameful and a sign of weakness	Crying is a very important human response built into our bodies. Crying is the display of our pain and is basic to our humanity. Other people have probably shamed me for crying so it is their shame I am feeling.
Making a mistake	I feel stupid, therefore I am stupid	Who hasn't felt that awkward when one does something a bit thoughtless careless and daft – but one cannot sum up a complex self like this. My annoyance is probably driving this feeling and my compassion can actually get stronger if I used it right at these moments.

'I must'

Over 2,500 years ago the Buddha said, 'Our cravings are the source of our unhappiness.' He also suggested that it is our attachment to things, our *'must haves'* and 'must bes' and 'others must be as I want them to be' feelings and beliefs that lead to suffering – not least because life is not like this. All things are transitory and it is coming to terms with that and living in 'this moment' that matters. Look out for feelings that indicate you are 'must-ing' yourself. As we become depressed, and sometimes before, we can believe that we *must* do certain things or *must* live in a certain way or *must* have certain things, e.g., others' approval, or achieve certain standards, e.g., weight loss.

By gaining control over our musts, 'got to haves' and cravings, we are gaining control over our emotional minds. Whatever your own particular 'musts', try to identify them and turn them into preferences. Recognize that reducing the strength of your cravings can set you free, or at least freer, and remember that there is often an irony in our 'musts'. For example, at times we can be so needing of success and so fearful of failure that we may withdraw and not try at all. If you go to a party and feel that 'everyone *must* like you,' the chances are that you'll be so anxious that you won't enjoy it and even may not go. And if you do go, you may be so defensive that others won't have a chance to get to know you.

Disbelieving and discounting the positive in personal efforts

If we have been threatened or experienced a major setback, we may need a lot of reassurance before trying again. This makes good evolutionary sense: it is adaptive to be wary and cautious. We even have a saying for it: 'once bitten, twice shy.'

The problem is that in depression this same process can apply in an unhelpful way. If we have experienced a failure or setback, we may think we need to have a major success before we can re-assure ourselves that we are back on track. Small successes may not be enough to convince us. However, getting out of depression often depends on small steps, not giant leaps. Typical automatic thoughts that can undermine this step-by-step approach are:

- I used to do so much more when I was not depressed. Managing to do this one small thing today seems so insignificant.
- Other people could take things like this in their stride.
- Because it is such an effort for me, this proves that I am not making any headway.
- Anyone could do that.
- Small steps are all right for some people, but I want giant leaps and nothing else will do.

Remember what we have said about depression – your brain is working differently. Perhaps the levels of some of your brain chemicals have got a little too low. Perhaps you are exhausted. Therefore, you have to compare like with like. Other people may accomplish more – and so might you if you were not depressed – but you are. Given the way your brain is and the effort you have to make, you are really doing a lot if you achieve one small step. Think about it this way. If you had broken your leg and were learning to walk again, being able to go a few paces might be real progress. Depressed people often wish that they could show their injuries to others, but unfortunately that is not possible. But this does not mean that there is nothing physically differ-ent in your brain and body when you are depressed than when you are not.

If you can do things when you find them difficult to do, surely that is worth even more praise than being able to do them when they are easy to accomplish. We can learn to praise and appreciate our *efforts*, rather than the results.

A crucial thing to remember is that you are training and stimulating your brain. By focusing on small things that you can appreciate and give yourself praise for, you will stimulate important positive emotion areas of the brain. *Although understandable, it is not helpful to keep dismissing these opportunities to stimulate your brain in a positive way.* Try not to get caught up in debates with yourself about whether you deserve it, whether you should do more and so on. Focus on it as 'physiotherapy for your brain'; exercising and stimulating key systems in your brain over and over again as often as you can.

Disbelieving the positive from others

Another area where we disbelieve the positive is when others are approving of us. To quote Groucho Marx, 'I don't want to belong to any club that will accept me as a member.' Even being accepted is turned into a negative. Here are some other examples:

- When Steve was paid a compliment at work by his boss, he thought, 'He's just saying that to get me to work harder. He's not satisfied with me.'
- When Ella was asked how she had been feeling when she returned to work after being ill, she concluded, 'They're just asking what's expected. They don't really care, but I guess they'll feel better if they ask.'
- When Peter passed a nice comment on how Maureen looked, she thought, 'He's just saying that to cheer me up. Maybe he wants sex'.

> • Paul sent in a report at work, even though he knew there were one or two areas where it was weak. When he got approving feedback, he thought, 'Deceived them again. They obviously didn't read it very carefully. No one takes much notice of my work.'

Rather than allowing himself to keep on thinking so negatively, Paul was encouraged to ask his boss about his report, especially the shaky areas. He didn't get the response he expected. His boss said, 'Yes, we knew those areas were unclear in your report, but then the whole area is unclear. In any case, some of the other things you said gave us some new ideas on how to approach the project.' So Paul got some evidence about the report rather than continuing to rely on his own feelings about it.

From an evolutionary point of view, the part of us that is on the look-out for deceptions can become overactive, and we become very sensitive to the possibility of being deceived. Moreover, fear of deception works both ways. On the one hand, we can think that others are deceiving us with their supportive words and on the other, we can think that, if we do get praise, we have deceived *them*. Because deceptions are really threats, when we become depressed we can become very sensitive to them. But again we can try and generate balanced alternatives to these ideas. For example:

Even if people are mildly deceptive, does this matter? What harm can they do? I don't have to insist that people are always completely straight. And life being life, some people are more deceptive than others. But I can live with that. To be honest I can be deceptive too – it is part of being human.

As a rule of thumb, it can be useful to take people at face value unless experience proves otherwise.

All-or-nothing

All-or-nothing thinking (sometimes also called either/or, polarized or black-and-white thinking) is typical when we are threatened. If we might be under a threat we often need to weigh this up quickly. Animals often need to jump to conclusions (e.g., whether to run from a sound in the bushes), and it is easier to jump to conclusions if the choices are clear – all-or-nothing. So our threat system can go for 'better assume the worst' and 'better safe than sorry'. See if you can spot these in the list below.

- My efforts are either a success or they are an abject failure.
- I am/other people are either all good or all bad.
- There is right and there is wrong, and nothing in between.
- If I'm not perfect, I'm a failure.
- You're either a real man or you're a wimp.
- If you're not with us, you're against us.
- If it doesn't go exactly as I planned or hoped, it is a fiasco.
- If you don't always show me that you love me, you don't love me at all.

All-or-nothing thinking is common for two reasons. First, we feel threatened by *uncertainty*. Indeed, some people can feel very threatened by this. They have to know *for sure* what is right and how to act and they may try to create the certainty they need by all-or-nothing thinking. Sometimes we may think that people who 'know their own minds' and can be clear on key issues are strong, and we admire them and try to be like them, but watch out. Hitler knew his own mind and was a very good example of an all-or-nothing thinker. Some apparently strong people may actually be quite rigid. Indeed, I have found that some depressed people admire those they see as strong individuals, but when you really explore this with them, they discover that the people they are admiring and trying to be like are neither strong nor compassionate. They are rather shallow, rigid, all-or-nothing thinkers who are always ready to give their opinions. A lovely motto someone gave me once was 'indecision is the key to flexibility'.

There is nothing wrong with sitting on the fence for a while or seeing things as grey areas. Even though we may eventually have to come off the fence, at least we have given ourselves space to weigh up the evidence and let our rational minds do some work.

The other common reason why we go in for all-or-nothing thinking has to do with *frustration* and *disappointment* (see Chapter 21). How often have we thrown down our tools because we can't get something to go right? When you get frustrated you tend to take a more extreme view. It is emotions that drive this view, so balancing of all-or-nothing thinking and our tendency to make extreme judgements of good/bad or success/failure can be very important in recovering from depression. The state of depression itself can reduce our tolerance of frustration and push us into all-or-nothing thinking, so we have to be aware of this and be careful not to let it get the better of us.

All-or-nothing thinking can be unpleasant for other people too. Tim talked about his mother who was depressed and how she found frustration very difficult. 'Small things would set her off and then you would never know what mood she would be in.' Tim could identify this as black-and-white and rigid thinking. 'Things had to be just so and if they weren't she'd get angry, anxious or withdraw.' Tim understood that this related to various stresses in her life. Nonetheless, seeing this allowed Tim to reflect on himself and he decided he didn't want to be like that. When he felt frustration mounting in him he would begin his soothing rhythm breathing, consider if his thoughts and feelings were rather black-and-white and practise being compassionate and tolerant in that context.

Overgeneralization

If one thing goes wrong, we can think and feel that everything is going to go wrong – our emotions go on a rollercoaster. When we overgeneralize like this, we see one setback or defeat as a never-ending pattern of defeats. Nothing will work; it will always be this way.

- a student received a bad mark and had a heart-sink disappointment feeling and concluded, 'I will never make it. My work is never good enough.' (linked to anger, frustration and anxiety)
- a friend had told Sue that she would come to her party, but then she forgot the date. Sue thought, 'This is typical of how people always treat me. No one ever cares.' (linked to anger, frustration and anxiety)
- Dan broke up with his girlfriend and thought, 'I will never be as happy again as I was with her. I will always be miserable without her.' (linked to sadness)

So it's important to be aware of the arising of feelings and meanings and the thoughts that tumble along with them.

In Table 10.2 we can explore some typical balanced and compassionate alternatives for working on our tendencies for overgeneralization. Notice that we always start with being under-standing and kind for the distress we feel.

TABLE 10.2 ALTERNATIVES TO DEPRESSING THOUGHTS

Depressing thought	Balanced and compassionate alternatives
Things will never work out for me	When I am upset it is typical for me to think like this – so I can be wise and kind to myself by recognizing it is my upset that is doing the thinking
	'Never' and 'always' are big words. I have thought like this before and things did work out – at least to a degree
	Let's take some soothing rhythm breaths and slow myself down a bit and give myself some space to think
	Now what would I like a really kind and compassionate person to say to me right now (really spend a moment on this idea and go with that)
	Rather than just blanking out everything I could think that things might go okay
	Predicting the future is a chancy business. Maybe I can learn how to make things go better. I don't have to load the dice against myself
	If a friend had a setback, I would not speak to them like this. Maybe I can learn to speak to myself as I might to a friend.

Egocentric thinking

In this situation, we have difficulty in believing that others have a different point of view from our own. The way we see things must be the way they see things – e.g., 'I think I'm a failure, thus so must they.' We discussed this on page 207, in the section 'Putting thoughts into the minds of others'.

But there is another way we can be egocentric in our thinking. This is when we insist that others obey the same rules for living and have the same values as we do. Janet was very keen on birthdays and always remembered them. But her husband Eddie did not think in these terms; he liked to give small presents as surprises, out of the blue. One year, he forgot to buy a present for Janet's birthday. She thought, 'He knows how important birthdays are to me. I would never have forgotten his, so how could he forget mine? If he loved me, he would not have forgotten.' But the fact was Eddie did not really know how important birthdays were to Janet because she had never told him. He was simply supposed to think the same way as Janet.

In therapy together with Janet, Eddie was surprised at how upset she had been and pointed out that he often brought her small surprise presents, which showed that he was thinking about her. He also mentioned to her – for the first time – that she rarely gave gifts except at birthdays, and to his way of thinking, this meant that she only thought about giving him something or surprising him once a year!

All of us have different life experiences and personalities, and our views and values differ, too. These differences can be a source of growth or conflict. It is because we are all different that there is such a rich and varied range of human beings. Unfortunately, at times we may downgrade people if they don't think or behave like us. On the book stands today, you will find many books that address the fact that men and women tend to think differently about relationships and want different things out of them. This need not be a problem if we are upfront about our needs and wants and negotiate openly with our partners. It becomes a problem when we are not clear with them about our wants or we try to force other people to think as we do.

Dwelling and ruminating

As we noted on pages 113–4, dwelling and ruminating on the threats and losses in our lives can be a source of maintaining your brain in a state of threat and stress. All the ways of thinking noted above can feed into 'dwelling and ruminating'. Some people also think that this is a way to solve problems and, if limited, thinking things through can of course be helpful. However, going over and over things that upset you or make you angry or anxious is not helpful. The steps are:

- Practice noticing your ruminations when they start up.
- Become mindful and notice the paths your thoughts tread – pull back to your observing kind and curious mode.
- Make a commitment to gently refocus your attention – maybe with an activity or bring to mind a helpful image or something that is more likely to stimulate positive feelings in your brain.

KEY POINTS

- The way we think about things can lead us further into depression rather than out of it.
- When we are depressed, our brains change in such a way that we become very sensitive to various kinds of harm, threats and losses. It is (or was) adaptive for the brain to go for an 'assume the worst' and 'better safe than sorry' type of thinking when under threat. In these situations, control over our feelings is given more to the threat system in our brain and less control is given to the rational, kind and compassionate systems (see Chapters 2 and 3).
- There are some typical types of thoughts that are encountered in depression. These include jumping to (negative) conclusions, emotional intolerance, 'I must', dismissing the positives, all-or-nothing thinking and overgeneralizing. We can try to work with these.
- One way to help is to recognize the typical styles of depressive thinking and open our hearts to generating compassionate balanced alternatives; to deliberately switch our attention, thinking and behaving away from the threat system into a more balanced and compassionate system.

EXERCISES

Exercise 1

Review the different types of thinking outlined in this chapter. Consider which ones seem to apply to you (see Appendix 2 for a quick overview of some typical types of threat-focused thinking).

- If you have written down your thoughts, consider which kind of depressive style each thought may be an example of – for instance, is it like jumping to conclusions, or emotional reasoning, or all-or-nothing thinking? You may find that one of the styles (e.g., all-or-nothing thinking) crops up in many different situations. That is certainly one of my styles when under stress.
- Use your rational/compassionate mind to generate alternatives; think of questions to put to yourself. Do you have enough evidence for your view? Is this a balanced view? Would you put it to a friend like this? If you are to be really kind now, what would you think? Are you trying to force a certainty when none exists? Are you disbelieving the positives? Are you frightened of believing in the more balanced and compassionate alternatives?
- Consider how you might help someone you like generate alternatives to, say, all-or-nothing thinking or jumping to conclusions. Practise being gentle with yourself rather than harsh and critical, and practise seeing things in grey rather than insisting on black and white.
- Work on emotional balance and feeling tolerance as noted above.
- Focus on what you can do rather than what you can't. Have the motto, 'The secret of success is the ability to fail.' (See Chapter 21 for further discussion of this motto.)
- Ask, 'How am I looking after myself? Do my thoughts help me care for myself?' Slowly build on your insights.

KEY POINT

Always have a go at spending a few moments on your breathing and then trying to shift to the compassionate self or bring to mind your compassionate image (see Chapter 8). Once in that frame (even if only slightly) it might be easier to generate and think about compassionate alternatives.

It can also help to be mindful of your thoughts – note them in your mind and stand back from them – view them from the balcony as it were – watch the mind shift to black-and-white thinking or over-generalizing. It can seem odd and difficult at first, but with practice it can be very interesting. There is no forcing or trying to make yourself change your mind – just be open to the possibility for change and see what happens.

11

Writing things down: How to do it and why it can be helpful

Learning *to write* about your thoughts and feelings, especially to begin with, can be helpful. Here are some of the reasons why.

- **Writing down is slowing down.** The first reason is that writing slows our thinking down and helps us to focus. It helps to stop those half-formed but emotionally powerful thoughts whizzing around out of control.
- **Attention.** Writing things down helps concentrate our attention and enables us to stand back a little. Seeing the words coming on to the page helps us to distance ourselves from the thoughts, as we have to focus on the process of writing.
- **Catching thoughts**. By slowing down and focusing we may discover all kinds of thoughts 'lurking in the background'. One way of catching our thoughts, and inner meanings we put on things and feelings, is by being gently curious and asking ourselves some questions such as those I outlined on pages 107–8 Also, having felt something, you stop and say, 'How can I account for what

I feel? What am I thinking?' This can help to pinpoint and identify our thoughts. The more you slow your thinking down, especially by writing, the more likely you are to 'catch' the key thoughts and meanings that are associated with what you are feeling.

- **Clarity**. Writing down is an excellent means of gaining clarity. When you have written your thoughts down, you have a record of them in front of you; something you can look over calmly to see how your thoughts may be understandable given your depression and life difficulties, but not helpful to you – and if you dwell on them they will make you feel worse.

- **Gaining a perspective**. Seeing your thoughts written out in front of you may well help you see that your depression is pushing you to be overly negative (loss- and threat-focused) and losing perspective. This is much more difficult to see if you just work with your thoughts in your head, because it is hard to gain the distance that is achieved by writing them down.

Thought forms

Thoughts forms offer ways of helping us to organize our thoughts and to distinguish between situations that trigger our feelings and moods, the kinds of thoughts and feelings that pour through our minds (often in a chaotic way), and then how we can re-focus our attention on generating helpful alternatives. Thought forms are just useful guides to help our practice and develop our minds: see Appendix 1 for some ideas.

My advice here is: keep it simple. Use whatever kind of form suits you, rather than struggling with something that you find too complex – provided it does the job, of course. The most basic thought-alternative form is simply a page divided into two columns. You write your unhelpful, threat-focused thoughts in the left-hand column, and helpful, compassionate alternatives in the right-hand column. These depressive thoughts might be triggered by an event, or might come on as your mood dips. The key point is *catching* what these thoughts are and offering a balanced and compassionate alternative to them.

Table 11.1 shows an example of a completed form.

TABLE 11.1 COMPLETED THOUGHTS FORM

Depressing thoughts	Balanced alternative thoughts
Here I am just lying in bed again	I have to admit I am not feeling too good right now
Can't see the point of getting up	Even though it will be a struggle, if I can try to gently encourage myself to get up and move around a bit this often helps
Things are bound to go wrong	If I can achieve a couple of things I'll feel better
Nothing is worth doing anyway – I won't enjoy it	Sure, I don't enjoy things much because I am depressed – the trick is doing things to overcome depression. I know I can enjoy things when I am not depressed. So I will do my best to work against my depressed brain state
Degree of belief: 70%	Degree of belief: 40%

Rate your belief

You will see that at the bottom of each column in this example there is a figure for 'degree of belief'– that is, *how much* do you believe what you have written down? Some people find that if they rate how much they believe something this can be helpful for seeing that beliefs are not black and white, all-or-nothing. As time passes and you start to feel better you'll be able to look back and see how the strength of your beliefs has changed with your recovery. Other people don't find this particularly helpful, because they feel it is artificial in some way. Once again, find what works for you.

Make up your own column headings

You can make up your own column headings for different tasks. For example, sometimes it can be useful to write down in two columns (1) the reason why you believe and then (2) in the other column the reasons to change that view, or consider the advantages and disadvantages of a particular belief. You might prefer to label the two columns 'what my threat- or loss-focused and/or self-attacking mind says' and 'what my rational and compassionate mind says'. For all these variations you can use the two-column format and simply change the headings to suit.

Adding more columns

In the thought forms given in Appendix 1 you will see other columns. In addition to the two noted above, we also have a column for writing down any critical *events* that might have triggered your distressing thoughts and a column for describing distressing *feelings*. This helps to give you a more complete picture; it will help your progress if you can be clear on what kinds of things tend to trigger your change of mood, arouse negative thoughts and feelings, or what those emotions and feelings actually are.

Rate change

It can sometimes be useful to rate the change in the strength of your beliefs and in your emotions after you have been through the exercise. For that, we might add a third column to the simple two-column form. Table 11.2 shows the same examples we used above, with the third column added on.

TABLE 11.2 CHANGING THOUGHTS

Depressing thoughts	Helpful thoughts that operate against the depression	How I feel now compared to before
Here I am just lying in bed again	I have to admit I am not feeling too good right now. Even though it will be a struggle, if I can gently encourage myself to get and move around a bit this often helps . . . (etc.)	Yes, I can see that this might be helpful and a way forward
Can't see the point of getting up	Even though it will be a struggle, if I can try to gently encourage myself to get up and move around a bit this often helps.	
Things are bound to go wrong	If I can achieve a couple of things I'll feel better	
Nothing is worth doing anyway – I won't enjoy it	Sure, I don't enjoy things much because I am depressed – the trick is doing things to overcome depression. I know I can enjoy things when I am not depressed. So I will do my best to work against my depressed brain state	I feel maybe 5% less depressed by compassionately refocusing my thoughts

Try as best you can, with an encouraging, supportive (not bullying) tone in your mind to carry out your plan to get up and out of bed, move about and do something active, no matter how small. You might rate how you feel having done this, compared to how you were feeling before you started. Note the difference. You could even compare how you feel now with how you might feel if you had not done anything at all but stayed in bed. The point here is that the more you yourself see the value in these kinds of exercises the more you are likely to have a go.

Adapting the basic idea to suit yourself

Once you have got the basic idea of the importance of writing things down and slowing your thinking down, you are prepared to start working on your thoughts, feelings, and moods. However, the exact framework you choose to do this should be something you decide for yourself: it's important that you are happy with the form you use.

Different forms will be useful for working on different things. I have started us off here with a fairly basic thought-recording form; but please tailor it to suit you. Experiment with these forms and try out designs of your own. However, always keep in mind the basic point of all this: that is, to help you stop hitting your brain with lots of negatives, to get a better perspective on things and start giving your brain a boost and some warmth.

Compassionate reframing

Ideas for generating alternatives are given in Chapters 9–11 and throughout this book. In Appendix 1 there are also various worked-out examples to offer you some more ideas – but these are only ideas. Sometimes it is helpful to take a few soothing rhythm breaths and focus on your compassionate self or image. You are trying to shift the position in your mind to where your thinking comes from – stepping into the compassionate frame of mind, as it were – and then from that position (or mind) starting to think about alternatives. You can also imagine compassionately trying to help someone, such as a friend you care for, to think in a different, more balanced way. How might you focus on strengths and courage, on coping and getting through? What would your voice tone be like? *The key is to shift position*. You will be very familiar with what your threat, loss and critical mind says, because that part of you will be active a lot of the time, but can you tune in to your compassionate mind, attend to it and develop it? Writing things down can give you the space and distance to start to do this.

Compassionate letter writing

There is now increasing evidence that writing about our feelings, expressing and exploring our feelings in writing (so-called *expressive writing*)[1] can be very helpful for some people. Indeed, we can put into words on paper things we might struggle to think about in our heads or express to other people. We will explore some types of writing here so that you can see which one helps you.

Writing about oneself

Choose what you want to write about: your life in general, or a particularly difficult time in your life that you had trouble coming to terms with, or problems that you are experiencing right now. The idea here is to express your thoughts and feelings on paper, writing about what has happened or is happening to you. Imagine that you're writing to a very compassionate person who completely understands what you feel.

Sometimes writing like this may stimulate different feelings in us. Again the key here is to go step by step and explore what is helpful to you. If you feel that there are things that you really don't want to face on your own, be honest about that and think about whether you want to obtain professional help to guide and support you, or talk to a friend. Remember all these exercises are intended to be helps and guides for you, and you'll need to judge just how helpful they are for you.

Another approach to writing is to begin to think about yourself and your feelings from different perspectives. Because we use different aspects of our minds when we write, we can sometimes find that in the process of writing, new insights and meanings emerge in our minds that help us clarify things. Practising doing this can help you access aspects of yourself that may help you understand your feelings better, learn how to tolerate them without fear or worry of acting them out, and perhaps tone down more depression-focused feelings and thoughts. But keep in mind what I have said many times before – this is an invitation, a 'try it and see'.

Writing about yourself from another's point of view

Sometimes it is useful to try shifting perspective on how we see ourselves. One way of doing this is to write a short letter about yourself, from the point of view of someone close to you who cares about you. I'm going to use the example of a fictitious person we will call Sue, but when you write your letter substitute your own name, of course. Such a letter might include:

- *I have known Sue for about twenty years. To me, he/she has been*
- *I find Sue*
- *I think Sue struggles with*
- *I like Sue because*
- *Sue's strengths are*
- *It would help Sue if she could*

This exercise is designed to help you develop the habit of considering other perspectives on yourself. If you like, show what you have written to someone you are close to and trust, and see what they think.

Some people find this very helpful, others do not. One person noted that 'I actually don't know anybody that well who would be able to write in detail about me.' So here you might want to *imagine* a friend, and what you would like them to say about you. If you find it is too easy to dismiss positives then you might want to try practising some of the imagery exercises we talked about in Chapter 8, or the behavioral work in Chapter 12.

Writing compassionately to yourself

In this exercise we are going to write about difficulties, but from the perspective of the compassionate part of ourselves. There are different ways you can write this letter. One way is to get your pen and paper and then spend a moment engaged with your soothing breathing rhythm. Feel your compassionate self. As you focus on it, feel yourself expanding slightly and feel stronger. Imagine you are a compassionate person who is wise, kind, warm and understanding. Consider your general manner, voice tone and the feelings that come with your 'caring compassionate self'. Adopt a kindly facial expression. Feel the kindness in your face before moving on. Think about the qualities you would like your compassionate self to have. Spend time feeling and gently exploring what they are like when you focus on them. Remember it does not matter if you actually feel you are like this – but focus on the *ideal* you would like to be. Spend at least one minute – longer if possible – thinking about this and trying to feel in contact with those parts of yourself. Don't worry if this is difficult, just do the best you can – have a go.

When we are in a compassionate frame of mind (even slightly), or in the frame of trying to help a friend or someone we care for, we try to use our personal experiences of life wisely. We know that life can be hard; we offer our strength and support; we try to be warm and not judgemental or condemning. Take a few breaths then sense that wise, understanding, compassionate part of you arise. This is the part of you that will write the letter. So we write this kind of letter from a compassionate point of view. If thoughts of 'Am I doing it right?' or 'I can't get much feeling here' arise, note or observe these thoughts as normal comments our minds like to make, but refocus your attention and simply observe what happens as you write, as best you can. There is no right or wrong, only the effort of trying – it is the practice that helps. As you write, create as much emotional warmth and understanding as you can. You are practising writing these letters from your compassionate mind.

As you write your letter, allow yourself to *understand and accept* your distress. For example, your letter might start with

> *I am sad. I feel distressed; my distress is understandable because ...*

Note the reasons, realizing your distress makes sense. Then perhaps you could continue with

> *I would like me to know that ...*

For example, your letter might point out that as we become depressed, our depression or a distress state can come with a powerful set of thoughts and feelings – so how you see things right now may be the depression view on things. Given this, we can try and step to the side of the distress and write and focus on how best to cope. We can write

> *It might be helpful to consider ...*

A second way of doing this is to imagine your compassion-ate image writing to you, and imagining a dialogue with them and what they will say to you. For example, my compassionate image might say something like

Hi Paul

Gosh, the last few days have been tough. Isn't it typical of life that problems arrive in groups rather than individually. It's understandable why you're feeling a bit down because ... Hang in there because you are good at seeing these as the ups and downs of life, and that all things change, and you often say at least we are not in Iraq. So you have developed abilities for getting through this and tolerating the painful things.

You will note that the letter points to *my* strengths and *my* abilities. It doesn't issue instructions such as, '*You must* see these things as the ups and downs of life.' This is important in compassionate writing. You don't want your compassionate letters to seem as if they are written by some smart bod who is giving you lots of advice. There has to be a real appreciation for your suffering, a real appreciation for your struggle and a real appreciation for your efforts at getting through. The compassion is a kind of arm round your shoulders, as well as refocusing your attention on what is helpful for you.

AN EXAMPLE

Here's a letter from someone we'll call Sally, about lying in bed feeling depressed. Before looking at this letter, let's note an important point. In this letter we are going to refer to '*you*' rather than '*I*'. Some people like to write their letters like that, as if writing to someone else. See what works for you but, over time, use 'I'. You could read this letter and substitute 'I' for 'you'.

Good morning Sally

Last few days have been tough for you so no wonder you want to hide away in bed. Sometimes we get to the point of shutdown, don't we, and the thought of taking on things is overwhelming. You know you have been trying real hard, I mean you haven't put your feet up with a gin and tonic and the daily paper. Understandably you feel exhausted. I guess the thing now is to work out what helps you. You've shown a lot of courage in the past in pushing yourself to do things that you find difficult. Lie in bed if you think that it can help you, of course, but watch out for critical Sally who could be critical about this. Also you often feel better if you get up, tough as it is. What about a cup of tea? You often like that first cup of tea. Okay, so let's get up, move around a bit and get going and then see how we feel. Tough, but let's try.

So you see the point here: it's about understanding being helpful, having a really caring focus but at the same time working on what we need to do to help ourselves.

Writing as you at your best

Another way to write these letters is to imagine the part of yourself you like, the self you would like to aspire to more of the time (as long it's not the aggressive kick myself past of course!). Then try to bring that 'you' to mind – recall 'you at your best', 'you as you would like to be' and then write from that part of you.

Guide to letter writing

When you have written your first few compassionate letters, go through them with an open mind and think whether they actually capture compassion for you. If they do, then see if you can spot the following qualities in your letter.

- It expresses concern and genuine caring.
- It is sensitive to your distress and needs.
- It is sympathetic and responds emotionally to your distress.
- It helps you to face your feelings and become more tolerant of them.
- It helps you become more understanding and reflective of your feelings, difficulties and dilemmas.
- It is non-judgemental/non-condemning.
- A genuine sense of warmth, understanding and caring permeates the whole letter.
- It helps you think about the behavior you may need to try, to get better.

Depressed people can struggle with this to begin with, and are not very good at writing compassionate letters. Their letters tend to be rather full of finger-wagging advice. So we have to work and practise being compassionate. The point of these letters is *not* just to focus on difficult feelings but to help you reflect on your feelings and thoughts, be open with them, and develop a compassionate and balanced way of working with them. The letters should not offer advice or tell you what you should or should not do. It is not the advice you need, but the support to act on it.

Writing to others

Another way we can use letters is to express to ourselves our feelings about people. Usually these letters are not sent. If you feel you want to send them, it's best to keep them for a week or two and think carefully before you do anything about it.

The purpose of this letter is again to articulate your feelings. You can write about your needs or sadness, disappointment or anger, or how you want to be loved or things you find it difficult to express. The point about writing these things down is that we think in a different way when we write.

Writing can help in ways that allow us to make sense of things and come to terms with them in a different way. For example, Kim felt very angry with her mother who was a career woman. As a child, Kim had been looked after by a number of different nannies. For some years Kim felt under pressure to tell her mother what she felt. She also felt she couldn't have a genuine relationship with her mother until she cleared the air, and that she was being weak in not speaking honestly. However, we talked about this and the importance of taking the pressure off herself 'to prove herself' and confront her mother. She wrote some moving letters that were never sent, and at the end of the process felt that a lot of the pressure to confront her mother had gone. In a strange way this actually made it easier for her to think about having a conversation with her mother about the key issues. Kim came to see that the degree of anger she felt blocked her in many ways, because it was less about anger and more about wanting recognition from her mother that was important. The writing helped with the anger and then Kim was able to think about how to have a quieter conversation about the sadness in Kim's life because of the effects of her mother's career.

Grief

Sometimes if we are grieving it can help if we write letters to the dead person, saying goodbye or whatever else we want to say. Goodbye letters can sometimes be quite emotional but also helpful in articulating and expressing our feelings.

As with all these exercises, take one step at a time and only do things that are helpful for you, or that you can see will be helpful if you stick with them. If you feel you grief is overwhelming then this might be a time to think about professional help from a counsellor or psychotherapist. Or simply take very small steps, but do it reasonably often, and build up.

Forgiveness

The last 10 years have seen a lot of research on forgiveness.[2] However, there is a lot of misunderstanding about it. Forgiveness is about letting go of our anger. The person we forgive we may never like, never want to see. We might never condone their actions. Forgiveness is simply putting down our weapons and our desire for vengeance, and walking away. We say, 'It ends here.' Of course there may be a lot of thoughts such as, 'I must not let them get away with it,' 'It is too unfair', 'I am weak if I do not pursue this,' 'If I were a proper person I would do something about this.' The problem is that living with anger often isn't going anywhere and that is very depressing. The only person we are hurting is ourselves and our brain, because we are constantly stimulating threat systems in our brain. Anger that is unhelpful like this simply makes us feel powerless.

Forgiveness is a way in which you can bring peace to your mind. We could fill a whole book looking at how to work on forgiveness.[2] If you go on to the Internet you will be able to explore lots of sites on forgiveness. Check them out and see what works for you; some are interesting and helpful, and some not. But at a straightforward level, forgiveness letters are simply ways to help you acknowledge your anger and upset and forgive, let go, move on, walk away. As one patient told me:

> *I realized I had spent a lot of my life hating my mother and yet also wanting her to love me. She just wasn't up to it. When I realized that actually she was quite a damaged person and simply wasn't up to being as I wanted her to be, I felt more sorry for her and able to forgive her. To be honest I pulled back quite a bit and I think she would like me to have seen her more, but I found a comfortable distance for me. Recognizing this and letting go of my anger and my need set me free. And you know, wherever she is now (she died a few years ago), I genuinely hope she's happy.*

Importantly, keep in mind that the point of these letters is not to stir up difficult emotions but to be compassionate about them and learn how to think about them in compassionate and balanced ways.

Gratitude and appreciation

So far we have rather focused on writing about difficult things. However research has also shown that it's very helpful if we can spend some time thinking about things we appreciate, like and feel gratitude for.[3] When we are depressed it can be quite difficult to have feelings of gratitude. Nonetheless if we focus on those feelings it will stimulate parts of the brain that are associated with positive antidepressant feelings. You can start by thinking of a person or key phase in your life, or someone who is showing you some kindness no matter how small, and think about gratitude. The feeling of gratitude is not a grudging or a belittling feeling at all, but a feeling of pleasure and joy that the other person was there and helped you in some way.

Gratitude is not associated with a feeling of obligation. The moment we feel obligated by somebody else's kindness it is difficult to feel gratitude. Focus on the behavior. One patient noted that although there were things that angered her about her husband, just focusing on her gratitude for him helped her feel more balanced and happier.

The same goes for appreciation. Take your pen and a fresh sheet of paper, and write about the things you appreciate and like in your life. They might be quite small things like the first cup of tea of the day; the blue of a summer sky; certain television programs; the warmth of your bed; a relationship; or part of your job – absolutely anything that gives you feelings of appreciation and liking. Notice how we often let these pass. Bear in mind why you are doing this as an exercise – it is to balance up your systems and to stimulate part of your brain that will help you counteract the feelings of depression. Recall that depression will force you into a corner of your mind so that you always have to walk on the shadowy side of the street, so we have to practise refocusing.

KEY POINTS

- To combat depression, we can call on different parts and abilities of ourselves: our rational minds and our compassionate/friendly minds. Writing helps us slow down and think in different ways.
- By calling on these aspects of our minds and trying to activate them, we are making our brains work in certain ways that can counteract depression.
- We can learn to write about our difficulties reflectively and with compassion by putting ourselves in the compassionate frame of mind when we write. This can take practice. Using a letter-writing approach can be helpful.

EXERCISES

Exercise 1

Write down your depression thoughts about a particular situation. Look at them carefully.

As you think about alternative ideas, take a rational/compassionate approach. Try thinking about what you might say to a friend who is in a similar situation. You might also consider how you think when you are not depressed.

To begin to generate alternative thoughts, look back at the ideas on pages 187–9 and focus on:

- What is it helpful to attend to (e.g., from memory or in your current situation). Remember the old saying 'is the glass half full or half empty?' – practise attending to the half-full aspects too.
- What is a fair, logical or reasonable way to think and reason?
- What would be the helpful and supportive things to do in this situation?

Exercise 2

Write some compassionate letters for yourself, or engage in writing that expresses your feelings.

Even if you don't have much faith in the alternatives you think of at first, the act of trying to generate them is an important first step. As with all exercises it is what you think will be helpful to you that is key, because different people find different things helpful. Make sure that all of your efforts to help yourself meet the 'friend and compassion test'. This means that any of your alternative thoughts are considerate, helpful behaviors that you would be prepared and pleased to offer to friends and that you can see are evidence of compassion. Logic and common sense is not always useful to us; it's when we feel it is helpful in our hearts that matters.

12

Changing your behavior:
A compassionate approach

As we saw in earlier chapters, the depressed brain state can be
a kind of 'go to the back of the cave and stay there' state. We
want to pull the covers over our head and wish the world would
go away. When we feel like this it helps to take a compassionate approach: in other words, to be very understanding of such
feelings but also to think what might be triggering this feeling
and how to break out of it. Maybe we have been working too
hard and are exhausted, or maybe life events, setbacks and
conflicts have taken the wind out of our sails. Sometimes a mild
depression tells us we are exhausted and we really need to find
a way to slow down and get some rest, let our bodies recuperate. Humans are like other animals – we need chill-out time.
It is amazing how, when people take longish breaks from work,
they often say they feel themselves slowing down, and the pace
of life is easier. We must admit to ourselves that, through no
fault of our own, we are living in a 'rush rush, hurry hurry' society where we can get rather exhausted. Learning to take time
out, respect our body and rest it as much as possible is important, and I agree – it is easier said than done. In particular, one
of the problems of being a single parent is the sheer workload,
and demands that can be exhausting. If burnout and exhaustion are behind the depression, it's important to see this and

to address it in appropriate ways – without blaming oneself for being tired!

However, as we get depressed we can also stop doing various activities and disengage, and this adds to a depression cycle rather than helping it. We find resting is not helpful. When we are depressed, daily activities can seem overwhelming. In these situations it can be very useful to *operate against the pull of depression.* We need to encourage ourselves to do more not less, but the emphasis is on *encouraging* not bullying ourselves. This helps us to activate our drive system. It helps if we organize activities in such a way that they can be approached step by step. In the last 10 years or so therapies for depression have been developed which focus specifically on changing behavior.[1] There are also self-help books dedicated to this type of 'change your behavior, change your mood' approach.[2] It's important, though, that you see this as helping you, not just as putting on a mask and carrying on regardless.

Tasks and goals

When therapists are trained, they are often taught to focus on three things: the bonds and relationships between patient and therapist; the tasks that need to be undertaken; and the goals and aims of the therapy. In helping yourself to get out of depression, you can take the same approach. The bonds and relationship you have with yourself have been the focus of earlier chapters, so now let's look at tasks and goals.

Tasks

Often, as we move forward out of depression, there are various tasks that we can set for ourselves on our step-by-step journey. Here are some examples:

- Learn to tune into and monitor your thoughts and feelings.
- Write down your thoughts and feelings.
- Try tape recording ideas that are good alternatives to your negative thoughts on a tape. When you feel down, play these alternatives to yourself.
- Learn to be honest with yourself.
- Learn how to take big problems and break them down into smaller ones.
- Set yourself small things to do that operate against the depression each day.
- Increase the time you spend talking with friends.
- Make the phone calls you need to make to sort things out.
- Learn to be more assertive or less self-attacking.

These are not easy things to do, so you may have to work hard. When we are depressed our thoughts and feelings are very dismissive – they may say things like, 'This won't work for me; don't be silly; I can't do it; can't be bothered; I'm too angry; it's too difficult'. These are all very common thoughts. The way to deal with them is to expect them, to notice them, but focus on the task anyway. If you put a certain time aside, e.g., five minutes, plan to focus your time on the task. You might also think about whether this feeling is actually linked to angry rebellion and you are really saying, 'Oh, sod it. I just don't want to do it, so why should I!' If that is true, then honestly acknowledge it – be compassionate and understanding of such feelings, but then take a breath and think about how to actually help yourself move forward. Think also that there may have been many times in life when you predicted that things would not work out but they did.

Goals and commitments

Having small and achievable goals can be helpful as these are the things you want to achieve. At first, depressed people usually just want to feel better. But this large goal needs to be broken down into smaller ones. These smaller goals might be:

- To do a little more each day.
- To be more assertive with some other person(s).
- To spend more time on something I enjoy.
- To join a club or charity where I can get involved with other people and feel useful.
- To spend more (or maybe less) time with my children.

The most important commitment is to put effort into transforming your depression by training your mind in helpful, compassionate *actions*. You do this in the knowledge that:

- The way our brains have evolved over many millions of years can be very tough on us and give a host of unpleasant feelings and moods.
- That is absolutely not our fault – we did not design our brain, choose our genes, or how our early relationships shape us.
- But it is up to us to try as best we can to work with our minds to change our mental states.

Commitment is linked to the value we put on things. For example, if I ask you not to express your anger for a week, or to go out even if you're depressed, you might be uncertain. What about if I offered you £10? Okay, £100? Not enough? Okay, £1 million. Of course I can't do that, but think about it – if there is a really big pay-off you might put a lot of effort into something. We have to be honest about this. Like a person training to get physically fit, some days will be harder than others – but the clear goal keeps them going. For working on a depressed state of mind, focus on how it will help you to get better and really make that your goal – think of all the benefits – imagine (and see) yourself as 'feeling better' and what you are doing now you are better. It is easy to let these slip from one's mind when it gets tough. It can be useful to set yourself a couple of goals at the beginning of each day or week. Start by setting small goals – the smaller, the better. If things are difficult or you don't reach your goals, ask yourself some questions.

- Were the goals too ambitious?
- Could I have broken them down further?
- Did I run into unexpected problems?
- Did I put enough effort into achieving them?
- In my heart of hearts, did I think that achieving them wouldn't really help?
- If it did not go as I wanted, am I being compassionate with myself?

Behavioral experiments

Many therapists encourage us to try what we call behavioral experiments. This means trying out different things, keeping an eye on what works for us, how we might do things differently to make them work better for us, and tailoring them to our needs. This does not mean doing things simply because we're told to, but trying to see the point of what we're doing. For example, if you want to get physically fit you might go to the gym and really push yourself even though it's not entirely comfortable. You learn what works for you and put up with the discomfort because you understand what you're trying to achieve. Indeed, the discomfort may actually inspire you because you feel it is helping you move forward in your goal of 'getting fitter and stronger'. We can approach depression like this too.

Take staying in bed. If staying in bed helps you feel better, all well and good, but often in depression it does not. We simply use bed, not to rest and regenerate our energies, but to hide away from the world. Then we feel guilty and attack ourselves for not doing the things we have to do. When you are lying in bed, you may tend to brood on your problems. Although bed can seem like a safe place to be, it can actually make you feel much worse in the long run. The most important step is to try to get up and plan to do one positive thing each day. Remember, your brain is telling you that you can't do things and to give up trying. You will slowly show that part of yourself that you *can* do things, bit by bit.

Occasionally, however, because depressed people often bully themselves out of bed with thoughts such as, 'Get up, you lazy bum, how can you just lie there?', it can be useful to try the opposite tack. This is to learn to stay in bed for a while, at least one day a week, and enjoy it – read a magazine or listen to the radio and allow yourself to feel the pleasure of it. To practise being able to lie in bed without feeling guilty can be helpful for some people. Imagine that you are exercising that pleasure area of your brain, which really needs exercise.

Designing experiments

It is useful to work on and against our depressive ideas by setting experiments: that is, testing things out and rehearsing new skills. A useful motto here is, 'Challenging but not overwhelming'. Remember – design your experiments – things to have a go at – to take you forward step by step, rather than rushing into something that has a high risk of failure. Don't worry if the steps seem too small. If things go a bit pear-shaped, remember it was just an experiment and think about how to learn from it.

Experiments don't always work out as we hope they will. When I was a shy young student at college, a good friend encouraged me to ask a woman to dance at our college dance. It was noisy, but I got my request across. She turned to her friend, looked at me, looked back at her friend, laughed – and they both got up and walked to the bar! Oh dear. On another occasion I had learned some assertiveness and was in a shop queue when an older man pushed to the front of the queue. People were irritated. I need to do something here, I thought. I'm a psychologist and an assertive one. I left my position at the back and said to the man, quite kindly I thought, 'Excuse me, look, I'm sorry but there is a queue.' He looked at me and then said, 'Why don't you eff off, you four-eyed git, before I smash your face in.' My response was of course to say, 'Absolutely – look – I'm off right now!' So even the best-intended plans don't always work out!

If we try things and they don't work out, we can try to find out why. Was there anything about it that was a success? For example, you did try and you can learn to cope with these setbacks and try again in the future. One can learn not to be so fearful of failing or rejection – it is unpleasant but nothing more. My college friend thought it was funny that the girls walked off but said, 'That's typical, you've just got to keep trying. Somewhere in the hall a girl will want to dance with you, you've just got to find her. On attempt 252 maybe.'

We also need to think whether we were attempting too much. Were our expectations too high? In the case of tackling the aggressive man the answer is probably yes – he was a big fellow, and I am by nature a coward. Did your negative thoughts overwhelm you? Did you really put the effort into it that you needed to?

People can generate and write down alternative thoughts and

ideas and behaviors. They may be very casual about it and just look at the words without thinking their meaning through, or trying to put *feelings* of kindness and understanding into those alternatives. In the back of our minds might be a thought, 'This approach can't work.' So we stack the experiment against ourselves before we begin.

So we may need to use the courageous part of our compassionate mind to tell ourselves in a friendly, supportive way:

> *Look, I know this is hard, and yes, it is a shit being depressed, but let's not stack things against myself. Let's give it a fair go. After all, what have I got to lose? If I were helping a friend, I'd know how tough it is but I'd also encourage them to give it a go. Let's go through this step by step.*

Getting out of depression takes effort, and this is especially true if you are trying to help yourself. It is the same with getting physically fit. It would be no good putting on your trainers and running to the garden gate and back – you have to push yourself more than that (assuming you don't live in a stately home where the garden gate is a mile away). It is very understandable to find this tough going, and it may be that there are times when we need some extra help from friends or professionals. There's no point in berating ourselves if we've tried our best and have found it too hard.

Blocks to becoming active

To become more active, it helps to decide on a specific activity and the time you are going to do it. For example, go shopping at 10 a.m. on Tuesday. Visit a friend at 2.30 on Wednesday afternoon. When the time comes, go for it. Each day, do some things that invite you to operate against depression. Make a plan for the week, and when you get to the time do whatever it is you've chosen to do. Try to engage in each activity in a *spirit of encouragement and support*.

You may well have some extremely understandable but unhelpful or irritable thoughts: 'Nothing I do to help myself will help me – so it is not worth trying.' If you do, be compassionate and shift to your compassionate self (see pages 149–155). Recognize that all over the world depressed people think like this, because that is how the depressed mind thinks– so it is perfectly understandable to think like this. But it is only one possible pattern in your mind, so consider also:

- Am I defeating myself before I start? Probably if I am honest. Huff.
- Let's get helpful here and try to be supportive.
- Do I really have enough evidence to say this or that can't work, or is this just how I feel about it?
- What have I got to lose by trying? If I put effort into this and it doesn't work out, I'll certainly be no worse off and might have gained something.
- If I try, at least I'll know I made the effort even if things don't work out.
- I can go one step at a time. If I break my problems down into smaller ones, they may not seem so overwhelming. I don't have to try to do too much at once.
- I may feel better if I try to do something rather than nothing.
- I can praise myself for effort.

Now try this. Spend a moment on your soothing breathing rhythm and connect with your compassionate self, no matter how minimally (see pages 149–55) Read through these ideas (on page 253) with as much warmth, care and concern as you can, and as if you really wanted to help a friend. How do they seem to you now?

Learning how to do things we don't want to do

To reach our goals in life we often have to do things we don't want to. People who want to be successful at sport, playing an instrument or passing exams have to practise and study even when they don't want to. Many of us feel very anxious when we start learning to drive a car. When I started, my leg shook so much I could hardly push in the clutch! However, we accept those things – because of our goal to be able to drive and be mobile. And of course there are many small things that we may not want to do such as getting up to go to school or college, studying for exams, going to work, or getting the children up and out for school. Even making the effort to socialize can seem like a hurdle.

Step 1: Develop your vision

When engaging in disliked activities, focus on the benefits of doing them (rather than the difficulties), and think about how you will feel if you complete a task. Think how your actions can take you nearer to your goals, while avoiding things won't actually help you get better – although you may temporarily feel less anxious (or whatever).

Karen felt tired and a little anxious about going to the shops. So she created in her mind a vision of herself coming home with the bags of food and making something enjoyable to eat with the family and tried to hold that in mind while doing the shopping. She saw that as an achievement. It really helps if we can think of a goal and commit ourselves to it. Otherwise what's the point of engaging in difficulties unless you can really see the benefits and focus on those? That's true for all things in life, of course.

Sue kept in mind how good she would feel in a few months when she had left her husband and worked through his threats. 'It was keeping that vision of being free and living alone, doing my own things, that helped get me through and take difficult decisions,' she said.

Step 2: Develop the feelings of support and helpfulness

Focus on creating inside you *feelings that will help you*. When engaging with activities you're not too keen on, spend a moment really trying to contact and create within you your compassionate self. Then take yourself gently by the hand and engage in the activity. When we talk about getting up to do things, this is not to bully you out of bed or into doing things but to encourage you to get up, because lying there and brooding on problems may only make you feel worse. Getting up and doing things takes you closer to your goal of recovery. But test it out, try it a few times and see how you go. Think about how you can make this 'acting against your depression' with kindness more effective for you once you understand the value of doing it.

Working on blocks to helpful compassionate behavior

Compassionate behavior is aimed to help you grow, develop, nurture and overcome difficulties in your life. It is very easy for us to view compassion and kindness as being about giving in, about not pushing ourselves, and *sometimes it can be this*. I am all for making life as easy as possible if it helps me. But we need to be wise about this because if we are honest sometimes backing off, giving in, or taking the easier route is going to make life much more difficult; that's not compassionate. David Veale and Rob Willson in their book *Manage Your Mood* have identified a number of obstacles to working on helpful and compassionate behavior.[2]

Doing things only when you feel motivated to do them

Sometimes that works, and there are times when we feel like doing things and times when we don't, but be honest with yourself if it's just avoidance. Will there actually be a time in the near future when you know you will be motivated? Maybe it is useful to act against this lack of motivation. Learn how you can do things even when you're not motivated because then you are free from the 'whimsies' of your motivational system. Learning to do things in an unmotivated way can be a useful skill.[2]

Waiting to feel better

If you are feeling very tired, then it is a good idea to check with your family doctor whether there could be a physical reason for your tiredness. Tiredness is one of the most common symptoms that present to family doctors today, so ensure you get the evidence that your tiredness is indeed related to your depression. Sometimes if you are recovering from a physical illness or you have been exhausted, waiting to feel better and allowing your body to recuperate is helpful. But at other times simply waiting to feel better is not helpful and the way to feel better is actually to do more things. For example, there is no point in saying, 'I will ride my bike or get fit when I feel fit and energized'. The reason for doing these things is because I don't feel fit and it is the doing of those things that makes me fit and energized (hopefully!). We must not put the cart before the horse.

Waiting for medication to work

You might think, 'My doctor told me I need medication; indeed this book has talked about depressed brain states, so I just need to wait for the medication to work.' Sometimes this can be helpful, but we can also change our brain states through our activities. Your medication will not retrain you, teach you, or help you build up your coping skills – only you can do that. These skills we are discussing here can help you now and in the future to put control back in your own hands. Your medication might work better if you also work against your depression.

When I have more confidence I will do more

This is also a 'cart before the horse' issue.[2] Think of any activity such as learning to drive. What comes first, confidence or your anxious practice? Confidence comes from the doing, not the other way round. If you have had confidence and have lost it I'm afraid the same applies; we regain confidence through the doing.

Frankly I can't be bothered

Who hasn't felt that from time to time? But in depression, sadly, it can be for most of the time. As I noted briefly above, if we're honest sometimes these feelings can be tinged with anger or, 'Why should I, it's too much effort.' We might feel angry with people around us, and fed up, and it's easy to withdraw from them. One of the difficulties for some depressed people is recognizing just how much anger or resentment interferes with their lives in all kinds of ways. Here again the trick is to act against that anger, and not to allow your anger to dominate your behavior, by giving up or withdrawing. Acknowledge your anger honestly and then think of some activities that would help you. Be honest if you tend to 'cut off your nose to spite your face'. This is actually rather common, so there is nothing to feel ashamed about once you're honest about it. Keep in mind to be honest but also kind about these thoughts and feelings – they are all very human things, really.

Breaking down large tasks into smaller ones

Depressed brain states can tone down some of our thinking abilities. The depressed brain state interferes with our planning and straight thinking abilities, so we have to plan things in different ways than we might normally do. Suppose you have to go shopping. It would be natural for a depressed person to think about all the hassles before they start, feel overwhelmed, and not go. Okay, we know that is how depression thinks so how can we act against it? One way is to practise the step-by-step approach and focus on one step at a time.

So first look in your cupboards and make a list of what you need. When you've done this, give yourself some praise. Think of a phrase that's fun for you, such as, 'Okey-dokey – done' or, 'Okay, that's cool – I've done step one.' Keep an eye open for angry thoughts like, 'But this is so simple I should be able to do it easily.' Well, if you weren't depressed you would, just as if you didn't have the flu you could probably run easily, and if you didn't have a broken leg you could probably walk upstairs easily. The brain state of depression makes our daily activities difficult, so acting against it is hard work. Keep in mind that after all, you are one step further ahead than you were before you made the list.

Next, get your bags and other things together to go to the shops. On the way, focus on the fact that you are now prepared for shopping. Again notice the various thoughts that can pop into your mind about how difficult this is, how tired you feel, how you probably will forget something. Keep in mind that we expect those thoughts because that's how depression thinks. Be mindful and notice the thoughts, recognize them as expected and natural, and then refocus your attention on your activity and intention. To the best of your ability, be kind and gentle with those intrusive thoughts and feelings.

When in a shop, work your way slowly around until you have everything on your list. Oh, they have run out of a key thing you wanted? Note your frustration, recognize it as natural, be kind to it and then refocus your attention on how best to cope with that annoyance and the thing you wanted not being in this shop. Notice if depression gives you a stream of thoughts 'I knew this would happen; it is typical; what a useless shop; why does this always happen to me!' And of course we don't need to feel depressed to have those thoughts! Again be mindful – notice them, smile at them and return your attention to the task at hand – be kind to these thoughts – don't fight with them or try to stop yourself having them. Remind yourself that millions of people throughout the world are probably having the same thoughts as you.

We have used shopping as an example, but of course you can use any activity you like. Here are the steps:

- Break the activity down into small chunks or steps.
- Notice what would be helpful to do for each step.
- Notice distracting thoughts and feelings; treat them kindly but give focus to doing the activity.
- Smile to yourself when you achieve each step.

> • Notice frustrations along the way; be kind to those frustrations and refocus your efforts on achieving your goal.
>
> As with most things in life, practice helps.

Planning positive activities

Often, when we feel depressed, we think we have to do all the boring things first. Sometimes, boring chores are unavoidable, but it will really help you if you also plan to do some *positive activities* – simple rewards that give (or used to give) you pleasure. For example, if you like sitting in the garden with a book, going to visit a friend, taking a walk, or swimming, then plan to do these activities.

Sometimes depressed people are poor at including positive activities in their plans for the day. All their time is spent struggling to get on top of the boring chores of life. They may feel guilty going out and, say, leaving the washing up undone. But we need to have positive activities. If we don't, it is like drawing on a bank account without putting anything into it. The positive things you do can be seen as depositing money in your account. Each time you do something that gives you pleasure, no matter how small that pleasure is, think to yourself: that's a bit more in my positive account. Another way to think about it is stimulating these emotion systems inside of you. They need to be 'worked', like muscles do. If we don't stimulate our positive emotion systems then we are not stimulating the cells in those systems and eventually they might not be able to give us the positive feelings we want. This is why we can think about what we are doing as a kind of *physiotherapy for our brains*.

If you think like this it will help you get around blocks to doing positive things, such as thoughts like 'I do not deserve this', 'I am being selfish', or 'I must attend to other things first'. We may have grown up being told we deserve this or don't deserve that. But this is not about deserving, it is about exercising your body and brain to help them work more effectively for you. You can always choose not to do positive things once you are free to.

In Chapter 7 we explored focusing on things you like and enjoy, and learning to appreciate things. To start with these are often small things such as your first cup of tea of the day. Learning to train our attention to focus on pleasures is important. For example, you might like walking, but even though it is a beautiful day, because you are not practising focusing your attention on it, your mind is full of your problems and how you are not feeling so good. When engaging with positive activities, focus your attention on what you are enjoying, no matter how small that experience of enjoyment is. Have a go for a while and see what happens for you.

Coping with boredom

Some depressions are related to boredom. Through no fault of our own our lives have become repetitive and boring. Sometimes this appears unavoidable. However, again the key issue here is to diagnose boredom and then take steps to challenge it.

One of my patients had gradually slipped into a lifestyle that involved going to work, coming home, watching TV and going to bed, having given up meeting friends and planning activities with them. Slowly, step by step, he began to think of things he would *like* to do, and then tried to see if he could do at least some of them. One thing was joining the local football club and getting involved as a social member. At first he found making the effort to get to meetings tiresome, but he got to know a few people and that encouraged him. Another was joining a local charity group and helping with fund-raising.

A recent patient experienced life as rather meaningless, but had the idea that somehow life should be meaningful all by itself. But meaning is something we need to create, and we do this through our activities and commitment to goals. Finding things you can do to help others can often make life meaningful. Meaning rarely comes from simply wanting to pursue pleasures.

Women who feel trapped at home with young children are particularly vulnerable to boredom and lack of adult company. We are a highly sociable species, and sharing and talking with others is important for our well-being. Again, the main thing for people in this situation is for them to recognize that they are bored and begin to explore ways of getting out more and developing new contacts. They could perhaps contact mother-and-baby groups, and ask their friends about other activities. If social anxiety is a problem, people who are depressed like this could try to do a little more each day in making outside contacts and/or contact their family doctor to ask if there are any local groups who might be able to help them with social anxiety and getting out more. The reasons that we may have fallen into a lifestyle where we are not stimulating our positive emotion systems enough may not be our fault at all, but we will have to try to take control over the situation, step by step.

Increasing activity and distraction

Sometimes, when people feel very depressed or uptight, they can also feel agitated. At these times, trying to relax does not work. Their mind won't settle down to it. Then they need to distract themselves with a physical activity. Any kind of activity – digging the garden, jogging, aerobic exercises, decorating and so on – can be helpful. Physical activity can be *especially* useful if you are tense with anger or frustration.

Creating personal space

Occasionally there may be a problem in creating 'personal space'—that is, time to be spent on oneself. We can feel so overwhelmed by the needs of others (e.g., the family) that we allow no 'space' for ourselves. We become over-stimulated and want to run away. If you find that you need time on your own, don't feel bad about it but see it as important to think about. Talk to those close to you and explain this. Make it clear that this is not a rejection of them: rather, it is a positive choice on your part to be more in touch with yourself.

Many people feel guilty if they feel a need to be alone doing the things that interest and are important to them, but it is important to negotiate these needs with loved ones. Most importantly, do not assume that there is anything wrong with you for wanting space or that there is necessarily anything wrong with your relationships. Relationships can become claustrophobic from time to time. If you know that there is space for you within your close relationships, this may help to reduce possible resentments and urges to run away. Keep in mind that we humans evolved into small groups *living in the open*. Thousands of years ago we would not be trapped in a house with one person or children. It is very natural for us to want to spend time alone. Carol found that wherever she went in the house sooner or later one of the family would have a request: 'Where's my shirt?, 'Where are you, mum?' She couldn't even get any peace in the loo! It helped to explain to her family that she needed rest time and this would be helpful to her.

Knowing your limits

Depressed people can become exhausted from overwork and then can't cope with the demands placed upon them. They notice that they were failing and becoming overwhelmed, feel ashamed about their failings and become more depressed. Most depressed people are real battlers but sometimes they allow themselves to over-extend because they can't say 'no'. To be frank that is not helpful to you. I have certainly got caught in that one too.

Think of ways that you might replenish yourself, but most importantly, don't criticize yourself for feeling burned out. Acknowledge it honestly and think through steps that might help. Are there enough positive things in your life? Can you do anything to increase them? Can you speak with others about your feelings and seek their help? Can you take time out or pass on some of the chores? Burnout can occur if we have not created enough personal space. Limits are personal things and they vary from person to person and change from time to time and situation to situation.

Looking after our bodies

Dealing with sleep difficulties

Sleep varies from person to person. My daughter and I have never been particularly good sleepers, whereas my wife and my son can fall asleep almost anywhere. In addition, the ease of getting to sleep and our need for sleep change as we grow older, so our sleep patterns are personal to us. Although it's annoying, try not to worry about not getting enough sleep. Famously, Margaret Thatcher only slept for four hours a night! Sleep problems can take various forms. Some people find it difficult to fall asleep, others wake up after being asleep for an hour or two. Other people wake up in the early hours, and there are also those who sleep extremely lightly.

Think of sleep as another behavior that needs managing. A milky drink before bed may help. Make sure that your bed is comfortable and the room well ventilated. Plan for sleep. Don't do what I used to, which was to work late into the night and then find I couldn't sleep because my head was buzzing with the things I had been working on. In planning for sleep, think about relaxing (and try to relax) half an hour to an hour before bedtime. Listen to relaxing music or do a relaxation exercise. If possible, read a book that takes you out of yourself (but not one that scares you or is particularly mentally involving). Avoid arousing (exciting or scary) TV programs. If appropriate, ask your partner for a soothing massage. Take gentle exercise during the day.

Among the things to avoid is alcohol. Having a drink (or two) may seem helpful, but usually isn't. It leads to disturbed sleep patterns, and you may wake early in the morning with mild (and, if you drink heavily, not so mild) withdrawal symptoms. Catnaps during the day can disrupt night sleep. If I sleep for longer than 15 minutes during the afternoon it can really mess up my night's sleep. If you wake early, get up and avoid lying in bed, ruminating on your difficulties. As a poor sleeper, if I wake early I tend to get up and work. Of course, at times this leaves me feeling tired, but I have come to accept this as my style. If your sleep pattern is very disturbed, you may find an antidepressant helpful. Some people have found that going without sleep for a whole night and not catnapping the next day can help lift their mood, but this is best done under supervision. There are some good self-help books on the market for sleep problems. Do discuss with your family doctor though, because sometimes tiredness and not sleeping can be linked to things like anaemia (or other physical reason) and a dose of iron tablets might help.[3]

Body work

An important aspect of compassionate behavior is looking after, nurturing and caring for your body. Your body is like a garden, and to function well it needs looking after. It can become exhausted and *needs pampering*. Learn to care for your body and treat it with respect. Teach it how to relax, exercise it and feed it good things – not junk food and high-sugar foods, especially if you are depressed.

I always advise trying to find a sympathetic family doctor with whom you can have a frank and open discussion about your depression. In 1992 the Royal College of Psychiatrists in Britain mounted a 'Defeat Depression' campaign to increase the awareness and skill of family doctors in this area of psychological problems.

Very occasionally, depression can arise from a number of physical conditions. These include:

- problems with the thyroid gland
- anaemia
- diabetes
- chronic fatigue syndrome (CFS; also known as ME)
- vitamin deficiency (e.g., B12)
- hormone problems
- stroke
- complications with other medications.

It is important to have these and other things screened out as soon as possible. However, one should also recognize that most depressions are not triggered by a major physical condition, although there may be more subtle problems.[3]

Changing the way you treat your body

Eat a healthy diet and drink plenty

People who are depressed often have a very poor diet. Work out a balanced diet including fresh fruit and vegetables and a high percentage of carbohydrate (e.g., pasta, bread, potatoes). This is because these foods release their energy slowly and may help to boost certain chemicals in the brain that are depleted when we are depressed. You may wish to take advice on this.[4]

There is increasing evidence that weight loss itself can affect various brain chemicals. Consider if your depression came on or got worse as you lost weight. Some research has also shown that eating large amounts of sugar and other refined foods might increase irritability in some people, so try cutting out cakes and other sweet things.

Some people like to take extra vitamins. The evidence for these helping depression is not clear, but provided you are not doing yourself any harm (e.g., too much vitamin A can damage your liver), these may work as a placebo if nothing else – that is, you may become less depressed simply because you believe in the vitamins, not because they have actually had a direct effect on your brain chemistry. A sympathetic family doctor will advise you on this.

We often don't drink nearly enough and so toxins can build up in our bodies making them feel sluggish. The ideal is two litres a day so that your urine is fairly clear but don't drink too much too quickly. Drinking water can also help weight loss. Again it is very useful to talk to your doctor about this. If anxious, avoid the stimulating caffeine drinks of coffee and even tea, and try green teas.

Supplements

Because depression is so common in our societies, the Internet is full of remedies. These include things like omega-3 fatty acids, folic acid, S-adenosyl methionine (SAM-e), St John's wort and many others. Evidence that some of these may be helpful is gradually accumulating.

The problem is that the quality of products obtained via the Internet can't be guaranteed. Some of these supplements can interact with medication or have side effects. So if you want to explore them you will need to discuss things with a qualified person, usually your family doctor or a nutritionist. Provided you obtain appropriate professional advice, then experimenting and seeing what works can be helpful.

As with much in this area, we desperately need more research. We also know that people can have very individual responses to all kinds of medications and supplements. What is helpful for one person may not be helpful for another, because biologically we are all slightly different. Evidence tells us that many people pursue the alternative therapies for depression, but if you choose to explore this path, tread cautiously.[3]

Taking exercise

There is increasing evidence that exercise can be very beneficial for mild to moderate depressions because it tends to boost the production of certain chemicals in the brain. A patient of mine who had a bipolar illness (and was taking lithium and an antidepressant) found that if he woke up in the morning feeling down, a vigorous swim in the local pool helped to lift his mood. When we become depressed we tend to do less, and if you can encourage yourself to take exercise, this can be helpful. It may give you a sense of achievement, in addition to being good for you and boosting certain brain chemicals.

Reducing your alcohol intake

Alcohol can have a depressant effect, and it is usually helpful to reduce your intake, especially if you tend to drink to control your moods. Sometimes people use alcohol to get to sleep; as we have seen, this can be detrimental. Altogether, alcohol is a bad way of managing stress and depression.

Stimulants and other drugs

If you are taking stimulants, try to stop. This applies even to mild stimulants such as coffee. Occasionally, I've found that some of my depressed patients drink vast amounts of strong coffee, sometimes more than 10 cups a day. Many stimulants can have depressant or anxiety-increasing side effects.

If you are using illicit drugs, try to get off them as they will not be doing your body any good. Some cannabis smokers lose motivation and become depressed and apathetic, and if there is an underlying sensitivity, it can also lead to more serious mental health problems. In fact, abuse of all drugs, including painkillers, needs to be considered here. If you are taking a lot of painkillers, you should see your family doctor and plan to reduce your intake.

Tranquillizers

Taking the odd tranquillizer from time to time can be helpful. However, if you have been using tranquillizers for a long time, you should think about coming off them. You must not come off them too quickly, however, but rather reduce your intake slowly. It is important to obtain medical advice from your family doctor, who might refer you to a psychiatric nurse or psychologist. There are also self-help groups and books to help with tranquillizer withdrawal.

Learning to relax

Sometimes this is easier said than done. Have a look back at pages 130–2 for some suggestions. There are also a variety of books and self-help tapes on relaxation on the market, as well as classes and groups. Explore these and see if you can find one that suits you.

Overview

Compassionate behavior means engaging the world in a certain kind of way, which often means acting against our depressed feelings For this we can develop compassionate courage. We also need to treat our bodies carefully; after all, they are the foundation for many of our feeling states. I suspect that in the years to come we will learn much more about the relationship between our diets, various additives in our food, the chemicals in the atmosphere and how these effect our moods. But we can try our own experiments. Provided you discuss with your family doctor or a qualified professional then you may want to experiment to see if certain types of change in eating, exercise or supplements help you. My view about depression is that it affects mind and body and we should treat them both kindly.

KEY POINTS

- There are many forms and causes of depression.
- Because of these differences we need to have a variety of different approaches to depression.
- It can be helpful to plan activities step by step. Break problems or tasks down into simple steps and follow them one at a time.
- Include some positive activities in your life. At times, you may need to increase your social contacts, at other times reduce them to create personal space. Much of this is about working out your own needs.
- The type of thoughts we have can affect the way our brains work. Sometimes, certain thoughts can be controlled by distraction.
- Don't assume that you have to become an inexhaustible supplier of good works. No one can be. Learn to work out your limits. If you think that there are very few things you can't cope with, the chances are that you are not working within your own limits.
- Finally, treatment often needs to be aimed at how our bodies are working. It may require us to take seriously the possibility of using an antidepressant to help us get going again. We may need to change our lifestyles (e.g., take more exercise, improve our diets, cut out the coffee, learn how to relax, distract ourselves).

EXERCISES

Exercise 1

- Make a list of the points in this chapter that you think are relevant to you.
- Clarify in your mind:
  - How are you treating your body?
  - How do you organize your activities? Can you plan to do things step by step?

Exercise 2

Make a list of the positive things you would like to include in your life. These can be quite simple: for example

- I would like to see my friends more.
- I would like to go to the movies more.
- I would like to have more time to myself.

Consider ways that might make some of these things happen.

PART THREE

Developing Supportive Relationships with Ourselves

13

Stop criticizing and bullying yourself: Treating yourself with compassion

Humans are able to think about themselves as if they were thinking about someone else. We have feelings and make judgements about ourselves; there can be things that we like or dislike; we have relationships *with ourselves* that can be healing or unhelpful and even abusive. If we are honest we can think or say things to ourselves, and feel emotions (anger and contempt) towards ourselves, that we wouldn't dream of directing towards other people. We recognize that if we treated others like that it would be abusive. But we treat ourselves like that, especially if we fail in some way, make mistakes, do things we regret, or just feel bad. At the times we need compassion, we actually give it to ourselves least. Because we believe that somehow being critical, harsh, disliking or even hating ourselves is deserved or can be good, we continue to do it. However, self-criticism, especially feelings of anger, frustration or self-contempt, is bad for your brain (see pages 28).[1]

This chapter encourages you to develop a more helpful and considerate response to yourself. Your sense of yourself is always with you, from the moment you wake up to the moment you go to bed. It makes sense to learn how to have a relationship that is friendly, supportive, healing and stimulates the positive emotion systems in our brain rather than the threat systems.

In depression, thoughts and feelings about oneself can become very negative. I say 'can' because this is not always the case. For example, I recall a woman who became depressed when the new people who moved in next door played loud music into the early hours. She tried to get the authorities to stop them, but although they were very sympathetic, they were not much help. Slowly she slipped into depression, feeling her whole life was being ruined and there was nothing she could do. However, she did not think her depression was her fault or that she was in any way inadequate, worthless, weak or bad. Her depression was focused on a loss of control over a very difficult situation.

Sometimes depression can be triggered by conflicts and splits in families or other important relationships. The depressed person may feel defeated and trapped by these relationships, but not to blame for them. Sometimes depressed people feel bad about being depressed and the effect this is having on them and others around them, but they do not feel that they are bad or inadequate as people; they blame the depression.

Nevertheless, many depressed people have a poor relationship with themselves. A poor relationship with oneself can pre-date a depression or develop with it. This chapter will explore the typical styles of 'self-thinking and feeling' depressed people engage in, and consider how our relationship with ourselves can be improved. All the styles discussed here can be seen as types of self-bullying. As you will see, we can bully ourselves in many different ways.[1]

Social comparison and self-blame

We live in a world that is very judgemental and treats us rather like objects.[2] At school, being chosen to play on the football team, getting our first job and so on, we are surrounded by people who can do better than us, who we feel are more attractive, more capable, and so on. What is worse – in schools, through our media and in workplaces, we are constantly encouraged to compare ourselves with others – are we as good as them; as clever, attractive or slim; or as wanted? My research has looked at how people can feel under pressure to strive to keep up and avoid being judged as inferior. You will not be surprised to learn that the more people feel under pressure to avoid being seen as inferior compared with others, the more vulnerable to stress, anxiety and depression they are.[3]

Social comparison can be helpful because it helps us copy each other – adopting the same values, wanting the same things and trying to improve ourselves. If we fail at an important task, such as an exam or the driving test, we can feel better if we find out that others have failed too. We might feel guilty at feeling pleased they failed too, but it's only natural to feel better when you think you're the same as others.

Depressed people can feel that others are more talented or lucky. As children they may have felt that parents favoured their siblings, or they may feel that their siblings had an easier time growing up.[4] Sometimes depressed people have many unresolved problems about these early relationships. They may feel that they have always lived in the shadow of a sibling – were less bright, less attractive and so forth. Sometimes parents and teachers have compared them unfavourably with others –'Why can't you be like Sam or Jane' – or maybe they had parents who were always comparing them with others. For example, when Jane came second in class, her father's reaction was always disappointment: 'What's the matter with coming first?' His motto was, 'Second is the first loser'. Such children grow up in an atmosphere of constant striving to compete with others to win parental approval; they never feel good enough. If you look back at pages 28–9 you can see how this can stimulate the drive system by trying to be 'better and better or have more and more' and never being satisfied or content. That is not your fault, but it is something you might wish to work on, to learn how to be more content and understand the roots of your striving and social comparison. Maybe it is searching for love and acceptance that underlies your striving?

Jim went to university and did well, but his brother Tom was a more practical person and not cut out for the academic life. However, instead of being happy with himself, Tom constantly compared himself with Jim and felt a failure. He would say, 'Why couldn't I have been the bright one?'

Babs' mother was often ill, and as the older daughter she took on responsibility for caring for her. However, she didn't feel appreciated for the role and grew up feeling secretly resentful, but always putting other people first and presenting herself as a nice person. Her anger at the situation, added to thoughts of how 'compared with her', her siblings had an easier life, fuelled her depression.

Even though social comparison can give us lots of problems, it's interesting that sometimes we don't compare ourselves with Mr or Ms Average or people who are similar to ourselves. Jane, a mother of two who devoted herself to looking after her children, had a number of friends who went out to work even though they had children too. Jane thought, 'I'm not as competent as them because I don't go out to work, and I have to struggle just to keep the home going'. When I asked her if she had other friends with children who did not have outside employment, she agreed that most of her friends didn't. However, it was not them she compared herself with, but the few who did have jobs. Part of the reason for selecting people like this is that we slightly envy them; we want to be like them.

Sometimes when we compare ourselves unfavourably with others, we also think that other people will have the same judgement of us. Other people will see us as inferior or bad in some way – that we are not as good as other people (recall 'Mind reading' on page 207). This can be quite a major problem if we have to open our hearts and share our difficulties.

A young mother's comparison

Diane felt really depressed after the birth of her child. She found it difficult to feel 'affection' for her new baby. She thought that her reaction was different from that of all her friends and therefore there was something wrong with her to feel this way. She was angry and frightened about her depressed feelings and envied what she saw as her friends being happy mothers. As a result, she never told anyone but suffered in silence, feeling different from them and cut off. Had she opened up to others (rather than feeling shamed by her comparisons) she would have found that these are sadly not uncommon experiences, and are no fault of her own – hormonal readjustment can be really unpleasant and play havoc with our minds.

One of the big benefits in working in group therapy is the degree to which people are prepared to share their problems. Often when one person is brave enough to own up to certain types of negative feelings or experiences, other people feel able to share. Indeed, sharing is much easier when we no longer compare ourselves unfavourably with others but realize we are all in this same boat of living in a world of suffering and hardship.

Even those with status can feel inferior

Social comparison is one reason why people who seem to have quite prestigious positions in society can become depressed. I worked with a doctor who had done well during his training yet, when he qualified, found the work stressful. He thought that he was doing much worse than his colleagues. Compared with them, he did not feel confident or on a par. As a caring GP he took more time with his patients and then struggled to keep up – but then blamed himself.

Balancing social comparison

Although it can be very difficult to avoid making social comparisons, here are some ideas to think through to help you think about how social comparison works within you.

- **When you compare yourself with others, choose a target who is most like you**. In other words, avoid comparing yourself with those who are clearly a lot better in certain ways. If a comparison turns out badly, consider the reasons and evidence why this comparison may not be an appropriate one for you. We have different genes, backgrounds, talents and abilities – it is not a level playing field.
- **Think about the reasons for your comparison**. Although comparing ourselves with others is very natural, recognize that it can be harmful and keep in mind why you want to do it – what's the point of it for you? If it has value, such as giving you something you can try to copy, or it inspires you, that's fine, but if it depresses you – not fine.
- **If you do compare and feel down, avoid attacking yourself**. Try to remember that there are always people

who are better at doing certain things or have more, but it does not make you a failure or inadequate because you can't do these things or don't have as much.

- **Think of your life as your own unique journey, with its own unique ups and downs and challenges**. Although you might want to live the life of someone else, this is not possible. Focus on you as yourself rather than you as compared with others.

- **If you are depressed, avoid labelling yourself as in-adequate because you think others don't get depressed**. Sadly, many people do get depressed and anxious.

- **Spend some time refocusing and thinking about how social comparison can be hurtful for so many of us**. It is understandable, but think of ways of dealing with it that are kind to yourself.

Self-blame can come from fear

Self-blame and criticism are strongly linked to depression. When people self-blame and self-condemn, there is often a sense of the fear (e.g., of being rejected for mistakes or for not being good enough) and loss. Sometimes we learn to self-blame because we are frightened. Consider this on a world scale. Over thousands of years humans have been very frightened about what life can throw at them. Their children can die of numerous diseases, there can be famines and droughts and all kinds of unpleasant things. In societies throughout the world humans often imagine and then appeal to various gods who might be able to control bad things. Then they have to get them on side and they usually do this by sacrificing, appeasing or promising obedience to the chosen god. Problems arise if this does not work. The following year the diseases still come and so do the droughts, famines and other bad things. People rarely give up on their god as a poor bet; more commonly they blame themselves. They feel they must have done something wrong, or not done things sufficiently right, and have caused offence or displeasure to the god. Self-monitoring one's behavior, to check if it is acceptable – and then self-blaming if one thinks it is not – are common if we grow in fear of others. Sometimes in these societies if the gods do not help out there is a blaming of other people, 'Maybe it was those people who broke the traditions and caused the gods to abandon us' – and so starts a round of persecution born out of fear.

When we believe that powerful others and people can help, love or hurt us – and when we're children it is parents and teachers who can indeed do those things – it is natural for us to monitor ourselves, trying not to make them angry with us or to withdraw support and affection. Because we are monitoring ourselves, if things go wrong, we blame ourselves. If parents are in a bad mood, we might wonder what we have done to upset them. Thus a natural style of self-monitoring and self-blaming can become a style we carry through life. It is useful to remember that a style we learned out of fear – wanting to please and blaming ourselves, wanting to be loved or protected and not harmed – can become a style we use in all kinds of situations. We may never have learned to see the origins of our self-blaming style as being rooted in fear and wanting love.

If you tend to blame yourself, often worrying if you've upset people, not done well enough or have various faults – always try to think about what you are really frightened of. Next, write down the reasons why these might be linked to your fears (of rejection, or people becoming angry). You might not be fully conscious of them at first. Consider if these styles have been picked up in childhood. If so, with your compassionate self-focus, consider the possibility that you are blaming yourself not because you really are to blame, but because it feels *safer* to self-blame and to protect yourself – just like the people who blame themselves if their gods don't come through for them. If it is about fear, safety and protection, then be honest about this, rather than thinking your self-blame reflects any truth about you!

Taking too much responsibility

Blaming occurs when we look for the reasons or causes of things – why did such and such a thing happen? When we are depressed, we often feel a great sense of responsibility for nega-tive events and so blame ourselves. As noted above, the reasons for this are complex. Sometimes we self-blame because as chil-dren we were taught to. Whenever things went wrong in the family, we tended to get the blame. Even young children who are sexually abused can be told that they are to blame for it – which, of course, is absurd. Sadly, adults who are looking for someone to blame can simply pick on those least able to defend themselves.

Sylvia was a harsh self-blamer. Her mother had frequently blamed her for 'making her life a constant misery'. Her mother was herself a depressed and angry person, but Sylvia accepted her mother's explanations at face value – as children do. Not surprising, then, Sylvia took this style of thinking into adulthood and tended to blame herself whenever other people close to her had difficulties. Yet when Sylvia looked at the evidence, she real-ized that her mother's life was unhappy for a number of reasons, including a difficult marriage and money worries. As a child Sylvia could not see this wider perspective, but believed what her mother told her. Sylvia had to learn that her self-blame was a style she had picked up in childhood, and practise a more balanced approach. Sometimes, of course, this is quite frightening because it raises a number of other issues about the kind of person she is and the anger she might now feel.

When people are depressed, their self-blaming can become extreme. When bad things happen or conflicts arise, they may see them as completely their fault. This is called *personalization* – the tendency to assume responsibility for things that are either not our fault or only partly so. However, most life events are a combination of various circumstances. When we are depressed, it is often helpful to stand back and think of as many reasons as possible about why something happened the way it did. We can learn to consider alternative explanations rather than just blame ourselves.

The responsibility circle

Many of the things that happen to us are due to many reasons. Here is an example to help you think about this. Sheila's husband had an affair, for which she blamed herself. Her thinking was: 'If I had been more attentive, he would not have had an affair. If I had been more sexually alluring, he would not have had an affair. If I had been more interesting as a person and less focused on the children, he would not have had an affair.' All her thoughts were focused on herself. However, she could have had alternative thoughts. For example, she could have thought: 'He could have taken more responsibility for the children, then I wouldn't have felt so overloaded. He could have spent more time at home. If he had been more attentive in his lovemaking, I might have felt more sexually inclined. Even if he felt attracted to another woman, he did not have to act on it. The other woman could have realized he was married and not encouraged him.'

One can then write down these various alternatives side by side and rate them in terms of *percentage of truth*. Or one might draw a circle and for each reason allocate a slice of the circle. The size of each slice represents the percentage of truth. In Figure 13.1

you can see how this worked for Sheila. The two circles represent a depressed view and a more balanced view. Note how some situations often have many causes. Sheila's more balanced,

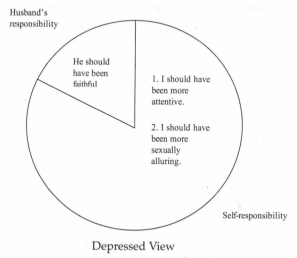

Husband's responsibility

He should have been faithful

1. I should have been more attentive.

2. I should have been more sexually alluring.

Self-responsibility

Depressed View

Husband's responsibility

Self-responsibility

Husband helped more in the house and shown more interest in me

Husband could have

Husband can be impulsive and not think through the consequences of his actions

I could have taken more interest in sex

Husband's style

Husband is responsible for own sexual conduct

Husband's responsibility

Other women could have said 'No' to a married man

Differences in sexual interest and drive

Opportunity was available

Other women's responsibility

External factors

Relationship factor

Alternative View

Figure 13.1 'Responsibility circles'.

'alternative view' circle seemed more true to her once she had considered it.

The next thing to do is to go around the circle carefully and think about it in as compassionate, warm, kind and understanding a way as you can. Try and create those feelings in your mind as you consider the alternatives.

Think about the fact that if we take too much responsibility on our own shoulders then we are *robbing* other people of theirs. In parent–child relationships this can be very important. If parents feel guilt and blame themselves for their children's difficult or bad behavior, how are the children ever going to learn to take responsibility?

Tess had been depressed when her son Sam was born. Later on, she always blamed this for Sam's difficult behavior. The family therapist spotted this and noted that Sam had few boundaries because Tess always blamed herself for his behavior. She could not confront Sam and help him become responsible for himself and his behavior.

Compassionate behavior is about giving people what they need, not necessarily what they want. When it comes to responsibility, don't be greedy and claim more that your fair share!

The same principle can apply when we blame others. We may simply blame them without considering the complexity of the issue, and label them as bad, weak and so forth.

Self-blame and control

One reason we might self-blame is that, paradoxically, it might offer hope. For example, if a certain event is our fault, we have a chance of changing things in the future. We have (potential) control over it and so don't have to face the possibility that, maybe, we actually don't have much control. In depression, it is sometimes important to exert more control over our lives, but it is also important to know our limits and what we cannot control. Sheila had to face the fact that she could not control her husband's sexual conduct. It was his responsibility, not hers. We have to be careful that, in self-blaming, we are not trying to give ourselves more control (and power) than we actually have (or had). We will look at this in regard to shame and abuse on pages 388–89.

Avoiding conflict and anger

Another reason for self-blame is that it may feel safer to blame ourselves than to blame others. By self-blaming we might avoid conflicts and expressing our own anger. You will need to be honest about this – how frightened of your anger are you? How much do you think it could turn you into an unlovable person? Remember the example above of the blaming ourselves if the gods don't help out or seem punitive (see pages 281–2) – sometimes we can be very frightened of anger and conflicts, and it is out of fear that we self-blame.

It may be that self-blame keeps the peace and stops us from having to challenge others. If, when we were children, our parents told us that they hit us because we were bad in some way, we might have accepted their view and rarely argued. This attitude can be carried on into adulthood. The other person always seems blameless, beyond rebuke.

People can be in conflict and in dilemmas about blame. One part of the self can feel angry, but another part can feel sorry or disloyal to (say) a parent. There can be a real desire to avoid conflict, and not wanting to be seen as ungrateful, aggressive or bad. The problem is, of course, that conflicts are part of life.

Sometimes we recognize that we are not totally blameless in something, but when it comes to arguing our case, the part that is our responsibility gets blown up out of proportion. We become over-focused on it and feel that we have not got a leg to stand on. However, most things in life have many causes, and the idea here is to avoid all-or-nothing thinking. By all means, accept your share of responsibility – none of us is an angel – but don't overdo it. Healing comes from forgiving yourself and others.

Expecting punishment

When bad things happen, depressed people sometimes feel that they are being punished for being bad in some way. It is as if we believe that good things will only happen if we are good and only bad things will happen if we are bad. If bad things happen, this must be because we have been bad, or simply are bad. When Kate lost a child to sudden infant death syndrome, she felt that God was punishing her for having had an abortion some years earlier. But millions of women have abortions and don't suffer this event, and vast numbers who suffer this sad event have not had abortions.

In depression the sense of being punished can be quite strong, and quite often, if this is explored, it turns out to relate to a person's own shame about something in the past. For instance, Richard's parents had given him strong messages that mastur-bation was bad. When he began doing it when he was twelve, he enjoyed it but also felt terribly ashamed. For many years, he carried the belief that he was bad for enjoying masturbating and sooner or later he was going to be punished for it. When bad things happened to him, he would feel that these were 'part of his punishment'.

To come to terms with these feelings we usually have to admit to the things we feel shame about and then learn how to forgive ourselves for them. It can be difficult to come to terms with the fact that the principles of 'justice' and 'punishment' are human creations. There is no justice in people starving to death from droughts in Africa. Good and bad things can happen to people whether they behave well or badly.

The fear of punishment can also come when we have had parents who frequently lost their temper and became very aggressive. Abigail's mother could be loving but at times would have rages and be physically aggressive. Clearly, those events created intense fear in Abigail. It is quite understandable that if there were conflicts or things went wrong, Abigail's threat-protection system would spring into action and she'd have an internal fear that something very bad or threatening was going to happen.

Expectations of punishment can operate at an emotional or gut level. It is important to stand back from that and realize what's happening inside. We can then practise our soothing rhythm breathing (see pages 123–4), and recognize that our feelings make sense, but we can allow ourselves to be gentle with them now.

Note that Abigail had the classic problem of wanting love from a person who could also be dangerous. This is very tough, because different parts of her brain are in conflict. The part that wants to be close to a loving mother and yearns for protection pulls her forward while the threat self-protection system pushes her away. These are difficult and confusing feelings to have to deal with and can really scramble our minds. If Abigail gets close to people this might reactivate her fear that people she's close to can blow up at her.

Some people can fear the punishment of Hell. But here's how I see it. If you believe in Heaven then it's kind and loving people who go there, right? And these are people who do not like others to suffer. So Heaven is full of those who would work to stop the suffering of others – so if Heaven if full of such souls, who could rest knowing people suffer in Hell – so how can Hell exist? For me it is our own minds that create these fears.

Self-criticism

Some people believe that self-criticism is the only way to make them do things. For example, a person might say, 'If I didn't kick myself, I'd never do anything.' Or they might believe that unless they are critical and keep themselves on their toes they will become arrogant, selfish and lazy. They use their self-bullying part to drive them on – sometimes in rather sadomasochistic ways. Such a person may believe that threats and punishments are the best ways to get things done. In some cases, this view goes back to childhood. Parents may have said things like, 'If I didn't always get on at you, you wouldn't do anything', or 'Punishment is the only thing that works with you'. They may also have been poor at paying attention to good conduct and praising it, and rather more attentive to bad conduct and quick to punish. As a result, the child becomes good at self-criticism and self-punishment but poor at self-rewarding and valuing. See Table 13.1 for ways to look at this differently.

In depression, however, self-criticism can get out of hand. The internal bully / critic becomes so forceful that we can feel totally beaten down by it. Then, when we are disappointed about things or find out that our conduct has fallen short of our ideal in some way, we can become angry and frustrated and launch savage attacks on ourselves. Research has shown that it is the emotions of anger and contempt in the attacks, not just the kind of things you think or say to yourself, that really do the damage in self-attack.[5]

It–me

The late Albert Ellis pointed out that self-criticism can lead to an 'it–me problem': 'I only accept *me* if I do *it* well.' The 'it' can be anything you happen to judge as important. For example, if you are a student, the 'it' may be passing exams. You might feel good and content with yourself if you pass or do well, but become critical and unpleasant with yourself if you do less well. Your feeling of disappointment fuels negative feelings of yourself. Or the 'it' might be coping with housework or a job: 'I only feel a good and worthwhile *person* if I do these *things* well.' Success leads to self-acceptance, but failure leads to self-dislike and self-attacking. Not only may you feel like this, but you might have beliefs where you think it's true: 'I'm not worthwhile if I can't succeed at things'.

This kind of thinking means: 'I am only as good as my last performance'. But how much does success or failure actually change us? Do you really become good (as a person) if you succeed and become bad (as a person) if you fail? Whether we succeed or fail, we have not gained or lost any brain cells; we have not grown an extra arm; our hair, eyes and taste in music have not changed. The consciousness that is the essence of our being has not changed. It is like water that can carry good or bad things but the water itself is not those things. Of course, we may lose things that have importance to us if we fail. We may feel terribly disappointed or grieve for what is lost and what we can't have. But the point is that these things will be more difficult to cope with if our disappointment becomes an attack on ourselves and we label ourselves rather than our actions as disappointing. It is very helpful to pull back and reflect on feelings of disappointment and consider if these feelings have somehow got linked to your feelings about yourself. If so, imagine your mind separating them and saying clearly 'I am upset about this or that – but this is not about me or the essence of me'.

Another key way to work on this 'it–me' problem is to separate *self*-rating and judgements from *behavior* rating and judgements. It may be true that your behavior falls short of what you would like, but this does not change the complexity and essence of you as a *person*. We can be disappointed in our behavior (and we can all do some daft, thoughtless and unhelpful things), but as human beings, we do not have to rate ourselves in such all-or-nothing terms as 'good' or 'bad', 'worthwhile' or 'worthless'. If we do that, we are giving away our humanity and turning ourselves into objects with a market value. We are saying, 'I can be treated like a car, soap powder or some other thing. If I perform well, I deserve to be valued. If I don't perform well, I am worthless junk.' But we are not things or objects. We are living, feeling, highly complex conscious beings, and to judge ourselves as if we are just objects carries great risks.

Self-attacking

Recent research has suggested it is our emotions and response to self-criticism that are associated with depression.[5] Our research has also shown that people criticize themselves for different reasons. Sometimes it's because they want to drive themselves to be better, but at other times it's out of rage and hatred and just wanting to hurt themselves.[6] We might make a mistake, have an argument with somebody, or eat too much and put on a few pounds, and realize that we could have behaved better. We might offer a mild rebuke to ourselves, or try to learn from things. However, when we attack ourselves there are emotions of frustration and anger and sometimes even contempt and shame. It is these feelings that we put into our self-criticism that turn it into much more of an attack on ourselves.

When self-criticism becomes *hostile* and activates basic beliefs about ourselves (of being weak, bad, inadequate, hopeless, and so on), then depression can take root. We all have a tendency to be self-critical, but when we become angry, frustrated and aggressive with ourselves and start bullying and labelling ourselves as worthless, bad or weak, we are more likely to slip deeper into depression. In a way, we become enemies to ourselves; we lose our capacity for inner compassion. It is as if the self becomes trapped in certain ways of feeling and then (because of emotional reasoning) over-identifies with these feelings. We think our feelings are true reflections of ourselves: 'I *feel* stupid / worthless, therefore I *am* stupid / worthless.'

Here are some ideas about how to work with these difficulties:

- If I am honest, my self-criticism and attacking happens because I feel frightened about my mistakes or areas where I feel inferior. This fuels my frustration and anger with myself. Maybe I need to come to terms with what I am actually frightened about. (Spend some moments quietly reflecting on how your self-criticism links to your fears. What is the fear that underlies your criticism and anger with yourself?)
- How can I be compassionate to that fear?
- To sum up a person (e.g., myself) in simple terms of good / bad, worthwhile / worthless is all-or-nothing thinking. It is compassionate to appreciate that there are some things I can do quite well and some things I don't do as well as I would like.
- All humans are fallible; we make mistakes, mess things up, behave selfishly – all we can do is try our best to improve. Self-attacking does not really help me with this (see Table 13.1).
- Because I *feel* stupid and worthless does not make it true. I'm confusing a feeling with a sense of self.
- The idea of worth can be applied to objects such as cars or soap powder but not to people.

- I don't have to treat myself as an object, whose only value is what I achieve or do.
- If I say 'worthless', it is just one of a number of possible feelings that I, as a human being, can have about myself. I can try and put these critical feelings in perspective.
- I would not treat a friend like this – and anyway I am on the path of compassion, so that is what I am trying to develop step by step.
- If I had a chance to change the world I would not issue a command that everyone who fails should feel worthless – quite the opposite (a patient came up with this idea, which I think is very interesting and helpful).

Remember these thoughts and reflections have to pass the 'compassionate friend' test: Would you say this to a friend? Would you help a friend in this way? Would you agree that it is a kind and nurturing thing to think, say or do?

Self-hatred

As I have mentioned, it is the fear-linked and hostile emotions lurking in the self-criticism that often do the damage. Getting more insight into these emotions and some control over them can be very helpful. At the extreme, some depressions involve not only self-criticism and self-attack, but also self-hatred.[8] This is not just a sense of disappointment in the self; the self is actually treated like a hated enemy. Whereas self-criticism often comes from disappointment and a desire to do better, self-hatred is not focused on the need to do better. It is focused on a desire to destroy and abolish.

Sometimes along with self-hatred are feelings of *self-disgust*. Disgust is an interesting feeling and usually involves the desire to get rid of or expel the thing we are disgusted by. In self-hatred, part of us may judge ourselves to be disgusting, bad or evil. When we have these feelings, there may be a strong desire to attack ourselves in quite a savage way – not just because we are disappointed and feel let down, but because we have really come to hate parts of ourselves.

Kate could become overpowered by feelings of anxiety and worthlessness. When things did not work out right, or she got into conflicts with others, she'd feel intense rage. Even while she was having these feelings, she was also having thoughts and feelings of intense hatred towards herself. Her internal bully was really sadistic. She had thoughts like: 'You're a pathetic creature, a whining, useless piece of shit.' Frequently the labels people use when they hate themselves are those that invite feelings of disgust (e.g., 'shit'). Kate had been sexually abused, and at times she hated her genitals and wanted to 'take a knife to them'. In extreme cases, self-hatred can lead to serious self-harming.

Kate's difficulties came to light in therapy, and for these types of extreme problem, therapy may be essential, but they are helpful to think about on your own too, because it is important to try to work out, and see if your bullying, self-critical side has become more than critical and has turned to self-dislike or self-hatred. Even though you may be disappointed in yourself and the state you are in, can you still maintain a reasonably friendly relationship with your inner self?

If your internal bully is getting out of hand, you may want to try the following: In as warm and friendly a way as you can manage, say to yourself:

- I understand that my self-hatred is highly destructive – certainly not very compassionate.
- Am I a person who values hatred?

- If I don't value hatred and can see how destructive it is, maybe I can learn to heal this part of myself.
- I know perfectly well that, if I cared for someone, I would not treat them with hatred.
- Am I as bad as Hitler? No? Then maybe I need to get my hatred into perspective.
- Maybe I have learned to hate myself because of the way others have treated me. If I attack myself, I am only repeating what they did to me.
- I can learn to be gentle to my hatred – just be in compassionate self mode and then see how hate covers up hurt and fear. Gosh, that might be tough! But that is the compassionate path I'd like to take, even if it is small steps at a time.
- First, I commit myself to recognizing my self-hating part as understandable but unhelpful, linked to hurt – and then build on my desire to heal it.

We need to consider, too, that *we hate what hurts us or causes us pain*. Rather than focusing on hatred, it is useful to focus on what the pain and hurt is about. If you discover that there are elements of self-hatred in your depression, don't turn this insight into another attack.

The tough part in all this is that you will need to be absolutely honest with yourself and decide whether or not you want hatred to live in you. When you decide that you do not, you can train yourself to become its master rather than allowing it to master you. However, if you are secretly on the side of self-hatred and think it's reasonable and acceptable to hate yourself, this will be very difficult to do, and it will be hard to open yourself to gentleness and healing. For some people, this is a most soul-searching journey. But as one patient told me:

*The hard part was realizing that, whatever had happened
in the past and whatever rage and hatred I carried from
those years, the key turning point had to be my decision that
I had had enough of my hatred. Only then could I start to
take the steps to find the way out.*

And, of course, it is not just with depression that coming to
terms with and conquering hatred can be helpful. Many of our
problems of living together in the world today could be helped
if we worked on this. We all have the potential to hate – there is
nothing abnormal about it. The primary question is, how much
will we feed our hatred?

Developing compassionate self-correction to replace harsh self-criticism

In this difficult and painful life, when we make mistakes, things
don't work out, or we do things we deeply regret, learning to
be kind to ourselves is the most important lesson to help us with
depression. The first thing is to decide if you are actually frightened of giving up the self-criticism and self-bullying. If you ask
people to imagine what life would be like if they gave up self-
criticism and self-bullying altogether, they can actually be quite
puzzled and even frightened. They may believe they would not
achieve anything; would become lazy, arrogant or unkind. It's
almost impossible for them to believe that they wouldn't become
lazy because they have a genuine wish to do well and a genuine
wish to be kind.

The first thing is to make a distinction between what I call
compassionate self-correction and shame-focused self-criticism or
self-bullying. They are outlined and contrasted in Table 13.1.
Compassionate self-correction is based on being open-hearted

and honest about our mistakes with a genuine wish to improve and learn from them. No one wakes up in the morning and thinks to themselves, 'Oh, I think I will make a real cock-up of things today, just for the hell of it'. Most of us would like to do well, most of us would like to avoid mistakes, most of us would like to avoid being out of control with our temper. We need to recognize that our genuine wish is to improve. Self-criticism, on the other hand, comes from a fear- and anger-based place. It is concerned with punishment and is usually backward-looking, related to things we have done in the past. The problem is you cannot change a single moment of the past, you can only change the future.

To appreciate the differences between compassionate self-correction and shame-based self-attacking, imagine a child who is learning a new skill but is struggling and making mistakes. A critical teacher will focus on those mistakes, point out what the child is doing wrong, appear slightly irritated, imply that the child is not concentrating or could do better if they try. The focus of that style of teaching is based on fear and shame – to make a child frightened or to feel bad if they don't do well. In contrast, consider a kind teacher who focuses on what a child does well and shows them how they can improve and learn from mistakes, and genuinely takes pleasure in the child's learning. Which technique do you think will help the child the most? Which one would you prefer?

If you do things wrong or make mistakes there is going to be regret, and momentary flashes of irritation, anger and perhaps calling yourself names. The point is though, how long do you stay here? How quickly can you switch to a compassionate refocusing?

TABLE 13.1 DISTINGUISHING COMPASSIONATE SELF-CORRECTION FROM SHAME-BASED SELF-ATTACKING

Shame-based self-attacking	Compassionate self-correction
Focuses on the desire to condemn and punish	Focuses on the desire to improve
Punishes past errors and is often backward-looking	Emphasizes growth and enhancement
Is given with anger, frustration contempt, disappointment	Is forward-looking
Concentrates on deficits and fear of exposure	Is given with encouragement, support, kindness
Focuses on a 'global' sense of self	Builds on positives (e.g. seeing what you did well and then considering learning points)
Includes a high fear of failure	Focuses on attributes and specific qualities of self
Increases chances of avoidance and withdrawal	Emphasizes hope for success. Increases the chances of engaging with difficult things
Consider example of critical teacher with child who is struggling:	Consider example of encouraging, supportive teacher with child who is struggling:

Overview

The way we treat ourselves is quite complex, but the basic question is, can we be a friend to ourselves when things go wrong and we mess up? It is easy to criticize – critics are ten a penny. Compassionate self support is harder but well worth working for. One patient reflected on her depression and eventually recognized that her depression was strongly linked to her self-condemnation. 'I condemned myself into depression,' she said. 'That was all that was in my head, but now there are compassionate alternatives and different feelings about myself.'

KEY POINTS

- We can attack ourselves without really realizing what we are doing. Our feelings and moods seem to carry us along into certain styles of thinking and evaluating ourselves.
- If we are to climb out of depression, we may have to take a good look at ourselves and decide to deal with and heal our self-criticisms, anger and self-hatred.
- The hard part can be helping ourselves to focus on the need for inner healing. Once we have done that, we can then start to focus on what we need to do to be healed. Often the first step is to sort out our relationships with ourselves.

EXERCISES

Exercise 1

The first steps are to use our rational and cognitive approach to examine self-criticism. The next exercises will use a more compassion-focused approach to work with our inner self-critic. So we can begin:

- Consider whether you have an underlying sense of inferiority, with a sense of being not quite up to it compared to others. (To be honest, many people do have that lurking sense and it's when it gets out of hand that it becomes really problematic.)
- Think about whether this is because you have a sense of disappointment, and if related to disappointment is it a sense of fear of, say, rejection or being left behind?
- If so, when something happens and you feel bad about yourself, ask yourself: 'What am I saying about myself? What does this mean about me?' Write down these thoughts. Try to clarify the key streams of thinking:
  - what you think others might be thinking about you
  - what you are thinking about yourself.

Look at those thoughts and then:

- Consider in what ways you might be using: all-or-nothing thinking, emotional reasoning, disbelieving positives (see Chapter 10).
- Using your 'thought form', focus on the fourth column (see Appendix 1). Use your rational/compassionate mind to generate alternative views about yourself.
- Consider how you might help someone like yourself deal with self-attacking and bullying themselves, and then apply this to yourself. Learn to be gentle with yourself.
- Imagine a really caring person advising you. What would they say? Look at the evidence and think of alternatives. Ask yourself: How am I looking after myself with these thoughts/feelings? Do my thoughts help me to care for or look after myself?' In this way, slowly build up your insights.

Exercise 2

You probably have a sense of the kind of things you say and feel about yourself when you are in that frustrated or disappointed self-critical state. You know what your inner critic says and the kind of attacks it launches. It might have grown from childhood or even started as someone else's criticism of you. We are now going to work with this inner self-criticism and bullying in a different way, first using our compassionate image.

- Set some time aside and then sit or lie comfortably and engage in your soothing rhythm breathing. Create your compassionate self inside of you (see pages 149–51). Imagine that you have all of the ideal qualities of kindness, wisdom (you know how difficult our evolved brains are), strength and maturity, and are never condemning. It is you at your best and how you would most like to be. Spend some minutes really focusing on those, remember to adopt a compassionate facial expression and if possible a relaxed body. Feel yourself expanding as if you are becoming powerful in a calm, confident and very benevolent way. When you feel some degree of contact with those feelings you can try this exercise. Imagine your self-critical side as a person, as if you could take it out of your head and look at it. Now, in front of you, imagine yourself being critical to yourself. See the facial expressions and look at the emotions that self-critical part of you directs at yourself. Now see beyond those emotions, to the disappointment or the fear. Extend your compassion to your critical self. You're not arguing or trying to change the critical self, and it doesn't matter how your critical self wants to respond, even by devaluing what you're doing or ridiculing it. Continue to feel compassion for it and watch what happens. Offer it as much compassion as it needs. One patient told me her self-critical side lifted two fingers to the compassionate self, with words to go with the gesture, but she stayed in compassion mode and gradually the self-critic 'got smaller and then seemed rather sad, really'.

- A variation on this can be to engage in your soothing rhythm breathing and then imagine your compassionate image (see page 156) standing next to you and then both of you extend compassion to your critical self. Again, note what happens. If feelings emerge, be mindful of those feelings and stay with them.

- A third exercise involves writing a compassionate letter to one's self-critical side or inner bully. The letter might look like this:

Dear inner critic,
I know that you get frustrated and upset and become angry with me. This is because you are frightened of what will happen if we don't succeed/achieve/change etc. Actually, like me, you want to be respected, loved, cared for or admired – the basic human wants. The thing is, you worry that all these things will slip through your fingers unless we get our act together. Look, I understand your fear. I also understand that your response is to panic and lash out like this. I'm very sorry you feel so vulnerable. It's not your fault but this attacking

actually contributes to our feelings of vulnerability and depression, and so it's time to learn how to be gentle and kind in these situations. We can learn to do the things that will genuinely move us forward in life. In your heart you know this. So I'm not going to attend to the things you say as much as I used to, okay? I used to get caught up in them and believe that these thoughts had some truth to them, but they don't really – it's just that we're frightened of rejection. But if I am honest and compassionate I can learn how to cope with rejection if it comes.

Writing these letters can help you develop a different attitude to your self-critic, and become more aware of when that part of you – linked to your feelings of anger, frustration and fear – kicks in. That then becomes the signal to switch to your soothing breathing rhythm and compassionate-balanced focusing.

As with all these exercises, go one step at a time and only engage in things that you find helpful to you, and can see the point of. One of the key elements of helping ourselves is to work out what is helpful to us, because what might be helpful to me may not be helpful to you and vice versa.

In this case imagine your inner critic, and then from your compassionate self recognize that you do not need to keep this 'voice from the past'. It was not there to really help you. So now imagine that you are leaving it and see it gradually move away and grow smaller, smaller, smaller. You are creating in your mind 'letting-go conditions'. If this is too difficult and you think it could be a major source for your depression, then maybe professional help would be useful for you.

Sometimes the voice of the critic might remind you of someone who was unkind or even abusive to you. Here you might need a more assertive response. Remember, compassion is not submissive or weak. Finding what works for you can be key here.

14

Depressed ways of experiencing ourselves: How compassionate re-focusing can change our experience

The last chapter focused on thoughts and feelings against the self. This chapter explores how we label ourselves and think and feel about ourselves in unkind ways. Learning to spot and counter these ways of experiencing ourselves can help with depression.

Self-labelling and the different types of self

Most of us have had the experience of feeling bad, inadequate and useless at times. These feelings usually arise when we are disappointed by our actions, have failed at something or have been criticized by others. As we grow up, our parents, teachers, siblings and peers *label* us in various ways and may call us things that are hurtful. We may be told that we are a nuisance, bad, unlovable, stupid. Or perhaps overprotective parents say that we are not able to make our own decisions or cannot cope by ourselves. Over time, we develop various ways of thinking about ourselves as being a certain kind of person – that is, we come to *label and describe ourselves in various ways*. Now the label can colour the experience.

We can often label and experience ourselves differently in different roles. For example, suppose you write to a pen friend

– how would you describe yourself? Suppose you are applying for a job – how would you describe yourself? If you are writing to a dating agency, how would you describe yourself? Finally, if you are writing to a priest or someone similar to confess something and seek forgiveness, how would you describe yourself then? The chances are that each letter would say different things about you, because we humans are very complex and have many different qualities and parts. In fact many psychologists suggest we have many *different types of self and potential selves within us*. We can play different roles with different people. With some people we might be light and humorous, but with others we might feel irritable and tense, and with others again we have a sense of unease or anxiety around them. And of course different situations seem to draw out or activate different aspects of ourselves. I am happy to talk to an audience about my specialist field, but put me in a car and tell me to drive to London and you'll fill me full of dread and anxiety.

When we become depressed, the richness, variety and vitality of our many and potential selves drain away and we start thinking of ourselves in rather simple terms, or labels. The labels might be triggered by life events. For instance, you might be rejected by someone you love and then label yourself as unlovable. Or you might fail at some important task and then label yourself as a failure. Negative *labels* are often sparked off by negative *feelings*, which in turn may be strong echoes from the past.

Self-labelling is essentially a form of name-calling. In depression, we come to experience ourselves as if that label (e.g., weak, inadequate, worthless, bad) sums up the whole truth about us. It can feel *as if we are* the label: our whole self becomes identified with the label. The judgements, labels and feelings that we have about ourselves when we are depressed tend to be the same the world over. Whether we live in China, the United States or Europe, depression often speaks with the same voice. Here are some of the words depressed people typically use to describe themselves:

bad	inadequate	outsider	unlovable
empty	incompetent	rejectable	useless
failure	inferior	small	victim
fake	loser	ugly	weak
hopeless	nuisance	unattractive	worthless

Consider for a moment a person you care about. How do you think they would feel if you started to call them these names? Whenever they made a mistake, you called them incompetent or a failure. Of course, it would make them pretty miserable or they'd sack you as a friend. It is no different from your own self-treatment, though. It is easily done but very unhelpful. The trick is to learn to be kind and balanced in our relationships with ourselves when the going gets tough, when we fall over, when we make mistakes, when we are rejected.

However, *we can train our minds* to realize that the feeling and label of being 'worthless or useless' is only one of many possible sets of judgements. There are others, such as: honest, hard-working, carer, helper, lover, old, young, lover of rock music and chocolate, gardener. Our depressed negative judgements, which seem so certain and 'all or nothing', can also be examined for their accuracy and helpfulness. Although depression tends to push us towards certain types of extreme judgements, it is helpful to think that these are only parts of ourselves. Like a piano, we can have and play different notes and can play them in different combinations. We are far more complex than our depression would have us believe. Consider the typical kinds of labels you put on yourself and then reflect on the following:

- As a human being, I am a complex person. I am the product of many millions of years of evolution, with an immensely complex genetic code and billions of brain cells in my head. I am also the product of many years of development, with a personal history. One of the things evolution has given to all of us is the ability to operate in **many** different states of mind and in different roles. Therefore to judge my whole self, my being and my essence, in a single negative term is taking all-or-nothing thinking to extremes.

- When I am depressed, it is natural and understandable that I tend to **feel** bad and inadequate, but this does not **make me** bad or inadequate. To believe it does would be a form of emotional reasoning. I might feel worthless (that is what depression does to feelings) but this does not make it true. These are the thoughts linked to my fears and anxieties and frustrations but they are not truths.

- Although I tend to focus on negative labels when I am depressed, I can try to balance these out with other ideas about myself. For example, I can reflect that I am honest, hard-working and caring – at least sometimes. I can consider alternative labels and inner experiences. When depressed it is easy to focus on the negatives, because that's what depression does. The trick is to refocus my attention on the things that I appreciate about myself, even if they are difficult to see at times. The act of practising helps me take control of my mind rather than letting depression determine what I think and feel.

- How do I see myself when I'm not depressed? Okay, maybe not as good a person as I might like, but certainly not as I do now.
- Although depression likes simplistic answers to complex problems and tends to see things in black and white, good and bad, I don't have to accept this view but can try considering the alternatives.
- The essence of me is really my conscious self. Consciousness is like a spotlight that can shine on many things. It can cast shadows, the light is not the things it lights up – just like me! (See page 121.)

So our labels reflect inner feelings and the way others have labelled us, but we must be careful not to think that the feeling captures the self. The feeling is not yourself – it is (just) a feeling in your consciousness (about yourself) that you are having in this moment. Let's look at some typical examples that operate in depression.

The empty self

Some depressed people can see themselves as *empty*. Depression tends to knock out many of our positive emotions, and it is not uncommon to find that people lose feelings of affection for those around them. Hence they feel emotionally dead, drained and exhausted. As one patient told me, 'I am just an empty shell'. This is an example of allowing our feelings to dictate our thoughts. The *feeling* of being empty and alone is not the same as actually *being* an empty shell.

When dealing with these distressing feelings it can be helpful to recognize that they can be a natural symptom of depression.

Depression can knock out our capacity to feel. Thus, it is not you, as a person, who *cannot feel*; rather, you are *in a mental state of not feeling*. As soon as your mood lifts, you will feel again. Try not to attack yourself for your loss of feelings, even though it can be desperately sad and disappointing (see page 411). Indeed, if you focus on the sadness of it, rather than the badness, you might find that you want to cry, and crying might be the first glimmerings of a return of feelings. If this happens, put time aside to allow yourself to cry, check out if you have fears of crying and think about what they are. Think about how you may address those fears. Consider how in the past you have coped with these feelings, and you may have more courage than you are acknowledging.

Sometimes the experience of emptiness is linked not to negative things about the person but to the absence of positive things. Paula explained this feeling to me: 'I've never felt bad about myself really. I think I'm not a bad person on the whole, but I just feel that I'm a "wallpaper person".' She felt neither lovable nor unlovable; she just didn't feel anything strongly about herself one way or another. She revealed a history of emotional neglect by her parents. They had not been unkind to her in an aggressive way but were simply not interested in her. With no one in her life who she felt valued her, Paula had been left with feelings of emptiness and drifting through life. When she looked at the advantages and disadvantages of this idea of being a "wallpaper person", she discovered that, although it gave her a feeling of emptiness, it was also serving a useful purpose: *it protected her from taking any risks*. She had a motto: 'nothing ventured, nothing lost'.

This view of the self was also a safety strategy protecting Paula from the fears of going out into the world to try to achieve things and change her sense of herself. Changing things we feel safe and familiar with can be difficult and frightening – even if those things are not good for us.

One way to approach this is not to think of getting rid of anything. We can keep our old beliefs as long as we like, if we feel safe with them, but we can also try to build new ways of thinking and feeling and gradually see if we like those better as they become safe and familiar. Feel free to hang on to your beliefs as long as you feel you need them. Try not to feel that something is going to be taken away from you, leaving you vulnerable. But also allow yourself to *outgrow your old beliefs*.

Here are some ideas for building new self-experiences:

- Compassionately prepare yourself to take risks and learn how to cope with failure, disappointment and possible rejection (see Chapter 22). This will be much easier if you learn the art of being kind to yourself in the face of setbacks. We can start with small steps.
- Focus on times when you do have some feelings for things – maybe the music you enjoy, or watching a movie.
- Develop your mindful attention (Chapter 7) and note how your mind pulls your thoughts this way and that – so, far from empty.
- Consider that emptiness is a form of emotional reasoning, such as 'I feel empty therefore I am,' which, of course, does not make it true (see pages 213–15).
- Consider that what you are calling emptiness might actually be loneliness or a kind of lostness – unsure what you want to do or where to go in life. If so, be honest about that and gently accept it, but also see it as a specific problem to be worked with.
- Engage in your compassionate self work and imagery (see Chapter 8). Sometimes working to help others – making that a life goal – can give us a new sense of purpose.

As we have seen, a key step forward is to act against the feeling or thought that seems to be causing us trouble. Let's think why you are not empty. Consider your fantasies, dreams, desires and preferences. The pattern of your preferences makes you a unique person. For a start, you probably want to feel different from how you do now. That must mean that you desire to achieve a certain state of mind – not to be depressed any more.

Let's begin by looking at your preferences. What kinds of films do you prefer and what kinds do you tend to avoid? What kind of music do you like and what leaves you cold? What kind of food do you like and what makes you feel sick? Would you prefer to eat a freshly baked potato or a raw snake or a cockroach? Simple and silly ideas perhaps, but you do have preferences. What kinds of people do you like and feel comfortable with? Which season do you like best? What kinds of clothes do you prefer? If you say that you have no preferences, try wearing a salmon pink top with fluorescent green trousers that don't fit! The point is not so much that you are empty but that you may, for example, lack confidence to do the things you want, or be feeling very tired, of feel trapped in a lifestyle that is boring. You see, the label does not help you — but working out the actual problem might.

Think about what could happen if you started working on your preferences and developing them. This means not only thinking about your preferences but also acting on them, so it might lead to some anxiety. If so, write down your anxious thoughts and compassionately think how to shift them – see if your fears are exaggerated. How could you take steps to overcome your anxieties?

Suppose you admit that, however mild they might be, you do have preferences, and emptiness is in your feelings not fact. But then you might say, 'Yes, but I don't have any qualities *that another person might find attractive*.' That's another issue – that's not about you, but how you relate to other people. If this is what you think, then your feelings of emptiness may possibly be more related to loneliness. Or perhaps it's a problem of confidence. Have you shared your preferences with others? If not, what stops you? What would it take for you to turn to someone you know and say, 'I'd like to do this or that. Would you?' If you find that you have thoughts of, 'But they may not want to, or they might think that I was being silly or too demanding,' the problem is less one of emptiness and more one of confidence. It may be true you have a problem with confidence, and it's also true that if you do not practise expressing your preferences and desires it can sometimes be difficult to know them yourself. How can you learn what you like and enjoy if you don't try things out and discover you like this but you don't like that?

It may also be that you are being unrealistic. Do you want to be attractive to some people, or to everyone you meet? Are you too focused on social comparison (see pages 276–81)? Do you believe that, because your parents didn't seem that interested in you, nobody will ever be?

Here are some more balanced, helpful ways of thinking about this:

- Telling myself I'm empty is a form of emotional reasoning.
- I can learn to focus on my preferences and start to share these with others. It may be difficult, so I'll go one step at a time, but at least I'm on the road to developing.
- I may be discounting the positives in my life and saying that some things about myself don't count. If so, what would they be?
- I might be self-labelling here and not appreciating that all human beings are highly complex.

- Maybe it is not so much that I am empty but that I am lonely and I have difficulties in reaching out to others.
- Maybe it is a problem with confidence. If I felt more confident in expressing myself, would I feel empty?
- Am I attacking myself by saying that nobody could be interested in me without giving them much of a chance? If so, how could I give them a chance?

Feeling a nuisance

Nearly all of us humans want the approval of others. This often means that we want to be seen as having things (e.g., talents and abilities) to offer others, and it may be easier to care for others than to be cared for. One problem that can arise is that, when we have needs that can only be met by sharing our difficulties with other people, we feel that we are being a nuisance and may not deserve to be cared for (see Chapter 18). People can be riddled with guilt and shame about needing help. In their early life, their needs may not have been taken seriously. One patient of mine – whose motto was, 'A problem shared is a problem doubled'– was constantly monitoring the possibility that she was a burden to others. This led to guilt and feeling worse, which, of course, increased her need to be cared for and loved.

The fear of being a nuisance is a common one, but also a sad one. Of course we can feel like a nuisance in a whole variety of ways. Maybe we are physically unwell, are not as competent as others in the group and so on. Sometimes we may have difficulty in being fully open about our needs and asking others for help. Instead, we tend to 'beat about the bush' when it comes to our own needs and feelings, and send conflicting messages to others. People's sex lives can be full of these kinds of worries in approaching one's partner for a sexual encounter.

Sometimes patients come to therapy but feel awkward, and instead of getting down to the business of trying to sort out what they feel and why, they constantly worry about burdening me. They may feel they are not entitled to be in therapy, that their problems are not serious enough, that they are 'making mountains out of molehills'. Rather than allow us to come to a view on this together, they've already decided that they're being a nuisance to me. I explore this fear of being a nuisance quite early on. Sometimes it relates to shame, sometimes to a fear that I won't be able to cope with their needs because these are too great and complex. At other times it relates to trust: they think that, while I will be nice to them on the surface, secretly I will be thinking that they are time-wasters, that I will deceive them about my true feelings.

Concerns of being a nuisance and being a burden can be upsetting, so it's useful to consider the following points.

- All humans have a need for help from time to time.
- Am I labelling and criticizing myself for having these needs rather than facing up to them and understanding what they are?
- What does my compassionate/rational mind say about that?
- What is the evidence that other people won't help me or want to share with me if I ask them?
- Am I predicting a rejection before it comes?
- Am I choosing to ask people for help who I know in advance are not very caring, or would have difficulty understanding my feelings?
- Am I saying that all my needs must be met before I can be helped and therefore thinking in all-or-nothing terms?
- Are some of my needs more important than others? Can I work on a few specific problems or needs at a time?

- Can I break my needs down into smaller ones, rather than feeling overwhelmed by such large ones?
- Can I learn to be more assertive and clear about my specific needs? Would that help me?

There is another aspect that can be useful to consider. Sometimes we know that we are in need of healing or help and that we have to reach out to others, but we don't know what for or what exactly our needs are. That takes some thought, but if you do become clearer on these issues, *consider what you will do to help yourself if you do find someone who can meet some of your needs*. This is quite an important question. Of course, you might feel happier with some of your needs having been met, but how will this change you? How will you use these met needs for personal growth? When we think about this we sometimes recognize that we are looking for other people to help us develop confidence, or help us feel better. In fact, although others can be very helpful in this regard, these are things we need to work on for ourselves as well.

Sharon was afraid to ask her husband to spend more time with her and to be more affectionate. She thought that this would interfere with his work and that she was simply being a nuisance to him. However, as she explored these needs and considered how she would be different if they were satisfied, she realized that she actually needed his support and approval to boost her own self-confidence. Then she would be more able to go and find a job. By thinking what she would do if some of her needs were met – that is, how this would change her – she recognized two things: first, that there were things she could do for herself to help boost her own confidence (such as not criticizing herself and learning to be more assertive); and second, she recognized that she could be clearer with her husband about the fact that she wanted him to help her gain confidence to go looking for work.

Sharon also realized that seeking more affection from her husband might not be a burden but would actually strengthen the relationship, and this was something she could test. On reflection, she saw that her husband might well benefit from talking more about his feelings and needs, too. She was able to see that her needs could be joint needs. When she spoke to her husband about this, at first he did not really understand. But she stuck to her guns, and later he, too, came to see that he had been so focused on work that he had become lonely himself and felt their relationship was drifting. Not knowing how to address that, he drifted further into work. Moreover, he admitted that he knew that Sharon had felt down but was not sure what to do because she only spoke about her feelings in a general way, not the problems that lay behind her feelings – how she was bored and lonely in the house and she wanted to get out and find a job. To not burden her when she felt down, he had stopped sharing his own problems with her. We can stop sharing for fear of burdening others! Relationships flourish precisely because we share our needs and grow together, not because we hide them.

Fakery

Related to emptiness but different from it is the feeling that one is a fake. From an evolutionary point of view, deception and fakery have been very important behaviors for animals and humans. Quite a lot of animal behavior actually depends on fakery and bluff. Faking and bluffing can be very protective. It is also important to note that children have to learn how to lie. The ability to lie and fake things is actually an important social skill. However, when we become depressed we can feel as if everything we've done has been a pretence or a fake, or simply the result of luck. Depressed people begin to devalue their previous or current successes. The reasons for this vary. Sometimes they are perfectionists and think less of things that they feel are not up to standard. They know that there are flaws in their actions or achievements, but become overly focused on them. They think that they were pretending to be more competent. When a professor who held an exalted position in the academic world won a prestigious prize he became depressed, because he felt that he had fooled everyone and that all his writings were of little value. Success did not fit with this self-identity. There was also a fear that he might not maintain his reputation, people would find errors and it would collapse; people would then be very disappointed in him.

When depressed, we may also start to worry about whether the feelings we had for others in the past were genuine, or we were fooling ourselves. However, depression is the worst possible time to start making these kinds of decisions because it reduces the capacity for positive feelings, and we often become less affectionate. In addition, feeling that we are deceiving others can lead to guilt, which we then try to cover up (see Chapter 18).

When Brenda became depressed, she became preoccupied with having fooled Nick into marrying her and that she was now faking love for him. When she came to see me, we had a conversation that, boiled down to its essentials, went something like this:

Paul: *When you got married, did you think that you were faking your love for Nick?*

Brenda: *No, I wouldn't put it like that. I was, to be honest, more unsure about him and more worried than I let on, but we got on okay and I thought it would work.*

Paul: *Marriage can be a scary time, so maybe you had mixed feelings and were unsure of what to make of those feelings.*

Brenda: *Yeah, I guess so. It was a big step to get married and I was worried about whether I was making the right decision.*

Paul: *Do you think that being understandably worried about making the right decision means that you were being deceptive?*

Brenda: *I'm not sure.*

Paul: *Okay, well, let's put it this way. If you are being deceptive with Nick, is it possible that this is because you are confused in your mind and not sure what you really feel about him?*

Brenda: *Oh, yes, all my feelings seem confused right now.*

Paul: *Okay, well, let's see this problem as one of confusion rather than one of deliberate deception. Right now you may not feel a lot of love for Nick, but we aren't sure why that is. Maybe there are things you are resentful about, or maybe there are other reasons, but if we work through these, step by step, we might get a clearer picture of what you feel. The problem is, if you just attack yourself for feeling that you are deceiving Nick, then you will feel guilty and find it more difficult to sort out your feelings.*

This gradually made sense to Brenda. It turned out that, because she had not been passionately in love with Nick from the start, she felt in her heart that she had deceived him and this made her feel terribly guilty. To overcome her guilt, she would do things in the relationship that she did not want to do (e.g., sex, going out), but she also felt resentful for giving in. She felt rather used by Nick. Slowly Brenda began to see that her main feelings were actually anger and resentment. Once she stopped feeling guilty for having deceived Nick and faking love, she could move on to sort out the genuine problems in the relationship. To do this, she also had to recognize that love is complex and not at all like the movies make out. Brenda discounted the positive in her life by only focusing on her negative feelings and on the times she felt confused about her feelings for Nick rather than on the times she enjoyed being with him. Working on the resentment actually strengthened their relationship.

Sometimes people feel that they have no choice but to fake things. For instance, they may feel that they have to fake love, to hold together a relationship or a family or, as in the following example, a career. Mike faked a liking for his boss who, he thought, could sack him if he did not make a good impression. He came to hate himself for being (as he saw it) weak. However, he could have looked at it differently. He could have said, 'I understand that I need to hold on to this job and I don't have that much power to do this other than creating a good impression and getting on with my boss. Actually, I am a very skilled social operator.' This is not to say that it's okay to fake – that's a personal decision. Rather, we need to be honest about it, understand the reasons for it and avoid attacking ourselves for it. If we want to reduce the degree to which we fake things with others, we need to learn how to be more self-confident, compassionate with ourselves and others, and assertive. That will be hard to do if we are attacking and running ourselves down.

The fear of being a fake is not only associated with guilt (as it was for Brenda) but carries the fear of shame (Chapter 17) and being found out. Some people live in constant fear that, because they are living a pretend life, they will be found out, ridiculed and shunned.

Here are some ways to think about dealing with feelings of being a fake:

- It may be true that I may have been lucky in some things, but this cannot account for everything I have achieved. I must have some talent, even if it is not as great as I would like.
- Sometimes I fake things because I am confused and/or frightened. It would be better to work on this confusion and fear rather than simply attack myself for the fakery and pretence.
- Faking or not faking is rarely all-or-nothing. There are degrees of faking and some are actually helpful.
- If, since I feel like a fake, I believe I am a fake, this is emotional reasoning. I could be more balanced in my thinking here.
- Feeling like a fake is often a symptom of depression. My depression may not be giving me an accurate view of things or myself.
- If faking is upsetting me, it would be better for me to understand my reasons for it. I might then be in a better position to change. If I attack myself for faking, I will feel much worse and need to fake more, not less. Let's be compassionate here and see what lies behind these feelings.

Fakery and deception are more commonly experienced in depression than is often recognized, and the question of fakery and deception often goes to the heart of many social dilemmas. We can feel intensely guilty when we know that we are not being fully honest and genuine. Or we can feel very vulnerable when we are not confident of our behavior or performance and think others might spot the flaws and regard us as fakes. The problem is that, in many situations, there is often no one genuine feeling but many different feelings. If you have a row with your partner today, this does not mean that all the other good times you had together were fake. If you are depressed, this does not mean that the other times when you felt good or achieved things were a pretence; it means that you can feel different things at different times and when in different states of mind.

Be honest with yourself

Self-honesty can be very difficult and in fact we may never actually achieve it because so much of what goes on in the mind is actually outside of our consciousness – this is not our fault of course! Nonetheless it is important to try, and this will become easier once you learn self-kindness, to replace self-criticism and take balanced positions on things (avoiding black-and-white and either–or thinking). When it comes to expressing feelings and behaviors to others my main thought is whether it is helpful or destructive. Sometimes we are kind to others when we don't really feel like it, because we know that it is good for them or they will like us. Sometimes we have to learn more assertiveness or to become skilful social players, recognizing that at times hiding our feelings is actually a quite useful protective ability.

The key issue is not to be critical but to think what would help you to be more able to express your feelings if that's what you want to do, or accept that you may not be able to in certain contexts. For example, Karen carried a lot of anger towards her mother over various things in her childhood. Over a number of years she planned what she wanted to say and would sometimes ruminate on her anger, but when she saw her mother she was always kind and polite. Then her mother became very ill, and it was clear that Karen was never going to express her feelings. Developing compassion for the dilemma Karen had been in, giving up telling herself 'I should've told her earlier!', which also had some degree of self-anger, was helpful. Karen learned and developed compassionate acceptance, that she wasn't honest with her mother, but had chosen to protect her mother. Like all things in life there were advantages and disadvantages, and she could come to accept that. Indeed, Karen was able to think about her caring and polite side and her self-sacrifice in a positive light instead of an angry, self-critical light.

KEY POINTS

- We often experience ourselves as if we could be summed up in single words (weak, empty, inadequate, unlovable, fake, etc.).
- The labels may vary from person to person, but most of them imply a negative rather than a positive judgement of ourselves.
- When negative feelings and labels become central to the way we experience ourselves, they can influence much of what we feel and think (look back at page 28).
- It is helpful to recognize that these labels are often based on anger, frustration, disappointment, fear or loneliness, or may come from what other people have said to you and how they have labelled you.

EXERCISES

Exercise 1

Look at the labels that appeared listed on page 306 and see if you think that any of these apply to you. If not, maybe there are others that might apply. Examine whether you tend to sum yourself up in single words. Single words can't really describe your complex feelings and thoughts though, can they?

Exercise 2

Begin to use your compassionate/rational mind to generate alternatives to these single labels. For example:

- Label says: 'I am a failure'
- Compassionate/rational mind says _____
  (create a compassionate expression as you read through below)

'This label comes from feeling depressed, and when I am depressed, I tend to think in a lot of negative ways. For example, I tend to discount the positives in my life and indulge in emotional reasoning. Sure, right now I feel bad – but let's not turn that bad feeling into an attack on the whole of me. Successes and failures come and go in one's life, but these are not the essence of a person. My feeling is more one of anger, frustration and disappointment and everyone's entitled to those feelings. I would not label my friends like this if they had setbacks and disappointments; I would be understanding of their feelings. Perhaps I need to learn to do that to myself as well. What evidence is there against this label? Am I being all-or-nothing here? If I was helping a friend in a similar situation, what would I say to them?'

Work out if this kind of compassionate reasoning is helpful to you. Be aware that you might tend to undermine your efforts to switch into a more compassionate, gentle and balanced approach. Ask yourself, 'What have I got to lose by really focusing on these alternatives for a while and seeing if they help?' Remember, in depression we are usually very good at focusing on the negatives. Negative beliefs from childhood and stress hormones incline us to focus on the negative. The task now is to develop the ability to look for the positives. The more you practise attending to the positives, the better this will be for your mood and reducing stressful signals.

Exercise 3

When did you first start to think of yourself in this way? Is it the depression speaking, or was it other people who told you these things that labelled you? If it is others, then follow these steps.

1 Take a piece of paper and write down some times you can recall where others labelled you in a certain way, or by their actions gave you the impression of what they thought about you. Sadly people label other people all the time, and it's how we deal with it that's important.

2 Consider what might have been in the mind of the labellers or name-callers or people who judged you or criticized you. Did they have your their best interests at heart? Really think about this now. Were they doing this from a position of genuine caring and concern about you? How did it benefit **them** to label you in this way? Did it stop them having to blame themselves? Were you simply an easy target? Were they people who tended to be somewhat bullying and easily frustrated in many other situations? In thinking about this then consider what is in it for you to buy into their views. Maybe you did at the time out of fear, confusion or the hope they would love you – but maybe these people are not reliable judges – and if we are truly honest you know that in your heart.

What we are trying to do here is to help you not to take these judgements at face value. This can be hard, because sometimes we feel we should accept the judgements of others, especially our parents. Not to do so can feel like a bit of a rebellion or even a betrayal – so you might have to have a go at this one a few times.

3 Sometimes it can help to imagine yourself having a conversation with your compassionate image and talking through these situations. Remember these are *compassionate* discussions, the kind of conversation you might have with someone in your situation who you really care about and who you want to see free of suffering. When engaged in this work, try to create kind, understanding feelings in yourself. You may then wish to think about whether the time has come to grow away from the labels that others have given you, to become your own person. Allow yourself to think of letting go these labels if you don't need or want them. What effort would

that take? What would the advantages and disadvantages be? What would stop you doing this?

4 Here is an exercise that you will have read a few times now. Engage your soothing rhythm breathing and take up a relaxed posture. Create feelings of compassion within yourself, imagining yourself to be a mature, wise, caring, warm person who does not get flustered. Remind yourself of you 'at your best'. Adopt a kind facial expression and allow yourself to note that feeling. With that kind facial expression, imagine the part of you that labels you standing in front of you. Look at its facial expressions and the motives behind the labelling. Extend your compassion to it, see the fears behind the labelling. Whatever the labelling part of you says, whether it tries to ridicule you or put you down in some way, remember you are the compassionate side, the wise side, you've seen this all before and are not taken in by it. Continue to send your compassion to this part of you and see what happens. If you feel too drawn in to the labels, pull back and refocus on the compassionate self until that feels stable again – then repeat.

5 In the next part of the exercise we will do exactly the same except this time we will focus on the part that has been labelled and is feeling bad, empty or beaten down in some way. Again, look at that part and extend your compassion to it, not in a sorry or pitying way but simply with a desire for it to recover from its suffering and to flourish. Then, using kind thoughts, focus on the belief that it can and will recover.

Experiment with different exercises, perhaps combining them, and seeing which ones seem to work for you. The more effort and reflection you put into your practice, the more you are likely to benefit because you are taking control to retrain your mind. Remember the essence of yourself is like your consciousness, your spotlight – not what it illuminates. The feelings are feelings *in you* but are not the essence of *you* (see Chapter 7).

15

Further ways of helping ourselves change

This chapter explores some other options for working against depressive thoughts and feelings and trying to change our brain states. It might be helpful to try some of the exercises in the previous chapters first, so that you have some experience of identifying your thoughts and generating alternatives, before you try the ideas here, so see how you go.

Flash cards

Flash cards can be used as reminders of the sort of useful things that you tell yourself when you are feeling depressed. To make a flash card, take a blank postcard or a similarly sized piece of paper. On one side, write down one of your most typical negative thoughts; then, on the other side, write down some key helpful alternatives to this. Repeat this exercise for the depressing or anxious thoughts you usually have.

For example, suppose that you have the thought: 'I will never get better.' On a day when you don't feel quite so bad, write out this thought on one side of a card. On the other side, write down what you imagine you might say to a friend who had such a thought, or how you imagine someone who cares for you might speak to you. Remember, consider these ideas not with a cold mind but with as much warmth and friendliness as you can muster – as if someone who cares about you is encouraging you to make your journey out of depression. Here are some alternatives to try:

- This is a very distressing idea. However, it is very common for depressed people to think and feel like this so it is natural and normal to feel like this because I am depressed.
- I can therefore just be mindful of this thought and feeling and see it as being produced by the depression. I can let the idea be there without running away trying to avoid it or dwelling on it and assuming it is true.
- This is typical of all depression – it always looks on the dark side. I am one with others on this.
- Because I feel like this, it does not make it true or a fact. The evidence is that people do recover from depression. I can be accepting of this thought, see it as an understandable thought – but not a fact. I can stand to the side of it.
- Although I (understandably) want to feel really well right away, I might be trying to achieve too much. Maybe I could aim for a little improvement and work with that, step by step.
- Focusing on the idea 'I will never get better', although understandable, will make me feel worse. It would therefore be preferable to focus on what I can do rather than what I can't. How can I act against this belief and practise redirecting my attention and my behavior?
- It could be a good idea to distract myself from dwelling on these thoughts, perhaps by listening to the radio, taking myself out for a walk or doing some gardening. While doing this I will try to focus my attention mindfully on the activity.

- If I learn to go step by step, I might learn to get more control over my depression. Let's really give it a go and see how far we can get.

When you look at these ideas, how do they seem? Are there ways of discounting them running through your mind – as is typical in depression? Are you thinking, 'Yes, but', or 'This might be okay for other people but not for me' or 'It's too simple'? If you are having these thoughts, remember – this is the depression speaking. What have you got to lose by trying? How might you be kind and understanding to your dismissive thoughts, but not let them decide your actions or take control? What happens if you read them through but focus on 'hearing them in your mind' in as kind and warm a way as you can? Why not have a go?

Let's try another typical depression-maintaining thought that involves self-labelling: 'I am a bad, weak or inadequate person for being depressed. I never thought it would happen to me.' Your flash card might list some of the following:

- There is nothing bad, weak or abnormal about me because I am depressed. Up to one in five people could have times when they feel like me.
- Many celebrities and people in high places (film stars and politicians) have suffered from depression. Depression can't be about weakness if all these people can get depressed, too. Winston Churchill suffered from depression, which he called his 'black dog', and he was hardly a weak person. It is to do with our brain design.
- I would not speak to friends like this. I would try to understand and encourage them. Labelling them (and me) bad or weak does no good at all. It is just another form of bullying.

- When I get depressed, I focus on all my bad points. This is usually to do with my frustration or disappointment. The time has come to learn to be kind and understanding of my setbacks and my frustrations.

You can carry your flash cards with you, in a pocket or handbag, and take them out to give you a boost and help. Some people find pinning cards up in particular places around the house can be beneficial. For example, a woman I know who wanted to lose weight and had trouble controlling her snacking put a card on her refrigerator. It read:

So you feel like a snack right now? But think about this. Do you really need it? Would you feel better if you resisted the urge? Have a cup of tea instead. Hold on and you will be pleased with yourself tomorrow.

By reading this every time she was tempted to snack, she gained that little bit of extra control.

Compassionate cards

A slight variation of the above flash card idea is the following. Find a postcard or photograph that you really like, with a picture that gives a calm and soothing impression. One woman chose a picture of a mountain which she thought conveyed strength and calmness. Another chose to make her own card from some paintings and coloured paper. Choose any picture you like – it might even be one that makes you smile. Since you know what your depression thoughts are, you don't need to write those. All you need to do is write down your alternative compassionate thoughts (maybe like the ones we tried above) on the back of the picture. When you are happy with this, then look at your picture, create a soothing rhythm in your breathing and adopt a kind facial expression. Read your alternatives, then flip the card and look at the picture and try to feel soothing and acceptance for you. Try that a couple of times. You can use your card when you're feeling distressed – don't forget that slight smile and kind facial expression because this will be stimulating muscles in your face and feeding back into your brain. With practice, you may find it helpful. As for all of these ways of working with your depression, try them out and see how you get on. Introduce you own ideas for working on your depressed brain state.

Preparing yourself for stressful situations

If you know that you have something stressful coming up, you can prepare for it in advance. You can use flash cards as reminders for coping. For example, suppose you are going to have people over for a meal. One response might be, 'Oh God, it's too much. I'll never cope.' You could write down some key coping thoughts before the event:

- Maybe it won't be as bad as I think. Let's get the evidence.
- I can break down what I have to do into small steps. Each small step might be 'do-able'.
- Filling my head with 'can't do' thoughts is understandable but it would help if I refocus my attention and thoughts (see pages 190–95).
- I can develop a plan of action. I can rehearse the relaxation skills while I'm doing it and see if that helps me.
- I can learn to accept and tolerate my anxiety and feelings without running away. I can remind myself I have coped with these in the past. It's the body getting into its anxiety routine. I understand that this is extremely unpleasant, but not dangerous.

- I can focus my attention on what I'm doing. If I start to criticize myself, I'll say, 'Look, I'm doing okay' and really focus on that – and okay means 'okay', not necessarily marvellous.
- When the guests arrive, I can give them drinks and ask them about themselves. People like to be asked things about themselves; the focus does not have to be on me.
- If I feel tense during the meal, I can work on my relaxation. I can get up, go to the kitchen, or go outside for some air. I am not trapped here. I am free to go where I want – it's my house.
- I can deliberately practise imagining it going reasonably well, and feeling pleased, rather than only imagining it going badly. The aim is to show myself that I can cope and this is all I want to do right now. I will avoid all-or-nothing thinking (i.e. it has to be great or it's a failure).
- Each step of the way, I will focus on doing okay. I can do my best to keep my inner helper with me and praise myself for any small success.
- Practise making a real commitment to change and take on the challenge. Think about and build an image in your mind of how you will feel when you do.

The aim of this kind of work is to help you to prepare for things that you might find difficult. The more you try focusing on coping, the easier it may get.

If emotions could speak

Some depressed people say that they do not have clear thoughts going through their minds, only feelings. I remember once driving to work feeling rather down. At first, I could not focus on anything in particular, so I used the technique of, 'If my feelings could speak, what would they say?' I tried to get my 'down' feeling to tell me what was wrong. As I followed this idea, I found that I could begin to identify what my down feeling was about. It said, rather out of the blue, 'Your life is going nowhere. You're getting old now and your chances have gone.' As I followed this thought, I recognized that it had been triggered by playing cricket. Through my thirties, I had been too involved with work to play the game, which I had enjoyed in my youth, but had taken it up again in my mid-forties. Although I'd been a reasonable player when I was at university, I wasn't now. Compared to the younger players, I was a lumbering oldie with a poor eye for the ball. I suddenly realized that I was grieving for my lost youth! If fact, my thoughts were not really accurate about what I was really feeling. I was not actually worried about my life going nowhere (I was doing quite well, in fact) but was upset about losing my youth. Sometimes our thoughts are *not* actually accurate reflections of our feelings. When we allow our feelings to speak freely, they can take us to some strange and interesting places.

So if you can't identify thoughts but you can identify feelings, say to yourself, 'If my feelings could speak, what would they say?' Speak out loud the things that come into your mind; let the ideas flow. As you allow your thoughts to flow, be aware of them but avoid trying to direct them anywhere. Be mindful. See what comes up, what passes through your mind when you focus on the feelings. Be prepared to draw a blank sometimes, or for thoughts not to make much sense. The idea here is to allow yourself to go on your own journey of guided discovery.

Speaking with different parts of ourselves

So far we have talked about having depressing thoughts, anxious thoughts, angry thoughts, rational thoughts, compassionate thoughts and so on. Sometimes it is helpful to think of these thoughts as if they represent different parts of ourselves, and use an approach that allows us to name these various 'parts' or types of thoughts (see pages 87–8). Self-critical thoughts can be called the 'internal bully', self-supportive thoughts can be named the 'inner helper', 'compassionate image, friend or nurturer' and so forth. If we give space to these inner selves (types of thoughts), it allows us to observe and listen to the different types of conversations going on inside us. The point is that we are not one-dimensional beings, and in many situations we can have a mixture of thoughts and feelings.

Sometimes we can learn to pay attention to what different parts of us are saying by using different chairs. For example, sitting in one chair we become one part (e.g., the angry self, or anxious, sad or critical self). We give full voice to the thoughts, concerns and feelings. Then we get up, take a few steps and a soothing breath and sit in a facing chair and become the wise, compassionate self who has listened intently, is understanding and helpful. Pay close attention to the thoughts that flow here. If not much comes then imagine speaking to someone else for a moment – someone you care for – and also make a note to practise becoming the compassionate self more often.

Something else you might find helpful is a 'playful' style, playing each part as if you were trying to win an Oscar. This is not at all easy when we are depressed, but this does not mean we cannot be playful and take our inner thoughts less seriously.

A word of caution – if your self-critical side is not only your own disappointment and put-downs but also reminds you of someone who was very hurtful or harmful to you, then your compassionate side needs to be assertive and stand up to the 'voice from the past'. This can be tough and may need to be worked though with help or a therapist. As always, only go with these exercises insofar as you find them helpful to you (see page 303).

Changing depressive images

When we are depressed, we often feel as if we are in a deep hole or pit and our internal images are very dark and harsh. Because this internal world can blacken our lives, it is sometimes helpful to work with these images directly. If you feel in a deep hole, imagine a ladder coming down to you and that you are climbing out, rung by rung. Practise the imagery before sleeping. It would be nice to jump out in one go, but that's only possible for a superman or superwoman and I have yet to meet one of those. Each time you succeed at something, that's one more rung up the ladder.

If your inner image is dark, try imagining getting some light in by installing some windows, or build a door and get out. Try not to accept the image passively, but start to change it so that it becomes more healing.

Carol had thought about getting out of a difficult relationship and coping on her own, but her internal image was always of living in some dark, cold place that nobody ever visited and which she never left. She thought that some of her dark images might have had their origins in being left in a cot in a dark room as a child. By focusing on one of these images and using active imagination (i.e. moving into the image), it became clear how dark this image of being out of the relationship actually was. Then it became possible for her to explore and change the image. She imagined what she could do in this place to change it, how she would like her own place to look, how she might decorate it, what pictures she might put on the walls, what flowers she might buy, what friends she might invite around, and so on.

The key thing about images is that, once you have a sense of them, you can work on how you would like them to change. Avoid simply bringing the image to mind and then feeling worse because you are not working to change it. It is changing the image that is important.

Sometimes people enjoy painting. People who are depressed tend to paint dark pictures, but it can be helpful to paint healing ones. Think about the kinds of images that are healing. These may be of a country scene, or of water – a seascape, for instance. Again the key idea is to acknowledge the dark images but also to introduce light and healing.

Changing values

We learn some of our values and attitudes because important people in our lives have told us that some values are good or punished us if we did not conform to them. Our attitudes towards sex, religion or the expression of anger are often learned in this way. Sometimes we adopt values by copying others, even those in society in general. For example, there is concern today that thinness is so highly valued as a female trait that many young women are getting caught in over-restrictive diets that can spiral into eating and weight problems. We take certain of these values into ourselves (i.e. we *internalize* them) and they become our own values and the ways that we judge ourselves.

Getting out of depression sometimes means that we have to re-examine our values and our attitudes. This may be enormously difficult and painful because we may lose our sense of who we are and have to accept new risks. To make matters worse, we may feel a great sense of disloyalty in changing our values from the ones our parents have given us. Sometimes we cling to values that are quite harmful to us because, in the back of our minds, we still hope to succeed with them and make our parents (or others) proud of us.

Sam had a high need to achieve and do well because his father had told him that only achievement counts in the world. Sam knew that his style of pushing to achieve, achieve, achieve and his intense self-criticisms were doing him no good, and he also worked out that the voice of his inner critic sounded very much like his father. And yet, despite this insight, he could not let go of the idea, 'If I don't achieve anything, I am worthless.' For him to give up these values required him to give up the idea that he would, one day, get it right and prove himself. That had always been his hope, and to abandon that seemed like letting his father down and leaving himself with nothing in life to aim for. It took a long time for him to see that, while achieving things was nice and gave him a buzz, it was not helpful to base his whole self-worth on it; that putting all his eggs in one basket was a severe restriction on his sense of worth; and that his father had been wrong to imply that Sam was nothing without achievement.

To help you explore these sorts of issues, write down two columns. In the first, write down the values that you think that you have learned from others. In the second, list the values you would like to impart to someone you love – e.g., a son or daughter. Table 15.1 shows an example.

Far from being weak or no good, depressed people are often following their values to the letter, bending in every conceivable way to make them work. If they fail at this, they don't re-examine their values but attack themselves vigorously. In fact, it is the strength of their efforts to maintain their values that can, at times, drive them into depression. The main problem here is that, although they may 'fight' the depression, do all the things they believe they should do and stick rigidly to their (learned)

TABLE 15.1 ATTITUDES AND VALUES

Possible attitudes/values I have learned from others in my life	Attitudes I would like to impart to someone else (e.g. a child or friend) to help them be happy
You should not express anger	It is important to be able to express your feelings and not hide them. Anger can be turned into assertiveness. It is also about being honest with yourself and others
Other people's needs are more important than your own	Everybody's needs are important. If you only attend to others, you will become out of touch with your own needs and become just a servant. Eventually you will get depressed and be less able to care for anyone
Being depressed is a sign of weakness	Depression is a painful state of mind that needs to be understood. Throughout history, many millions of people have been depressed

values and judgements, they end up enduring their depression but not actually changing it. They think that, with a little more effort, they will win through. But challenging depression may mean exploring values and attitudes that are no longer useful, such as our tendencies to overwork or over-commit ourselves. Working hard to get well may mean working hard to change some of our attitudes – not just following them more vigorously.

Life scripts

Another way to think about attitudes and values is to tackle them in the form of *life scripts* or as typical roles we easily slip into. These offer us an identity – a sense of the person we are. For example, think for a moment about what kind of person you are. Try completing this sentence

I am the kind of person who _____

You may have many endings, not just one.

What did you come up with? Did you have things like:

I am the kind of person who cares for others/is a hard worker/should never show anger?

or

I am the kind of person who always loses out/gives in/gets left behind/fails at the last hurdle?

or

I am the kind of person who waits to be chosen rather than actively chooses/does not show off?

Perhaps you had much more positive ones too. The point about life scripts is that they are like parts in a play. At times, it can seem as if we are performing a part written by someone else. We might even blame fate. Over the next few days ponder on how you might answer this question and see if any new ideas come to your mind. See if one of your life scripts – a role you play, such as 'do as others want', or 'Mr Angry' seems to repeat. If so, write these repetitions down and think about where this script might have come from. Gently consider what you would have to do to change it, how might you act in different ways if you had different values. To begin with, *play* with a few ideas.

Another life script you might try is:

I am the kind of person who is not or does not _____

Here you might write

I am the kind of person who is not selfish/deliberately hurtful to others for fun

or

I am the kind of person who does not enjoy sex/put my needs first/cheat on others and so on. Forming an identity often means discovering things we think we are and things we think we are not.

If you identify a life script – a style of living that makes you 'you'– think about how you might wish to change it. What would you need to do? Can you go some way towards being more as you would like to be? Recall that change can be slow, step by step.

KEY POINTS

- You can make flash cards with depressing or upsetting thoughts and then compassionately note those and generate alternatives to act as reminders and to refocus your mind.
- Allow your emotions to speak. Give them a voice and then explore their inner meaning.
- Use empty chairs to enable yourself to express out loud the various types of thoughts that might be going through your mind from the different posts of yourself.
- Consider some of the images that you have in your mind when depressed and introduce more soothing and healing images.
- Consider some of your basic life values and attitudes and decide if they are useful to you. For those that aren't, change them by thinking about the values you might want to impart to someone else. Those values are more likely to be your own genuine values and attitudes.
- All of us live out various roles or 'life scripts'. These can be changed if we give ourselves the space to consider what they might be and how we might tackle them step by step.

EXERCISES

These have been discussed within the chapter (e.g., making flash cards). The key point is to be as supportive and encouraging as you can and to see this as something to practise.

PART IV
Special Problems Associated with Depression

In this section, we will apply the ideas discussed in Parts II and III to specific problems in depression, some of which may apply to you and some of which may not. The chapters in this section can be worked through in order, but it's not essential. If you don't understand certain sections, skip them and come back to them later. Some chapters cover the same ground and similar issues, but from different points of view.

16

Approval, subordination and bullying: Key issues in relationships

Approval

We begin Part IV with the issue of approval because desires to be approved of, accepted, included, wanted, recognized, appreciated, valued and respected are often at the heart of many of our personal conflicts and worries when we're depressed. When we explore other problem areas, such as shame, anger, disappointment and perfectionism, we will find that the issue of approval from others and fear of the opposite – criticism, rejection or marginalization – is often in the background, if not in the foreground.[1]

Before we explore how needs for approval are often tied up with depression we need to understand one thing. Humans have evolved to be a very social species whose very survival has depended upon the care, support and friendship of others. We even have special systems in our brain that monitor what we think others think about us, and will often try to work out if people like or don't like us. Seeking approval is something all humans do. Otherwise, the fashion industry would get nowhere! Think, for a moment, what our world would be like if no one cared what others thought of them, if no one worried about gaining approval – and yes, there are some people who seem to be like that.

Feeling cared about and wanted can affect us in many ways. When we face crises or tragedies in our life it's our ability to turn to others and feel supported and comforted by them that can help us get through. The problem is that because of early life difficulties or current life stresses, we can come to feel so alone and different that we become very dependent on other people's approval and support. There is also good evidence that for some people not having anybody to talk to or share feelings with may be associated with depression.

We also know that in an effort to feel accepted and win approval people can sometimes become very submissive and focus on pleasing others. In that way they get out of balance with self-development and social connectedness. Yet other people who really would benefit from talking about their feelings and opening up to others actually close down and withdraw as they become depressed. This is sometimes due to feelings of shame, fear of being misunderstood or a sense of being a burden, or sometimes because, for them, being with other people means they would have to put on an act.

Competing for approval

Much of our competitive conduct is related to gaining approval – whether it be passing an exam, winning a sports competition or beauty contest, or even having friends say nice things about our cooking. We often do these things to court other people's approval, to feel valued. Children compete and compare over the latest cool clothes, music or video games. We want other people to see us as able, competent, or cool, to raise our status and standing in their eyes. Be it with bosses, friends or our lovers, we want them to think well of us. We also have a need to belong to groups and to form relationships, and so avoid being seen as inferior or rejected. Indeed, people will do all kinds of crazy things to win the approval and acceptance of others, be this of friends, parents or even God.

We can start to feel a bit depressed if we feel this competition is going badly and that compared to others we're not doing so well. This takes us back to social comparison, discussed in Chapter 3 on pages 276–81. Feeling that other people are doing better than us can stimulate our envy and rumination and sense of inferiority. This in turn can drive the desire to win approval.

Approval and self-judgements

We are biologically set up so that other people's approval and acceptance can help us feel good and their disapproval and rejection feel bad. However, we are likely to meet both during our lives and so we need to work out how to deal with both. Unfortunately, our need for approval can become a trap when we pursue it to an excessive degree. We can become rather submissive – overly trying to please others (people pleasers), panicky if we don't and – worse still – self-critical. We also might not be able to cope with conflicts and disappointments in relationships. Even our nearest and dearest can be disapproving some of the time, or fail to notice things about us that we would like them to give special attention to. Sometimes they are just in a bad mood, of course. For example, Liz had a new hairstyle and hurried home to show Carl. He had liked her old hairstyle and was unsure about the new one, so he was cagey about whether he liked it or not. Liz felt deflated and started to think, 'I thought he'd really like it but he doesn't. Maybe I made a mistake. Perhaps other people won't like it either. Why can't I do anything right?' Liz started to feel inadequate with herself and angry with Carl. Note how Liz's disappointment turned into:

- All-or-nothing thinking: 'He doesn't like it,' rather than 'He's unsure' or 'He likes it a little' or 'He may come to like it when he's used to it.'
- Overgeneralization: 'Others won't like it,' instead of 'I like it and the people in the shop said it looked good. Just because Carl is unsure doesn't mean that everyone won't like it.'
- Self-criticism and self-attack: 'Why can't I do anything right?' instead of 'A hairstyle is a hairstyle and not evidence that I do things right or wrong.'

Can you see here how Liz's disappointment and frustration is fuelling this self-criticism? Liz could simply recognize the disappointment and leave it at that, rather than use those feelings to be critical of herself.

A helpful way to cope could be to compassionately recognize and accept this as disappointment.

Oh, this is disappointing as I was hoping Carl would like it – so it is understandable to feel a bit deflated. He usually comes round, but even if not, I like my hair and it is helpful for me to start accepting what I like even if others are less sure. This is helping me become more my own person and this can help our relationship.

So learning to cope with this difficulty is actually an opportunity for growth.

Some people have feelings of inner emptiness if they do not constantly gain the approval of others. Wants, wishes and what were once thought to be good ideas seem to evaporate the moment another person does not go along with them or seems to disapprove. If this is the case for you, think about the possibility that you can start to find your own self by exploring your own preferences. Search inwards rather than outwards. Review the section on the empty self on pages 308–13. Ask yourself what things you can value that do not depend on other people's approval. Even if someone disagrees, this is not 'all-or-nothing' – it is not the case that they are right and I am wrong.

Mind reading

When we become depressed, we can need so much reassurance that we become extremely sensitive to the possibility that others do not like or approve of us – they might be deceiving us. Sometimes we may engage in what is called *mind reading*[2] (see pages 207–8). In this situation, rather small cues of disapproval are seen as major put-downs or rejections. A friend hurries past in the street and does not seem to want to talk to you. If you are depressed, you might think, 'My friend does not really like me and wants to avoid me,' rather than, 'S/He seems rushed and hassled today'.

If you are unhappy with someone's attitude towards you (perhaps because they were critical or ignored you), it is helpful to reflect and balance your thoughts. You can go through a number of steps. Remember, the first step is always to be understanding and kind to what we feel. If somebody criticizes you or doesn't praise you when you were looking for it, acknowledge that this is upsetting. The more we are honest about our feelings, the more we will be able to work with them kindly. Once you have been kind, understanding and accepting of your feelings of disappointment or upset then it's possible to stand back and think about your situation in a range of ways. Remember that standing back and using your compassionate and rational mind requires you to consider some questions in a kindly way, with a genuine desire to help you find balance in your thinking and not become more distressed than you need be. Try some questions like these. Ask yourself:

- Did the critical remark or look really represent a major put-down?
- In truth, is it my anger that has got to me – even if I am not voicing it?
- Was that really to do with me or were they just in an irritable mood today?
- How would I have felt about it if I was not depressed?
- Am I mind reading and thinking that the person thinks more negatively about me than they actually do?
- Am I assuming that a small disruption in the relationship is a sign of a major breakdown in it?
- Am I thinking in all-or-nothing terms or overgeneralizing? For example, am I saying, 'If someone cares about me, they must never ignore or criticize me.'
- What will I think about this event in a week's or month's time – am I likely even to remember it?
- Am I expecting others never to have a bad day and be grumpy or irritable?
- What is the most helpful thing for me to focus on now?

The subordinate self

The subordinate approval trap

The subordinate approval trap often begins when you feel low in self-worth but you work out that you can feel better about yourself if others approve of you. You set out on a life's task of winning approval – which, on the face of it, sounds like a good idea, but the way you seek to gain approval might involve various unhelpful things. For example, you might try to be what another person wants you to be. You might avoid owning up to your own needs or feelings. You might hide your anger. You might be overly accommodating, hoping that the other person will appreciate this. You might do things you don't really want to do but don't want to risk criticism or disapproval. This is a matter of degree, of course, because we all engage in these behaviors to some extent, but when we get depressed or when we are vulnerable to depression it can be to quite a large extent. Sadly, what can happen is that other people may get used to you simply fitting in, and the odd nod of disapproval can have you hurrying back to please them. You end up feeling like a doormat and worthless. You may also feel rather resentful after all the effort you put in. What do you do? Well, you'll go back to your old strategies. You know how to deal with feeling worthless – you try to win other people's approval, right? – and so around and around we go, as Figure 16.1 shows.

Figure 16.1 Feeling worthless circle.

Getting out of this circle requires that you are aware that you are in it, and that it is, to a degree, you who are setting yourself up for it. Next try to compassionately change the idea that you are worthless. Remember that this is a self-label (see Chapter 14) and is likely to be kept in place by your inner critic (see Chapter 13). Remind yourself that 'worthless' is a label and unhelpful. For the longer term your compassionate mind can support you in a journey of growth and change. This might start with gradually thinking about, recognizing and of valuing your feelings, learning simple acts of self-assertiveness, learning to see how you can enjoy some time alone and doing things you *want* to do.

Understanding and coping with disapproval

Of course, approval may matter a lot when it helps us get a job or get on in a relationship. Again *we're all like this to a degree* – so it is a matter of degree. However, a serious difficulty arises when we make negative judgements about ourselves if we don't get the approval we want. Here's an example: You put what you thought was a good idea to others at work, but they are not impressed and said that it was poorly thought out. A flush of feeling that sweeps through you directs your thoughts to:

- Oh no! They must think I'm not very bright.
- This is terrible. I've damaged my reputation.
- I should have thought it through more.
- I am stupid to have opened myself up to such criticism.
- Why do I always put my big foot in it?

What has happened here is that the disappointment and concern with the criticism has sent a flush of anxiety through you. If you are new to the team you may (understandably) want to impress them. We need to be kind, understanding and accepting of the anxiety and then not let our more extreme thoughts go through our minds unexamined or untested out. It helps to learn to cope with this because the chances are you'll want to offer another idea at some point and don't want to be so anxious that you can't say what you want to say. Here are some compassionate and rational balancing ideas – but you may think of others that suit you better.

- These meetings are an anxious time, so it is only natural to feel anxious and cagey about this event. **It's quite normal** – the key thing is how I cope with this normal anxiety.
- Well, it's disappointing that my idea didn't catch on, but reputations are not damaged in single incidents like this. Maybe I'm upset because my pride's been hurt a little. I can live with that.
- Other people get criticized, too – not just me. This is how these meetings are.
- Nothing risked, nothing gained.
- The critic in the meeting tends to be like this with others – a bit bullying really.
- If I can learn to cope with this type of criticism, rather than telling myself how bad it is or how stupid I am, I'm going to be better able to cope in the future and it will increase my confidence.
- Even if I fail, this does not make me a stupid person. And in any case, failure is not all-or-nothing. There are parts of my idea that are still good – I just need to work on them more.
- My disappointment is masking the positive aspects of my self and what I can contribute.

You could also be honest with yourself and think about whether your desire to impress did indeed mean that you were a bit rushed and didn't think out your idea very well. If that's true then it's a useful learning experience. Be honest about that and move on with it. You might also notice some anger in being criticized.

When we make mistakes or get criticized it's helpful for us to refocus our minds and not ruminate on them. What can we learn from the experience and how are we going to change our behavior in the future to be helpful?.

A loss of identity

When we feel ourselves to be subordinate to others, that we are being used by them in a way we do not like, all kinds of changes happen in us. Beth and Martin had a good sex life. Martin was always keen, and at first Beth took this to mean that he really fancied her and she was a 'turn-on' to him. That made her feel good. However, gradually she came to think that, in other areas of their life together, he did not seem so caring. Eventually she had the thought, 'I am just a body to him'. This thought, of being used by Martin, and being highly subordinate to his sexual needs, had a dramatic effect on her. She lost all interest in sex, became resentful of Martin and wanted to escape. Moreover, she felt that he had gradually taken over her identity and that she had lost her own. However, Beth's thoughts got out of perspective as she became more depressed. Slowly she was able to change her thinking:

- It remains true that Martin fancies me and I don't need to discount that aspect of our relationship because I am angry with him.
- I can talk to Martin and tell him that I'm unhappy with other areas of my life.
- I can take more control in my marriage. If I feel exploited, maybe it's because I'm not asserting my own needs enough.

- Martin is not really an unkind man, but he is rather thoughtless at times. I need to help him be more attentive.
- Maybe it's my resentment and unexpressed anger that are also causing problems here.

It had been Beth's feeling used and unappreciated that had sparked off her negative feelings, but she had not had an opportunity to focus on them, challenge their extreme nature and take more control in her marriage. When she did this, she saw that there were indeed problems in the marriage, but she felt more able to try to sort them out. And perhaps she had rather allowed Martin to be inattentive for too long. What Beth also realized was that she and Martin needed to engage in more mutually enjoyable activities, not just sex.

A loss of identity can occur when we are in conflict about whether to live for ourselves or for others. Such conflicts can become all-or-nothing issues, rather than being faced as *difficulties in balancing* the various needs of each person in a relationship.

Nell gave up her job to have children and support her husband, but she gradually found this less and less fulfilling. Over the years, it had become accepted that her husband Eric should do all he could to advance his career, and in the early days, this had seemed like a good idea. But when he was offered a good promotion that involved relocation, Nell became depressed. What had happened?

Nell felt that she had lost her identity, she didn't know who she was any longer and she wanted to run away. She didn't want to move to another city but, on the other hand, felt she was being selfish and holding Eric back. Although for many years she had voluntarily supported him in his career, and at first had valued this, she gradually had come to think of herself as merely his satellite, spinning around him, and simply fitting in with his plans. However, she felt it was wrong to assert her own needs, and she was very frightened of doing or saying things that might be strongly disapproved of. Even her own parents said that she should do what she could to support Eric, and she worried about what they thought of her. As she became less satisfied with her position in the family, she found it difficult to change it because she thought she was being selfish and 'ought' to be a dutiful housewife. She thought that doing things that might interfere with her husband's progress would make her unlovable. But relocating and leaving her friends was a step too far. As for Eric, he was stunned by Nell's depression, for he had simply come to expect her to follow and support him. He had not learned anything different. In fact, Nell's depression was a kind of *rebellion*. But notice that this style had simply emerged between them and was *nobody's fault*.

The first thing Nell had to do to help herself was to recognize the complex feelings and deep conflicts she was experiencing. I recommended that she watch the film *Shirley Valentine* – in which a housewife goes on holiday to Greece with a woman friend, leaving her husband behind, and then decides to stay on. I suggested she could consider her depression as a kind of rebellion: not as a weakness or personal failure (as she did at first), but as something that was forcing her to stop and take stock of where she was and where she was going. An important idea was to see the depression as making her face certain things, and although painful, could be an impetus for change. When she gave up blaming herself for being depressed, and telling herself that she was selfish for not wanting to move house, her depression lessened. We then did some of the exercises for the empty self (see pages 308–13).

Sometimes people feel that they have to accept a subordinate position because they have lost confidence in other areas of their lives. This was certainly true for Nell, so the next thing was to explore her loss of confidence with her. She wanted to go back to work, but felt that she was not up to it. Underneath this loss of confidence was a lot of self-attacking – for example, thoughts of, 'I'm out of touch with work', 'It's been too long', 'I'm not good enough', 'I won't be able to cope', 'I might do things wrong and make a fool of myself.', 'Everyone is more competent than me'. Nell had also become envious of her husband's success and his independent lifestyle, but again, instead of seeing this as understandable, she told herself that she was bad and selfish for feeling envious.

Confidence is related to practice. Think of driving a car. The more you do it, the more confident you will be. If you rarely drive, you won't have the chance to become confident. It is the same for social situations. Women who have given up work to look after children can sometimes feel afraid of returning to work later in life. If this happens to you, think of whether you lack confidence because of a lack of practice. Be kind and compassionately gentle towards that. Avoid the tendency to criticize yourself. Work towards building your confidence compassionately, step by step. Get the evidence, rather than assume that you wouldn't be able to cope. If you give up too quickly, it may be because you are self-attacking.

Conflicts over how to live

If you can come to terms with a possible loss of approval, this will place you in a better position than before your depression. Other people will not be able to frighten you with their possible disapproval. Always keep in mind, though, that wanting approval is absolutely natural – and the need may increase when we are stressed or depressed. It does for me. It is how we manage this that is key, not whether we have those feelings or not.

Kim was married to a wealthy businessman. Before she came to see me, she had been given medication and told that her depression was biological. She herself could not understand her depression – after all, she had as much money as anyone could want and her husband was not unkind. She thought she should be happy, but instead she felt weak for being depressed. Within a few sessions, Kim began to talk about how she had come to feel like a painted doll. She had to appear with her husband at important functions and often felt 'on show'. Her husband was often away on business trips, and when he returned home tired, she felt that he used her to relax. She began to express her own needs, wanting to go to university and wear dirty jeans, as she said – but she also thought that her needs were selfish and stupid for a woman in her position and would court serious disapproval. She believed that, because her husband could provide her with any material thing, she was being ungrateful and selfish for wanting to live differently. She said, 'Many people would be delighted to have what I have'. She also had many self-critical and self-doubting thoughts about going to university, for instance, 'I'm too old now', 'I wouldn't fit in', 'Others will think I'm odd', 'I'm not bright enough', 'I'll fail'. Of course, she didn't try to discover the evidence for any of these beliefs, and the depression was taken as proof that she would not be able to cope. They were more fears than facts.

When Kim began to help herself to get out of her depression, she started to:

- Learn to take her own needs seriously.
- Change the self-labels of 'ingratitude' and 'guilt' to 'want to develop'.
- Avoid discounting the positives in her current life (e.g., 'Nobody is interested in me for myself', 'I'm only a doll for my husband').

- See her depression as a signal that her life needed to change, rather than as a sign of weakness.
- Understand how her thoughts were driving her further into, rather than out of, depression.
- Talk more frankly with her husband.
- Find out whether she could cope with university.
- Avoid attacking herself (especially in social situations).

Today I would do more compassion work too. Some people who feel highly subordinate to others can also feel so inferior that they think they don't have the power to change. Once they can give up seeing themselves as inferior and inadequate, they open the door to change.

In a way, Kim felt as much subordinate to a way of life as to any particular person. Sometimes it is making money that causes problems, or maintaining a certain lifestyle. A couple may have become so dependent on money-making that intimacy falls away and tiredness rules. Both partners feel trapped by the demands to 'keep going'. Sadly if relationships are subordinated to the need to make money, there is often a reduction in intimacy and happiness. There is increasing concern about these problems in our society today. The fear of losing a job can lead to working long hours; or there may be a need for two salaries. It is helpful to openly acknowledge this as a modern issue to be faced. Put time aside to 'feed' the relationship without this being seen as a burden. Gardens will grow whether you tend them or not but, if untended, you might not like the look of them as the years go by. Plan activities that are mutually rewarding and enjoyable. Spend time together on positive things, and show each other appreciation for sharing those things. Try to build on the positives rather than being separated by the negatives.[3]

Non-verbal communication

Our need to feel approved of by others begins from the first days of life. For example, babies are very sensitive to the faces of their parents. If babies are happy and smile at their mothers and they smile back, the positive feelings between them grow. But if a mother presents a blank or angry face, the baby becomes distressed. When mothers and babies are on the same wavelength and approving of each other, we say that they are 'in tune' or are 'mirroring' each other. Indeed, in adult life, approval is signalled not only by the words people use but by the types of attention they give, the smiles, facial expressions and nods. A smile or a frown can say a lot, and a hug can do much to reassure us. When we get depressed we can become sensitive to non-verbal communication.

Not only can we withdraw into ourselves and become rather unappreciative of others when depressed, but our own non-verbal communication can be very unfriendly. We look grumpy and fed up most of the time, and rarely think about how this will affect others. Yet when others become distant, we feel worse. Unless you are very depressed, it is often helpful to try to send friendly non-verbal messages – to smile and be considerate of others. You may protest, 'But aren't you suggesting that I cover up my feelings, put on an act?' The answer is yes and no. Yes, to the extent that you need to be aware that a constantly grumpy appearance is not a good basis for developing positive relationships – a depressed attitude can push others away. Moreover, if you smile and be friendly, this can affect your mood positively. However, the answer is also no, to the extent that, if there are problems that you need to sort out, then they need sorting out – don't hide what you feel. Being grumpy or sulky and making no effort to be friendly actually sorts out very little – it can lead to brooding resentment in you and others.

Entrapments

We can get ourselves trapped in relationships and then feel depressed and stuck because we don't want to upset people (see page 57).[4] Steve had been made redundant, but a colleague he had worked for previously had set up a new business and invited Steve to join him. Steve had some doubts but needed the money and didn't want to let his colleague down. A couple of weeks into the job, Steve's concerns were realized. However, he felt his colleague had been very kind to help him out and that he would be turning his back on that kindness if he left – even though he now disliked the job. Steve became trapped by a sense of obligation, not wanting to let his colleagues down and also frightened they would see him as ungrateful. Gradually his sleep deteriorated, he became tired and anxious at weekends. Eventually, he was honest with his colleague who was very sad to see Steve go and tried to work out how to make the job better. However, Steve eventually found a job far more suited to his skills, and his depression receded in his new job. Sometimes our fear of upsetting people can trap us.

Of course there are many reasons for feeling trapped. For example, we may be in relationships we don't want to be in but don't have the money or alternatives to see a way out. Here it's important to recognize the feelings of entrapment and then find people to talk to – perhaps a family doctor – to explore how to cope and resolve the difficulty. Recognize that feelings of entrapment are not uncommon in depression, that these feelings are not your fault, and that while they can be difficult, they are resolvable. Be cautious of thoughts such as 'I shouldn't feel like this', 'There is no way out', 'Things can't change'. These are understandable feelings and thoughts, but if we are kind to them, acknowledge them but also explore around them, seek help, don't take them at face value, we can never tell what lies ahead.

Giving approval

We can be so busy trying to gain approval and do things to please other people that we forget how to show appreciation of what they give us. For example, Lynne had a great need to be approved of. When I asked her how she showed that she valued her husband Rob, she said, 'By doing things for him, keeping the house clean'. My response was: 'Well, his approval of you makes you feel good, but what do you say to him about how you value him?' Lynne went blank, then said, 'But Rob doesn't need my approval. He's all right. Life's easy for him. I'm the one who is depressed.'

When they were together, Lynne and Rob tended to blame each other for what they were not doing for each other:

> Lynne: *You never spend enough time with me.*
> Rob: *But you're always so tired.*
> Lynne: *That's right – blame me. You always do.*
> Rob: *But it's true. You're never happy.*

Around and around we went. Neither Rob nor Lynne could focus on how to offer approval to the other. Instead, they continually focused on their anger and thus there was little to build on. They rarely said things like 'You look nice today' or 'It was really helpful when you did that' or 'I thought you handled that well' or 'You were really kind to think of that'. Lynne tried to earn approval but was not able to give it. It was painful for her to come to see that, in placing herself in a subordinate position, she felt that others should attend and approve of her, and she would work hard to get this approval, but she did not need to show approval of others. She saw them as more able than her and believed that her approval of them did not matter.

Depression can make us very self-focused in this regard. Sometimes depressed people are resentful of their partners, and giving approval and showing appreciation is the last thing they want to do. Don't blame yourself for this but be honest and see what steps you can take to change. It can be useful, therefore, to consider how we can praise those around us – not just do things for them, but show an interest in them and recognize that all humans feel good if they feel appreciated and not taken for granted.

Being bullied

It is one thing to be criticized and to learn how to cope with it, but it is another to be on the receiving end of bullying. There is much literature on bullying and depression and an Internet search will reveal a lot of information, including advice on what to do. You could look at *www.bullying.co.uk* as a start. If you feel depressed because of bullying and want to escape, then recognize this as a normal response to bullying (our brains shift to threat mode big time) but get help; feeling bullied is even linked to suicide.

There is now much evidence that being on the receiving end of a lot of criticisms and put-downs (sometimes also called high expressed emotion) is associated with mental ill-health.[5] These criticisms and put-downs can be verbal or non-verbal, or even physical attacks. Although it is common in depression to over-estimate the degree and implications of criticism, it can also be the case that put-downs are not exaggerated. The problem then becomes whether anything can be done to change the situation or whether it is best to get out of the relationship.

Bullying and intimate relationships

Mark rarely said positive things to Jill, and acted as if he were disappointed in her. In therapy, he rarely looked at her but instead scanned the room as though uninterested in what was going on. Even when he did say some positive things to Jill, they were said in such a hostile and dismissive way that you could understand why she never believed him. The problem here was not only Jill's depression but also Mark's anger (rooted in his own childhood) and difficulty in conveying warmth. Many of his communications bristled with hostility and coldness; he saw depression as a weakness and was angry at Jill's loss of sexual interest. She came to dread Mark's moodiness and how he would look at her.

Sadly, Jill and Mark had become locked into a rather hostile and disapproving style. She experienced him as a disapproving, dominant male, and her life was spent trying to elicit his approval and get some warmth from him. When she failed, she blamed herself and became more depressed, with a strong desire to escape the relationship – which also made her feel guilty and frightened. She held the view that she should make her relationship work, regardless of the cost or how difficult it was. She prided herself on not being a quitter. But sadly, only if she subordinated herself to Mark's every need could she elicit approval from him. Moreover, she came to believe that all men were like this.

Problems such as these often require relational therapy. However, if you blame yourself for the problems or are ashamed of them, this might stop you from seeking help. If you feel frightened and are not sure where the next put-down is coming from, whether in a close relationship or at work, it is possible that you are caught up in a bullying relationship. The degree of your fear can be a clue here – although consider whether you would be fearful if you weren't depressed, because sometimes we become fearful of others because of depression. I have certainly come across many couples who fight a lot, feel resentful and so forth, but are not necessarily frightened of each other. So fear may be a key.

The first thing is to be honest with yourself and consider if a frank exploration of your relationship and its difficulties would be beneficial. Sometimes it is the bullying partner who feels ashamed about examining feelings of closeness and how to convey affection. Mark, for example, came from a rather cold and affectionless family and felt uncomfortable with closeness. He acted towards Jill in the same way that his father had acted towards him and his mother. As Jill came to recognize this, she gave up blaming herself for his cold attitude, and although this did not in itself cure her depression, it was a step on the way. She learned that trying to earn approval from a person who found it virtually impossible to give was, sadly, a wasted effort. Eventually the relationship ended.

So the lesson to be drawn from this is, don't blame yourself for another person's cold attitude towards you. If you do, you are giving too much power away to the other person. Research has shown that a woman still living with an abusive partner will often blame herself for the abuse inflicted on her, but will come to see it as not her fault if she moves away. Try using the 'responsibility circle' (pages 284–6) and see how many things you can think of that might be causing the problem. What are the alternatives for the other person's cold attitude?

Coping with violence

Obviously a more serious form of bullying is *domestic violence*. If this is happening to you then don't suffer in silence; don't self-blame or feel ashamed as sadly many people can suffer from this in their relationships. Reach out for help; for example, contact a national centre for domestic violence and speak to someone who can offer you support and advice (e.g., *www.ncdv.org.uk*). Remember the cardinal rules: honesty to your experiences, kindness and compassion for what you are experiencing, work out what you need to help you, give up self-blame and reach out to others.

Bullying at work

There is increasing concern today at the amount of bullying that goes on in families, schools and at work (see *www.bullying.co.uk*). Being on the receiving end of a bully's attacks can be pretty depressing. As a society, we need to learn how to be more accepting of others and less unkind. As individuals, we also have to learn how to protect ourselves as best we can from the effects of bullying.

You can sometimes spot a bully because you will not be the only one who experiences his or her behaviors as undermining. It can be useful to get the views of others – get the evidence that it is not just you. For example, in the case of Jill and Mark, many of their mutual friends saw Mark as a 'difficult' person. When Jill thought about this evidence, it helped her to give up blaming herself.

Bullies at work can be very upsetting, because you can dread going to work or feel yourself stirred up each morning. If this is the case for you then try talking to someone such as your union representative or works doctor or another manager. Talk to others about how they cope, see if you can learn anything and also so that you don't feel alone with it; maybe form an alliance with others. If you are able to move away, do so. The key thing is to avoid shaming self-blame for your reactions – rather work with them in as helpful a way as you can.

One key problem is *rumination*. We often ruminate on the bully – what was said and what we should say, and how angry we are and having to face them again! Over and over it we go. That is very understandable but will constantly stimulate your threat and stress systems. If you can spot yourself ruminating, note this as understandable but not helpful – and switch to a compassion focus as outlined in Chapter 8.

If sexual harassment is the problem, specific individuals may be picked on. Others may not experience the bully in the same way. If this happens to you, again, obtain support from others and be as assertive as possible. Raise the issue as openly and frankly as you can at work. Don't be stopped from raising the issue with thoughts of, 'It's only me'. You may need legal advice. The more you are able to discuss this with others, this easier it may be to work out how best to cope.

KEY POINTS

- Wanting the approval of others is natural and makes the world go around. However, sometimes it is easy to become fearful of disapproval and then we can get caught up in a subordinate approval trap, becoming more subordinate, trying to be pleasing to others and sacrificing our own needs and wishes.
- We can become subordinate to the lifestyles of others, or even to a lifestyle we may have chosen at one time. This can lead us to feeling that we have lost our own identities.
- As for other aspects of depression we have discussed, the key is not to self-blame but be open and think through the main issues that might be linked to your depression.
- Sometimes we will need to reach out for the help and support of others, sometimes learn to be more assertive and sometimes develop courage to make change in our lives. All these will be easier (though not easy) if you are kind and supportive of yourself.

EXERCISES

You can explore how you deal with disapproval and criticism in a series of steps.

- First, begin with a relatively minor example of criticism. Bring that to mind. Now reflect on the feelings and thoughts that passed through you. Stand back from them, take a 'view from the balcony' as it were and clarify those feelings and thoughts. Think whether there are underlying fears, (e.g., that the person does not like you) or links to your past – do they remind you of an unkind parent, teacher or school bully? This helps you start the process of being kind to your sensitivity to criticism. You will be able to say to yourself, 'It's understandable that I feel upset by the criticism because . . .'

- Take a few soothing rhythm breaths and allow yourself to slow down for a moment. Imagine yourself to be a compassionate person; feel your inner kindness and wisdom grow; bring a gentle and kind expression to your face; feel yourself expanding and becoming like a wise authority. From that position, consider ways in which you can think about the criticism and your reactions in a different way.

- If you find it helpful, write down alternative ways you can think about the criticism, which might include recognizing your sensitivity, balancing your thoughts so that you don't see this as a major rejection, recognizing the role of your own anger, remembering that these feelings pass, criticisms and arguments are part of everyday life, the other person might be grumpy. Would it help you to consider forgiveness (see Chapter 20)?

- Keep in mind that while rumination is easy to fall into and very under-standable, if you keep going over and over your upset, hurt or anger these repetitions in your mind are often unhelpful to you. Become mindful when they start up and watch them kindly.

- Be honest with yourself about whether you need to learn assertiveness. Sometimes we can struggle to be assertive because in our heads we become too angry or frightened, and rather than thinking about how to offer clear messages if we are upset by criticism, we just imagine getting our own back, or having a major fight. Since that is overwhelming, we can be stuck ruminating. If you feel like that be kind to yourself, smile at it and then think about what a compassionate and helpful approach would be.

- Think about how you deal with approval. Sometimes people who want approval are dismissive when they actually get it. It is almost as if they have to be constantly seeking but must never find; as if they don't know what to do with it when they get it. Think whether that's true for you, and if you have a tendency to constantly move the goalposts. If so, be kind to yourself but also make a decision to pay attention to small signs of approval such as smiles or small acts of friendship towards you. This is definitely a case where 'small is beautiful'. This helps us to give up trying to be some sort of super being and win super approval.

- As we have often said, the secret of success is the ability to fail (see Chapter 21). The secret of gaining approval is the ability to deal with criticism and disapproval. This is always tricky but if we can learn to tolerate criticism without ruminating, or deal quickly with our anger or fear, we will be better placed to deal with the ups and downs of relationships. It's tough, so go step by step.

- Put time aside to write a compassionate letter(s) to yourself to explore your issues about approval and how to work with it (see pages 233–9).

- Last but not least, if you are in a bullying relationship, be honest about it, speak with others and acknowledge that sometimes it's important to get away from the bully. Use your compassionate and rational mind to help you think through how to do that and to develop the courage you'll need.

Understanding and healing shame in depression

Of all the emotions that are likely to reduce our ability to be helped, to reach out to others and to treat ourselves with kindness, shame is the most important and destructive. Indeed, people can feel ashamed about being depressed, and desperately try to hide it from others. If we can recognize our inner shame and work to reduce it, we will do much to heal and nurture ourselves.

In general, shame – like embarrassment, pride, prestige and status – is related to how we think others see and judge us, and how we view ourselves. We call these *self-conscious emotions* because they relate to our feelings about ourselves.[1] The word 'shame' is thought to come from the Indo-European word *skam*, meaning to hide. In the biblical account, Adam and Eve ate of the apple of the tree of knowledge, became self-aware and realized their nakedness. At that moment, they developed a capacity for shame and the need for fig leaves – or so the story goes. Part of their shame was fear that, having transgressed against God's instructions, they would be punished.

Shame is now regarded as one of the most powerful and potentially tricky issues in helping people with depression, because it often involves concealment or an inability to process 'shameful' information. People don't easily reveal or talk about things they feel ashamed about – they're worried about what others will think of them. Indeed, some people are ashamed of depression itself and this is why, sadly, they don't seek help.

The elements of shame

Shame is a complex phenomenon, with various aspects and components. Among the most important ones are the following:

- **Social or externally focused thoughts and feelings**. These are beliefs that others see us as inferior, bad, inadequate and flawed; that is, others are looking down on us with a condemning or contemptuous view. This is linked to stigma and what we call external shame.
- **Internal negative self-evaluative thoughts and feelings**. These include beliefs and feelings that one is inferior, inadequate or flawed. Many of our self-attacking thoughts and feelings (e.g., I am useless, no good, a bad person, a failure) are in essence shaming thoughts and self-evaluations. This is called internal shame.
- **An emotional component**. The emotions and feelings of internal and external shame are various, but include anxiety, anger, self-disgust and self-contempt. Some people describe shame as a form of 'heart-sink' – the kind that sweeps over us when we're hoping to succeed at something and then find we have failed!
- **A behavioral component**. Shame is related to the submissive response (that we share with other animals) where we can feel small and looked down on, avert our eyes and try to make ourselves look smaller. There is a strong urge to hide, slink away, avoid exposure and run away. Sometimes we just want to cry. Often we can find

it hard to think or speak. Sometimes, though, when criticised, we can show a much more dominating response of anger and want to retaliate against the one who is 'exposing' us or suggesting we're inferior, weak or bad in some way.

- **A bodily or physiological component**. Feelings of shame are stressful and activate our threat and stress systems. Shame also affects our mood chemicals and is not helpful in trying to foster positive moods.

The most powerful experiences of inner shame often arise from feeling that there is something different and inferior, flawed or bad about ourselves. We may believe that, if others discover these flaws in us, they will ridicule, scorn, be angry and/or reject us. In this respect, shame is fear of a loss of approval in extreme form.

We can feel paralysed by shame and at the same time acutely aware of being scrutinized and judged by others. Shame not only leads us to feel inferior, weak or bad in some way, but also threatens us with the loss of valued relationships – if our shame is revealed, people won't want to help us, be our friends, love or respect us. A typical shame-based view is, 'If you really got to know me, you would not like me'. A major feeling in shame can be aloneness. We can feel isolated, disconnected and inwardly cut off from the love or friendship of others. Shame can give us the feeling that we are separated (different) from others, an outsider.

Feeling ashamed and being shamed

It is helpful to distinguish in our minds internal shame (how we judge and feel about ourselves) from external shame (the feelings we have about ourselves when we think others are looking down on us). Let's look at this distinction with an example. Recall Anne from Chapter 9 (pages 190–3) who burnt her party dinner. She may be very concerned about what other people think, and worry that they may see her as incompetent and inadequate in some way. Her attention is focused on what is going on in the minds of other people and her social standing in *their minds*. This is external shame because the source of the criticism and the attention is outside (external) of herself. If she is *self*-critical and harsh *on herself*, maybe calls herself names and feels irritated with herself, then she will also have internal shame. The source of the criticism and put-down is coming from within our own minds. Table 17.1 outlines these distinctions and shows how they are linked to our key fears.

However, it is possible that Anne could be upset because she believes others look down on her but is not *self*-critical and accepts she's not a particularly good cook. Anne might have

TABLE 17.1 SELF-CRITICAL THOUGHTS AND FEARS[2]

External shame	Internal shame
How I think others feel and view me	*What I feel and think about myself*
These new people will see that I'm disorganized	I'm so annoyed with myself for forgetting such a basic ingredient
They'll not be very impressed with my cooking abilities or my organization	What's the matter with me? Why can't I get my head in gear?
They'll feel let down at having to eat a takeaway	The meal I cooked would have been so nice and impressed them.
I've probably blown it with them — they'll now always see me as a bit scatty and not take me seriously	I've really let myself down again by being careless and not paying attention
Anne's key fear is: I'll not be able to make close friendships with people who respect me	*Anne's key fear is:* I'll not be able to make close friendships with people who respect me. I'll be marginalized and lonely

external shame but no internal shame. If Anne is convinced by the genuineness, if people reassure her, that they don't mind the meal being overcooked, she will quickly calm down, because she trusts others to still like and care about her. The kindness of others is soothing. Internal shame, however, is less easily dealt with because it's our own internal judgements, evaluations and feelings – and these we can find more difficult to settle. This is why it is important to learn *self-kindness*. Look back to pages 190–3 and note some of the suggestions for working on this problem.

In depression it is common for people to have both types of shame. They feel others see them as inferior, bad or inadequate; and they also see themselves as inferior, bad or inadequate. When you are working with your own sense of shame, then, it is useful to be clear about:

- What you think others are thinking and feeling about you.
- What you are thinking and feeling about yourself.

When you do this, you will see how often shame feelings are related to fears of loss of approval. In this chapter we will focus mainly on internal shame; that is, the kind of things you say to yourself that trigger feelings of shame in you, make you behave submissively and undermine your confidence.

Shame can affect us in many ways and we can defend against it in many ways. The first thing to recognize is that we feel insecure in the minds of others in some way. We're not sure whether they accept us or not. If we grow up knowing that others are accepting, validating and forgiving, we tend to be less bothered by shame than if we grow up in neglectful, harsh, rejecting or critical environments. If shame is a major problem for us, learning how to deal with it compassionately can help.

The focus for shame

According to the psychologist Gershen Kaufman,[3] there are at least three areas in which shame can cause us much pain. We can feel shame about *our bodies*, shame about our *competence and abilities*, and shame in *our relationships*. There is an additional aspect that is especially common in depression: shame of *what we feel, or the things that go through our minds*. Let's briefly look at each of these.

Shame about our bodies

Some people don't go to see their doctors because of shame. There are all kinds of conditions that people regard as shaming: piles (haemorrhoids), impotence, bowel diseases, urinary problems, eating disorders, drink and drug problems. Shame, perhaps more than any other emotion, stops us from seeking help. There is general agreement that doctors could be more sensitive to shame, how to spot it and work with it.

Sadly, too, people who have various disfigurements – from mild acne to severe burns – can also feel shame, especially if others laugh at them, reject them or appear repelled by the way they look. But people cope with these in different ways (see *www.changingfaces.org.uk/Home*).

People who have been sexually abused often have an acute sense of bodily shame. They can feel that their bodies have become dirty, contaminated and damaged. In extreme cases, these individuals may come to hate and even abuse their own bodies. Talking about the experiences and feelings of abuse can in itself produce strong feelings of shame, and for this reason people may hold back from discussing them. Healing this shame involves coming to terms with one's body and reclaiming it as one's own (see below).

Concern with the way we look is, of course, a driving force behind fashion. However, some people feel so awkward and ashamed of their bodies that they will do almost anything to themselves to avoid suffering these feelings. People might spend hours body-building at a gym, and put great effort into dieting to make themselves thinner. Make-up and plastic surgery may also be used to avoid feelings of body shame. In the West today much depression emerges out of feelings of shame and unhappiness with the shape and size of our bodies – hence the huge dieting industry, which offers hope of change. Sometimes we can over-hope, in the sense that we might believe something like, 'If I lose weight then people will like me more and I will be happy'. If we try and fail, as people often do (I can't tell you how often I have tried to lose weight) then again that can feel shaming.

Georgie struggled to lose weight. She lost a couple of pounds then put them back on again. This caused a dip in mood and she was very down on herself and then ate more.

The issue about helping ourselves if we are overweight (and that includes me – unfortunately) is learning how not to shame ourselves if we don't do as well as we would like. We learn to be kind and understanding of our setbacks, while also trying to encourage ourselves to try again. If we are shaming of ourselves, we are much more likely to give up. Sometimes we need to simply learn to come to terms with the size we are and develop self-acceptance. At times, a bit of 'What the hell' in our lives can be helpful! (See page 501.) Think about joining a slimming organization because here you might receive help, guidance and a lot of understanding and support from other members. Talking to others helps us to see that we are all struggling with the same things – it not just ourselves – so we don't need to cover up or hide away.

TABLE 17.2 USING OUR RATIONAL AND COMPASSIONATE MIND

Rational mind	Compassionate/friendly mind (kind, warm tone)
Empathic understanding	
My thinking is understandably clouded by my frustration and disappointment and also wanting to be like others. So the task now is how best to cope with this understandable disappointment.	*It is understandable I feel frustrated because I put a lot of effort into losing weight and want to look slimmer and fit into those clothes.* *It is understandable that my attention will be on my weight because we live in a social world that makes so much of it!*

Here Georgie shows that she recognizes the problem as frustration clouding her feelings and thoughts. She is compassionate because she recognizes (is sensitive and sympathetic to) her frustration and disappointment as understandable and reminds herself why she feels like this. So she doesn't dismiss her feelings but accepts her disappointment with understanding – it is unhelpful to tell ourselves we should not feel what we do when we clearly do.

Shifting attention	
I can choose where I put my attention and I can do that according to how it will help me with my frustration 'in this moment'. *Put time aside to practise redirecting attention in kind and compassionate ways.*	*If I stay focused on my weight I will become unhappy – so it would be helpful if I redirect my attention to other things.* *I can be mindful (see Chapter 7) of how these thoughts and emotions are playing in my mind. I can bring to mind the things that make me happy in life; these might be my relationships (bring to mind a picture of someone smiling at me) or things I do, or my garden.* *I can engage in soothing rhythm breathing, put myself in my compassionate self mode and just be compassionate to my distress – feeling kind. I can bring to mind a compassionate other image and imagine compassion and kindness flowing to me.*

Here Georgie is practising directing her attention in a different way and not letting her frustration dictate what dominates her mind. She is taking control and making choices about her attention and focus.

Reasoning and thinking	
Having a weight problem is very common because of the world we live in – that is not my fault. Humans evolved in times of great scarcity. We are designed to go for more and more rather than limit ourselves – so dieting is hard work.	*With a friend I would help her to realize that it doesn't matter to me about her weight, I am interested in the quality of her as a person, whether I can trust her, share my values and stories with her. I would support her by recognizing how difficult*

Because of our genes, different people lay down fat at different rates and also some find limiting their food easier than others — that's not my fault.

weight loss is, particularly in this world surrounded by wonderful foods, that the food industry has spent billions of pounds making us want to eat, and encourage her to accept the ups and downs of trying.

It is easy for me to compare myself with thin women, because that's what all the magazines and our culture wants me to do, but actually this way of comparing myself to others is not helpful to me. The fact is I'm fatter than some people and slimmer than others.

Here Georgie is learning to reason and think about the issue rationally and fairly and then with warmth and kindness, thinking of how she would talk about this if it happened to a friend. She is recognizing that her compassionate, caring side sees things and thinks about things in a different way to her angry, frustrated, vulnerable side.

Helpful behavior

I can work out what went wrong and develop a plan to learn from the experience.
The secret of success is really linked to the ability to fail. When I do not fear failure I'm free to succeed.

It is understandable why I might feel I don't want to be bothered trying to lose weight any more! This is my frustration and vulnerability talking. However, if I'm kind to myself and allow myself to settle down I know I'll come around again and have another go. So many of us have these battles. If it helps me I can ask people to come and help me, or join a support group. Let's see if I can work out another plan.

Here Georgie is thinking about compassionate behavior — behavior that will help her move forward, develop, learn from mistakes, grow and develop confidence. Compassionate behavior is about kindness, but is also about encouraging and being supportive in changing our behavior, taking on the challenges of change and not avoiding difficulties.

To generate compassionate feeling, Georgie can now look through her alternative thoughts, engage in her soothing rhythm breathing and focus on the words but imagine a compassionate image, or a compassionate voice speaking the words. Here it is not so much convincing herself through evidence, but focusing on the kindness, support and understanding in these alternatives that is key.

Shame about our competence and abilities

This kind of shame relates to performing physically or mentally. For example Pete would become very angry with himself when he was unable to make things work. When household appliances broke down, he took it as a personal criticism of his abilities and manhood if he could not fix them. When his car wouldn't start, he would think that, if he were a proper man, he would be able to understand mechanical things and would be able to fix it. He hated taking it to the garage and showing his incompetence to the garage staff, and so always asked his wife to take it.

In my own case, my poor English has often been a source of mild shame. My teachers at boarding school would write in my report that I was lazy and careless. I could spend hours on a piece of work, reading over and over it, and feel confident it was 'spelted' correctly, only for it come back covered in red marks with comments like, 'Slapdash, Gilbert!' – which then triggered that dreadful heart-sink feeling. Dyslexic children often experience much shame and feelings of being defective and inferior. The main point here is that attempting to do things and failing can be a source of shame. It is made worse when we rate ourselves as bad, and attack ourselves for failing. As a rule, it is easier to cope with the criticism of others if we don't attack *ourselves*. If we do, then there are attacks from the inside and outside and that can feel a very unpleasant place to be in! The next time you feel embarrassed at a failure, check to see if you are self-attacking and bring your rational/compassionate mind into play. My own experiences made me very aware of the power and pain of shame and why kindness and compassion are such helpful antidotes. I am also very grateful to copy-editors!

Shame in relationships

None of us like criticisms – although who is doing it and how it is done is important. However, when our shame sensitivities are touched we can become alarmed, anxious, defensive, angry, sulk or give in quickly. This can give us difficulty owning up to our vulnerabilities, for fear that, if others became aware of them, we would be marked down as weak and inadequate. Fear and shame of criticism can make relationships difficult because we find it hard to ride the ups and downs of relationships.

Some people feel awkward when wanting to express or respond to affection in the forms of gentleness, touching and hugging. It is as if there is an invisible wall around them. In situations of close intimacy, their bodies stiffen or they back away. Some may hide their shame by clinging to the idea that, 'Grown men don't do that sort of thing' or that to be tender is to be 'soft' and 'unmanly'. This can cause problems in how they act, as intimate friends, lovers and fathers. For example, children often seek out physical affection, and it can be very hurtful to them if their fathers push them away when they try to get close.

Shame about what we feel

We sometimes conceal our true feelings out of shame. We can be ashamed of feeling anxious, tearful or depressed or angry – as if the very fact that we have these feelings means that there is something wrong, flawed or unlovable in us. People with shame about their feelings can't believe that others have the kinds of feelings or fantasies they do.

For many years, Alec suffered from panic attacks. He dreaded going to meetings in case the signs of his anxiety showed. He was so ashamed of his anxiety that he did not even tell his wife. Eventually he broke down, became depressed and could not go to work. Then the story of his long suffering came out. From a young age, his father had told him that real men don't get anxious; they are tough and fearless. When Alec had been anxious about going to school, his father had been dismissive and forced him to go – shaming him in the process. By the time he was a teenager, Alec had learned never to speak of or show his inner anxieties.

Susan, who was married, met another man to whom she felt strongly sexually attracted. She flirted with him and would have liked the relationship to become sexual, but she felt deeply ashamed about her desires and believed that they made her a very bad person. As she came to understand that sexual feelings are natural, and to explore what it was about the relationship that so attracted her, she discovered a desire for closeness that she could not get from her husband. This, of course, raised the question of what she could do about that; but it helped stop her being ashamed of her feelings and allowed her to accept that she, like other human beings, wanted closeness and could find a whole range of people rather sexy.

Jenny's mother had told her that sex is dirty – something that men enjoy because they are more primitive and superficial than women. Later, when Jenny had sex, she could sometimes push these thoughts aside, but afterwards she was left with the feeling of being dirty and of having betrayed her mother's values. When she monitored her thoughts during the day, she noticed that, whenever she had sexual thoughts and feelings, she would also have thoughts at the back of her mind of 'A good woman doesn't have these feelings. Therefore I'm dirty, and if my mother knew what was going through my mind, she would be disgusted and disappointed with me.' She then distracted herself from her sexual feelings and turned them off.

These were not clear thoughts as I have written them down

– they were more sensed, and Jenny had to stop and really focus on 'what am I actually thinking here?' to get a handle on them. However, once she had come to recognize that she was having these kinds of thoughts (and she had to really focus to 'catch' them going through her mind), she was able to say to herself:

> This is my sexual life and it does not belong to my mother for her to control. If I feel sexual, this is because I feel sexual, and it has nothing to do with being dirty. My sexual feelings also give me energy and are life-enhancing. I don't need to act out my mother's sexual hang-ups in my own life.

Andrew was ashamed of his homosexual desires. Brought up within a strict religious framework, he thought that these feelings were a sin against God and that he was a bad, worthless human being for having them. Although it was a struggle, he began to explore the possibility that there were alternative ways to think about and explore his sexuality – without being ashamed of it.

Gary was ashamed of his anger and rage. When he became angry, he felt terrible and unlovable. He said that he just wanted to act like a decent human being, and, more than anything, he felt that his anger made him a horrible person. Indeed, his self-criticism often told him that he was horrible, ungrateful, selfish and self-centred. As a result, he could not explore all the things that hurt him and the reasons behind his anger. Instead, he simply tried to keep a lid on his anger rather than acknowledge its source, go in to accept it and work out how to heal it. The dip in mood for feeling (or at times expressing) anger is more common in depression than is sometimes recognized. Indeed, Freud thought anger was central to depression.

At times, Patricia felt very tearful, but she would not allow herself to cry – she was too ashamed. Leo hid the extent of his drinking out of shame. Zoe was too ashamed to talk about the fact that her husband was abusing her. Amanda could not go far from her house just in case, when she needed to use the bathroom, there was none available and she would wet herself. There are many, many examples. For a moment let us feel compassion for all those who suffer with shame.

Crying

We often use the expression – 'it's a crying shame' – to denote perhaps that shame can involve tearful feelings and wanting to be loved. Let's look at crying and shame, because some depressed people really struggle with this. They see crying as a sign of weakness or of falling apart and are ashamed. Table 17.3 shows some shaming thoughts and balanced / compassionate alternatives.

TABLE 17.3 ALTERNATIVES TO SHAMING THOUGHTS

Shaming thoughts	Rational and compassionate alternatives
Crying is a sign of weakness	Crying is a sign of pain and hurt, not of weakness
	Maybe it is our ability to cry that makes us human
	When we lose the ability to cry, we may lose the ability to feel and to heal
	Even if others see crying as a weakness, this does not make it true. Maybe they also have a shame problem about it
	After all, if we were not meant to cry, why do we have the physical capacity for it?
	Crying is often about feeling sad or lonely, and this is an important message to listen to
	The more I can acknowledge my tears, the more in touch with my feelings I may become
	So now let me be mindful with my tears – see what they are about – stay with them and be kind to them

Sometimes people don't realize (or have not had a chance to learn) that feelings can be complex; one can have *different* and conflicting feelings towards the same thing or person. Some people believe you should never be angry or want to leave a person you also love; that they should never annoy you to the point you want to shout at them, but that is the way of life.

If we have learned to hide our feelings in early life, then professional help may be useful to help us start to explore them more. But remember we all have feelings and some of them can seem very powerful – indeed overpowering or explosive. If you feel like that then that is not your fault (it's to do with the way our brains are, and depression states) and once you give up self-blame you are freed up to seek out ways to help yourself.

Frightened and ashamed by our thoughts

Ever been in a high building or on the edge of a cliff? It is quite common for people to experience a feeling of being drawn towards the edge of high buildings with the thought of jumping off. This can be a bit frightening and we may wonder why we would have such frightening thoughts. But the fact is, given this tricky brain of ours, we can sometimes have thoughts that are in direct contrast to our true wishes. These thoughts and fantasies are called *contrast thoughts*. For people who have obsessional disorders, where such thoughts and images are common – they are called obsessional contrast thinking – thinking in complete contrast to one's actual wishes. Another example is that we might have a violent thought about someone we love. Having sexual thoughts or desires that seem odd or outside the norm can also be frightening. Contrast thoughts can intrude into our minds, can be distressing but are common.

If people feel ashamed of their contrast thoughts they may try to hide them or not think about them (which normally makes them worse), or ruminate on why they had them. Sometimes they can worry about acting out their thoughts, and this can link to a condition called obsessive compulsive disorder. Some people think that having a thought is as bad as an action. To address the shame aspect, you might consider that writers of horror stories write down their bizarre (and at times very violent) fantasies and thoughts and can *make a lot of money out of them* – whereas depressed people can be frightened of theirs. The writers know how bizarre our minds can be, while some depressed people think we should always be rational and reasonable. The fact is we have difficult minds to work with, and our minds can be filled with all kinds of odd ideas and fantasies – through no fault of our own! Learning how to notice them, accept them and let them pass, seen as products of our odd, evolved brains, can sometimes help. If they are more persistent you may find it helpful to talk with your family doctor.

The origins of shame

There are a number of theories about the origins of shame. According to one view, evolution has equipped children to enter the world as social beings with an enormous need for relationships, care, joyfully shared interactions and recognition. The treatment we receive at the hands of those who look after us will have a major effect on whether we move forward with confidence (the result of the many positive experiences encountered while growing up) or with a sense of shame, of being flawed, not good enough, lacking value or worth. Research has shown that the way the caregiver and infant interact has important impacts on the infant's nervous system, emotions and sense of self.

Shame can arise from at least three different types of reactions to the treatment we received from our parents or others who have cared for us in our early lives:

- thwarted efforts to be recognized as good and able
- pressure to conform
- direct attacks, puts-downs and rejections.

The need to be recognized as good and able

Consider the following scenario. Three-year-old Tracy sits quietly, drawing. Suddenly she jumps up, rushes to her mother and proudly holds up her drawing. The mother responds by kneeling down and saying, 'Wow – that's wonderful! Did you do that?' Tracy nods proudly. 'What a clever girl!' In this encounter, Tracy gets positive attention, and not only experiences her mother as proud of her, *she also has emotions in herself about herself – she feels good about herself.*

However, suppose that, when Tracy went to her mother with her drawing, her mother responded with, 'Oh God, not another of those drawings. Look, I'm busy right now. Can't you go off and play?' Clearly, this time the way that Tracy experienced her mother, the interaction between them, and the feelings in herself about herself were quite different. Tracy would be unlikely to have had good feelings in herself, and may have had a sense of disappointment and probably shame. Her head would have gone down and she would have slipped away. Thus *a lack of recognition* and a dismissal of ourselves, when we display something attractive to others, can be shaming. Experiences like this happen in even the most loving of homes and children learn to cope with them; but if they are common and arise against a background of insecurity and low parental warmth, they can, over time, be quite damaging.

One of my patients who read this section said that it brought back memories of herself as a child, when she would be sent to her room to play and 'just keep out of the way'. Throughout her life, she had never felt wanted and had developed a sense of being in the way and a nuisance (see pages 313–16).

Donna's parents were very ambitious. They wanted the best for her, and wanted her to do her best. If she came second or third in class, they would immediately ask who came first and indicate that coming second or third was okay but not really good enough; with a bit more effort, she could come top. Donna came to believe that nothing other than coming top was good enough to win the approval from her parents that she so desired. Anything less always felt like a disappointment for them and herself. You can guess what this all led to – an underlying belief and emotional sensitivity that, unless she did everything perfectly, she was flawed and had let herself and others down. Donna was rarely able to focus on what she had achieved, but thought only about how far short she had fallen.

Indeed, throughout life we seek the approval of other people, especially those close to us. If friends come to dinner we want them to tell us they've had a lovely meal – not that our meal was okay – average, they've had better and worse. We meet a new lover; we want them to say that our lovemaking was great – not that it's average – they have had better and worse. The desires to create positive feelings in the minds of others is all very human – and we can feel a sense of shame if we struggle to do this.

Pressure to conform

We all have a very strong desire to conform and be accepted. We want to feel that we *belong* somewhere. We follow fashion and express the same values as others so that we can signal that we are one of the group. We follow gender stereotypes. We are highly motivated to try to be valued by others rather than devalued. All around us are values and standards to which we are supposed to conform if we don't want to be shamed and stigmatized. The awful Chinese practice of foot binding, and other such practices of mutilation, can be kept in place via cultural shame to conform.

We may even try to avoid shame by going along with others, showing that we are made of the 'right stuff', even if, in our heart, we know that our action is immoral. Keith told me that getting into fights was often more to do with avoiding the shame of not fighting than with any real enjoyment in, or desire for, a punch-up; yet no one in his group wanted to 'break ranks' and point this out. Conforming to cultural values to avoid shame is a powerful social constraint. To risk exposure to shame is to risk rejection and not belonging. The pressure to conform can lie behind our cruelty to ourselves and others.

Direct attacks

We also know, of course, that children and adults can be shamed directly by being told that they are stupid or bad, that they don't fit in or are unwanted, and by being physically attacked. Indeed, some people will deliberately use the threat of shame, and the human built-in aversion to it, to control others. Shame does not only arise because approval and admiration are withheld; direct verbal and physical attacks can shame, too.

Let's look at this in more detail, because it will reveal something of the power of emotional memories. Imagine a child called Joe who has annoyed a parent. The parent shouts at Joe and tells him he is a stupid boy. Joe will have the following experiences: a triggering event and then awareness of the arousal of anger in the mind of the other (in this case the parent). That anger will be picked up by Joe's brain as threatening and dangerous, which will activate anxiety – even panic. Without thinking, Joe's brain will automatically be trying to work out the best defensive responses, such as anxiety, wanting to run away, head-down submissiveness and/or freezing. Note also that in that moment no one comes to help Joe; he is alone in this very threatening situation.

A host of different emotions and urges to do things (such as run away and hide) are being welded together. There is the awareness of anger in the other; there is the awareness that somehow his own behavior may have caused this threat from the parent to arise; there is intense anxiety arising in himself; there is a sense of aloneness and being isolated; there is an awareness that no one will rescue him; and of course there are the verbal labels of being 'stupid'. All these come together in that experience to form the core of an *emotional memory*. Like any powerful emotional experience and memory, it will influence our thoughts and feelings about ourselves and others, and our behaviors. The key point is to think about what Joe is learning about himself and others here. How easy will it be for Joe *not to* develop beliefs that he is stupid and that this 'stupidity' could get him into trouble? Not easy.

If the parent apologizes and explains their behavior, and at other times shows affection and praise, Joe can put this down to parental anger and not to himself, or that he is basically okay but needs to be careful at times. Problems arise if this does not happen, and Joe's most intense emotional experience of his parent is of anger and being labelled. Now in the future, criticism and anger in others could activate those emotional memories and feelings in Joe, including anxiety and a sense of aloneness. These feelings might flush rapidly through his body if someone is critical of him.

The point is, we can see how shame experiences can lay down powerful and complex *emotional memories* which can be triggered again in the future. Sometimes when we experience shame, and those heart-sink feelings, it is useful to think about the kinds of early experiences that might have made us vulnerable and then to practise compassion for those memories (see the exercises at the end of this chapter).

Sexual abuse

Sexual abuse has been found to be linked to chronic depression. In many cases where this is so, the people who were abused will often feel intense shame and be self-blaming and accusing – even though they were children or young adolescents at the time.[4]

The reasons for this are complex but can be a sort of self-protection because blaming the abuser can feel dangerous or confusing in some way. Clearly abuse can't possibly be a child's fault, because, as David Finkelhor pointed out some years ago, before anything happens, before the child is even involved, things are going on in the mind of the abuser. For example, there is the 'desire' in the abuser, and willingness to take advantage of a smaller person who will be in a relatively powerless position. The abuser has to overcome any moral scruples, and in today's society clear messages of wrongdoing. They need to manipulate the child into a position where they get them alone and can engage in the act, and they may overcome the child's resistance either with fear or some placating tactic: 'It's okay, this is a loving act really'.

In this book on depression we can't explore in too much detail how to tackle feelings of this kind of shame and self-blame. There are a number of books that specifically address this painful area.[5] There are also phone and Internet helplines, some of which are listed in Appendix 3. What we can say is that, using a compassionate approach, there are a few things that might be helpful to consider. First, as noted above, abuse begins in the mind of the abuser. Second, if you think about the size and power discrepancies between the child and an adult or older person, it's clear where the power is. Third, we need to address the issue of shame, because sometimes people feel that only if they can convince themselves they were not to blame can they not feel ashamed. Books that put a lot of emphasis on why you are not to blame can sometimes imply that that's the only way to heal oneself of shame.

But in fact there is actually nothing to be ashamed about in sexual abuse. It may be tragic, terrifying, betraying, confusing, sad or 'just was'. Those are some of the ways people will describe how they experienced it. As Carolyn Ainscough and Kay Toon note in their book, there are different experiences.[5] Some children are traumatized and terrified by aggressive threatening abusers. Others are seduced into going along with things that they're unsure about, or they might find their bodies behaving in what appear to be aroused ways. Keep in mind that sometimes we find our bodies acting aroused – because that's what bodies do. If I'm absorbed in a scary movie, even though I know perfectly well it is only a film I can't necessarily stop my body from being anxious. Bodily feelings don't obey any logic. And of course sometimes children can confuse affection in these interactions and go along with things – so it is not your fault.

There's a more important point still, far beyond blaming. This is that there is nothing to be ashamed of in being abused. It is sadly common throughout the world and has been for many thousands of years. It is a tragedy, something that might have been very frightening, a betrayal, a confusion, and a grief, but once you decide not to be shamed by it, you can become compassionate to your experiences and kind to your suffering.

Sometimes we won't let go of shame and self-blaming because it's a way for us to feel in control. If we really understand that it was not our fault and *we had no control*, this can be very frightening. Sometimes people say self-blame is the only way to make sense of it. I am all for making sense of things if they are genuine but there is no point in making up explanations – and when you would not make those blaming judgements if you were thinking about another child in your position. Our lack of control is the reality and the question is how we are able to be honest, humble and acknowledge some of our limitations in this life. This is not easy, so do reach out for help.

Another problem is that our efforts to shame perpetrators can cast a shame shadow over the survivors. As one abused person said, 'Society regards sexual abuse as disgusting, therefore if people knew my past they would see me as disgusting.' Indeed it is not uncommon for people to feel ashamed because they are worried about how other people will see them if they discover their past.

Because of this, people can feel ruined or damaged; anger they might feel towards the abuser can be directed at themselves because of the sense of being scarred. They don't like themselves because they feel that other people wouldn't like them if they knew. However, it can help to open our hearts to the fact that hundreds of thousands of children in the world are abused, and have been throughout history. Indeed, in some places in the world today, marriage between young girls and older men is still allowed. Sexual desire towards children or family members creates tragedies and traumas but, I would suggest to you, not shame, and in your compassionate, wise mind I suspect you know this already – if you tune into it.

Let me show this to you. Consider that if you knew of a child or young person going through these experiences, would you want to point the finger, call them names and shame them? I doubt it. It is far more likely that you would want to reach out to them with gentle support, kindness and rescue. For those children who are suffering today we wish for them to be free of their suffering, not for them to be ashamed.

If you are struggling with these experiences, and you believe that they may well be part of your depression, then open your heart to recognizing you are one of many; there is nothing shameful in what happened to you. Remember abuse has been part of the human condition for thousands of years. Note too there are many trained people out there who are skilled and keen to offer compassionate help. Most reputable support helplines are completely confidential. You can ask about your situation and see if you feel safe enough to realize that, whatever the circumstances of your abuse, good therapists will never shame you but will help you work through it so that you can gently heal and value yourself. The key thoughts are openness and honesty, kindness and understanding for yourself. Compassionately work on any self-blaming or self-dislike, and reach out for help – your family doctor may also be able to help you with this.

The shaming loop

As we enter depression, we can get caught up in various circles of negative thinking and behavior, and shame can lead to several forms of self-perpetuating difficulties. At times, these can give rise to what I call a *shaming loop* (see Figure 17.1). This is particularly true of teenagers, adolescence being a time when the approval of peers and the potential for shame can have particularly significant effects. Many children are prone to being teased; some, sadly, more so than others. Coming to terms with teasing can be important for adolescents, and there are positive ways to do so, such as finding other friends or learning to ignore the teasing. Some individuals, however, turn to all kinds of things to ensure that they are not rejected in this way. Simon, for example, told me that he stole from local shops to give things to 'friends' so that he would be accepted and win some status or prestige from them. Sadly, through much of his adult life he had felt that he had to give 'tokens' to others before they would accept him.

It is not always the case that feeling inferior leads to social withdrawal – but it can do, especially when people label and attack themselves. When feelings of inferiority do lead to social withdrawal, then such individuals are also more likely to be

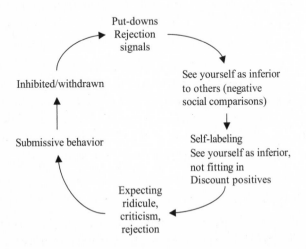

Figure 17.1 The 'shaming loop'.

rejected because they signal their feelings of inferiority to others. Unfortunately, adolescents in particular, but also adults, do not find withdrawn behavior attractive. The very thing that these people were hoping to avoid – being seen as inferior and being rejected – can happen because of the way they behave.

Heading shame off at the pass

If shame is so powerful, how do we cope with it? One way is to avoid it, by avoiding being seen as inferior, weak or vulnerable. You never put yourself into a situation where you could feel it. While the methods below may work for a while, problems can arise if they are adopted over the long term.

Compensation

This involves efforts to prove to yourself that you are good and able, and to avoid at all costs being placed in an inferior position. Sometimes we engage in vigorous competition with others to prove our own worth to them and to ourselves. It is as if we are constantly in a struggle to make up for something or prove something. Of course, we are trying to prove that we are not inferior, bad or inadequate and thus can be accepted rather than rejected. A therapist colleague told me (kindly) that this is why I write so much – but then, hey, we are all neurotic and it is how we use our neuroses that's important. I like writing now because I have copy-editors who can save me from shame!

Concealment

This occurs when individuals hide or avoid that which is potentially shameful. Body shame (including shame of decay and disease) may lead to various forms of body concealment. In the case of shameful feelings, we may hide what we feel. Other people are always seen as potential shamers who should not be allowed to peer too closely at our bodies or into our minds. When we deal with shame in this way, much of our lives can be taken up with hiding – even hiding things from ourselves. We can repress memories because they are too painful and shameful to know and feel.

Laughter may be used to distract from shame. We may make jokes when we feel mild shame, to divert others' attention from it. When it is used to stop us from taking ourselves too seriously, joking can be very useful; but laughter employed to avoid shame often feels very hollow underneath. Some comedians use shaming humour which can actually be a cover for their own fragilities or anger.

Concealment can sometimes produce another form of shaming loop. For example, Janine would become defensive and irritated if the members of her therapy group began to talk about issues that touched her shame. This made the other group members irritated in return. They felt she was not being honest or facing up to her problems. This actually caused Janine to feel even more shame, and so she closed down even further. Thus her way of trying to hide her shame actually produced more shaming responses from others.

Violence

As I noted above, anger and blaming others can be a response to external shame: 'If you shame me, I'll hit/hurt you.' This is retaliatory shaming. Violence, especially between men, often arises as a shame avoidance strategy – a form of face-saving. In some male gangs it is the most important and powerful source of violence. Shame violence and feelings of humiliation can be acted out in many ways.

Ray had been caught stealing at school. When his father found out, he gave him a 'good thrashing'. What happened here is that Ray's father felt shamed by his son's conduct, believing that his son had disgraced him and the family. Not able to recognize or deal with his own shame, the father had simply acted out his rage on his son. This, of course, compounded Ray's shame and anger. Had Ray's father not felt so ashamed of his son, but instead been concerned to help him, he might have been able to sit down and explore what this stealing was about.

Natalie and Jon had a disagreement in public, and Natalie contradicted Jon. When they got home, he threatened her, saying in a very menacing way, 'Never show me up in public again, or else!'

Usually, shame and counter-shaming interactions do not reach the stage of violence. Nonetheless, they can involve a good deal of blame and counter-blame. Each person attempts to avoid being placed in the bad or wrong position. You might recall the inter- action between Lynne and her husband Rob from the last chapter (see page 360).

Projection

Projection is used in two ways. The first is mind reading, where you may simply project your own opinions of yourself on to others. If you think that your performance is not very good and label yourself as a failure, you believe that others will think the same. You assume that you are not very lovable, so you take it as read that others will think so, too. You feel that crying is a sign of weakness, so you think everyone else does, too.

A more defensive kind of projection involves things about yourself that you are fearful of or have come to dislike. You hide these from yourself, but see them in others. It is the other person who is seen as the weak, shameful one – not you. Condemning homosexual desire, for example, may be a way of avoiding acknowledging such feelings in oneself (which are feared), seeing them only in others who may then be attacked. Sometimes bullies hate the feelings of vulnerability in themselves and so they attack others in whom they see these feelings. Some bullies label others in the same way that they would label themselves if they could ever reveal their own vulnerability or hurt. Such people project those aspects that they see as inferior in themselves. Racist and sexist jokes can be a result of this.

If people criticize or attack you, it is possible that they see something in you that they don't like in themselves. For example, Sandra sometimes cried about feeling alone. Her husband Jeff would become quite angry at this, which Sandra took as a criticism of her crying. But it turned out that, as a child, Jeff had himself been criticized for crying. Not only did he view Sandra's crying as a criticism of himself (he thought it meant she was not happy living with him), but he also hated the feelings of vulnerability that might lead to *him* crying. Thus, Sandra's crying reminded him of things he was ashamed of in himself.

So, if people put you down or try to shame you about something (perhaps for crying or failing or needing affection), ask yourself: How do *they* cope with these things? How do they cope with crying or failing? If you reflect on this and recognize that they don't allow themselves to cry, or that they become quite angry when they fail, or that they have problems with affection, then it is wise to consider that perhaps they are criticizing you because they can't cope with these things themselves. Whatever you do, don't get caught up in the idea that they are right and you are wrong.

Shame, humiliation and revenge

We touched on humiliation a little above in the section on violence. Humiliation is similar to and different from shame. Both involve painful feelings, of being put down, harmed or rejected. We believe that the other person (parent, partner, boss) is sending signals that we are unacceptable, inadequate or bad in some way. This is external shame, but in humiliation we focus on the 'badness' in the other, not in ourselves.

Feelings of humiliation, where we feel unfairly criticized or injured, can ignite powerful desires for revenge. Indeed, you can tell the extent to which you feel humiliated by the intensity of your thoughts about the injustice done to you and the strength of your desire for revenge. For some people, their fantasies of revenge are frightening and so they are hidden away. In such cases, acknowledgement of anger is a first step. For others, the anger and desire for revenge are constantly present, and they need to discover ways to work through the humiliation and let it go.

You may be vulnerable to feelings of humiliation now because of things that happened to you in the past. However, sitting on a lot of desires for revenge is not helpful to you. This is not to deny that very harmful things may have been done to you; rather, it is to say that if these feelings are not worked through, they can lead to a lot of mistrust of others and a tendency to constantly want to get your own back. This is a very lonely position and will keep your threat system stimulated by your vengeful thoughts. You can take the first steps to change by acknowledging your pain and hurt and deciding to seek help. You may also need to grieve for past hurts and losses.

It is one thing to have a desire for revenge on someone we do not care about, but what happens if it is someone you *do* want to have a close relationship with? Ted's father knocked him about as a child, and yet Ted also loved his father and wanted to be close to him. In therapy, Ted found it extremely difficult to recognize the feelings of humiliation that his father had inflicted on him and his own desire for revenge. Until he did recognize this, he was not able to move on to forgiving himself, for his vengeful thoughts, and forgiving his father.

Blocked revenge

Sometimes a strong desire for revenge that is blocked can be associated with depression. For example, someone has been physically attacked in the street or seriously injured in a car crash, but the guilty person gets off with a light sentence or evades arrest altogether. When we feel a grave sense of injustice that we cannot put right, we can feel terribly frustrated and defeated. People who experience blocked revenge can be caught up in awful ruminations and feelings, often leading to difficulties in sleeping. This continual brooding keeps the stress system highly active, as they go round and round in circles. Even if they know this, they may be understandably reluctant to give up their preoccupation. Professional advice and support may help.

Becoming assertive

Sometimes dealing with shame is about becoming assertive. For example Kimberly often felt shamed by her husband's put-downs until she learnt to stand up to him. In working with depressed people we can find that shame and self-criticism can be covers for anger and that when they are honest about their anger the shame changes. For example, Anne's mother was emotionally neglectful and very critical, but insisted that she was a wonderful mother. So wonderful, in fact, that Anne was never going to be as good as her at anything! Part of Anne loved her mother and was frightened of losing her support or igniting her criticism, but it was not until Anne acknowledged that there was also a part of her that would like to 'smash her smug little face in' (and give voice to that in therapy) that she was able to begin to think about assertiveness – being compassionate and understanding to that anger was key to helping with shame.

Overview

Shame is a very important emotion, but like all emotions such as anxiety, fear and anger it can become problematic. It can become too easily triggered, too intense and last too long (because of how we ruminate on our sense of shame). It can be associated with unpleasant memories, bodily feelings and a flawed sense of ourselves.

How we learn to recognize and work with shame is key to healing our shame, learning from it, growing from it and moving on. In this chapter we have seen a whole range of ways in which we can experience shame and deal with it compassionately. Shame is part of the human condition.

KEY POINTS

- We all have the potential for shame.
- There are two types of shame. External shame is linked to the feelings we have if we think others are looking down on us, are critical, or see us as not worth bothering with. Internal shame is experienced when we are harsh and critical with ourselves.
- Shame grows in us when we label ourselves as bad, inferior, inadequate, etc.
- Shame can be focused on many things – on our bodies, our actions, our feelings. The origin of these feelings may be recent or in the more distant past.

- Shame can arise when we want to feel good about ourselves, loved, wanted and valued, but seem unable to elicit this from others and encounter criticism or rejections.
- Shame can be a paralyzing experience, and we may spend a good deal of our lives trying to conceal it or make up for what we think is shameful.
- Recovery comes from gradually acknowledging what we feel ashamed of, learning to treat it with compassion, and recognizing that many depressive styles operate in shame (e.g., discounting the positives, all-or-nothing thinking, overgeneralizing, self-labelling and even self-hatred).

EXERCISES

Exercise 1

Complete the following sentences:

- I feel ashamed about myself because _____
- I feel ashamed of myself when I do/fail to do _____
- I feel ashamed of myself when I feel, think or fantasize about _____
- I feel ashamed of myself because in the past I _____

Now that you have outlined some of the things you feel ashamed about, you can start to use your rational/compassionate mind to face these honestly and heal them.

To start with, write down some alternatives to the thoughts of shame you might have. For example:

I am not a bad/inferior/worthless person because _____

Here, focus on compassionate understanding, compassionate attention, compassionate thinking and compassionate behavior, and then generate compassionate feeling. Remember to open your heart to common humanity, that many humans have these kinds of difficulties.

Exercise 2: Opening to your compassionate mind

In this exercise, spend some moments quietly and engage your soothing rhythm of breathing. Feel yourself slow down. Focus on your compassionate mind (see pages 149–55). Remember this is what you imagine yourself to be – a deeply compassionate person. Imagine yourself expanding because not only are you compassionate, kind and gentle but you are also an authority and have wisdom; create within yourself a sense of strength and warmth. Allow yourself to have a kind facial expression and body posture. When you are happy with that method, imagine you can see in front of you the shame-self or the part of you that is feeling shame. See the eyes cast downwards. Allow compassion and kindness to engulf that part of you. Offer as much compassion as it needs. If your mind wanders or you feel it being pulled too much to the shame aspects, stop, pull back, regain your soothing breathing, refocus on your compassionate qualities of wisdom, strength, warmth and being non-judgemental, and then start again.

LETTING GO WITH GRATITUDE

Sometimes as people sit with their compassionate postures and imagine the shame aspect they can see this part of them shrinking and moving away. This can be very helpful. Imagine that the part that feels shame is shrinking and moving away – getting smaller and smaller until it vanishes. But it is leaving *with gratitude for you* – with gratitude for you because you are releasing it and letting it go. You are not holding on to it any more. It can rest. It is the same basic ideas that we used with our tension; see pages 130–2.

Exercise 3

Try using healing compassionate imagery. Imagine yourself when you feel ashamed – nothing too major to start with: what is (or was) happening to you? Imagine that someone who cares about you has come to help you. What do you need from them? Ask for it. Imagine what they say to you – maybe they put an arm around you (if you like). Let their compassion sympathy flow to you. Decide how you will change to heal and grow from your shame feelings. Next, imagine how you would act if you were less shame-prone and think about the steps to take to make this come true.

Exercise 4

Sometimes it can be very useful to write a compassionate letter about things we are ashamed about (see pages 235–9). Remember this letter is written from the point of view of a wise, compassionate, gentle and kind self. Keep in mind that we all just find ourselves in this life, have been dealt different hands that we have to play as best we can. With this understanding and compassion, engage with your shame. Focus on compassionate attention, remembering times we have shown the more positive aspects of a personality. Consider your compassionate thinking and reasoning, and try to write a letter with a real desire to give understanding, compassion and gentleness. Sometimes these letters are difficult to write and you might have to try several times. Experiment and see how you get on, keeping clear in your mind that your goal is to bring compassion to your shame feelings.

Exercise 5

When we are ashamed we can back off from people and withdraw, so anti-shame behavior – operating against shame – is by engaging with others rather than withdrawing. You might also think about something positive you might do that your anxiety or shame might hold you back from. This might involve taking the first steps to initiate positive activities with other people. Decide if you are a person who waits to be chosen or are a chooser. Exert more control over positive choices, not just vetoes. Being able to stand up and resist things you don't want to do is important, but also consider being assertive in a positive way, to think about what you would like to do and how to make that happen rather than letting your lack of confidence hold you back. In this exercise choose something positive, it doesn't have to be very big, and go for it – learning to be kind, encouraging and supportive along the way.

Understanding and coping with guilt

Differences between shame and guilt

So far we have talked a lot about not blaming and not being self-critical, because condemning and blaming does not help us – but learning to be open to our limitations, mistakes and unkindnesses and be genuinely committed to improve and repair is very important for us in developing compassion (see Table 13.1). Guilt and the ability to be able to tolerate guilt can help us here.

Appropriate feelings of guilt are seen as more positive than shame because they are linked to wanting to avoid hurting others, the ability to think about *other people's* feelings, to moral concerns and genuine effort to make amends.[1] Guilt can obviously link to the legal meaning, that is, to mean one has 'caused something' to happen – but here I am going to contrast the psychological meanings of guilt and shame.

- Guilt has a different focus from shame. In guilt we usually focus on the *harm* or *hurt* we have caused other people by our actions, thoughts or feelings. Guilt can link to feeling *responsible* for others – to make them happy or protect them from harm. Shame, you will recall, is more about harm to oneself (being a bad, defective or unattractive person in some way).

- Guilt tends to focus on specific events – 'I feel guilty because I did *that* or thought *this*'– whereas shame is focused on feelings about the self, such as being inadequate, flawed or unattractive.
- In shame we want to hide and cover up, but in guilt we want to repair things and put things right.
- Guilt (often) arises where there are conflicts over things that we want, or want to do, that may harm others. Guilt is commonly associated with conflicts where one person's gain is another person's loss.
- To feel guilt, you have to be open to the suffering of self and others; to have empathy and sympathy and to experience feelings of sadness and sorrow (in contrast to shame's anxiety, anger or denial) if you have hurt someone. These are not pure emotions because mostly we have blends of both.

To clarify these distinctions, consider the reactions of two men, John and Tom, both of whom have affairs. When their respective wives discover their infidelity, John thinks,

Oh dear, my wife will give me a hard time now. Maybe she won't love me so much. Suppose she tells our friends? How will I face them? I think I had better hide for a while and be extra nice.

John's focus is not at all on the pain he has given his wife, but only on himself. His main concern is the damage the discovery may do to him (external shame) and maybe he is not a nice person (internal shame). His response is shame-based. Tom, however, feels terribly sad for the hurt he has caused his wife and the damage he has done to the relationship. He recognizes how bad he would feel if the situation were reversed and feels remorse. Tom may also worry about his wife loving him less and what his friends might think of him if they found out, because principally he is focused on the harm he has done and the hurt he has caused and how he can help his wife. His response is guilt-based.

Some guilt feelings are often related to a certain kind of *fear*. The fear is the same kind of fear we might feel if we hear that someone we love has been hurt – it is based on a worry for and about them. When we have done something that has caused hurt or harm there can be feelings of sorrow and sadness, and these in turn are linked to feelings of remorse and regret. It is these feelings that make us want to put things right. For example, John may not feel very much sorrow for what he has done, because he is focused purely on the damage to him that may follow from the discovery. John's fear is that others will not like him. Tom, however, feels deep sorrow to see his wife so hurt.

You will note from this example that although Tom feels guilt and is far more in touch with the pain he has caused than John, he is unlikely to be free of shame. Suddenly, confronted with a deeply hurt wife, he may (perhaps for the first time) really appreciate how hurtful his actions have been, and this could trigger negative (shame-related) thoughts. Although this chapter is going to focus on guilt, we should be clear that guilt can trigger shame (and self-attacking thoughts, e.g., 'I am a cheat and a bad/unlovable person'); indeed, in depression it commonly does. Both guilt and shame are *self-conscious* emotions – meaning that they focus attention in on the self. The heightened self-consciousness of guilt can easily tip into shame and negativity when we are depressed. Guilt, as a trigger for shame, is important to spot.

Caring and guilt

The American psychologist Martin Hoffman sees guilt as related to sympathy and empathy: you need both to feel guilt.[2] Sympathy is when we are emotionally moved by another's upset or hurt; the wince if we see someone fall heavily or cut themselves. Empathy is our ability to put ourselves in the shoes of others and think about things from their point of view. However, without caring concern or some sympathy, empathy can be put to dark uses. Advertisers need some empathy to know how to hook us in to buy their products. Bullies might know how to really upset us because they can work out our soft spots and play on them. There is more to guilt than just empathy, and adult guilt must always involve some capacity for compassion and a desire to care for others – or at least not cause harm. This is why guilt cannot be understood purely by our thoughts. If we don't care about others, why would we be bothered with guilt? One does not need to care for others to feel ashamed, but one does to feel guilt. Indeed, one reason we can behave so badly and hurtfully towards others is because we don't have any interest in caring for or about the person. Similarly, if we stop caring or feeling sympathy for ourselves, we can also treat ourselves very cruelly and unkindly.

Guilt as moral emotion

I will explore how guilt can become a problem, especially when it is fused with shame – which it often is in depression. However, we should also be clear that guilt is an extremely important moral emotion. Guilt feelings can enable us to feel for others and be sensitive to hurting other people and truly want to make amends. Guilt is very much something to be open about, own and tolerate without turning it into a feeling of being a bad person (i.e., shame). We can learn to accept that sometimes our behavior is not so good! Guilt is when we focus on the other person(s) and care about them and our impact on them. Shame, however, is about our sense of ourselves.

Caring, reputation and approval-seeking

Guilt requires some emotional capacity for caring. It is not related to a status hierarchy or to feeling inferior in the way shame is. Guilt evolved along with our capacity to care for others. However, before we look at this more closely we need to clarify something important about our motives for engaging in caring behavior towards others. Not all acts of caring involve genuine feelings of care or sympathy. In fact, many don't. Sometimes we are kind and nice to others because we want them to think well of us. We want to have the reputation of being nice, caring people. We are caring because we want to be liked, loved or admired. This is approval-focused caring. If we fail at this, what we feel may be not guilt (because our motives weren't focused on the other) but shame: 'Oh no, I forgot Bridget's birthday party. She will think *I am* really thoughtless and be angry *with me*. Why *am I* so forgetful? *I am* stupid to make these mistakes.' You see how much is focused on the self?

Let's think about Tom and John again. Suppose John decides that he must be extra nice to his wife because in that way he might *win back* her love, or make life easier *for himself*, or because he might feel better *about himself* – this is approval- and shame-based caring. Tom, however, wants to help *his wife* to feel better. This is guilt-based caring. When we try to make amends only from shame, those around us can sense we are being nice for our own self-interests! So, in response, they might reject us.

So we can see that caring for others (being nice to people) and putting things right when they go wrong can be motivated by a desire to make ourselves feel better (shame-based) or to make others feel better (guilt-based). However, as in so many things, the picture is rarely black and white; in most cases it is a matter of balance, and our caring behavior is not purely of one or the other kind. Let's look at this more closely.

Rescuing heroes and self-sacrifice

For many people, doing a good turn for others and helping out when needed feels good, especially if others show gratitude and appreciation of our efforts. Letting our friends or family down, on the other hand, can feel bad. Trying to earn others' gratitude and thus feel good about ourselves is a typical human thing to do; we like to feel needed. For some, though, this desire can become exaggerated.

For example, David had fantasies of developing a loving relationship with a woman by rescuing her from a difficult life situation. The fantasy was vague. It could have been that she was lonely, or in a bad relationship with another man. He wanted to be someone's knight in shining armour and rescue her. The key point was that he felt that if he found a woman who needed him, then her *gratitude* to him would be the basis for love. He needed to be needed. As you might imagine, he was far more uncertain that he could be loved simply for himself – he had to be useful to a woman before she would love him. You can also imagine the kind of person he felt he had a chance with. He never thought he'd get anywhere with strong and able women, and he felt they would overpower him easily. Gratitude and appreciation are of course important aspects of affectionate relationships; but sometimes people set out to put themselves in relationships where they can earn gratitude – almost expect it, even – because getting others' gratitude and appreciation is the *only way* they feel loved.

As for the partner – they do not want to be related to someone only out of gratitude – that becomes unpleasant!

Looking at the same desire negatively, we need others to be in difficulty so that we can rescue them. Some theorists see this style as developing in childhood, where children try to heal the wounds and difficulties of their parents and so to make their parents love them out of gratitude. This style can be called the *rescuing hero*. However, also note how our fantasies can involve obtaining other people's appreciation, gratitude or admiration for being able to make things better for them. How much of it is really approval-seeking? Saving the world from a disease or alien invasion is the stuff of many of our fantasies as children and (judging by Hollywood movies) adults too. We want to be heroic saviours.

Rescuing heroes are prone to burnout, exhaustion and hiding their negative feelings towards others. They may have problems with being assertive in pursuing their own wants and desires, through always trying to be 'so understanding' of others. Sometimes they try to avoid the more angry and aggressive feelings in themselves because they fear this makes them unlovable. Various writers have claimed that some people can care or love too much, and are vulnerable to depression because they behave too submissively. In fact, many books have been written on how guilt arises from an overdeveloped need to be nice, and can get in the way of healthy lifestyles. However, as many spiritual traditions point out, it is not really possible to love too much. In my view the problem is more commonly one of needing to be seen as, and to feel oneself to be, a caring person. We are too submissive and fail to look after our own needs.

If you think you are a bit of a rescuing hero and always try to look after others, the first thing is to be kind to yourself about this – let's face it, it's not a bad trait to have. Once you are kind and accepting of this tendency in yourself, the next thing is to think about how to bring more compassionate balance into your life. This may require you to spend some time gently thinking about what *your* needs are – then act on them, step by step. If you are into list-making then make a list of the ways you could bring a better self–other balance into your life. Or you could write yourself a compassionate letter on how to be more balanced and less of a rescuing hero.

For example, Tina always put her young children first and was often tired when her husband got home. She was not keen on getting babysitters, so their going out together had fallen away, as had their sex life. Her husband had gradually disengaged because she was very much 'mother hen' with the children and wanted to do most things with them – so he felt a bit excluded. Tina came to realize that she was putting too much of her self-identity and sense of being a 'good person' into being the 'perfect mother'. This was linked to feeling she had not been properly cared for as a child herself, but she came to see that she was neglecting her own needs and those of her marriage. Slowly she acknowledged she needed more help from her husband, especially at night, and also needed some space for her own interests. At first her husband was a bit annoyed because he felt she was pushing him even further away – but she had anticipated this and was able to accept his feelings and agree that maybe she had overdone the mothering role, but now needed his help. Step by step, and keeping a compassionate focus, they worked it out together. As she felt more able to have time and space for herself and she let her husband help out more, they rekindled their affections and thought more of themselves 'as a team'.

Guilt, caring and depression

When people become depressed they can lose the capacity to *feel caring* towards others and then feel deeply guilty and ashamed about this. Sometimes when people become depressed they face up more honestly to the fact that some of their caring and 'putting others first' has been motivated by the wish to be liked, loved and approved of, and not necessarily from care or compassion for others. Third, guilt and the concern not to hurt others can create many complicated dilemmas in life that can also be traps. Let's look at these links.

Losing the capacity to 'feel' for others

Depression knocks out many of our abilities for positive feelings. We can lose interest in ourselves, and in others too. Becoming aware that we have neither the energy to care nor feelings of caring can be a blow to our self-esteem.

Sam had been a caring man for his family and friends, but when he became depressed he felt unable to show interest in his family. His anxiety stopped him from doing things with them, like going on holiday, which previously he would have planned, organized and enjoyed. When one of his children informed him he was going to be a new grandfather he felt inwardly dead about it. Our conversations went something like this:

Sam: *I just don't feel anything for anyone any more. I don't know what has happened to me. When Julia told me she was expecting I didn't feel anything. I know my reaction must have hurt her and I felt terrible about it. I would so much like to be there for her, but it just seems such an ordeal. My first thoughts were, 'Oh God, I am going to have to take the responsibility*

> *of being a caring grandad. I don't want the hassle of that.'*
>
> Paul: *Well, sadly, depression can do this. And even when we are not depressed we can have such feelings and thoughts. But when we are depressed our inner resources are low and the body simply does not have energy to put into caring feelings. If there is no fuel in your car it does not matter how much you push the accelerator, it won't go anywhere. This does not mean the car is bad or deficient, only that the fuel tank is empty. We need to have a way of thinking about your loss of ability to care for others, 'to be there for them', so that your guilt does not become another source of self-attacking.*

Working with this aspect of Sam's depression was focused on his guilt feelings about not feeling for others close to him. It turned out that he was often prone to guilt feelings and was normally very loving and sensitive to others. Sam was experiencing guilt for his lost abilities to 'be there for others' and was aware of how much his depression was hurting others. Yet he felt he could not do anything about it. Nor could he address some of his anger and difficulties in relationships because to do so felt like a betrayal and (of course) made him feel more guilty. His guilt feelings turned to shame; for example, he told himself he was selfish and an unlovable person. Therapy focused on seeing the depression as a brain state that turns off certain positive emotions.

Mothers can be especially prone to guilt when they lose loving feelings for their children. They tell themselves, 'I should not feel like this, I should always feel loving towards them'. Concern that their feelings and behaviors are harming their children can be a source of painful guilt. If this triggers negative ideas of the self such as 'I am a bad mother', then there is guilt and shame.

If you suffer from these kinds of feelings, then, as with so much I have tried to outline here, the key message is clear – *the loss of feelings is not your fault – it is sad and painful but absolutely not your fault*. We can be kind to our loss of feelings, and work out how best to walk the road of self-understanding and healing our minds.

Feeling a burden to others

Some depressed people feel that they are being a burden to others (see pages 313–16). They may even feel that others would be better off without them. This is a dangerous way of thinking, because it fuels suicidal thoughts. It is *never* true, because suicide leaves those left behind in states of sadness, loss, anger and confusion; they'll never forget. If you think like this, let me state clearly: this is the depression talking, and *it is never true*. Sadly, I have seen the damage a suicide can do to families for years to come. And when people recover from depression they are very relieved they did not harm themselves. If you think others would be better off without you, then you need to be clear in your mind that everyone, including you, would be better off if you could recover from your depression – that's common sense – but, no matter how dark your feelings are, *no one* gains from a suicide.

So let's be honest about this. Sure, depression is burdensome – but so are many other types of illness. We do not need to pretend otherwise. And we may become dependent for a while. When we are children we could not survive without being dependent on others. When we get sick we often need looking after – life is like this. There are times when we have to take as well as give. Sometimes we have to learn how to cope with being cared for, for a while; to learn that sometimes we have just run out of fuel and then we can't give out as much as we would like. If you are haunted by feelings of being a burden, then seek professional help as soon as you can. Tell yourself,

This is my depression talking. There is nothing bad about me for feeling this way. However, I can focus on what I need to do to get well rather than how bad (guilty and/or ashamed) I am for being depressed. There are over 300 million depressed people in the world, so it can't be my fault if my depression makes me feel this way. Let's go step by step and focus on what I can do rather than what I can't.

This is what we worked on with Sam from pages 411–12.

Paul: *At the moment you're preoccupied with the fact that you don't feel pleasure in your daughter's pregnancy, right? And you feel sad at this loss and the possibility that it hurts her?*

Sam: *Yes.*

Paul: *Okay, suppose you were to put that to one side; to admit, as you have, that your feelings are not functioning that well right now; that's sad for you, but what might you do that she would like?*

Sam: *(thinks) Well, I guess I would normally send her a card or something.*

Paul: *Okay. How would you feel if you did that?*

Sam: *Better, probably, but it wouldn't seem genuine. I should do this because I really want to, because I feel something. (*Note the underlying belief that all caring should come from a deep feeling of caring. We could have explored this belief, and later on we did, but here we took a different track.*)*

Paul: *Sure, if you weren't depressed you might well feel something. But look, we know that at the moment you won't, so there is not a lot of point in telling yourself you should feel something. Your feelings may come back as you recover. The first step is helping you do things that you want to do, regardless of what you feel. Feelings will be the bonus of getting well. So even though there may not be much feeling in it right now, sending a card would be something you could do.*

Because Sam was preoccupied with his guilt feelings about not feeling overjoyed at his daughter's pregnancy, but felt indifferent, he had been paralyzed and unable to act in ways he'd normally do. This made him feel even worse. By breaking into this paralysis we were able to help him begin to make changes and not expect that his behaviors should be matched with passionate feelings of caring. He went to the shops and sent a card and some flowers. His daughter was touched by this, and it was a small step forward. This also indicates the importance of doing things and taking action, even when you don't really feel like it (see Chapter 12). So compassionate behaviour can be more important than compassionate feeling.

We also learned from this exercise that Sam had been telling himself that if he went through the motions of caring then this was not genuine caring, and if it was not genuine caring it was a fake, and if it was a fake it was worthless. Remember how some people can be tormented by the ideas that their behaviors are fake (see Chapter 14)? Sam gives another example of this.

Sometimes people lose affectionate feelings for others (and feel guilty) because of unresolved conflicts of anger or envy. I will discuss these in later chapters; here we simply make the point that whatever might be causing the loss of caring feelings, there are things that one can do and ways of thinking about the problem that need not lead you into self-attacking. Ask yourself:

- Am I expecting too much of myself?
- Am I expecting my feelings to work as they would if I were not depressed?
- How would I feel if I were not depressed or stressed out?
- Even though I may not have much feeling for it, are there things I could do that would help me feel better?

Guilt, dilemmas and traps

Few of us take pleasure in purposely hurting others, especially those we care about, but sometimes this is inevitable and we need to face that. Carol had stayed in a relationship for some years because she could not face hurting John. She was fond of him, but the love had gone out of the relationship some years earlier. Her mother had had a similar relationship with her father, and Carol had felt sorry for both of them. They had stayed together, her parents had told her, 'for the sake of the kids'. That of course put some burden on Carol, to think that mother and father suffered each other because of her. It is just as likely that there were many other complex factors in *their* psychology that made them cling to each other. For example, maybe they did not know how to build affectionate relationships.

Many children in such situations, far from feeling gratitude to their parents, can feel a sense of guilt. Carol was one of those people who felt it her role to make people happy. She was one of life's rescuing heroes. To be a cause of unhappiness (e.g., to John by leaving him) was almost unbearable. Also, as we noted above, guilt is most likely in times of conflict, where one person's gain is another person's loss.

No therapy can help people avoid dilemmas in life, and sometimes these are acutely painful. There are no right or wrong answers; no cost-free solutions. All one can do is help people think about their dilemmas in ways that allow them to move forward with them rather than get stuck in guilt and shame. In essence, Carol's psychology had set up a trap – sometimes called the compassion or guilt trap. She was not free to do what she wanted (to leave the relationship) because she felt too guilty about the pain she would cause John. Underneath this there was a bubbling resentment (for which she felt guilty) and depression. She could see no way forward.

Carol's therapy focused on issues related to her guilt and her inability to tolerate it. She had to acknowledge the painful fact that her guilt often led her to being dishonest in relationships. She would do things for others to avoid upsetting them. By the end of her therapy she had worked out that ending the relationship might be for the better. She would be sad about it, and John would be hurt, but if she stayed she would only get more resentful and depressed. Once she had faced the possibility that she could go, that she could face her guilt, sorrow and sadness, she felt less trapped. The therapy had loosened the bonds that were immobilizing her. I don't actually know if she did leave John, as their relationship had improved slightly through her being more honest with him; but she told me that she had more insight into what locked her into unhelpful relationships, and this released her a little. Maybe facing the fact that she *could* leave made the need to leave less urgent. I don't know.

Guilt and escaping

Just as we can feel a burden to others, so we can feel burdened and overloaded by the responsibilities of life. Not only may people lose interest in caring for others; as they get depressed they can have strong desires to get away from them, to escape. For example, a young mother who is not sleeping and has become exhausted may want to run away from everyone who is making demands on her. In our own studies we have found that desires to escape are strongly associated with depression.[3] (See pages 57–8.)

If you have strong escape desires, then remind yourself that these are common in depression. Try to work out specifically what you want to escape from. Do you need to create more space for yourself and look after your own needs more? Worksheet 4 in Appendix 1 addresses this issue. Guilt about wanting to escape can stop people exploring why they wish to leave, or what they need to do to change their current situation, or even whether they would indeed be better off leaving or taking time out. Guilt can lock us into circles of thought and feeling such as: taking on too much responsibility, we feeling burdened, then want to escape, then feel guilty; to cope with the guilt we try harder, but then feel more burdened – and so on. It's important to allow yourself to take an honest look at your life and see what needs to change to make you feel less burdened. Are you expecting too much of yourself? Do you take on things because you do not like to say 'no' – but then feel resentful and out of control? Have you become exhausted? Do you feel like this when you are not depressed? Imagine you were talking to a friend. How would you see it for them? How would you help them? What might a rational/compassionate approach be?

Being honest

Guilt can be like other emotions, such as anxiety or anger – we can feel overwhelmed. But fear and guilt can lead to dishonesty and serious difficulties. Abigail often felt a little intimidated by her husband and wanted to separate from him, but whenever she broached the topic he got angry and made her feel guilty. She withdrew more and more and started taking overdoses. One day she admitted, 'You know, I just hoped he would get fed up with me, find someone else and leave – that was my dream. I could not bring myself to be the one to walk out'. Abigail was also not entirely sure in her own mind if she wanted the relationship to end – but if her husband left her, that would relieve her of those doubts too. When she fantasized about him leaving her there was 'this enormous sense of relief'. She was also honest enough to acknowledge that part of her could then also play the hard-done-by victim.

These are not easy things to acknowledge in ourselves – they take courage – but we can be gentle and see that many people get caught in these dilemmas and struggle to be honest. It's not our fault – life can be tricky. However, once we give up self-blaming and face our sense of shame and guilt, and realize our dishonesty is not helpful, then we are more open to think how best to move forward. Ruminating on entrapment is a recipe for depression. In fact Abigail did eventually muster the courage to leave and some months later reflected on why she had not 'done it years ago'.

Guilt and a sense of deserving

People who are prone to excessive guilt will sometimes talk in terms of 'entitlement' and 'deserving'. Fairness and a sense of deserving are part of our psychology, but we must learn to keep it in balance. Some depressed people feel they don't deserve to be happy – that somehow if they are happy they will be punished for it. Folk who feel like this might have been made to feel guilty when they focused on their own needs and feelings. Some people can also feel tormented by guilt and shame because they can't enjoy their good fortune. Such a person may say, 'I've got so much going for me. I'm not poor, and I have a fairly good relationship with my partner, but I'm not happy. I feel so guilty that I can't appreciate things. Maybe I don't deserve them.' This is a bit like Sam from a few pages ago. Instead of working hard to find out exactly what they are not happy about, they keep telling themselves they 'should be happy' and feel worse for not being so. If this is the case for you, then write down what you are satisfied with in your life. Then write down the things you are happy with. Recognize that there are things that you are happy with and things that you may not be happy with. Next, note that if you are unhappy in one area of your life this can affect the feelings about other areas – that's natural. If you break a leg, it doesn't matter how well the rest of your body is functioning, the broken leg still hurts like hell and stops you doing lots of things. Telling yourself you shouldn't be in pain because at least you don't have cancer does not help much. Of course, learning to appreciate the good things in one's life is important in depression because it helps us avoid all-or-nothing thinking and over-focusing on the negative, and stimulates positive feelings. There is not much to be gained by feeling guilty for not being happy. You can see then that the question of deserving does not enter into it.

Some people can feel guilt at wanting to fulfil their own needs; wanting more affection or time to do things with friends. One patient thought that wanting more personal space was 'kind of greedy'. Owning up to and trying to fulfil one's needs are normal, natural and important. The key thing is how to balance the demands on us, while also looking after ourselves and not burning ourselves to a frazzle!

Fear of enjoying life

We might need to acknowledge that some of us can develop a fear of pleasure and enjoying life. Sounds odd, doesn't it? But consider Kerry. She has many memories of enjoying herself, then something bad happening. For example, she recalled enjoying playing with friends in a garden, screaming with fun. Then her mother came rushing out and told her how bad she was as she had forgotten to clean her room, grabbed her painfully by the arms, told the other children to 'go home' and threw her into her room. Kerry said, 'If I feel very happy I am sure I will pay for it tomorrow or something really bad will happen. I feel I must never let my guard down.' In Kerry's mind good feelings were associated with bad outcomes. You can see how Kerry had learned to be frightened of feeling good.

Patricia only felt people cared for her if she was in pain or unwell – indeed, only if she were ill did she think that her mother paid the slightest attention to her. In her mind was the idea that being happy or well meant not being cared for or about.

So there may be all kinds of reasons why we feel guilty or frightened to be happy. In a quiet moment it can be useful to write these down, in a gentle and honest way. Ask yourself, 'If I was frightened or concerned with being really happy – what would my concerns be?'

Remember, too, that it's relationships that make us happy, not material objects. People make this mistake time and again. Just because you are wealthy or healthy (although these help, of course) is no guarantee at all of being happy. Indeed, I would suggest that often it is not so much happiness that is key, but that we can learn contentment and how to be at peace with ourselves.[4] To help yourself with these problems you can:

- acknowledge that you may be wary of feeling happy
- write down possible fears and where these might have come from (why you are not allowed to be happy)
- think how you can test out these ideas and how to practise small steps for changing
- recognize that 'that was then, this is now' and it is time to retrain your brain
- make an effort to practise your 'change steps' allowing yourself to feel (a bit) happy each day.

Survivor guilt

Lynn O'Connor and her colleagues in San Francisco have studied guilt over a number of years and noted there are different
types of guilt. One of these is *survivor guilt*.[5] This type of guilt first
came to the attention of researchers when it was found that
people who had survived traumatic experiences such as being
in a concentration camp or taken hostage, or survived a disaster
could feel bad because they had survived while others had died
or been seriously injured. They asked themselves, 'Why did I
survive and others die?' Sometimes there was a feeling that they
didn't deserve to live, or didn't have a right to be happy when
others had died. Feeling happy made them feel guilty. A recent
study has found that people who have survived a life-threaten-
ing illness and knew others who shared the condition but who
did not survive, can feel not only sadness but also a depressing
sense of not deserving or, 'Why me?'

Guilt at being better off than others

Lynn and her colleagues also reasoned that this kind of guilt can
operate in many types of relationship where we find ourselves
better off than others: for example, from an awareness that we
have superior qualities, or better opportunities. Imagine that you
and a good friend take an important examination, say to go to
university or get a job, or you enter a competition like a beauty
pageant. You are both keen and share your hopes of passing or
winning. You pass but your friend does not – she fails. How do
you feel?

There are times when we know that we can't do anything to
help others; and knowing that others are suffering while you
feel helpless to do anything about it can be depressing, especially
if you are doing well yourself. Sonia had a good job in advertising

and was over the moon about it. Her husband Dave, however, was not doing so well. His firm was going downhill and eventually he was put on short time. Sonia started to feel guilty about her success. When she came home she didn't share good experiences she had at work or her sense of how exciting it was, because she felt it would upset Dave and make him feel worse. She was also worried that Dave would resent and envy her for her good job. She loved Dave, but she also began to resent his low mood and anger at how things had turned out for him. Then she also felt guilty at feeling resentful. After all, things were going well for her. The guilt of upsetting Dave with her own good fortune stopped her from sharing things with him. As time passed, she found that she would stay longer at work to be with enthusiastic people rather than in the more subdued mood that prevailed at home – but this also made her feel more guilty. Key beliefs were: 'I shouldn't want to spend more time at work when I know that Dave needs me at home. I should be there for him. I shouldn't enjoy my life when Dave is not enjoying his. I am selfish.' Sonia needed to clarify the issues and recognize that, for her, wanting to be with enthusiastic people rather than a husband afflicted by envious low mood is natural. For Sonia, the important point was to help her see that labelling herself as selfish and feeling guilty about feeling resentment were unhelpful.

In some families, induced guilt is rife. Sonia had grown up in a family with a mildly depressed mother. As she entered adolescence and started to go out at night, her mother would often tell Sonia how lucky she was and how much more difficult it had been for herself when she was young. 'I never had the opportunities you have', she'd say. Her mother would tell her how much she loved Sonia, not by noting how good-natured or talented Sonia was, but by pointing to all the sacrifices she (as her mother) had made for her! Sonia was unwittingly being trained to operate on guilt and gratitude. She came to believe that she should always put the needs of others first and that if others were suffering or needed her, she should be there for them. After all, she was so lucky, wasn't she? In therapy it is common to find that people who are sensitive to guilt, who feel uneasy with success and enjoying life, often have had depressed parents. They need to care for others, to help others; and quite often they gravitate into the helping professions.

As we have seen, then, when something good happens to some depressed people they often wonder if they 'deserve' it, have a right to enjoy it or are frightened to enjoy it. These thoughts are often not fully conscious, but are in the background of their minds. If you ever worry about showing off your talents because you fear that others will feel badly in comparison to you, and so you play them down, the chances are you are operating on some kind of guilt issue. You may also have a belief that others will *envy* you. 'If they see my good fortune or talents they will envy me or dislike me or try to pull me down.'

Just as some people feel they don't deserve their good fortune, and so sabotage their ability to enjoy life, so others are all too ready to use the idea of deserving to support and justify their good fortune. Some time ago the newspapers published the fact that a wealthy financier had been given a £3 million 'golden handshake'. When asked whether he was a 'fat cat', he responded with, 'No. I worked hard for my firm and deserve it.' No obvious guilt here. It looks like the banking system all over the world has been run by the 'give me more I deserve it, guilt-free' mob. How much more refreshing to have heard, 'Well, I have had the good fortune to be reasonably bright, with an ability for hard work; I've been given a good education and had the connections to get a good job.' As you see, the notion of 'deserving' is in the eye of the beholder.

Responsibility guilt

Many commentators note that we are surrounded by (some would say bombarded by) constant information about the need to be aware of the consequences of our behavior. We must be careful with our diet, be careful of our weight, look after our children properly, not buy commodities that might damage the environment or be made by child labour in the third world, be aware of our carbon footprints, open our eyes to the suffering in the world and recognize the terrible economic injustices – on and on. It is probably true that we are living at a time when we know far more about the consequences of our behavior than at any other time. Learning to be open to and live with these responsibilities without feeling burdened, becoming hopeless, controlled by guilt or going into a state of detachment and denial – these are interesting challenges for us. The depressing bit here though is usually social comparison – believing that we're doing less well than others at these things.

Lynn O'Connor and her colleagues have also pointed out that at times we take *too much* responsibility *for other people*, especially their feelings[5] (see pages 283–8). For example, some women blame themselves for their husbands' drinking or violence. One woman felt that her husband drank because he felt unloved, and that if she could love him more he would stop. Thus in her mind she felt guilty for not loving him enough to heal his inner pain. This kind of thinking, however, takes responsibility away from the other person and stops them having to confront their own problems. To put it negatively, we can literally rob people of their responsibilities. It is as if we were saying to the other, 'You are not responsible for your own happiness or bad behavior. It is all down to me. I am responsible for what you feel or do.' Put like that, it doesn't sound so good, does it? People can only grow and mature by taking responsibility for themselves. Although you may think that blaming yourself and feeling guilty is help-ful or protects them, it is unlikely to do them much good in the long run. It is the same with our children – a key challenge is how to enable them to take responsibility for their lives.

In such situations it can be useful to draw out a responsibil-ity circle (see pages 283–8). There may well be aspects of any situation that are indeed your responsibility and under your control; but always try to keep a balance here. Avoid all-or-nothing thinking: it's either me or them. Sometimes when people confront their own pain, especially if it's people you care about, you may feel sad for them. But this does not mean you have to feel guilty, as if you were not doing enough to help them. Support them, yes; but don't take on the responsibility for their change or healing their minds – only they can do that.

Saying goodbye

I discovered my own 'rescuing hero' side with a wise and kind supervisor who drew my attention to the fact that I was not discharging people from therapy as I should. He helped me discover my own thoughts along the lines of, 'Maybe I haven't done enough to help them. Maybe they will need me in the future.' I had mild guilt and shame feelings about discharging people because I might be abandoning them (letting them down), and so they would not like me.

When it comes to ending a relationship or separating from others, we often have many mixed feelings, and one of them can be the guilt of leaving and saying goodbye. Perhaps it is leav-ing friends or staff behind when we take a new job or maybe it is leaving a relationship that has had its day. Even parting with a beloved car can be tricky for some of us!

In the lives of some depressed people there is often a history of guilt at leaving their parents. When Ruth wanted to go away to study, one of the things that stopped her from going to her favoured university was the prospect of leaving her mother, who from Ruth's childhood had turned her daughter into her 'closest friend'. Although Ruth was close to her mother too, the relationship was fairly one-sided in terms of who was benefiting from it. Ruth remembered many occasions when she had not gone out with friends so that her mother wouldn't be lonely. Ruth had major guilt problems in separating from her mother, and thinking of her as 'being left alone'. But from the outside it was clear that unless Ruth had faced this, she would not have been able to claim her own life. Parents are responsible for their own lives and can cause children real problems by turning them into their carers or depending on them for friendship. For most animals, including humans, the role of the parent is to train their offspring to be able to enter the world, even at times to push them out into it. It is not to keep them away from it in relationships of dependence.

Grief and guilt

The biggest separation is, of course, death. When someone we love dies it is not uncommon to feel (at least a bit) guilty. We remember all the times we said unkind things; the times we could have done more for the person and didn't; the visits we could have made and didn't. This is all normal and not uncommon. We are only human, after all. However, sometimes there have been unresolved conflicts with the dead person and we feel painfully guilty that we were not able to sort them out before they died. Many Hollywood movies have been made in which relationships work out at the last moment before death and a reconciliation occurs. There are few dry eyes in the house, but that is Hollywood; real life is not often like this.

Guilt can be one of the many complicating factors in grief and can stop us working through our grief. The problem with guilt and death is that because the other person has now 'gone', we may see no way we can repair things or put them right. We feel blocked. If this is true for you, then getting counselling or therapy might help you move forward. As always, be aware of the negative self-attacking thoughts you might have.

Through talking to others, you may gain new insights and see possibilities for change. I remember a person early in my career who taught me a lot about how things can 'just happen' in therapy. We had been working on his relationship with his father and how they had not got on that well. When his father died, Ben felt intense sadness and guilt for a separation that had lasted for years and which neither had been able to heal. Then one day Ben had a dream about his father. I don't recall the details, but Ben came to therapy in a changed state of mind. He said something like,

You know, I can see now that both my father and I are proud men. Neither of us could share our feelings that easily. I see how much he suffered because of this. It seems so silly and pointless to me now. His death has brought home to me how important it is to say what we feel and not hide behind these barriers. By dying when he did, he has given me the chance to be different from him. In a way I guess that is a gift he has given me.

Ben was very tearful at this point. He had looked at his guilt in a different way, and had been able to learn from it rather than being paralyzed by it.

There can be times when a death is a relief. Maybe one has had to look after a dying person, whose death sets both free. Even this can induce guilt, however, as if we should not feel relief at the release from the burden of caring alongside the sadness of the loss. A hundred years hence, much that we see around us will be dead. This is the cycle of life. Death makes room for new life. The evolutionists have their views about it and the religious have theirs. The only point I am making here is that to feel relief at the lifting of a burden is natural to life. You may wish to focus on your sadness, but you don't need to be stricken by guilt.

Self-focused guilt

Can we feel guilty for things that harm only ourselves? The existential writer Irving Yalom, in his book *Existential Psychotherapy* – a fascinating work on these issues, including those associated with death – answers yes.[6] In his view, to believe that we have not lived to our full potential, that at times we have taken the coward's way out (my favoured way) and have not been 'true to ourselves', can induce what he calls existential guilt – that is, guilt for how we live our lives. We put up with things which in our heart we know we shouldn't tolerate. One of my own self-guilt areas is in having been a smoker. In my heart I knew it was bad for me but I couldn't face up to the effort and loss of pleasure to stop. I knew I was harming my body, and my family asked me to stop – and I was always going to, 'next week'. This type of guilt is helpful to own and face up to, because it helps us take steps to change. When we deny it or pretend we don't feel guilty for things we know can harm us, then we may be less likely to change. Having said this, it is usually better to find positive reasons to stop doing harmful things – guilt simply alerts us to the need for change.

Inducing guilt

Roy Baumeister and his colleagues have written about how guilt can work positively in relationships. Imagine what relationships would be like if we never felt it![7] Certainly, there are times when children and adults alike have to recognize the hurt they have caused others and learn to experience and cope with guilt; and there are times when adults have to point this out to their children. However, some people actually try to induce guilt in others, to make them do what they want them to do. For example, they might say to a lover, 'If you leave me I couldn't cope without you', or even 'I will kill myself'! They try to shift responsibility to others. This tactic may work to a degree, but you always run a risk here. If you are a guilt-inducer and go around telling people how bad they make you feel, or try to control them by inducing guilt and making them feel sorry for you (or bad about themselves), you will run into problems. You may end up with resentful others around you.

Again, one has to be honest here. Think of the last time you had a conflict. Did you say things you (secretly) hoped would make the other person feel guilty or ashamed? Even if you were successful, how would this help them feel closer to you or more keen to be with you? Think of people you know who make you feel guilty. Do you like being around them? Do you like being around people who make you feel sorry for them? Sadly, no. In the next two chapters we will look at dealing with conflicts and how to be assertive. Recognize your guilt-inducing tactics (which we all use from time to time). Once you are aware of them, then you can choose to be different and find new ways of sorting out your differences and conflicts with others.

Distancing oneself from guilt-inducers

Annie found that every time she got off the phone after talking to her mother she felt depressed. As we unpacked this mood change we found two other feelings: guilt and anger. Her mother had a knack of making Annie feel guilty (e.g., for not visiting enough), and always wanted to pour out her woes, with the expectation that Annie should do more for her. Annie felt angry at not being able to stand up to her mother. Despite this, she kept phoning, because she thought she ought to and felt guilty if she didn't; and so she kept stirring up low moods.

I suggested a ban on phone calls (I had to take the responsibility for this at first). Second, we looked at what was a reasonable level of responsibility and what was not. Annie acknowledged that her mother had always been like this and had alienated other members of the family too. Third, we discovered that Annie had a secret hope that one day her mother would change and give her the love and approval she wanted as a daughter. Accepting that this was unlikely was painful. Fourth, and later on, we helped Annie monitor her thoughts very carefully as she spoke to her mother on the phone, and to generate alternatives as they happened. During the conversation, she held a flash card on which she had written thoughts like:

I know Mum will try to make me feel guilty, but then she always has and she does it to others too. It's not me, it's her style. She is not going to give me the approval I want, so there is no point in secretly hoping and then getting angry. I don't have to feel responsible for her happiness, and in truth there is not a lot that I could do.

The key idea was helping Annie to keep a balance and break up her guilt–anger cycle. Sometimes it is important to keep our distance, and acknowledge that while we may feel guilty about this, we can tolerate it if we don't engage in excessive self-attacking or tell ourselves things like: 'I am bad or unlovable for keeping my distance.' And, of course, it can help to talk to sympathetic others or therapists if there are complex conflicts with guilt-inducers that you'd like to resolve.

Tolerating guilt

Carol's story, described on page 416, warns us about the unintentional dishonesty that can creep into our lives if we don't face up to our guilt feelings and simply act on them. Our feelings, such as anxiety, anger, jealousy, shame or guilt, are there because evolution has designed them that way. But we need to understand them, not just act them out. If every time we felt anxious we ran away, we'd soon end up with serious problems of managing our lives. If every time we felt angry we lashed out at people, we would not have any friends. With guilt as with so many other areas of life, it is often a matter of learning to cope with and tolerate our feelings. Indeed, if we can't tolerate at least a little guilt or shame, we will run into problems. If, in every conflict that produces guilt, we back down, we will soon feel overwhelmed and paralyzed. Sometimes therapy is about learning to tolerate our guilt feelings without becoming submissive!

There are some depressed people who are, in effect, intolerant of shame and guilt. They may feel these things acutely, but instead of working with the feelings, understanding them and learning how to accept them as part of life, they will do everything they can to turn them off and avoid feeling them. There are many reasons for this. Sometimes it is because these feelings have been overwhelming in childhood and they have not had the opportunities to work with them and accept them. And of course sometimes it is because these negative feelings trigger terrible (shame) attacks on the self in the form of self-criticisms and put-downs.

Anger and guilt

Usually, guilt does not involve anger at others. (This is another aspect that distinguishes it from shame and humiliation.) Sometimes people feel angry if they can't own up to their feelings of guilt and recognize that they may have hurt someone. Consider an example. Tom forgets Jane's birthday and when he gets home she's clearly upset about it. Here is a guilt scene:

Jane: *Tom, it's my birthday and you forgot. I feel really upset about it.*

Tom: *Oh, Jane, I am so sorry. You are right. I was so busy. It was really thoughtless of me. Let me put it right by taking you out tonight.*

Let's assume that Jane accepts the apology and the offer. Here Tom has acknowledged his guilt (at having hurt Jane), apologized and made an offer to 'put things right'. Jane, for her part, is not intent on punishing Tom but accepts and forgives. Obviously how he conveys his genuine feelings is important here.

But suppose it went like this:.

Jane: *Tom, it's my birthday and you forgot. I feel really upset about it.*

Tom: *Oh, come on, Jane, you know I have been so busy. I can't remember everything, I'm stressed out right now.* (Angrily) *Look, I am sorry, okay!*

In this scenario Tom can't cope with his guilt and feeling bad, so he turns it around and blames Jane, asking her (angrily) to accept the fact that his work took precedence over her. His 'sorry' is not a 'sorry' at all. The evening will now be affected by bad feelings, because Tom does not deal with his guilt but tries to cover it up. Many therapists would see this as turning guilt into shame, but it is also a form of guilt intolerance.

Another possibility is:

Jane: *Tom, it's my birthday and you forgot. I feel really upset about it.*

Tom: *Oh, Jane, I am so sorry. You are right. I was so busy. It was really thoughtless of me. Let me put it right by taking you out tonight.*

Jane: *Well, it's too late for that. I think you are a mean, thoughtless sod.*

In this scenario Jane does not accept the apology. Perhaps she thinks, 'If he loved me he would not forget', and acts on that assumption, maybe also withdrawing and sulking. She is intent on wounding Tom – inducing shame and guilt. This will get neither of them anywhere.

The point here is that because guilt often arises from conflict there is always the possibility either that the guilty person won't face up to it or that the one who feels hurt will escalate the situation into yet more hurtful conflicts. As a rule of thumb, when you hurt people with your thoughtlessness – and you will, we are not perfect – own up to it. This does not make you a bad person; far from it. It keeps you in touch with your caring feelings and compassion.

If you do feel sorry for your poor behavior, then it is useful to express this as sadness rather than as anger. If you express your apology in an angry, dismissive or cold way, people won't believe it's genuine. Many apologies fall flat because of the way they are given. As a general rule, if someone who has hurt you appears to be genuinely sorry, then it is helpful to accept it. Attacking them further is usually not productive.

Guilt and forgiveness

Among the ideas that can help you with guilt over things you have done in the past are those of forgiveness and acceptance. Forgiveness is discussed more fully in Chapter 20, but we can note here that inner forgiveness can be an important aspect of change. We could all benefit from the practice of self forgiveness because we can all look back and cringe at some of the unkind things we have done.

Kieran had walked out on his family 15 years earlier. As he grew older and matured, he was haunted by terrible guilt at what he'd done, but he could not face it; so he drank. It took him some time to recognize that when he married he was not emotionally mature enough to cope with a young family. So he had to face up to and grieve for the pain he had caused. Until he could confront this grief, sorrow and guilt, he could not come to terms with his life. His guilt had turned to shame, which paralyzed all good feelings about himself. He saw himself as a worthless inadequate who always let people down and who could never be trusted. Thus (he believed) he'd never be able to have a loving relationship. This kind of self-battery did him no good at all; nor did it help him to relate to others or to develop a more supportive relationship with his ex-wife and son, which he wanted to do. The self-battering was doing his wife and children no good either – of course the key thing was not to become so self-focused and absorbed but think how to help and repair things. Some self-forgiveness is needed. The steps to self-forgiveness often require us to fully acknowledge what we have done, face our guilt and pain and sorrow, learn from it, make amends if we can, and *give up attacking* ourselves. Here are some ideas:

- Recognize the behaviors (or whatever) you regret and be honest about them.
- Check out your thoughts and see if they are reasonable or if you are experiencing more guilt than is appropriate (see pages 283–8).
- Acknowledge that it is painful to own up to having done hurtful things to others, but that is a part of healing. There may be grieving to do.
- Focus on your behavior or the specific thing rather than turning it into a self-focused shaming experience (the 'Oh, I am bad' focus) – that is turning away from the other and in on yourself.
- Recognize that your self-criticism might be stopping you from moving forward and really facing this emotion work – so see shame-focused self-blaming as unhelpful here.
- Recognize you are a fallible human being – all of us can do things we later regret, or grow and mature and look back with sadness – feel part of the struggles of humanity.
- Do what you can to repair the harm you have done.
- Decide how you will learn from this experience and how it has 'matured you' as a person.
- Be prepared that truly facing our 'guilts' can be very 'sadness-inducing' and we might need to bear that sorrow.
- Practise compassion focusing for yourself.
- Be open to forgiveness, rather than thinking that you do not deserve it – see forgiveness as a healing process.

- Think about how by facing your guilt you are developing moral courage and trying to ensure better behavior in the future.
- Remember your essence is your consciousness that can experience many things (see page 21).
- Be clear that forgiving yourself is not about letting yourself off the hook or saying things do not matter. Self-forgiveness can be emotionally pretty tough at times because it requires our honesty and true recognition that we can be unkind.

KEY POINTS

- Guilt is a natural part of life. We can't go through life, with all its conflicts and difficulties, without feeling it. Guilt helps us to recognize our hurtful behavior. However, if it gets out of balance, it can be rather inhibiting to us in recognizing our own needs and may distort our relationships.
- Guilt often arises when we think have been hurtful to others, we haven't done enough for people, have had to say no to people, have got more than them or have to separate from them.
- We can learn to identify our guilt areas and clarify our typical thoughts and feelings.
- Especially important is when feelings of guilt trigger self-attacking (shame-related) thoughts and feelings.
- Sometimes we need to learn how to tolerate guilt feelings, and the sorrow associated with them, as part of life (like anxiety or anger), rather than trying never to feel them.
- If you feel guilty about being depressed, letting others down or being a burden, then remember that you would prefer not to be depressed – you are not a joyful depressive! If you feel suicidal for being a burden, then be clear: this is the depression talking – and seek professional help. You owe it to yourself to do what you can to recover from your depression rather than let it dictate your actions.

- Guilt is like any other emotion. For example take anxiety; sometimes it is important to heed anxiety and run away but sometimes it is better to tolerate anxiety and stay with something that is making us anxious. If we run every time we feel anxious we will miss out on many important things in life. It's the same with guilt. If we give in every time we feel guilty this is not always helpful. Indeed sometimes tolerating guilt and not giving in is a kind thing to do.

EXERCISES

Exercise 1: Identify your key guilt areas

- I feel guilty when I _____
- I would feel guilty if I were to _____

Guilt can be helpful or harmful, so let's think about this. Clarify if it is mainly guilt you are feeling, or shame. In what ways does acknowledging your guilt and working with it help you? You might think, for example, 'It allows me to recognize when I am hurtful to others, to face up to this honestly and make reparations if I need to. This is part of growing and accepting myself as a fallible human being.'

I am sure you can think of a lot of the good reasons why we should act out our guilt and be kind to others. However, we have much to balance here because, just as it is not always helpful to run away if we feel anxious, so it is not always helpful to act on guilt and just give in or apologize when the actual problem was due to many factors and shared responsibility (see pages 284–6). To balance our thoughts, in what ways does your guilt and acting out of (i.e. without thinking too much – just doing what your guilt feeling pushes you to do) not help you?

Exercise 2: What are the disadvantages and downsides of acting out of guilt?

Here are a few:

- By always giving in to others (e.g., to a child) I might spoil them and make them selfish and expecting others to meet every need.
- I might not be fully honest with others and this can lead to problems
- I might not learn how to negotiate my needs with others.
- If guilt always stops me I might not be able to see what my reasonable needs are or learn to be assertive.
- Doing things out of guilt can lead to resentment.
- If I turn my guilt in on myself I will feel shame and then more depressed.

So, when you feel guilty it can be helpful if you face it. But you can ask yourself the following questions:

- Am I trying too hard to be nice? If so, what am I trying to achieve by this?
- Am I taking too much responsibility for other people?
- Am I able to be assertive when I need to be, even if others may not be happy with that?
- Am I telling myself guilt is always bad (all-or-nothing thinking)?
- Am I trying to avoid painful dilemmas by not feeling guilty?
- Do I feel guilty if I succeed when others fail, and if so, does this hold me back with no real benefit to anyone?
- Do my difficulties with guilt block my growing?

Exercise 3: Some ideas for facing guilt

You can refocus on a compassionate approach by taking a few soothing breaths and switching to your compassionate self (see pages 149–55). With as much kindness and gentleness as you can muster consider the following:

- Guilt feelings are part of life – there is nothing wrong about me feeling them so I can learn to tolerate them with kindness.
- If I could tolerate my guilt feelings without acting on them, how might this help me improve things in my life? (Spend some time thinking this through.)
- If there are indeed grounds for guilt, what would be helpful and compassionate for me to do?
- If I'm honest, are other people really expecting too much of me?
- In fairness, am I expecting too much of myself?
- What would I say to a friend in a similar situation?
- Do I need to learn the process of self-forgiveness?

Exercise 4: A life review

Writing a life review can sometimes be useful. Start by writing: 'I have learned to feel guilty because.' Then, just for yourself, write your own story of how you think this may have happened. Then write, 'The challenge for me now to move forward on this problem is to.' You might also consider writing some compassionate letters to yourself (see pages 233–9).

Coping with anger

Strong feelings of anger are common in depression. Freud believed that unexpressed anger actually causes depression, as if anger can be turned inwards. He thought that people are angry with themselves to avoid being angry at others on whom they may depend. As we saw in our chapter on self-criticism, there can be a lot of self-directed anger and frustration in depression. However, we now know that, in some depressions, people become more angry and short-tempered with others, not less. In some of our own research we found women become angrier with themselves as they become depressed but men become angrier with themselves and others.[1] When we feel angry and on a short fuse it is often those weaker than ourselves that get it.[2] People can also be very fearful of their anger.[3]

There are four domains of coping:

- the anger that others direct at you.
- the anger you (want to) direct at them.
- the anger you see others directing at each other (e.g., children watching their parents fighting).
- the anger you direct and feel for yourself.

What triggers anger?

Anger is often related to feeling frustrated, blocked, thwarted, ignored or criticized. Something or someone is not as we want it or them to be. In evolutionary terms, anger gives us the energy to overcome the blocks to our goals, or to fight harder (counter-attack) in a conflict situation. Thus, anger can be a natural response, although unpleasant and undesirable.

Examples of some of these are threats, damage or losses to:

- our sense of self (be this physical or self-esteem)
- relationships and possessions that are important to us
- our plans and goals
- our way of life.

Obviously our sense of control is important here, and anger can be a way to try to regain control. It can rise quickly in us before we have much chance to think about it – thus the value of practising mindfulness.

Frustration

Frustrative anger occurs when things in the world don't go as we want them to – e.g., the car won't start in the morning so we can't get to work on time. Stress and depression can lower our tolerance for frustration and thus increase our susceptibility to feel anger. When stressed, we may feel generally more vulnerable to things that can damage or block us, and there are also some basic self-beliefs that can affect our tolerance for frustration – for instance, 'This shouldn't happen to me', 'This is going to seriously interfere with or block me in what I want to do'. Time pressures and things going wrong unexpectedly can lead to the familiar flush of irritable anger. Don't I know that one! However, people who are going to be able to cope with such things as the car not starting will note the flush of anger, and then quickly turn to coping (e.g., get a taxi). Those of us who struggle will personalize and may feel 'let down by the car' (how could you do this now!) and have a tantrum.

Coping then is making a commitment to try to cope with your anger in the following ways:

- Note the flush of anger as it arises in you.
- Break your focus (e.g., by switching to soothing breathing).
- Hear that kind voice of understanding in your mind.
- Recognize that anger is a perfectly understandable feeling (don't self-blame and start battling with yourself), but is not helpful in this moment.
- Keep in mind that it is not personal – it happens to other people too.

Really focus on coping and *what is going to be helpful to you right now*; for example, do you need to take yourself away from the situation (or person) until you are calmer; do you need to seek help?

Injury

We can feel anger when others pose a threat to us or injure us in some way. Physical or verbal attacks can lead to feelings of anger. Anger is likely to be greater if we think the injury was deliberate, or the result of carelessness, than if we think it was unintentional or unavoidable. The anger that we feel towards an intentional injury can be revenge, and the impulse is to harm (counter-attack) the other person verbally or physically. These feelings are common in group conflict and war. Even when people rationally realize that cycles of vengeance are doing no one any good, it can be hard to stop. Coping is similar to the above: noticing anger arising and then shifting attention, and making clear in one's mind that anger is not a good place to be acting or thinking from – don't forget that this takes practice though, so go easy on yourself but try your best.

Exploitation

A very common theme in anger is exploitation. This is when we think someone is taking advantage, using us or taking us for granted. As we have seen, most of us have a desire to feel appreciated and for relationships to be equitable. Be it in child–parent relationships, between friends and lovers, or even between countries, perceptions of being exploited or taken advantage of can lead to anger and its consequences. Assertiveness and dealing with the issue at hand are often important.

Lack of attention

Anger can arise when others don't give us the attention we want. They may ignore us or dismiss our point of view. For example, Emma wants Chris to spend more time with her and help around the house, but he says that he's too busy. Or maybe Chris says he will help but does not keep his promise. Emma feels angry with Chris. However, with this kind of anger, we rarely want to harm the other person, but rather behave (e.g., scream and shout) so that they don't ignore us. We want to renegotiate our relationship, not necessarily destroy it. Sometimes this requires a steady and constant compassionate addressing of the issues.

Envy and jealousy

This kind of anger arises when we think that someone is getting more of something desirable than we are. Linda thought that she would win the beauty contest, but she didn't, and she felt envious anger towards the winner. In envy, we want what someone else has, be this material possessions, a position in society, a popular personality, intelligence and so on. In jealousy, we think that someone we value might prefer to be with a person other than ourselves – for example, a married woman shows an interest in another man and her husband has pangs of jealousy. This type of jealous anger (if expressed) acts as a threat to the woman, suggesting serious consequences if she were to cheat on or leave her husband. Sexual jealousy is more likely to arise for someone who sees their lover or partner as a possession. Jealous people can also be very insecure and may come from backgrounds of sibling rivalry or having to 'battle' to win parental attention.

Lack of social conformity

This anger relates to the feeling that others should do as they are told. Parents become angry with children who disobey them. A religious person becomes angry if the members of his church do not obey the rules. We may become angry with our government over how they spend our money. The basic belief here is, 'Others should conform to and obey the rules of conduct that I believe are important'. The anger occurs because, in some way, we see the other person's conduct as potentially damaging to our own interests or way of life.

Sympathetic anger

This is when we feel anger by seeing harm come to someone else – for instance, when we see people starving and feel angry that this has been allowed to happen. The anger fuels the desire for us or others to do something.

The helpful and the unhelpful

There are two aspects common to all these situations: first, things are not as we want them to be; and second, we place a high value on the things that we are angry about. In helping ourselves with our anger, it is possible that we may discover that we are over-valuing something, drawing conclusions about a situation that may not be warranted or seeing more potential damage in a situation than there is. Anger can be *very helpful* because it alerts us to things that we need to defend or change. People can be inspired by anger (at, say, injustice) to change things, or to have their voices heard. It is usually when anger involves ill-will or desires to cause harm that we have problems – and of course this ill-will can be directed at oneself.

The shades of anger

Anger itself is not all-or-nothing, black or white – it is more shades of pink to red. For example, imagine a line that starts off white and gradually becomes pinker until the other end is red. At the white end, there is no feeling at all, nothing matters. At the other end, one is enraged. The trick is to be somewhere along this line where you can keep control, but not in the white area or the red area. Anger is like a car that we need to learn how to drive. You don't want to drive everywhere at 100 miles an hour, but neither do you want to leave the car locked in the garage because you are frightened of driving.

Sometimes depressed people do not know how to drive their anger. They continually lock it up and enter only as far as the vaguely pink area – at least as far as expressing their anger goes. This may work if you are confident in doing that and don't need to show your anger. But it is not so good if you do need to reveal it and feel weak and inferior if you back down too quickly. If you feel that your anger tends to get out of control, you can learn other strategies. Here are some to think about.

- Learn to become more aware of anger arising in you, and your trigger points.
- Recognize when you feel your anger is more in control than you are.
  Note that this is not your fault, but you need space not to let the sparks of anger get fuelled by your thinking or behavior – so learn containing skills such as:
- Learn to break contact with others if anger is too hot. 'Look, I'm going for a walk as I need to calm down a bit – sort my head out.'
- Practise being compassionate to your anger (not self-critical or condemning) while practising your anger coping skills as best you can.
- Practise switching your attention to your breathing or compassionate self or image.
- Not matter how silly or difficult it feels, create a compassionate smile on your face.
- When you are able, explore your thoughts and see if you can bring more balance to them.
- Avoid self-blame, condemning and self-retribution.

Anger is often defensive, in the sense that we are defending ourselves against a block to something or from criticism or being ignored or dismissed. When we behave defensively we often go for 'better safe than sorry' thinking, and our emotions are triggered quickly (see Chapter 2). This is why many psychologists think that beneath the veneer of our anger we feel vulnerable – not someone who is confident or strong.

Why anger expands

Why can anger feel so powerful? Why does it hit the red zone? It is not uncommon to find that what triggers anger can seem quite trivial. We might suddenly find that we are seething with anger over rather small events. It appears as if our anger has expanded. In some depressions, there are 'anger attacks', when people find themselves enraged for reasons they can't put their finger on. Some researchers believe that, in some cases, anger attacks are to do with the depression itself (and the biological changes associated with it). Some people on certain anti-depressant drugs can experience increases in irritability – for others they are more calming. If you find that you have become far more irritable and angry since starting an antidepressant, go back to your family doctor, who may recommend a change in medication.

There are also psychological reasons for 'blowing up' over a trivial event. Let's think about the example of Emma and Chris given on page 444. Suppose Emma says to herself, 'If Chris really cared about me, he would help with the housework'. Clearly the anger is not just about the housework but about the fact that Chris's lack of help is being taken as a lack of caring. Emma may also feel taken for granted. Thus, what seems like a trivial event actually has a much larger meaning.

When you think about the things that make you angry, it is useful to ask yourself some questions – invite your anger to speak to you, as it were. Okay, anger, now . . .

- What is it about this situation *that I really* value and feel could be damaged?
- Let's suppose I cannot change the situation. What does this say about my future.

- What am I saying about me if this (the source of the anger) happens? Am I drawing negative conclusions about myself?
- What am I saying about the other person? What motives am I reading into their action?

Another question that can be very useful is to ask is, 'In what way does this situation hurt me?' In depression, as a rule, it can be helpful to focus on the feelings of hurt rather than on the anger. If we focus on the anger, we could miss the fact that it relates to feeling vulnerable or damaged in some way. Indeed, by being angry we can sometimes block out deep fears of being abandoned, ignored and hurt. Behind anger in depression can be a lot of hurt, a need to grieve for past hurts and problems of shame. If we can work through the grief, the anger and the depression may subside.

If we focus on our hurts rather than on our anger, we might gain more insight into our anger. In Emma's case (see page 444), she saw that she believed that Chris's lack of help had the extra meaning of 'not being cared for', which led to the idea that maybe he did not value her or thought she was not worth caring for, which led to the idea that maybe he was right. This sensitivity may be from the past (e.g., feeling parents or friends did not care enough) but the key is that when Emma reflected compassionately she worked this out for herself. She realized that caring was not 'all-or-nothing' and that there were in fact many other instances that showed that Chris did care.

So our anger can expand when we overestimate the damage that can be done to us. Here's another example. Derek was working on a project that required help from others. However, they did not finish their own work on time and he became furious. His thoughts were, 'If I don't get this project in on time, that will be a very bad mark against me'. He had a fear of being seen as inadequate by his boss. 'They are making me look incompetent to my boss. This could affect my chances of promotion. Therefore, these people, by not doing their work on time, are shaming me and ruining my whole future.'

When Derek focused on his own fear of shame, he began to see that he often got angry with anyone who might 'show him up'. This led him to consider why the approval of those in authority (mostly men) mattered so much to him. This in turn revealed the poor relationship he had had with his father and his belief that, 'I must please those in authority, otherwise they will be angry and ignore/discount me'. These thoughts ignited many of the feelings and fears he had as a child. His anger was powerful because of the meanings he put on the situations that triggered it. Later, Derek was also able to see that his belief that 'his whole future would be ruined' led to a high degree of anger.

Derek learned to deal with his anger by making a number of flash cards:

- When I feel anger, I need to slow down and monitor my thoughts.
- If I don't slow down and monitor my thoughts, I am likely to see many events as a re-run of my childhood.
- When I get angry, I often overestimate the damage that can be done to me.
- What is the evidence that this situation is damaging? How can I cope with it by getting less angry?
- I don't have to feel ashamed by every block or setback.

Having the flash cards gave Derek that extra bit of space to avoid letting his anger run away with him. It helped him to take his foot off the accelerator. It's not magic but it is a help. You might want to write some out for yourself like Derek's.

Robert became enraged when he went to a hotel and found that he had been put in the wrong room and the young receptionist didn't seem to care. He ended up telling her that he didn't think the hotel should employ people like her. When he got to his room, he felt ashamed and depressed about his overreaction, sat on his bed and burst into tears. What had happened here? Later in therapy he was able to work out his thoughts as the following:

- Why can't people get things right?
- This receptionist obviously sees me as a fool and a soft touch.
- If I were manly, I would sort this out without any difficulties.
- People should respect me and not treat me this way.
- I must be seen as a weak, useless bastard.
- That's not fair – I'll show her that I'm somebody to be reckoned with.

Of course the anger is more of a rapid 'whoosh' than built up thought by thought – but the thoughts show us what is in the anger. In a few seconds the problem had grown out of all proportion and had become a question of respect, manhood and being seen as a soft touch. The receptionist's attitude had triggered Robert's underlying fear of being someone not worthy of respect and of his sense of inferiority – all of which he defended with rage.

Later, while still sitting on the bed, he recognized that he had behaved aggressively to the receptionist. He then thought:

- I'm losing control.
- What's happened to me? I used to be caring of others.
- Maybe I'm just a selfish person who has to have his own way.
- I am unlovable and bad for being like this. I hate myself for being like this.

So we can see how Robert's anger expanded because he had overestimated the damage to his self-esteem and had believed that this was a test of his manhood. In fact, it is not uncommon to find that depressed people can have rages and then feel intensely unlovable and hate themselves for it – they feel angry with themselves for being angry.

George became enraged with another driver while driving with his family. His children were frightened and started to cry so he screamed at them, too. Later, he felt ashamed and guilty. He thought that he had ruined their day and was a horrible man to 'go off like that'. At 3 a.m., feeling alone and unlovable, he started to think that they would be better off without him and contemplated suicide. George's anger was a sign that he was not coping and was feeling very vulnerable underneath the rage. He was in a depressed brain state, where anger is far more easy to activate. When things are tough like this, it is the very time to be gentle with ourselves. Indeed, the tougher things are, the more powerful compassion can be. Being kind to ourselves for being a little upset is one thing, but if we can be compassionate when we have a rage then that is powerful. Remember, this is not 'letting ourselves off the hook'. Indeed, sometimes we will feel *more* upset at the upset we have caused others when we give up self-blame and focusing on ourselves. We are kind because we mean to heal ourselves, and make genuine amends for any hurt we have caused.

So, understanding the values you place on the things that make you angry is a first step. Then consider the ways that you feel hurt and vulnerable. If you sometimes feel that you lose control, avoid globally attacking yourself and instead look for alternatives. The following are the ones that Robert eventually came up with for himself:

- Okay, I did go off the deep end and that is disappointing.
- However, I know that I'm not always or even usually like this.
- I need to recognize that I'm under stress right now and that my life is not easy, so my frustration tolerance is low.
- I need to learn to back off when my feelings are hitting the red zone. However, a low frustration tolerance does not make me a bad person – even if some of my actions are undesirable.
- I will help myself if I learn to be more assertive rather than aggressive. If I label myself as bad, I will only feel much worse, and when I feel bad and ashamed of myself, my frustration tolerance level goes down further.
- I can forgive myself for this, apologize to the hotel assistant if I need to and move on. Hating myself is failing to treat myself with compassion and recognize the stress I'm under. If I treat myself better, I'm more likely to treat others better.

You may have noted that the anger in the various examples outlined above could also be seen as 'shame anger'. The anger acts as a defensive measure against being put down, feeling small, discounted or rejected. Indeed, in situations when you feel anger, it is always worth thinking that shame may be part of your feelings. You can get into shame/anger spirals where you are angry at being shamed and ashamed of being angry. The first step to get out of this is to avoid attacking yourself (see Chapter 13).

Shoulds and oughts

One reason why we can feel anger is when we are using 'shoulds and oughts'. Robert, in the example above, had thought, 'Others *should* not behave this way'. Unfortunately, we can't write the rules for how other people will behave. If we are not careful, we can get stuck and simply go over and over in our minds what another person should or shouldn't do. A couple of times I have noticed my anger arising in airport queues, and my thoughts of, 'These queues are ridiculous, it's sheer incompetence; no one cares; they treat us like cattle' and so on. I don't like being trapped in queues – it's rather claustrophobic – so that fear can fuel my anger. Of course my anger does no good to anyone, and certainly not me or my blood pressure. I have to try to switch attention to the soothing breathing, create the compassionate smile, note how others are caught here too – it is not personal. One notices the anger and then *makes the choice* to try to refocus one's mind on helpful thinking *for one's own good*. At times, 'shoulds' are related to other thoughts, such as 'If X loved/respected me, he/she should/shouldn't'. You can work on these ideas by telling yourself:

- I would prefer that others did not do this.
- However, I cannot write the rules for their conduct.
- Each person is free to behave in their own way.
- If I don't like the way they are behaving towards me, I can learn to be assertive and put my point of view.
- I do not have to personalize every conflict situation and see it as a personal attack on my worth, selfhood, manhood or whatever.

Who is to blame?

In depression people frequently feel bad about themselves for getting angry. How can you treat yourself kindly if you have become so angry? Again, we need help from the compassionate/rational mind. It may help us with such thoughts as:

- It is indeed upsetting to become very angry.
- It may mean that underneath I am feeling very vulnerable.
- However, my anger doesn't make me completely unlovable as a person – that would be overgeneralizing, thinking in all-or-nothing terms and self-labelling.
- It is this particular action at this particular time that was rather harsh.
- Remember the times that I've been caring and not angry and how it's possible to do positive things for myself and others.

Sometimes, if we have been angry (especially with children), we feel so guilty that we think we have to make it up to them and start to allow them to do things that we would normally not allow – because of guilt. However, this can backfire because the children, being children, might start to take advantage of the situation, which can trigger our anger again. If necessary, apologize for your action and then work on gaining more control over it rather than acting out of guilt.

Hatred

Sometimes, because we believe that we have been very hurt or damaged, anger turns to hate. Then the desire is to harm others, and this can be frightening. Bella came to hate her mother because of a very physically and emotionally abusive past. She felt that her mother had 'an evil tongue'. She had fantasies about stuffing a pillow in her mother's mouth and watching her choke to death. However, she was desperate to be loved, and she took her hatred and murderous thoughts as evidence that she herself was evil. Her thoughts were:

- Hatred is bad.
- I should not feel like this.
- It is abnormal; others don't feel like this.
- I must be bad/evil for feeling hate so strongly.
- I can't reveal to others the depth of my feelings because they will think that I am evil, too.
- I hate myself for hating.

Her doctor, who had been treating her with drugs, had no idea of this inner life. This is not surprising, for such hate-anger is often not revealed if there is strong fear or shame associated with it. Bella was able to begin to challenge these thoughts and ideas:

We all have the capacity for hatred – it is not itself abnormal. Indeed, sadly, history shows the consequences of hatred, so there have been many who have felt like me. I am not abnormal. To call my hatred 'evil' is all-or-nothing thinking and self-labelling, and leaves out the hurt I have felt because of what happened to me. I did not wake up one day and think that it would be a good idea to hate my mother. These feelings have come from a lot of painful experiences, and it is understandable for me to hate someone who has hurt me so much. However, I do need to learn how to work with my hatred and come to terms with it. I need to learn how not to hate myself for hating. This is because my hatred hurts me and holds me back in my efforts to get well.

Avoid brooding

Brooding and ruminating is bad for our brains (see page 28). If we think about what anger is designed to do, and recognize that one of its functions is to help us to fight harder, we can see the danger of brooding on angry thoughts.[1] These turn on our threat self-protection fight/flight system, when stress hormones and other chemicals are pumped around our bodies, which become tense and alert. However, if no 'fight' or 'flight' happens, these chemicals can get up to mischief.

Allen was asked to take early retirement, and a new manager started to undo all the changes that he had introduced in his section. He had various arguments with his boss, but all to no avail. Allen became depressed and had serious sleep difficulties. I asked him to monitor his thoughts when he woke in the middle of the night. These turned out to be: 'The bastard. After all the years that I have worked there and this is how they treat me. There must be some way I can stop them. I can't just roll over and let this happen.' When these thoughts began to run through his mind, he became quite agitated and would pace about the house, going over and over them. If his wife tried to calm him down, he would snap at her and then feel guilty. Then he would say to himself, 'They're even breaking up my relationship with my wife'.

My discussion with him went something like this: 'When you have these thoughts, they activate your primitive fight/flight system and that's designed to hype you up – to fight or to run away. However, you've done what you can and there seems to be no way that fighting can help you now – especially at three in the morning.

You're left in a hyped-up state that has nowhere to go except in pacing about and snapping at your wife. You've recognized that, in reality, there is not much you can do.' Allen reluctantly agreed. 'So we have to find a way for you not to activate your fight/flight system because it drives you into depression.'

As Allen came to understand the processes that he was activating in himself, he was ready to start to explore alternatives. We wrote out some flash cards for him to read if he woke early:

- I am disappointed with this situation, but I have to face the fact that I have done my best and this is the way of the future.
- I have given the company many good years, and it has not been too bad really. I can be proud of that.
- Perhaps the time has come to let go and think about the next phase of my life.
- All these thoughts of fighting and getting my own back only hype me up and to no real purpose.

We might also care to reflect on a more Buddhist or philosophical view that all things are impermanent, nothing stays the same; the sea continually moves and if we try to stop things changing then we are on to a loser. Sometimes letting go (and grieving if we need to) can be one of our most important life tasks – and a tough one. With Allen we also examined the advantages and disadvantages of taking early retirement, including the fact that he would have more free time and that it would probably be better for his health. Once Allen let go and gave up fighting an unwinnable battle, he was free to explore other strategies – such as how to get the best deal for his retirement. It was not easy, but a year later, he told me that it had been the best decision he'd ever made.

So the key issue is to avoid brooding on anger. Work out strategies for coping. If there are things that can be done, do them. If there are others who can help you, seek their help. But brooding on injustice, going over the same ground over and over again, does not help. Giving up an unwinnable fight is one strategy, but at other times you may need to learn how to become more assertive and stand your ground (see Chapter 20).

Anger to avoid pain

Caroline was angry with her parents because she thought they did not love her enough. As long as she felt angry, she avoided the great sadness and need to grieve that were underneath her anger. Anger gave her some feelings of power. Sadness and grief made her feel very vulnerable.

Anger can be used to prevent the recognition of being hurt, but it is often hurt and shame that need healing and this often involves sadness. Some people may imply that all you need to do is to get your own back on the person who has harmed you or to stand up to them. However, although this can be helpful it is not always so. Underneath, we still have a wish to be loved and approved of. I remember a patient who had done quite a lot of work with another therapist on learning to stand up to her abusive parent and express her anger. However, despite this, she was still depressed and mistrustful. What she had not done was grieve for her lost childhood or allow herself to feel and accept the feelings of vulnerability in grieving.

You see, there are always two parents inside us. There are feelings and memories of the one we actually had, but also the desires, fantasies and hopes for the one we wanted – that ideal protective, loving, caring parent. We can work on coming to terms with the abusive parent and our anger with them, but we also need to work on grieving and letting go of the parent that we always wanted. We can do this by using our inner images and practise becoming the compassionate self – or sometimes through new loving relationships.

In working with anger in depression (and I stress 'anger *in depression*' because not all anger is like this), it is sometimes important to find someone who will help you move through the grieving process. In grief, we acknowledge our pain and vulnerability. In the grieving process itself, anger is often the first or a very early response – but we have to work through this stage rather than get stuck in it.

Bypassed anger: 10 common reasons for avoiding anger

Sometimes people try to avoid feelings of anger altogether. If you bypass anger, you might go straight to feeling hurt, but also feel a victim, a powerless subordinate. You will also bypass becoming assertive (see Chapter 20). You may feel that you have no power to do anything about certain situations. You might think that you feel hurt because you are weak, and you may not be able to focus on the fact that it is at least partly the attitude of the other person that is the cause. It is important to recognize your hurts without, at the same time, becoming a powerless victim.

Here are 10 self-beliefs that may stop you from exploring your anger and learning how to use it in an assertive way. Following each one, I offer some compassionate alternative ideas.

1: Others are more powerful than me. I will never win in conflict with them.

Compassionate alternatives: It's not about winning and losing. Even if I don't achieve the outcome I want, it is helpful to try to put my point of view. If I tell myself that I *have* to win, otherwise it's pointless, I am defeating myself before I start. If I attempt to put my point of view, at least I will have tried. Trying to be assertive means that I am less likely to be angry with myself if I don't get the outcome I want.

2: I learned in childhood that anger is bad.

Compassionate alternatives: Because my parents could not cope with my feelings of anger does not mean that anger is bad. Anger is part of human nature, and it can be useful. If we never felt angry about things, would we be motivated to change anything? Anger is really important because it reveals where I am hurting and what I value. True, aggression and lashing out are not good, but anger turned to assertiveness has many uses. Although my parents taught me that anger is bad, they may not have taught me how to be assertive. Perhaps they did not give me any positive ways to deal with conflicts – maybe the problem was that they did not know themselves. I need to learn this for myself.

3: When I am angry, I am bad and unlovable.

Compassionate alternatives: Of course, I might prefer never to be angry but that's not possible. In that moment, feelings of love might not be there, but that is like a storm that comes and goes and meanwhile the sky remains itself. To say that I am unlovable is all-or-nothing thinking and self-labelling and discounts the positive aspects of my life. When I think of being unlovable, I may be thinking of being unlovable *to someone*. Who is the person I feel unlovable to? If it is my partner, I can think of it this way: relationships are like boats. If my boat can only sail in a calm bay, it is not much of a boat. We need boats that will not capsize even if a storm blows up. If I see myself as unlovable when I feel angry, I am also saying that my relationship can't cope with the odd storm – but, in fact, clearing the air and being honest and frank with my partner is likely to strengthen my relationship, not ruin it.

Of course, it is true that, at the moments of conflict, you are not sharing loving feelings, but love is like the climate; it remains no matter what we do. Anger and conflicts are like wind and rain – they come and go. Just as one thunderstorm does not change a climate, so your anger does not make you unlovable. You can learn to survive conflict.

4: When I am angry, I am being disloyal.

Compassionate alternatives: Blind loyalty is rarely helpful and it is better to develop openness and respect. If I am respectful then I am also honest – because one can't be respectful in being dishonest about one's feelings. To feel disloyal is linked to guilt (see Chapter 18) but this does not mean I do not care for the other person. I also need to think if I am actually worried about being rejected for rebelling! Sometimes, when I confide in people I trust – about the anger I feel towards others close to me – I can have strong feelings of being 'disloyal'. However, confiding in others might help me to get my anger in perspective. If the person I am angry with has done things that have hurt me, keeping them hidden is really colluding in a secret rather than showing loyalty. I confide in others because I want to sort out my feelings. It is understandably difficult if I feel that I am 'breaking loyalties'. However, remember that people have done all kinds of bad things out of loyalty. If I show compassion, I can try to change things in a different way.

5: I must not hurt others.

Compassionate alternatives: Deliberately hurting others is not, by most people's standards, a moral thing to do, but the anger we are talking about here is not like that. Rather, I want to use my anger to draw attention to the fact that something is causing me pain or hurt, and change it. I have no wish to harm others just for the sake of it, but to help them see how they are hurting me and to stop them doing it. In this sense, my anger is defensive. Others are far less likely to be hurt if I explain my position and show respect for them rather than attacking them. It is also the case that I can't be held responsible for everyone's feelings – that's giving myself too much power. In any case, I might, in the long run, be more hurtful to them and our relationship if I am not honest with them about my feelings. Think in terms of respectful rather than hurting anger. This is not an excuse to act out whatever emotions I fancy – I will try to be emotionally polite as well as honest – thus as with all things it is a matter of balance.

6: I can't stand the feelings of anger.

Compassionate alternatives: Angry feelings can be frightening if I am not used to feeling them. I may block my angry feelings if I feel that I might lose control. However, I am far less likely to do this if I learn how to be assertive (see Chapter 16). Learning how to mindfully 'be with' my anger and learn acceptance and tolerance means that it will no longer frighten me and that will help me greatly.

7: I might lose control and damage people.

Compassionate alternatives: It is my responsibility not to do that. So I need to consider a number of things. First, am I seeing my anger as more damaging than it is? Am I secretly telling myself that I am a very powerful person and that everyone around is so fragile that they could not possibly cope with my anger? If so, I can try to think of the reasons why I might wish to believe that. Then work out the evidence for this belief and the evidence against it. Lashing out at people – going into the red zone – is not a good idea, but this is no reason to avoid being assertive with others. Let me think about times I have been angry but in control. Let me make a commitment to myself to stay in control but not in a way that simply silences me. Like driving a fast car, I can learn to drive at different speeds as are appropriate – I have just got to give myself a chance to learn. If I do go OTT and say hurtful things then I need to be honest about that, recognize my fallibility, also apologize and try to repair the harm I have done (see Chapter 18).

8: I might lose control and make a fool of myself.

Compassionate alternatives: It may be that I am prone to feeling shame if I express my feelings, so I can work on that. It may also be true that if I become very angry, I might say things that I do not mean or become tongue-tied. The main thing is to try to focus on the issue, that is the message I want to convey, rather than my anger.

If you have become angry, find out if you are having self-critical thoughts and calling yourself names (e.g., 'I'm stupid,' 'I'm a fool'). If so, recognize this is all-or-nothing thinking and discounting the positive aspects of your life. It would be helpful to remind yourself that your anger is one element that you might wish to change, but it does not make you a fool or stupid. We can all do and say foolish things from time to time – but we can also learn to tolerate and forgive ourselves for them.

9: I only feel I have a right to be angry if I am 100 per cent sure that I am in the right.

Compassionate alternatives: There are few things in life where one can be 100 per cent right. This is all-or-nothing thinking. Maybe no one is right or wrong, but everyone has a different point of view. Sharing these differences can be a source of growth. In any case my anger cannot be stopped simply by saying I have a right or I don't. I can also keep in mind that even if I feel I have a right to be angry, it does not mean anger is a useful response – sometimes forgiveness is.

10: I would be ungrateful or selfish to show anger.

Compassionate alternatives: 'Selfish' is, of course, a self-label and I am probably discounting all those times when I have given of myself. Even if I feel grateful to someone, this does not mean that there cannot be disagreements between us. I can show gratitude when the situation warrants it, but positive things can be achieved in not hiding my discontent.

Be cautious not to let your gratitude turn into a trap of obligation, for then you may feel more resentful.

Acknowledge if your anger is upsetting to others

Not so long ago when I was a stressed and my father had just died, I lost my temper big time with my computer at home which had suddenly decided it wasn't going to receive any e-mails or save files. I was under time pressure to get to work. In my explosion I said some very naughty words and threatened to completely kill, destroy and smash my poor computer that had been working well for years. Hearing this explosion of rage was of course very upsetting for my wife. Then I rushed out of the house and drove off far too fast – again, rather upsetting for my wife. A mile down the road that little voice kicked in, 'Gilbert you asshole! You are not supposed to get angry like that. Good grief – and you're writing a chapter on anger too – it was very upsetting to Jean – how could you!' However, thanks to my practice I think, I found there was a compassionate voice which soon recognized that I was actually quite distressed and simply said, 'You're very distressed right now, it's not your fault (and that felt sad then), but do pull into the side of the road, phone Jean and apologize and let her know your are okay.' So I did, and felt better. The point of the story is that is helps if we can quickly go to the compassionate self as anger arises in us and then behave as best we can. It is not easy, but if you're kind to yourself and own up to hurt if you have caused it, this will help you.

Overview

Anger is one of our main threat self-protective defensive emotions. It's one of our big emotions in our brain and therefore is easily aroused and can be tricky to control. This is not our fault at all, but it is important to learn how it is triggered in us and how to exert control. It might be linked to things from our past, the beliefs and attitudes about ourselves and other people we are carrying. We may use anger to avoid feelings of hurt, or to keep people away, or even to test them out.

Whatever the reasons for having difficulties with anger, and depressed people often do, the task is to be gentle with yourself about the problem and then think about how you can learn to manage your anger by either becoming more assertive or working on the things that make you angry. As with all of the ideas we are exploring together, be compassionate with your anger but at the same time do the best you can to work with it in a helpful way.

EXERCISES

Exercise 1

Write down your thoughts about the last time you became angry. Ask yourself questions like, 'What am I saying about this event?' 'What implications am I drawing?' 'What do I think this event (or the other person's attitude) says about me?' 'What am I saying about myself?' When you have written down some of your thoughts, explore whether you are engaging in any of the following: all-or-nothing thinking, overgeneralizing, discounting the positives, thinking in 'musts' or 'shoulds', and so forth (see Appendix 2).

Let's work through the example of Emma becoming angry with Chris over him not helping with the housework. The following are her main thoughts and the possible coping responses she came up with:

- I'm always left with the housework while he goes off with his friends.
  Well, actually he does help sometimes. I am overgeneralizing here. And I am ignoring some of the other positive things he does to help. Still, I do feel strongly that he should do more. I need to sit down with him to talk about it – when I don't feel so angry and upset.

- This is really unfair. If he cared about me, he would help out.
  Is doing housework the only sign of caring? Chris is behaving in a way that is traditional for males. His father was the same. I may not like it, but I may be exaggerating if I think this shows that he doesn't care about me. I need consistently to point out that this is a concern to me so that he can learn to change.

- He takes me for granted.
  I might feel taken for granted, but is this true? What evidence is there for and against this idea of being taken for granted? It might just be thoughtlessness and the need to help him be more attentive.

- Maybe that's all I'm good for. If I was more lovable, he would be more attentive.
  I recognized a problem about who does the housework. However, I'm going to feel much worse if I start to think Chris's lack of interest in housework is a lack of interest in me. It is this blaming myself and feeling unloved that is making me depressed. It could just as easily be a typical male attitude. I need to train him!

Exercise 2

If you tend to become too angry, try to spot the danger signs early. Think back to the last time you were angry.

- What was going through your mind? What were your early feelings? Was there any build-up to it? Could you spot the danger signs – feelings of getting wound up? If so, learn to say to yourself, 'I am entering my danger zone and need to back off – keep my distance'. If you find yourself getting too angry, move away from the other person. Blowing up at others is not helpful. However, if it is appropriate, come back to the issue that was behind your anger when you feel calmer. Don't avoid the issue but avoid the strong anger that might lead you to say things you later regret.

- Use the 'count to 10' approach. If you suddenly feel very angry, stop, then count to 10 slowly, then take a deep breath and change your facial expression. Learn to avoid acting when you have hit the red zone. You may also try leaving the room. The key idea is to distract yourself, and give yourself time to calm down sufficiently to stay in control.

- If any of the '10 common reasons for avoiding anger' (see pages 460–6) apply to you, make your own flash cards and try generating compassionate alternatives to these thoughts. Think of the advantages and disadvantages for changing them.

- If you are frightened of the feelings of anger, try expressing anger when you are alone. Get a rolled-up newspaper, stand by the side of your bed and hit your bed with it. As you do, speak (or shout) your thoughts about your anger. Allow yourself to feel your anger. Remind yourself that no one can be hurt by this exercise – the point of it is to help you become less fearful of the feelings of anger. When your anger has subsided, you may wish to cry. Allow yourself to do this. Then, and most importantly, before leaving the room lie on your bed and carry out a compassionate exercise. Think to yourself, 'This anger episode is over and I will let it go'. Imagine a stormy sea that becomes calmer. The idea is to recognize that you can become angry but will also calm down. Learning how to do this is important, because it helps you avoid brooding on your anger.

- At the end of the exercise, note that you were able to become angry and to calm down afterwards – imagine your compassionate image and feel warmth and kindness for you. Remind yourself anger is a part of us that's difficult, that's why we have compassion for it (we don't need compassion for things that are easy!). Over time, you may learn that the feelings of anger themselves need not be frightening, even though they may not be pleasant. But you were able to control your anger by directing it at the bed. This exercise is not designed simply to release anger but to allow you to experience it without fear. Go step by step, and learn that, even when you are very angry, you can still stay in control of your feelings. This is to help you become less frightened of your anger but it does not ignore the issue that you may need to explore what is causing your anger. Is it possible you're getting to boiling point because you find it difficult to be assertive in small ways?

- When you feel calmer, write down what you said when you were angry – what went through your mind? Explore to see if some of your thoughts were extreme and should be challenged. The next stage may be to recognize where you are hurting and what your anger is about. Then use your compassionate exercises from Chapter 8 to work on those issues.

20

From anger to assertiveness and forgiveness

We now need to think about what we can *do* when we feel angry given that, in depression, anger is often related to hurt, vulnerability or feeling blocked. What are compassionate ways to express and deal with the things that are linked to our anger? One way is to develop assertiveness.

Assertiveness

What is assertiveness?

Research has suggested that assertiveness is related to many types of behavior. Willem Arrindell and his colleagues in the Netherlands suggest there are at least four components to it:[1]

1 **Display of negative feelings**. The ability, for example, to ask someone to change a behavior that annoys you, show your annoyance or upset, stand up for your rights, and refuse requests. This is what most people are thinking of when they talk about 'being assertive'.

2 **Expressing and coping with personal limitations**. The ability to admit to not knowing or uncertainty about something rather than feeling ashamed to admit to it. Assertiveness also

links to the confidence to acknowledge making mistakes, and to accept appropriate criticism. This aspect of assertiveness also covers the ability to ask others for help without seeing this as a personal weakness.

3 **Initiating assertiveness**. The ability to express opinions and views that may differ from those of others, and to accept a difference of opinion between oneself and others.

4 **Positive assertion**. The ability to recognize the talents and achievements of others and to praise them, and the ability to accept praise oneself.

Assertiveness is practising how to be open and honest as well as able to offer personal views and values and reach out to others. Assertiveness takes practice, and we can feel more confident in some situations and with some people than with others.

Non-assertive, aggressive and assertive behavior

When people have problems in acting assertively, they are either highly submissive, fearful and prone to back down when faced with conflicts, or may become overly dominant and aggressive. Table 20.1 outlines some differences between non-assertive, aggressive and assertive forms of behavior, showing the contrasts in non-verbal behavior, feelings and thoughts.

Interestingly, non-assertive (submissive) and aggressive people can share similar beliefs. For example, both can think in terms of winners and losers. Aggressive people are determined not to lose or be placed in subordinate positions – 'I'm not going to let them win this one'. Depressed people can feel that they have already lost and are in a subordinate position – 'I can't win', or 'I always lose'. Sometimes this seems like a replay of how they experienced their childhoods. Parents were seen as powerful and

TABLE 20.1 NON-ASSERTIVE, AGGRESSIVE AND ASSERTIVE FORMS OF BEHAVIOR

Non-assertive	Aggressive	Assertive
Looks down or backs away	Stares and 'looks' angry, threatening	Meets eye contact but avoids 'the angry face'
Tries to signal 'no threat'	Wants to signal threat — to be obeyed	Wants to signal 'listen to my point of view'
Allows other to choose for self	Chooses for (and imposes on) self and others	Tries to reach agreement
Feelings		
Is fearful of the other	Is angry or enraged with the other	Tries to control both anger and fear
Hurt, defeated	Feels a victim and sense of injustice	Recognizes that one can't have everything one wants
Thoughts		
My view is not important	My view is the most important	All views have a right to be heard
I don't deserve to have this need, want or desire	My wants and needs are more important than other people's	Each person's needs and wants are important
I will lose	I will (or must) win	It is preferable for no one to win or lose but to work out how to give space to each person
I am inadequate or bad	I am good and in the right	Right and wrong is all-or-nothing thinking and labelling. It is preferable to work out what the issues are rather than labelling or attacking the person or oneself
Just here to please others	Others should do as I want	We should try to please each other in a mutually sharing and caring way
Self-attacking	Other-attacking	Avoids attacking

dominant and they (as children) felt small and subordinate. Depressed people can, however, be aggressive to those they see as subordinate to themselves (e.g., children). The important thing is to remind yourself that while it might have been true that, as a child, you were in the subordinate position, you don't have to be now. You can look after yourself and treat others as your equals. You are an adult now. You might use the motto, 'That was then. This is now'.

One way to feel more equal to others is to notice the 'all or nothing' of your thinking (powerful/powerless, strong/weak, winner/loser) and by considering that, 'It is not me against them. Rather, we each have our own needs and views'. To be assertive, then, is to not see things in terms of a battle, with winners and losers. This may mean that you have to be persistent but not aggressive. The angry-aggressive person wants to win by force and threat; the assertive person wants to achieve a particular end or outcome and is less interested in coercing others or frightening them into submission – and will often accept a fair compromise.

A second aspect of assertiveness is that it focuses on the issue, not the person. To use a sporting metaphor, it involves learning to 'play the ball, not the player'. In this case we speak of our wants or hurts without alarming others or employing condemning styles of thinking. For example, these are typical responses of someone who is angry and aggressive towards someone else:

- You are a stupid person (all-or-nothing thinking and labelling).
- You are always so thoughtless (overgeneralizing and discounting the positives).
- I can never trust you (all-or-nothing thinking and discounting the positives).
- You are a selfish bastard (just about all the styles!).

Of course we might all think these things, and say them too, but the point is to maintain our wish to find more compassionate ways to deal with things that upset us. Don't blame yourself, but refocus on your goal. Note that all these statements attack the other *person*, rather than addressing a specific issue or behavior. When people feel attacked, they tend to go on to the defensive. They lose interest in your point of view and are more concerned with defending themselves or counter-attacking. The assertive response focuses less on threatening or attacking the other person but more on specific issues, explaining our feelings and concerns and the quality of our relationships with others. Thus, in acting assertively we would explain in what way a particular action or attitude is hurtful. For example:

- When you 'behave' in that way, I feel hurt because I think that you don't care about me (you make clear your thoughts and concerns).
- If you 'say' things like that, I feel you are discounting my point of view.
- I feel much happier when you 'behave' like this (...) towards me.
- I accept that you feel like that, and understand why; however, my point of view is this.

Can you see the steps here?

1 Acknowledge your anger.
2 Recognize in what way you feel hurt (and, of course, try to discover if you might be exaggerating the harm or damage done).
3 Focus on what this hurt is about and your wish to have the other person understand your feelings and your point of view.
4 Don't insist that the other person absolutely must agree with you.

In assertiveness, we remain respectful of the other person. Winning, getting your own back or putting the other person down can have a negative outcome. In fact, even if you are successful (i.e. you win), the other person may just feel resentful and wait for a chance to get their own back on you! Winning can create resentful losers.

Avoiding spreading guilt

One word of warning. When you acknowledge your hurts assertively, this doesn't include making the other person feel guilty or ashamed. Sometimes people don't want to share with others what they want to change, but just want to make the others feel bad. When they discuss the things they want to change, they do it in a rather whining, 'poor me' way. Or they may say, 'It's all your fault that I'm depressed'. They may think, 'Look what they've done to me – I'll make them feel guilty for that. Then they'll be sorry.' This is understandable but not helpful. Getting your own back by trying to make people feel guilty is not being assertive. You may at times wring concessions from others, but usually people feel resentful if they have to give in because they have been made to feel guilty. I am sorry to say that some depressed people can do that – and children of depressed parents testify to it. All we can do here is be honest and try to spot our unhelpful behavior and change it.

Sometimes we might even do things to ourselves to try to make the other person feel guilty. After an argument with her mother, Hilary went home and took an overdose. Later she was able to recognize that she had been angrily thinking, 'She'll be sorry when she sees what she made me do'. Nobody can *make* us do anything – short of physical coercion. It was Hilary's anger that was the problem. Her mother had been critical of her, but at the time Hilary had not said anything, although she had felt anger seething inside her. Her overdose was a way of trying to get her own back. With some courage and effort, Hilary was able to be assertive with her mother and could say things like: 'Look, Mother, I don't like the way you criticize me. I think I'm doing an okay job with my children. It would help if you focused on what I do well, not on what you think I do badly.' This took her mother aback, but after that, Hilary felt on a more equal basis with her mother.

Sometimes depression itself can be used to attack others. Hilary also came to realize that, at times, she did feel happy but refused to let others know it. She wanted to be seen as an unhappy, suffering person, and that this was other people's fault and they should feel sorry for her and guilty. It was also an attempt to evoke sympathy from others – although it rarely worked. She had the idea that, if she showed that she was happy, she would be letting others off the hook for the hard times she had had in the past.

Sometimes there is a message in our depression. It may be to force others to look after us, or it may be to make them feel sorry for us. We find ourselves turning away from possible happiness and clinging to misery. Somehow we need someone to recognize our pain, apologize, or maybe feel sorry for us or rescue us – and we are not going to budge until someone does. It can be helpful to think carefully about how you want others to respond to your depression. It can be a hard thing to do, and you might see that sometimes we use our depression to get our own way or get out of doing things. Try not to attack yourself about this; you are far from alone in doing it. Your decision is whether to go on doing it or whether you can find other ways to make your voice heard. Using your own rational and compassionate mind can help you move forward.

Turn away from sulking

Another non-assertiveness problem is sulking, or passive aggression. In sulking, we don't speak of our upsets but close down and give people the 'silent treatment'. We may walk around with an angry 'stay away from me' posture, or act as if we are really hurt, to induce guilt. Indeed, our anger is often written all over our faces even as we deny that we feel angry. We have to work out if our sulking is a way of getting revenge on others and trying to make them feel guilty. Are we sulking in order to punish others? Always be kind to your sulking – but recognize it as a rather stuck state. Try to work out why you act that way. What stops you from being more active and assertive? What would you fear if you changed and gave up sulking?

You may feel powerless to bring about changes. This may be because you believe that direct conflict would get out of hand, or to show anger is to be unlovable, or because you think you would not win. However, sulking does have powerful effects on others. Think how you feel when someone does it to you. The problem with sulking is that it causes a bad atmosphere and makes it difficult to sort out problems. When you sulk, you give the impression that you don't care for others. Sulking is likely to make things worse. Another problem is that sulking often leads to brooding on your anger. The more you do this, the more you will want to punish others.

You'll find that, if you can learn to be assertive and explain what it is that you are upset about, you will feel less like sulking. It might be scary, but the more assertive you are rather than sulking, the more powerful you will feel. If in a sulk, be mindful – stand back from your feelings and how your body is pushing you to act and see what happens if you view those feelings compassionately – don't fight 'the sulk' but compassionately steer your way out.

Anger at failed assertiveness

A common occurrence is that we can become angry with ourselves for not being assertive. We have probably all had the experience of getting into a conflict with someone and not saying what we wanted to say. Then later, maybe going over it in bed that night, we feel very cross for not standing up for ourselves. We feel that we have let the other person win or get away with something. Afterwards we think of all kinds of things that we could have said but didn't think of at the time. Then we start to brood on this failure to be assertive and our self-criticism can really get going.

Roger was criticized in a meeting, which he felt was mildly shaming. He actually dealt with the situation quite diplomatically but, in his view, did not defend himself against an unfair accusation. Later that night and for a number of days afterwards he brooded on his failure to say what he had really wanted to say. These were his thoughts about himself:

- There you go again – letting people walk all over you.
- You never stand up for yourself.
- You've shown once again that you're made of mush.
- You've failed again.
- You're a really weak character.

Roger had a strong ideal of himself as a 'person to be reckoned with', but of course, he rarely lived up to this. As in the case of Allen (discussed on pages 457–8), who had to take early retirement, when Roger was out of the situation he started to activate his own internal fight/flight system and brooded on what he wished he had said. At one point, he had fantasies of revenge, of physically hitting the person who had criticized him. As with Allen, Roger's thoughts led to some agitation.

The following are alternative coping thoughts that Roger could have considered:

- First be understanding and compassionate to the distress.
- That was unfair of Harry to be critical of me, and upsetting. It is very understandable for me to feel like this, as no one likes to be criticized and I've always been a bit shy.
- However, my disappointment at not saying more has turned into an unfair self-attack which is not kind or helpful to me.

You will be aware by now that the most damaging aspects of Roger's internal attack were the thoughts of having failed and labelling himself as weak. These thoughts placed him in a highly subordinate position and were quite at odds with his ideal self (see next chapter). They activated a desire for revenge. Because of the way our brains work, it is quite easy to get into this way of thinking if we feel that someone has forced us into a subordinate position. We have to work hard to be compassionate with ourselves. Here are some alternative coping thoughts that can interrupt this more automatic subordinate thinking style:

- By globally labelling myself as weak, I feel bad. This is all-or-nothing thinking and ignores the positive aspects of my life. It makes me feel much worse. I was criticized – unfairly, in my view – but this is not the same as being 'walked all over'.
- It may be true that I need to learn how to be more assertive, but this is going to be hard to do if I take each failure to assert myself as evidence of weakness. There are many areas of my life where I have shown some

courage, but in any case, conflicts are often complex and cannot be reduced to simple ideas of weak/strong. Other people later agreed that the criticism was unfair, so they don't see me as weak.

- If a friend had been in a similar situation, I would not have attacked him or her in the same way that I attack myself – for I know that this would have made him or her feel much worse.

Read these through again but this time with as much warmth and understanding as you can muster. Do you notice how it feels when you put warmth into it? If we approach the problem compassionately and think about what would be helpful, we might identify a need to use assertiveness. We could then plan what we wanted to say (but didn't) and calmly try it out. The problem for Roger was that he never tried assertiveness but only felt disappointed with himself and then became angry. He never gave himself the chance to improve his assertiveness.

You can use these basic ideas in all kinds of relationships, including of course close ones.

Forgiveness

There is much research showing that learning forgiveness, and working through the difficulties of forgiving, helps our mental health.[2] If we carry a lot of anger for people we feel have hurt us in the past then this anger can sit in our minds and we often return to it – constantly stimulating our threat system. Deciding to walk the path to forgiveness can be a major way of moving forward. There are many aspects to forgiveness that we need to clarify. One cannot 'make' oneself forgive and sometimes we need time to heal – so no 'I should' or 'I ought' here.

Forgiveness is about taking the steam out of one's anger to others and in so doing no longer filling one's mind with angry, vengeful or victim thoughts. It is *not* about liking, wanting to, or feeling one should want to see or relate to the person you forgive. It is not about accepting that their behavior was okay when it was not. Forgiveness does not mean that what happened in the past does not matter, or forgetting. Rather, it is the effort made to give up the desire for revenge or punishment. In brief, these stages are:

- An **acknowledgement and uncovering phase** of harm done – this means facing one's hurt.
- A **recognition** of how 'holding on to one's anger and hurt' is damaging to oneself.
- A **recognition phase** of the personal benefits of forgiving. Spend time imagining what you would feel like if you let go – really see yourself in the future free from what you find hard to forgive.
- A **decision phase** to move and work towards forgiveness involving commitment to forgive.
- A **working through phase** involving the acceptance of others as fallible and flawed, that disappointment is inevitable
- An **outcome phase** acknowledging the benefits of forgiveness.

If forgiveness is an issue for you, it may be helpful to put time aside where you will not be disturbed, engage in your soothing breathing rhythm and then bring to mind your compassionate self or compassionate image(s) (see Chapter 8). Then gently work through each of the above phases. Make notes to yourself about your thoughts and feelings. You might like to write a compassionate letter to yourself on the benefits of forgiving and fears and blocks of forgiving.

Resentment and revenge

Forgiveness can be a lengthy process requiring the acknowledgement of much hurt. Some people may try to forgive without acknowledging their own pain and anger, but when they do this, resentment usually remains. Forgiveness can be a painful process. Learning how to forgive is about learning how to let go of anger. A need for revenge can be damaging to ourselves and our relationships. We may tell ourselves how justified we are to be angry *regardless of how useful this is*.

Judy felt much anger against her parents for their rather cold attitude, and blamed them for her unhappy life. In doing this, she was in effect saying to herself, 'I cannot be better than I am because my parents have made me what I am. Therefore, I am forever subordinate to them – for they held the power to make me happy. Therefore, I can't exert any power over my own happiness.'

Gradually Judy came to see that it was her anger (and desire for revenge) which locked her into a bad relationship with her parents. Forgiveness required a number of changes. First, she needed to recognize the hurt she felt, which to a degree was blocked by her anger. Second, she needed to see that she was telling herself that, because her parents were cold towards her, she was 'damaged' and destined to be unhappy – that is, she was giving up her own power to change. She realized that she felt a 'victim' to her childhood. Rather than coming to terms with this, she felt subordinated and controlled by it. While it is obviously always preferable to have had early loving relationships, it is still possible to move forward and create the kind of life one wants. As Judy came to forgive her parents (but not condone them), she let go of her anger and felt released from the cage in which she had felt trapped.

When we forgive, we are saying, 'I let the past go and am no longer its victim'. One patient said that, by giving himself the power to forgive, he was giving himself the power to live. Forgiveness is not a position of weakness. Some people find that 'letting go' feels like a great release. Remember you may never like or want a relationship with the person you forgive – rather, you let go of your anger.

Self-forgiveness again

We looked at self-forgiveness in the last chapter but because it is so important for us let us look at this once again. Self-forgiveness can go through the same phases as forgiving others:

- An **acknowledgement and uncovering phase** of how you might be self-critical and self-shaming. This means being fully open and honest with yourself and really attending to how you think and treat yourself unkindly.
- A **recognition** of how holding on to one's self criticalness and anger or disappointment with oneself is damaging to oneself? It is not stimulating those feeling systems that are conducive to well-being.
- A **recognition phase** of the personal benefits of recognizing oneself as a fallible human being and that learning to be more gentle, kind and forgiving is beneficial to one's moods and well-being (see also page 299 on the difference between compassionate self-improvement and shame-based self-attacking).

- A **decision phase** to move and work towards self-forgiveness, involving commitment to forgive. Make a decision that you are going to be a forgiving self-improver rather than a condemner (see Chapter 13).
- A **working through phase** involving the acceptance of yourself as a fallible human being who just 'found themselves here' trying to do the best you can.
- An **outcome phase** acknowledging the benefits of self-forgiveness.

Forgiving ourselves means that we treat ourselves with compassion. We do not demand that we are perfect or don't make big mistakes from time to time. There are many spiritual traditions that recognize the great importance of forgiveness.

Reconciliation

Some depressed people also have difficulty in reconciling and making up after conflicts have taken place. Couples and families with high levels of conflict but with good reconciling behaviors, and who value each other, tend to suffer less depression. When we reconcile and make peace, our anger and arousal subsides. Chimpanzees, our nearest primate relatives, actually seem better at reconciling their differences than some humans. Research shows that, after a conflict, they will often come together for a hug and embrace and they rarely stay distant for long.

So why is it difficult for some people to reconcile and make up? Some typical unhelpful thoughts that can make reconciliation difficult include:

- I must make them pay (feel guilty) for upsetting me.
- If I forgive them (or me) I am letting them (or me) off the hook.
- If I forgive them then I can't express my dissatisfactions.
- I'll have to be nice.
- Forgiveness is a position of weakness.
- It has more benefits for them than me.

If I apologize and want to reconcile, it means:
- I'm admitting I was in the wrong.
- I am giving in.
- I have lost.
- I am weak. Strong people do not apologize.
- Others will think I have taken full responsibility for the conflict.
- I am in a subordinate position.

In some cases, it is because as children we were never taught how to do it, and now as adults, we feel awkward about it. Perhaps neither they nor their partners know how to make the first move to make peace. Another reason is that one or both parties in the conflict will not reconcile until they are given the dominant position: they must win, get their own way and assert their authority. The one who reaches out to make peace is perceived as the one who has submitted.

For example, Angela said that, when she was a child, it was always her and not her mother who had to say she was sorry. If she didn't, there would be a very bad atmosphere between her and her mother, which she found intolerable. Her mother would sulk, sometimes refusing to speak to Angela until she had apologized. When she did, her mother would remind her of the conflict and how naughty Angela had been. At a time when

Angela was reaching out for acceptance, her mother would make her feel bad, ashamed and guilty again. Angela developed an expectation that, if she apologized, the other person would use this to make her feel bad about herself and would not accept her peace-making efforts without 'rubbing her nose in it'. She was therefore very frightened of conflicts because there was no way she could reconcile afterwards without always feeling in the wrong.

There are various alternatives to the above unhelpful thoughts and ideas. For example:

- I can apologize for my actions if I think I have hurt someone, but this does not mean that the conflict itself was all my fault. Indeed, it is preferable to think in terms of differences of opinions or desires rather than in terms of blame (see the responsibility circle in pages 283–6.
- Assertiveness is not about winners and losers but about being clear about the reason(s) for a conflict and attempting to resolve it.
- The ability to apologize and repair a relationship is a compassionate positive on my part, not a weakness.
- I don't have to grovel when I apologize, but rather to get together with the other person again because I care about the relationship.
- I can focus on the issue of coming together rather than on just relieving myself of guilt.

Reconciliation, like much else in assertiveness, is a skill that can be learned. It may be difficult at first, but if you set your mind to it, you will improve. Learning how to make up after conflicts makes them less frightening. It helps us stop ruminating on the anger and conflict and building up the other person into a real ogre! You learn that you can survive conflicts, they are a normal part of life and we may actually benefit from them. Making up is only a submissive position if you tell yourself it is.

Reconciliation in intimate relationships may involve hugs and other physical contact, but of course, you can't force this on others. If others are not ready to reconcile, all you can do is to state your position – that you'd like to make up. Be honest and offer an apology if you need to, and wait for the other person to come round in their own time. If they don't, avoid getting angry with them because they don't wish to go at the same pace as you.

One other thing that men especially need to be cautious of is encouraging their partners to prove that they are now reconciled with them by agreeing to have sex. If you do this, it is possible that your efforts at reconciliation will not be seen as genuine, but only as a tactic to get your own way. If your partner does not want to have sex, you may read this as 'Well, she does not really care for me, otherwise she would'. This can lead to anger and resentment again. If you feel that there is not enough sex in your relationship, this is best sorted out at some other time, calmly, and with no threat of 'If you loved me, you would'.

Overview

Feelings of anger and powerlessness can haunt you in depression because they stimulate the threat system. When that happens, the levels of stress hormones in our bodies increase. Healing then is about learning how to work with the feelings of anger and powerlessness, by being honest, learning assertiveness if we need to (and this may take some practice) and learning forgiveness. These are not easy steps, and in many spiritual traditions they can be seen as lifetime guides. If you practise developing your compassionate self, and really orientate towards developing that within you, this may help you in these tasks.

KEY POINTS

- It is the message or meanings in anger that need to be considered rather than the anger itself.
- In learning how to be assertive, we focus on the hurt and the issue(s) behind a conflict rather than attacking either ourselves or the other person.
- Non-assertive behaviors include aggression, inducing guilt, sulking and backing down fearfully.
- Anger at our own lack of assertiveness is a common experience. This self-directed anger can be more damaging to us than the lack of assertiveness itself.
- Because anger and assertiveness nearly always arise in situations of conflict, it is important that, after the conflict has passed, there is reconciliation and forgiveness. These may not take place if there are specific beliefs that stop them – for example, 'To apologize is to admit I was in the wrong, or that I am letting people off the hook'.
- Forgiveness is actually an assertive action because we give ourselves the power to forgive and thus release ourselves from feelings of having been a victim for which we must seek revenge.

EXERCISES

Exercise 1

Think of an area where you would like to be more assertive – maybe something small to begin with. For example, suppose you need a new pair of shoes. Go into the shop and spend time trying on several different pairs – then thank the assistant and walk out, without buying anything. Or think about something you might really like to do with a friend or partner and ask them. If they turn you down, then smile and be pleased you had a go. Notice, be mindful and compassionately smile at any tendencies to become critical and ruminating. Try something each day or as often as you can – practise, practise. If the issue is becoming more assertive in conflicts then:

- Avoid attacking the other person: that will put them on the defensive.
- Work out what you want to say, focusing on a specific issue.
- Be brief and clear.
- Be prepared to 'trade' and compromise.
- Avoid seeing either as signs of weakness.

Here's an example involving Emma and Chris, whom we met earlier (see pages 448–9). Emma was angry about Chris's lack of helping around the house. However, she waited until they were relaxed together and then said:

'You know, Chris, I wish we could spend more time together. However, I'm so busy with the house and it would be really helpful if you could lend a hand. I feel really left out when you go off to see your friends and I'm stuck here doing the ironing. It's not that I want to stop you going out but that I want to have more time, too. Look, I've worked out that, if you do more of the shopping and vacuuming I would have more time for myself. I'd really feel a lot better and not feel so taken for granted.'

Of course, this may not do the trick straight away, but it's a start. Sometimes it helps to rehearse what you want to say – that is, rehearse your assertiveness skills. Remember, it is a step-by-step process and does not have to go perfectly first time. By preparing what you want to say, rather than waiting until you get angry and rushing in with attacks, you are more in control and will often achieve more.

If you are prone to getting angry with yourself for not being as assertive as you would like to be, review the example of Roger on pages 479–81. Work out if you are attacking yourself. Then rehearse the types of assertive things you would like to say. Say them out loud. Get used to speaking them and hearing yourself say them. Avoid brooding on your anger and on all the really nasty things you could say. You know that you probably won't say them so there is no point in rehearsing them. Try out only those things that you think you should say.

An important aspect of acting assertively is 'slowing your thoughts down' to give you space to think. If you get into a conflict situation, don't feel that you have to respond immediately. One way to do this is to ask the other person to tell you more about what concerns him or her, rather than trying to defend yourself immediately.

You then might say to the other person, 'I can see how you could think of it that way, but this is how I see it'. Be factual rather than accusing. Stick to the issue at hand rather than trade personal attacks.

Spend time thinking about forgiving others and letting go of the past. Write down the advantages and disadvantages of doing this. If you could let go of the past (and any desire for revenge you might feel), how would this help you? What stops you? What are your thoughts here? Use your rational/compassionate mind to help you.

If you feel that some of the hurts from the past are very serious, and it is impossible for you to embark on this journey alone, think about seeking help. The moment you say, 'I no longer want to remain a victim of my past' you are taking the first step up and out.

Exercise 2

Try your compassion practice. First, sit or lie down somewhere comfortable. Go through a relaxation exercise of the type described on pages 130–3. Enter into your compassionate self mode and feel yourself expanding; focus on your kind and gentle facial expression. Sense how you think about things and the tone of your voice. Now imagine a person whom you want to forgive standing in front of you. See their facial expression and feel compassion for them. Remember that they just 'found themselves' here. If you find yourself being pulled back into your anger, break contact with the image, refocus on the compassionate self and begin again. As you feel compassion, notice what happens to the image that is the focus of your forgiveness. It might shrink or move away from you. Remember, you are healing yourself here because it's your holding on to your anger that's causing you pain. As your image recedes it is grateful for your letting go.

Remember that forgiveness doesn't mean that you like the person you have forgiven. You may never want to see them again. It's all about changing your emotional orientation.

Exercise 3

This time the focus is on a part of yourself you want to forgive. You can go through exactly the same procedure as in the previous exercise. When in compassionate self mode, imagine that part just in front of you. Then imagine forgiving that part of you with a compassionate heart. If you get pulled into angry critical mode, pull back into the compassionate self and focus on your breathing and sense of warmth.

Whatever works for you, use it. The idea is to develop the inner art of forgiveness. Forgiving yourself does not mean an end to trying to improve. It just means that improving and changing will be easier for you if you don't hang on to things from the past that cannot be changed.

21

Dealing with frustrations, disappointments and lost ideals

Many therapies focus on the importance of learning to cope with disappointments, setbacks and tragedies with forms of acceptance, coming to terms, not self-attacking and or not insisting on 'it must' or 'must not' – these are also old wisdoms.[1]

Our emotional reactions to frustration and disappointment depend on the importance we place on things. The most common are:

- When things don't work right or as we think they should.
- When we make (what we think are) avoidable mistakes. (I can get quite frustrated with myself if I bowl badly at cricket or drop that catch!)
- When others do not behave, or feel about us, as we want them to – e.g., don't show us enough respect, affection or break promises.
- When we ourselves lack an ability to do or achieve something we want.
- When we feel certain things – for example we feel depressed and lose energy, don't feel as positively about someone as we would wish, feel disappointed in ourselves because we lose the ability to feel affection or lose sexual feelings.

Shoulds and oughts

Disappointment is a major area where our shoulds and oughts (see page 454) come to the fore (as do our 'musts', see page 215). We can believe that things, ourselves or other people 'should be like this' and 'should not be like that'. The problem here is that, life being what it is, it does not respect our shoulds and oughts. Some of us feel that we should not have to die, and instead of coming to terms with it, rage about the fact that life 'shouldn't be like this'. Sometimes our shoulds stop us from doing the emotional work we need to do, to come to terms with things *as they are* and work out helpful solutions for dealing with them.

We can develop a strong sense of 'should' when it comes to our own attitudes – about ourselves, e.g., 'I *should* work harder', 'I *should not* make these kinds of mistakes', 'I *should not* be angry', 'I *should* love my parents and be more caring to them' and feeling very disappointed when things don't turn out as our 'should' says. Shoulds often involve anger and attempts to force ourselves to be different. When we rigidly apply the shoulds to ourselves, we inevitably end up bullying and attacking ourselves. It is as though we struggle to avoid accepting our limitations, setbacks or true feelings. In the 1940s the American psychotherapist Karen Horney called 'the shoulds' '*a tyranny*'.

When we apply shoulds to other people, we often feel angry with them when they disappoint us. Instead of seeing them as they really are, we simply say 'they *should* be like this' or 'they *shouldn't* be like that' (see page 454). Strong shoulds often reduce our tolerance for frustration, and as we shall see shortly, shoulds and oughts can lead to serious problems with disappointment.

When you're working compassionately it's always worth asking yourself, 'What's the fear, what's the threat behind my should, my ought or my must?' There are not that many: they boil down to the fear of rejection or being marginalized, being shamed, being hurt or criticized, or a loss of control. It is because the threat system is involved that we often have problems with frustration.

The problems of perfectionism

Depressed people are often surprised when I suggest that '*the secret of success is the ability to fail*'. So much in our society concentrates on succeeding and achieving things that we can become fearful of, or even *incompetent* at failing. Yet, if you think about it, success, like love, looks after itself. Most of our problems don't come from succeeding or doing well but from failing and not doing well. The way we cope with disappointment and setbacks can do much to throw us into depression, especially if we spiral into self-attacking and self-dislike. Learning how to fail without self-attacking can be a useful means of exerting more control over our moods. One reason why failure becomes a serious problem is because, perhaps without realizing it, we have become overly *perfectionist* and *competitive* people to whom the idea of failure is a terror.

Perfectionism relates to having high ideals and believing that we must reach them or else we are worthless and bad in some way. Research by the Canadian psychologists Paul Hewitt, Gordon Flett and their colleagues suggests that there are three forms of perfectionism:

- Self-orientated perfectionism: Here the focus is on high standards and the need to be perfect. When people fall short of these standards, they can become self-critical and experience a lot of frustrative anger.

- Other-orientated perfectionism: Here people demand high standards of others. They can become angry with others if others are not up to the mark. The other-orientated perfectionist may look for how far people fall short of a standard rather than how good they are.
- Socially prescribed perfectionism: Here people believe that it is others who expect high standards of them and that they will be rejected or shamed if they don't come up to those expected standards. This form of perfectionism is the most strongly linked to depression.

Doing your best

Some forms of perfectionism are very helpful. You would like your brain surgeon to be a bit perfectionistic! Most of us accept that trying to do our best is a good idea. If something is worth doing, it's worth putting some effort into it. The problem is: how much effort? Even if you work 20 hours a day, you might, in principle, say that you could have worked 21 hours a day. When we are in perfectionist mode, if we fail, we inevitably say we could have done more. The problem is clear – the goalposts keep moving.

It's similar for 'other-orientated' perfectionists. Even if you put a lot of effort into something, if it is not exactly what they wanted, they will say that 'you could have done more'. They can be very undermining – so watch out for them – they are often demanding and not always supportive of or able to appreciate one's efforts. Children, for example, will have problems in judging what is reasonable effort and what is not.

Regarding our own judgements about ourselves, it's not so much our desire for high standards – which can be driven by a passion to do well that causes trouble (see page 299) – it is when our perfectionism is driven more by fear of failure and fear of being criticized by other people and our self-criticism. Seeking high standards is important but once again it's what drives this and what happens in us if we don't quite make it; can we be self-accepting, kind, understanding and encouraging to ourselves in contrast to being very angry, self-critical and/or frightened of what other people think and will do? What is the true motivation for our drive to be perfect? If in our hearts we know that actually we drive ourselves because we are frightened, then we need to look at this – work on the fear. Research has shown that perfectionism is associated with a range of mental health problems, especially those linked with depression.

If you think you are a perfectionist then:

- Spend some time exploring in what ways perfectionism works for you. Do you put yourself up on the high wire trying to achieve too much?
- What are the advantages and disadvantages of your perfectionism style? Spend time on this really reflecting on these themes so that you can 'feel' how they are working in you.
- If you are not able to reach your standards, what are your greatest fears? Spend some time to note them – bring them to light.
- What feelings and thoughts do you have about yourself and how do you treat yourself? Can you distinguish being upset with an outcome and becoming self-critical in unhelpful ways?
- Is this linked to childhood?
- With kindness and openness, decide if this is helpful and, if not, how you might like to change things – to focus on your efforts and learn to value those – not just results.

- What would be compassionate attention, compassionate thinking, compassionate actions and behavior, and compassionate feelings in such situations?

Frank, an artist, told me how he would fly into rages and rip up his work if he could not make the image that he had in his mind appear on the canvas. This is an example of perfectionism driving us into low frustration tolerance. Even in sex, perfectionists may be more focused on how they perform than on getting lost in the pleasure of it. They have to 'do it right'. A patient of mine who used to go hiking, noted that he could have been walking anywhere; what seemed to matter more was how many miles he covered. He would set himself tests – 'Can I walk 20 miles today?' Even if it had been a bright and beautiful day and the countryside had been in full bloom, he would hardly notice this, because he was so intent in doing his set number of miles often as quickly as possible. Not very mindful!

At one level, we may see this as 'gaining pleasure from achievement'. Such pleasures are short lived, do not stimulate the contentment/soothing system, and because the next 'need to achievement' pops up quickly we lose the ability to take pleasure for each moment – to be fully present (see Chapter 7). Of course, in depression, there is often a sense of not achieving enough and certainly a loss in the ability to enjoy the simple pleasures of life.

The disappointment and dissatisfaction with performances that perfectionists feel can result in a number of difficult emotions: guilt, anger, frustration, shame, envy and anxiety. These negative emotions can make life a misery. Even if successful, we know this may not be enough because we might think that people are only interested in us because of our success and not because they really care. Various famous people can get depressed with problems like this – success does not really give that sense of connection and belonging that they were looking for. To get those feelings we have to retrain our brains and reach out to others.

Ask yourself: Why do I want to reach the standards that I've set myself? You have to be really honest in your answers. Here are some that others have given:

- *I want to impress others.*
- *I want to be a somebody rather than a nobody.*
- *I want to be loved and wanted.*
- *I don't want others to see the bad side of me or my flaws.*
- *I want to avoid being criticized and thought of as worthless.*
- *Life is pointless if you don't succeed.*
- *I must not let others down.*
- *There has to be something I am good at.*

It does not matter too much what your wants, wishes and hopes are, provided that you can cope with them not coming to fruition. If you say, 'I'd like to impress others,' that may be fine. But if you say, 'I must impress others, otherwise they will see me as inadequate and I will feel useless and rejectable,' you have a problem. And the reason why is that failure and setbacks will generate such anger with yourself and others that this can drive you into depression.

Here are some useful ways to cope with these difficulties. Keep in mind that some of your perfectionistic difficulties are fear-linked or simply bad habits. Make a decision to compassionately refocus your attention and practise the following:

- When engaged in activities such as walking, or cooking or sexual behavior become mindful (see Chapter 7).
- Take some soothing rhythm breaths and pay attention to the present moment. If out walking look at the sky, the trees and grasses – really attend to them; smell the air, playfully notice each step.
- If other thoughts drift into your mind that are not exactly about this moment (and they will) notice them kindly and bring your attention back to the sky, trees, grass etc.
- Remember to use your compassionate facial expression.

Personal pride and perfectionism

Some people with eating disorders, who become very thin, are often highly perfectionist and competitive. They have a pride in themselves because they exert control over their eating and weight. Often the problem starts when they get on the scales, see that they have lost weight and feel a thrill or buzz of pride from the achievement. To put on weight produces a feeling of deflation and shame. They can become obsessed with every calorie and type of food they eat. This is an example of shame-driven pride. They may feel ashamed of their bodies or believe that there is not much about them to be proud of but then they hit on the idea of weight loss, and the pride of losing weight drives them on.

When shame turns into pride, it takes a real struggle to change this. Helping these people to put on weight may be seen as taking away the only thing (losing weight) they feel good at. This kind of problem is a very different one from, say, panic attacks. Nobody wants panic attacks, so therapist and patient can line up together against the common problem. Anorexic people want to be thin; they want to maintain their perfectionist standards of not eating much.

It is the same with all forms of perfectionism and competitiveness, be it cleaning the house, playing a sport well, working long hours and so on. *The person does not want to give up these things.* However, it is the reactions to failure and setbacks that have to be changed. If the sports person becomes depressed because he or she is not playing well and loses confidence in him/herself, that is hardly helpful. Many talented sportspeople do not make it because of how they react to things not going well – they can't ride the ups and downs easily because anger and frustration disrupts their performance. They cannot refocus on the last.

'What the Hell' factor

There is an important motto for when we slip into perfectionism and overstriving – which is 'what the Hell'. The fact of the matter is that once you have tried your best – if it's not working – then 'what the hell' – you are not going to be taken out and shot by the Gestapo. It is finding that point inside you that lets you 'relax, ease back and let things be'. Obviously I am applying this to perfectionism when we overly strive and get into states of panic, fear and depression. People who are lazy may need much less of 'what the hell factor' – so it's always a matter of balance. But I and my own family have found that, at times, when things seem to be getting too intense, the ability to back off and think, 'Okay, I've tried my best so what will be will be' – 'what the hell' – is helpful. Technically this is called 'de-catastrophizing and keeping things in perspective' – but 'what the hell' – it works for me so I share it with you.

Frustration tolerance

It would be great if we never felt frustrated, but while we might be able to lower our frustration threshold, the key is our ability to tolerate and work with it. That requires us to become more observant of how and when it arises in us. Our ability to tolerate frustration can change, for many reasons. You have probably noticed that, some days, you can cope with minor problems without too much effort, but on other days almost anything that blocks you can really irritate you. This is what we mean when we say, 'He (or she) got out of bed on the wrong side today'. If we are driving somewhere in a hurry, we might see others on the road as 'getting in our way' and become angry. As our feelings and attitudes become more urgent, we start to demand that things 'should be' different from the way they are. Fatigue, tiredness and being under pressure are also typical everyday things that reduce our frustration tolerance. *And depression itself can lower our frustration tolerance.*

The degree of frustration that a person feels can relate to a fear of shame. For example, Gerry lost his car keys on the day he had an important meeting. He became angry with himself and his family because the keys could not be found. In the back of his mind, he was thinking, 'If I don't get to the meeting on time, I'll walk in late. Everybody will think I'm a person who can't keep to time and they will think I'm unreliable or careless.' At times, we may blame ourselves with thoughts like 'If only I were more careful, I wouldn't lose things'. Probably everyone could tell stories of how, when things are lost (e.g., the string or scissors are not in the drawer as expected), they became angry and irritated: 'Why are things never where they should be?' When we get depressed our frustration tolerance goes down and coping with that can be difficult. Again keep in mind that this is not your fault, it is the depression – but it is helpful to work out how to cope:

- Recognize that feeling 'on a short fuse' can be part of depression, and be prepared.
  Use your soothing breathing and monitor your thoughts mindfully – preparing to cope with your irritable mood today with efforts not to act it out.
- Try not to self-blame, as this will send you down in spirals – you may become frustrated with being easily frustrated.
- Advise others of this and assure them you will do what you can not to act it out.
- Take pride in the ability to feel without acting, to smile even though you are irritated inside. You're learning that you can have a choice about how you act.
- If you feel your frustration is a bit too hot to handle, take yourself out of the situation.
- Sometimes physical activity such as running or quick walking can be helpful.

Dashed ideals and fantasies

One of the most important qualities of us humans is that *we fantasize*. This means that we are constantly making plans and developing fantasies of how we want things to be. The problem with fantasy is that we often live in excess. We imagine we can do more than we can. Often I have fantasized and imagined I could complete a piece of work in a certain time only to discover I couldn't. Painters get frustrated when they cannot make the picture they are painting look like the one they have in their head. We often fantasize we are going to feel better than we do. For example, we might fantasize having a great fun holiday but it turns out to be just okay. Sometimes we fantasize about other people having fun lives and it is only us who are not. Fantasies can make us unrealistic in many areas of our lives. The way we create our fantasies, ideals, wishes, anticipations and expectations in our heads can be absolutely crucial to our abilities to cope with the ups and downs of real life, life that rarely matches our fantasies.

Petro was a very bright student and throughout his life his single parent (and school) had admired his ability and praised him. But gradually Petro developed an idea that he needed to do very well, make his mother proud of him, be successful (not like his father) and one day rescue her from their poverty. This became linked to his self-identity. He fantasized about his career and going to the top universities. His school rather fuelled these fantasies. The problem was as his examinations approached and he had one or two lower grades he started to panic – seeing all collapse around him. He slipped into depression and could hardly work at all, seeing himself as a failure – yet he was a very bright lad! However, he was grossly over-extended and up on the high wire of life. Oliver James discusses these issues in detail in his book *Britain on the Couch* – of how too many of our children are being set up with too high expectations and who either give up, or crash when they fall short.

We can be set up for disappointment because our ideals, hopes and expectations are unrealistic. Modern Western societies are very unhelpful here because they imply you can be anything you like if you work hard enough. *This is simply untrue.* Genes, opportunity and luck as well as effort have a big effect on how our lives turn out. Often we have to learn to play the hand we are dealt – and sometimes that is a difficult one. Learning to do that with compassion can help enormously. A serious thwarting of our life goals and ideals can trigger depression, especially if we see this as having a lot of social implications (e.g., loss of status, loss of a loving relationship) as well as implications for how our lives will be in the future. Thinking about depression often means that we have to ask ourselves several questions:

- What are our ideals?
- In what way do we feel thwarted in reaching them?
- How can we deal with the frustration and anger that comes when they are not met?
- What conclusions are we drawing about ourselves, others and the future?
- Are we caught up in a strong sense of 'should'?
- How might we ease down and become more balanced in our expectations and aspirations?

The disappointment gap

Spend a few moments thinking about your ideals. You'll explore this more clearly by writing down the ideal and the actual in two columns (see table 21.1). You can then think about what I call the *disappointment gap*. The disappointment gap leads to four possible outcomes:

- Attack and blame yourself.
- Attack and blame others.
- Give up.
- Accept reality without seriously attacking either yourself or others.

Because attacking is a common response to frustration, we can see that we have found a root source of our self-criticism – which is none other than our frustration. The more frustrated we are with ourselves, the more we may tend to bully and criticize ourselves. Keep in mind, as I indicated with the example above of Gerry (page 502) who lost his keys, that behind frustration can be feelings of threat, fear and anxiety – so always consider that as a possibility. Let's work through some examples and see how this works.

Brian had set his sights on an important promotion. For over a year, he had worked hard to put himself in a good position, and his bosses had indicated that the promotion was within his grasp. He began to anticipate and plan how the new position would make his work easier and more interesting and how the extra money would allow him to move house. Unfortunately, two months before the promotion was due, Brian's company was taken over and all promotions were put on hold. To make matters worse, the new company brought in some of their own personnel, and Brian found that the position he was going for had been filled by a younger man. He became angry and then depressed. All the plans, hopes and goals associated with the promotion seemed thwarted. He told himself that things never worked out for him and there was no point in trying to improve himself. He ruminated on the injustice of what had happened but had little power to change the situation – in effect, in his mind he kept fighting an unwinnable battle and thus saw himself as constantly frustrated and defeated. His *ideal* in contrast to his *actual* self looked like Table 21.1.

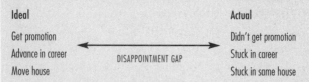

TABLE 21.1 BRIAN'S IDEAL–ACTUAL RELATIONSHIP

Ideal		Actual
Get promotion		Didn't get promotion
Advance in career	DISAPPOINTMENT GAP	Stuck in career
Move house		Stuck in same house

- **Attack self.** I should have seen this coming. I should feel confident enough to try to get another job, but I'm not. If I were more assertive, I'd make them give me my promotion. I'm weak for not coping with this.

- **Attack others.** They're just using me. They're unfair, and they should be fair and realize that this promotion was promised to me by the old company. They have snatched an opportunity away at the last moment.

- **Give up.** I can't get out of this. Nothing will change. My future is ruined.

Of course it's understandable why Brian felt bad about this lost promotion, but ruminating on his anger and self/other attacking made a bad situation worse. For him to come to terms with what happened – the fourth possible outcome – it helped for him to recognize his sadness about it (rather than block it out with anger) and the depth of his shoulds, and stop attacking himself. He soon realized that he could not have seen it coming and that it was not a matter of him not having been assertive enough. He gradually began to work out ways that he could get around this setback, waited a while and sought employment elsewhere. Coming to accept the situation and then working out how he could deal with it were important steps in his recovery. The more understanding, compassion and kindness one can bring to this situation the better – life can be very tough.

'It's all been spoiled'

Depressed people often have the feeling that things have been spoiled. Susanne had planned her wedding carefully, but her dress did not turn out right and it rained all day. This was disappointing, but her mood continued to be low on her honeymoon. She had thoughts like, 'It didn't go right. It was all spoiled by the weather and my dress. Nothing ever works out right for me. Why couldn't I have had one day in my life when things go right?' She was so disappointed and angry about the weather and her dress that she was unable to consider all the good things of the day, and how to put her disappointment behind her and get on and enjoy the honeymoon. She dwelt on how things had been spoiled for her, rather than living mindfully in each new moment of her unfolding life (see Chapter 7). Later, when she considered possible positives in her life, she was able to soften her all-or-nothing thinking and to recognize that she was seeing the weather and the dress as almost personal attacks. She realized how her anger was interfering with her pleasure. She also acknowledged that many kinds of frustrations and disappointments in her life are often activated by thoughts of 'everything has been spoiled'. She had to work hard to come to terms with her wedding 'as it was', but doing this helped to lift her mood.

The key process in these kinds of situations is:

- First, recognize the upset and disappointment.
- Then make a conscious decision that you really want to learn to calm down as soon as possible – that this is a life skill you would like to acquire and will train for.
- Then engage your soothing rhythm breathing – really focus on that.
- Then focus on being mindful and observing your thoughts and feelings – if you can, be curious: 'Oh, that's interesting, I'm thinking like that.'
- If you get 'pulled into your upset' then refocus on you breathing and either:
  – bring to mind your sense of being the self you would like to be (e.g., calm and compassionate – don't forget the gentle facial expression) and/or
  – bring your compassionate image to mind and imagine it with you, understanding the distress of your upset but there to help you.
- When you feel ready and able, think about how you might re-examine your thoughts and feelings and see them in a different way – what would a compassionate way of seeing them or thinking about them be? What might compassionate behavior be for you now? (See Chapters 8 and 9.)

- Keep in mind you are trying to turn on and stimulate your soothing system to help you in this situation (see Chapter 2).

The sense of things having been damaged and spoiled can be associated with the idea that things are irreparable and cannot be put right. In these situations, it is useful to work out how best to improve things rather than dwell on a sense of them being *completely* spoiled (which is linked to our anger). Of course, we might need time to grieve and come to terms with disappointments. One can't rationalize disappointments away. The feelings can be very strong indeed.

Sometimes we can feel we are spoiling things for others because (say) of our depression or mistakes etc. That takes us back into the realms of shame and guilt (see Chapters 18 and 19).

Loss of a positive relationship

When we fantasize about our ideal partners, we usually see them as beautiful or handsome, kind and always understanding. When it comes to sex, we may think that they (and perhaps ourselves too) should be like an ever-ready battery that never goes flat. When we think about our ideal lover, we don't think about their problems with indigestion, the times when they will be irritable and stressed or take us for granted, or that they could fancy other people.

As an adolescent, Hannah had various fantasies about what a loving relationship would be like. It would, she thought, involve closeness, almost telepathic communication between her and her lover and few, if any, conflicts. She believed that 'love would conquer all'. This type of idealizing is not that uncommon, but when Hannah's relationship started to run into problems, she was not equipped to cope with them because her ideals were so easily frustrated.

The early courting months with Warren seemed fine and they got on well and Hannah was sure that theirs was going to be a good marriage. However, after six months of marriage, they had a major setback. The negotiations for a house they wanted to buy fell through. Then, while they were trying to find another, the housing market took off and they found that they had to pay a lot more for one of similar size. Warren felt cheated by life, his mood changed and he became withdrawn and probably mildly depressed. Hannah, who was also upset about the house problems, was more concerned about the change in her relationship with Warren. The gap between her ideal and the actual relationship started to widen. This discrepancy in her ideal–actual relationship looked like Table 21.2.

Gradually Hannah began to recognize that their problems were not about love but the hard realities of living. There was

TABLE 21.2 HANNAH'S IDEAL–ACTUAL RELATIONSHIP

Ideal	Actual
Have fun together	Can't go out, short of money
Have few conflicts	Increasing conflicts
Always feel understood ←— DISAPPOINTMENT GAP —→	Don't feel understood
Feel close to each other	Feel increasing distance

- **Attack self.** Maybe I'm doing something wrong. If Warren cared for me, he would talk to me more. Maybe he doesn't love me any more. I get irritated with him so maybe it's my fault. He's lost interest in sex, therefore I am not sexually exciting any more. I should be able to cope better. Maybe I made the wrong choice of partner.

- **Attack other.** This is a different side to him. He should cope better and recognize my needs. He's being selfish and moody.

- **Give up.** There's no point in talking about what's wrong. We can't change the housing market. I'm stuck.

nothing wrong with her as a person or the relationship if Warren felt down. They had to learn to deal with their problems in a different way by encouraging each other to talk about their feelings. Hannah had often avoided this for fear that Warren would blame her or say that she was, in some way, part of the reason why he was feeling down. She also had to give up attacking him when he did not give her the attention that she wanted.

She slowly moved away from thinking that all problems in their relationship were to do with a lack of love. Warren had to acknowledge the effect his moods were having on Hannah and that he needed to work through his sense of injustice and belief that this was unfair and it shouldn't have happened. They eventually learned to build on the positives in their relationship rather than fighting over the frustrations. Tough work, but compassionate openness can help develop the courage necessary.

Disappointment and frustration with what we feel

So far we have discussed how we can be disappointed in things and people that block our goals and affect our relationships. Another key area of disappointment centres around *our own personal feelings*. Some depressed people go to bed hoping that they will feel better in the morning, and it is a great disappointment when they don't. Unfortunately, when depressed we often feel (understandably) disappointed and deflated when we wake up and don't feel any better but still anxious and tired. However, we can make matters worse by attacking ourselves, predicting that the day will go very badly and telling ourselves we 'should' be better. There are many other feelings that can be a source of disappointment. If this happens it can be useful to acknowledge this and engage in compassion under the duvet (see pages 151–2):

- When you first wake up, practise spending a moment to focus on your soothing rhythm breathing.
- Allow yourself to put on a compassionate facial expression. Don't worry if it seems odd or unnatural.
- Make a commitment to treat yourself with kindness today – to train yourself in this skill. If it feels very hard then that is a great opportunity for even a small bit of training to be helpful.
- Try not to fight with your thoughts or feelings, or force them to change, but notice them and be mindful of them as best you can.
- Keep in mind that feeling depressed is absolutely not your fault, it is sadly common and caused by many things.
- When you get out of bed and start to engage with the day go one step at a time, recognizing that you are doing the best you can. Make it a goal to be as supportive and encouraging of your efforts to cope with your depression as best you can.
- Some people prefer to get out of bed quickly without spending any time thinking about their thoughts or feelings. Again, practise and see which is best for you.

Let's widen our scope a bit and look at some examples relating to disappointments with feelings. The following problem shows clearly how difficulties can arise when our hopes and ideals are disappointed by our own feelings.

Don had suffered from anxiety attacks for many years and, as a result, felt that he had missed out on life. He developed a strong fantasy that, if someone could cure his anxiety, he would be 'like other people' and especially more like his brother who was successful in the art world. When I saw him, I found that his attacks were focused on a fear of being unable to breathe and of dying. However, by looking at the evidence that he was not going to die when he had an anxiety attack, and learning how to relax to gain more control over his attacks, he made progress. In fact, he did so well that he went on a trip to Europe. But when he came back, he went to bed, got depressed, felt suicidal and very angry.

We talked about the problem as one of unrealistic ideals. Don had the fantasy that if his anxiety was cured he would do a lot of things and make up for many lost years. In his fantasy, he would be like others, able to travel, be successful and, in his words, 'rejoin the human race at last'. He believed that normal people never suffered anxiety. He had hoped that there would be some magic method that would take the anxiety away, and that once it was gone, it would be gone for good. He explained that, on his European trip, he had suffered more anxiety than he'd expected.

We wrote out two columns that captured this situation, headed 'Ideal me' (i.e. without anxiety) and 'Actual me' (i.e. how I am now).

Ideal me	*Actual me*
Like others	Not like others / different
Able to enjoy life	Life is miserable
Confident / successful	A failure
Explorative	Frightened

←——— Disappointment Gap ——→

Our conversation then went something like this:

Paul: *It seems that you did quite a lot on your trip, but you feel disappointed with it. What happened when you got back?*

Don: *I started to look back on it and thought, 'Why does it have to be so hard for me, always fighting this anxiety?' I should have enjoyed the trip more after all the effort I put into it. I should have done more. It's been a struggle. So I just went to bed and brooded on how bad it all was and what's the point.*

Paul: *It sounds as if your experience did not match your ideal.*

Don: *Oh yeah, it was far from that.*

Paul: *Okay, what went through your mind when you found that the trip wasn't matching your ideal?*

Don: *I started to think I should be enjoying this more. If I were really better, I'd enjoy it more. If I felt better, I'd do more. I'll never get on top of this. It's all too late and too much effort.*

Paul: *That sounds like it was very disappointing to you.*

Don: *Oh yes, very, terrible, but more so when I got back.*

Paul: *What did you say about you?*

Don: *I'm a failure. I just felt totally useless. After all the work we've done, nothing has changed.*

Paul: *Let's go back to the two columns for a moment and see if I've understood this. For many years, you've had the fantasy of how things would be if you were better. But getting there is a struggle and this is disappointing for you. When you get disappointed, you start to attack yourself, saying that you're a failure and it's too late. That makes the 'actual' you seem unchanged. Is that right?*

Don: *Yes, absolutely.*

Paul: *Can we see how the disappointment of not reaching the ideal starts up this internal attack on yourself, and the more of a failure you feel, the more anxious and depressed you get?*

Don: *Hmm, yes.*

Paul: *Okay, it was a disappointment to have anxiety again. Were you anxious all the time?*

Don: *No, not all the time.*

Paul: *I see. Well, let's start from the other end so to speak. If you had to pick out a highlight of the trip, what would it be?*

Don [thinks for a moment]: *There were actually a few, I suppose. We went to this amazing castle set up on the hill . . .*

As Don started to focus on the positive aspects of his trip, his mood changed. He became less focused on the negatives and more balanced in his evaluation of the trip. I am not saying that you should simply 'look on the bright side' but suggesting you focus on the possibility that there may be some positives which offers some balance. It is easy to become focused on disappointment. By the end of the session, Don was able to feel proud of the fact that he had been to Europe, whereas a year earlier, going anywhere would have been unthinkable. He was not magically cured of his anxiety disorder. The more he focused on what he could do, rather than on how much he was missing out or how unfair it was to have anxiety attacks, the less depressed and self-attacking he became. Learning to be more mindful rather than fighting with, and being angry with his anxiety might also have helped him.

You might also notice something else here. If somebody has had a problem like this for a long time, it can become almost built in to their sense of self, their self-identity. Don believed that he was victim to anxiety and had missed out on life. This sense of *being a victim* to his anxiety was very strong and not easy to give up. If people see themselves as losers it can actually be quite difficult for them to see themselves as winners because it is too different an identity. Sometimes we have to be honest with ourselves and think whether we are trapping ourselves in an old identity. Are we really confident that we would feel okay about being a happy person? Can we allow ourselves to be happy in spite of difficult life circumstances?

Disappointment with oneself

We can feel that we have let *ourselves* down because we have not come up to our own standards or ideals. Here again, rather than accept our limitations and fallibility – that maybe we have done our best but it did not work out as desired – we can get frustrated and then go in for a lot of self-attacking. It is as if we feel we can't trust or rely on ourselves to come up with the goods. We start attacking ourselves like a master attacking a slave who hasn't done well enough. This frustration with oneself can be a major problem.

Lisa wanted to be confident, as she thought her friends were. She wanted always to be in a good state of mind and never feel intense anger or anxiety or be depressed. She had two clear views of herself – her ideal and her actual self (Table 21.3) – and these would go hammer and tongs at each other. She felt lazy because she couldn't get motivated.

Lisa's ideal self and her actual self were unrealistic. Her ideal self could not be met much of the time. Her actual self (which she identified as her depressed self) was prone to discount the positives, think in all-or-nothing terms and overgeneralize. Much of this was powered by frustration and fear.

It may be true that we can't rely on ourselves always to be anxiety-free, or make the best of things, or be a mistake-free zone. The main thing is how we deal with our mistakes and disappointments. Attacking ourselves when we feel the anger of frustration is not helpful and, in the extreme, can make us very

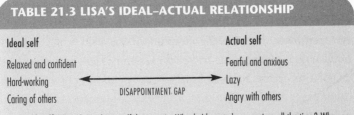

TABLE 21.3 LISA'S IDEAL–ACTUAL RELATIONSHIP

Ideal self		Actual self
Relaxed and confident		Fearful and anxious
Hard-working	DISAPPOINTMENT GAP	Lazy
Caring of others		Angry with others

- **Attack self.** Oh God, I've let myself down again. Why do I have to be so anxious all the time? Why don't I just get on and do things? I am a useless, pathetic person.
- **Attack others.** Why do others always seem so confident? I hate them. They don't understand how difficult it is for me.
- **Give up.** I had better not try too much because it will not work out. I'm bound to fail and let myself down. I just can't rely on myself.

depressed. Learning to accept ourselves as fallible human beings, riddled with doubts, feelings, passions, confusions and paradoxes can be an important step towards compassionate self-acceptance. When disappointments arise, can we be understanding and compassionate? Anyone can be compassionate if it is plain sailing, but can you do it in a storm and when things are going wrong? That would be really helpful.

A new baby

Fiona had wanted a baby for about three years. She would fantasize about how her life would be changed with a child, and she engaged in a lot of idealized thinking about smiling babies and happy families. However, the birth was a painful and difficult one, and her son was a fretful child who cried a lot and was difficult to soothe. She found it difficult to bond with him and, within a short time, became exhausted and felt on a short fuse. At times, she just wanted to get rid of him. She took such feelings not as a sad but not so uncommon experience of women after childbirth, but as evidence that she was a bad mother. When she could not soothe her son, she thought that he was saying to her, 'You're not good enough'. She thought that if she had been a better mother she would not have had a colicky child, and she would have been loving and caring from the beginning, regardless of her fatigue. She felt intensely ashamed of her feelings, and could not tell her family doctor or even her husband of the depths of her exhaustion or feelings of wanting to run away. She felt her feelings made her a bad person. The reality of life with her baby son brought a whole set of ideals crashing down around her head.

We can explore Fiona's ideal of her motherhood and her depression (Table 21.4).

TABLE 21.4 FIONA'S IDEAL–ACTUAL RELATIONSHIP

Ideal self		Actual self
Happy and relaxed		Tense and fraught; many sleepless nights
Feel loving towards my child	← DISAPPOINTMENT GAP →	Want to run away, feel aggressive
Be able to soothe him		He is difficult to soothe

- **Attack self.** I thought that I was a caring person but I feel so awful when he starts crying. I just want to leave him, to shut the door on him so I can't hear him. I can't cope, therefore, I'm a weak, inadequate and bad person. If people knew what was going through my mind, they would hate me, lock me up or take my son away. Maybe I don't deserve to be a mother. I hate myself for feeling this way.

- **Attack others.** Why does my son have to cry so much? He doesn't like me. If he'd only sleep like a normal child, it would be better. It's not fair. Why do others seem so happy with their babies? I hate them. It's not fair.

- **Give up.** There's nothing I can do. I should just passively accept this state of affairs or get away. No one could understand me.

Let's look at some kinder ways that Fiona might look at her situation, beginning with understanding and being compassionate to her distress. Here are some ideas for what she might reflect on and say to herself:

- **Compassionate understanding**. It's very understandable to feel upset about my baby's colic and how difficult it is to soothe him. That is indeed sad for me. Some women do seem to have an easier time of it. I was looking forward to this but in reality it is exhausting. It is understandable when you're exhausted like this to be on a bit of a short fuse and tearful.

- **Compassionate attention**. Although some women seem to bond easily with their babies, this is not true for all women by any means. Many women find babies who are difficult to soothe exhausting, and angry feelings are actually very common. Just like me. It's sad for them too. Lots of women's magazines write about these problems and they are also discussed on the Internet. It's clearly not my fault I'm having these difficulties and feelings. When I feel well I can be a caring person (bring to mind memories of caring).

- **Compassionate thinking**. There have been a lot of complex changes in my body and in my hormones as a result of childbirth and these can create all kinds of feelings in women, including myself. Many other women have these experiences too and so I am far from alone in this. If this happened to a friend I would be kind and understanding and see what help I could offer. Practising being kind and understanding to my distress is important too.

- **Compassionate behavior**. It will help me a lot if I face this problem honestly and discuss it with people who can help me, such as my health visitor or family doctor. They will be able to keep an eye on me and see if I need any extra help. I might also be able to talk to other women

> who have been in this situation and find out what has helped them. The most important thing is to say yes to the help on offer and not hide away in shame, because this is such a common problem for women.

The moment Fiona faces her sadness, stops attacking herself and recognizes that she is not alone but may need help, she is taking the first steps towards recovery. Becoming depressed after childbirth is intensely sad and disappointing, and you can experience many odd (sometimes even aggressive, overwhelmed or want-to-run-away) feelings, but try not to be ashamed about them. To the best of your ability, be compassionate and kind with yourself, and reach out to others and discuss your true feelings with people around you and in particular your health visitor or family doctor.

One more point to keep in mind. If we're having feelings of intense disappointment, say, there is often some bright spark who tells us to pull ourselves together, or who seems able to cope with everything. It may be someone in our lives who is being very critical of us, or who likes to tell us how well they coped with things and who can make us feel that we are a failure by comparison. Don't be too influenced by these people (it might even be a parent). What we feel is what we feel, and rather than attacking ourselves, it is preferable to look at the ways we can cope and sort out our problems in the ways that best suit ourselves.

Overview

It is human to want to achieve certain things and create fantasies in our minds. However, these fantasies can become unrealistic because life is often complex and difficult. In this chapter we have noted how we can produce all kinds of fantasies and can create all kinds of hopes, anticipations and expectations. If these don't come to fruition we can be disappointed. In our fantasies we often live a life of excess. Living in the *reality* of life can be tricky, but if we learn to be kind and compassionate, mindful and understanding, these can help us get through. Frustration and disappointment are not in themselves bad – indeed learning that we can't have want we want when we want it is important for our maturity and wisdom.

KEY POINTS

- We can be disappointed with all kinds of things in our lives such as blocks to major life goals, relationships and personal feelings.
- Our anger and frustration or disappointment can set in motion a train of thoughts that are either self-attacking and/or other-attacking.
- If we can learn to identify these thoughts early, we can take steps to work against them and work through them.
- As the anger grows in us, there is a tendency to use many of the thinking styles we have met in earlier chapters (e.g., all-or-nothing thinking, overgeneralizing, disqualifying the positives, dwelling on the negatives – see Chapter 10).
- Although disappointments are always upsetting, we can perhaps learn to limit their effects on us and prevent them from driving us into depression.

EXERCISES

Exercise 1

Think of the last time you felt disappointed and angry about something. Then write down your ideal thoughts and your actual thoughts in two columns. Find out if you do any of the following:

- **Attack self**. Write down any self-attacking thoughts that have been produced by this disappointment.

- **Attack others**. Write down any other-attacking thoughts that have arisen from this disappointment.
- **Give up** in a hopeless, irritated sort of way.
- **Develop acceptance** and see what you might do to improve or move on.

Exercise 2

Now that you have worked out how you tend to react to disappointments, first acknowledge your anger. Ask yourself:

- Am I going in for all-or-nothing thinking?
- Am I discounting the positives? What remains good or okay?
- Am I overgeneralizing by saying that everything has been spoiled?
- What would I say to a friend who had this disappointment?
- What would I like someone who cares for me to say to me?
- Spend a few moments thinking about how you would actually like to be able to deal with frustration and disappointments – would that be worth training for?
- Create in your mind the self you would like to become.

Further things to try

Self-feelings and judgements

Distinguish clearly between your actions and yourself (see Chapter 13). For example, ask yourself: If I fail an exam, does this make me – a person, my whole being, my totality – a failure? I might *feel* like a failure, but this does not make it true. Are you saying, 'I only accept *me* if I do *it* well'? If you fail at something you may have that heart-sink feeling, but the key thing is how quickly you can recover yourself and be kind and help yourself through this disappointment in your life – getting through and coping is the aim.

Shoulds, oughts and musts

Explore the pressure of the shoulds, oughts and musts in your life and how they can produce more emotional pain. Work out your preferred compassionate ways to spot and tone them down.

Shame

Are you disappointed because somehow you feel ashamed at not meeting your ideals? (If so, look at the shame exercises in Chapter 17).

Reality check

Although it may be painful it can help if, in a friendly voice, you ask yourself, 'Are my ideals realistic?'

Compassion work

When we are frustrated or disappointed, compassion can be very helpful. As I have indicated above, what you can do here is to focus on your soothing rhythm breathing and then work through what you feel would be compassionate attention, thinking and behavior to help you with your setback and frustration.

It is helpful if you recognize that you will be upset by things – this is simply natural. However, what you're looking out for is whether your frustration or anger becomes destructive by attacking yourself or others, or you have the heart-sink that pulls you down. Again, don't blame yourself for having the anger but do be gentle with it and at the same time bring more kindness and compassion into your frame of mind.

When you run into a major setback, or even if you are struggling with small setbacks, it can be useful to write a **compassionate letter** (see pages 235–9). This can help to get things in perspective and create the kind, friendly tone. Don't forget, this letter will be focusing on compassionate attention, thinking and behavior and looking at your courage and abilities – things we often forget and underestimate when we feel bad.

22

Summing up

Depression is probably one of the darkest winters of the soul. Researchers throughout the world are trying to work out why we have this capacity to feel as terrible as we do – and many have come up with various explanations. We know that there are many different types of depression, with different causes and factors maintaining it. In this book, we have looked at some common types of depression. Whatever else we say about depression, it is clear that there is a toning down of the *positive* feelings and a toning up of our *threat*- and *loss*-based ones. The emotions of anger, anxiety and dread were originally designed to protect us. It is when they get out of balance that they can have unhelpful effects. One evolved protective strategy is to slow down and hide – try to recuperate. In depression, however, this 'go to the back of the cave and stay there' is not conducive to our well-being. Our energy takes a nose-dive, our sleep is affected and of course our thoughts and feelings about ourselves, others and the world we live in are dark. But fundamentally, depression is a brain state and brain pattern to make us lie low when things are stressful.

We now know that depression is a potential state of mind that has evolved over many millions of years. Many animals too can show depressed states. We also know that depression is very much linked to the support and acceptance of others and ourselves. We have evolved to be motivated to be wanted, accepted, valued and have status in our relationships. Depression is marked by inner feelings of being distant and cut off from others, with a sense of emotional aloneness.

What comes through from our understanding about depression, and many studies on our human needs, is that we have evolved to be very responsive to kindness – from the day we are born to the day we die. I outlined some of the evidence for this in Chapter 2. Kindness soothes the threat system and indicates helpful resources. This in turn reduces the 'go to the back of the cave' protection strategy. This is why it is so important to learn self-kindness, because your brain is designed to respond to it. Depression also relates to our desire to feel in control of our lives rather than controlled. Here are some key ideas.

- Depression is a very varied problem. It ranges from the mild to the severe. Some depressions are associated with much anxiety, others with much anger. Some come on slowly, others quite quickly.
- Accept your depression as a brain state that has been triggered in you rather than feel ashamed of it, fight with it, hate it or condemn yourself. Once you accept it then you are freed to work compassionately with it. You can then take the objective view that by working in a certain way you may be able to shift this brain state. It is about healing our minds.
- There is an important psychological component to every depression, which this book has focused on, but this does not mean that psychological change is all you need to recover from depression. Some people benefit from medication and others require a change in social circumstances.

- Commonly, when we are depressed, we have problems in the way we think and experience ourselves and relationships. We may try to run from our painful emotions or ruminate on unhelpful emotions; our fears, moods and emotions take control over our thinking. Training our mind is a way of gaining control over it. But, like learning to ride a bike or do tricks with a football, it helps if we dedicate ourselves to the training.

- One key path of training is to make a commitment to develop one's compassion for self and others, and with this one's wisdom, emotional tolerance, strength and kindness. We can try to practise compassionate attention, thinking, behavior and feeling – each day!

- Compassion feelings can be difficult to experience because that system in our brain is toned down and/or we are frightened of it. It can feel overwhelming, or make us feel sadder; we may feel we don't deserve it or that we will let ourselves off the hook or become weak. So at first we need to work on compassionate thinking and compassionate behaviour. Think about compassion training as physiotherapy for your brain. It is then a question of step by step, working your exercises to increase your capacity to tolerate and feel compassion.

- Self-help books can be very useful, but of course sometimes we also need professional help. Self-help is no substitute for that. It may be that reading this book has encouraged you to consider whether you might benefit from therapy or other forms of help. If you think you might be depressed then contact your family doctor, who can talk things through with you, assess your symptoms and difficulties and if necessary refer you to a properly trained person.

- Shame can be one of the main reasons why you may be reluctant to seek help, but remember that depression is one of the most common problems that mental health professionals work with. You are far from alone. A similar case can be made for talking with friends; open up to friends, but choose people who you think will be able to understand you.

- Although you may need extra help, there are also many things that you can try to help yourself or at least avoid making your depression worse. To come back to my main point then, make a commitment to develop your abilities to be kind to yourself, able to reflect on your thoughts and your feelings using some of the ideas in this book, and engage in behaviors that have a chance to move you out of the depressed state of mind.

What is helpful?

Researchers are exploring what kind of self-help strategies depressed people find helpful. A review of this has recently been provided by two Australians, Amy Morgan and Anthony Jorm.[1] They broke these strategies down into three groups:

1 **Lifestyle strategies** include taking exercise, trying to maintain a regular sleep schedule, increasing activities that are potentially enjoyable (as opposed to boring or dutiful), and recognizing the need for resting. In general this means acting against the push and pull of depression and anxiety. Also important is body care, such as healthy diet and avoiding toxic substances such as drugs that have any influence on one's mood.

2 **Psychological self-help** includes focusing on rewarding oneself for small achievements, recognizing that many others suffer depression and visiting self-help websites (e.g., beyondblue, www.beyondblue.or.au is a particularly good one), trying to break difficulties down into smaller problems, practising mindfulness and monitoring one's thoughts.

3 **Social strategies** include trying to open up to other people, joining support and hobby groups and talking to somebody who has been through depression.

Interestingly, these researchers do not mention the importance of learning compassion to balance one's mind. Although the Buddha recommended this nearly 3,000 years ago we are only beginning to recognize its power. When you engage in any of these self-help strategies, do it in the spirit of self-support, kindness and compassion.

In addition, think about regularly exercising your brain in the ways described in earlier chapters. There is increasing evidence now that practice may change your brain over time.[2] However, like playing the piano or golf, you wouldn't expect to be good at it first time out. Regular practice, however, will improve your abilities. It is the same with compassion.

Keep in mind also that your compassion practice will have three components (see Chapter 8):

1 opening yourself to compassion from others (including the use of imagery)
2 compassion that you practise for others
3 compassion for yourself.

However, we have also looked at the way we can train our minds, direct our attention, thinking and behavior in a compassionate way which is conducive to healing depression; changing the brain state of depression from one of low positive emotion to more balanced emotion.

Don't get lost in unanswerable questions

When depressed we can feel life is meaningless – we are just oddities on a far-out planet; jumped-up DNA. Try not to get lost in this because 1,000 years from now we will see ourselves very differently. Many scientists are trying to answer the big questions: Why does the universe exist at all, rather than nothing? How can life evolve and why does consciousness exist? What is the meaning of life? We have no good answers! Your dog will never understand or be aware of existing in a material universe with planets. It will not have any notion of how your mind can think – because yours is so *different*. So there may be things way beyond our comprehension too, because our brains are limited. Don't set yourself unanswerable questions. We simply cannot answer a question about ultimate meanings in a life process. Rather decide what gives life meaning for you in *this lifetime*; you may or may not have other lifetimes or types of consciousness. All you can do is focus on this life – right here, right now. Trying to understand your mind and learning the art of compassion for self and others might not be so bad a goal to make life meaningful. Certainly the depressed mind state is the last place you should look for answers to complex questions.

Ten key steps that may help

1 Seek help if you need it, don't suffer in silence.
2 Go step by step.

3 Break problems down into smaller ones, rather than trying to do everything in one go.

4 Introduce more positive activities into your life.

5 Become more attentive and aware of your thinking and the ideas that go through your mind when you are depressed.

6 Identify your typical thinking styles (e.g., all-or-nothing thinking, discounting the positive aspects of your life). Note especially what you think about yourself, and how you label and treat yourself. Look out for your internal bully. Remember that this can drive you further into, rather than out of, depression.

7 Write down your thoughts to aid clarity and to focus your attention.

8 Identify the key themes in your depression (e.g., your need for approval, shame, unhappy relationships, unrealistic ideals, perfectionism). This will allow you to spot more easily your personal themes when they arise – and to challenge them.

9 Learn to work on your thinking with the use of your rational/ compassionate mind. The more you treat yourself with compassion and give up thinking of yourself in terms of inferior, bad, worthless, and so on, the easier it will be for your brain to recover.

10 Try to work on negative thoughts and developing new ways of behaving. However, also expect setbacks and disappointments from time to time.

Finally, remember:

- Your depression may be a state of mind you are in, but your depression is not you.
- Your anxiety may be a state of mind you are in, but your anxiety is not you.
- Your anger may be a state of mind you are in, but your anger is not you.

These states of mind are to do with how your brain was designed over millions of years. They are part of human nature.

Whatever judgements of 'you' that your emotions come up with, they are about as reliable as the weather. The more compassionate you are with yourself, the less you will be a 'fairweather friend' to yourself. If you can stay a true friend to yourself, even though depressed, you are taking a big step forward. You're on the way up

Bringing the themes of compassion practice together

Over the next few pages you will see some worksheets that are designed to help you focus on different aspects of compassionate self-help. In essence we are bringing together many of the ideas we have discussed throughout this book. We've covered quite a lot of ground, so when you look at the worksheets you may feel they are a bit overwhelming. Don't worry, however, just follow them through as best you can. You'll see that they make some logical sense. The key always is to focus on what you think would help you.

Developing your compassion practice

The worksheets at the end of this chapter help you work with specific events and practice. When we are distressed we want to find ways to work with that stress or upset without making it worse. This means we need to think about our attention, how we approach the upset, how we think about this and behaviors to try and deal with it.

This worksheet offers various prompts and ideas designed to help you to practise refocusing your mind and accessing your soothing/contentment system. When threatened or upset, it's easy to become focused on unpleasant feelings, worries or memories. Recognize them, but also rebalance your system.

Remember the depressed mind will pull our attention and thinking towards loss and threat. We have to make a commitment to focus, think and act against our urges to do nothing, to avoid things, or to dwell on the unhappy things.

Keep in mind that this can be hard and stay as kind and compassionate to yourself as you possibly can – no matter how well or poorly you think you do with any of the following.

One important aspect of practice is how to do it. Probably the best way to begin is to start in small steps, or as big steps as you feel able. We can begin with what we called on pages 151–2 'compassion under the duvet'. This means that before you go to sleep and when you wake up spend some time focusing your mind on your soothing breathing rhythm, adopting a kind and friendly facial expression, and creating your compassionate self. The act of imagining that you are this self can be helpful. Of course when we are depressed it can be extremely difficult to get any feelings, or even to bother. However, it is the effort and focusing your mind on compassion that matters. Don't worry if your mind constantly wanders – just bringing it back again is helpful. Try it for a week and see how you do. If you prefer, you can engage with your compassionate image.

Doing this for a couple of minutes each day (more if you can) might be enough to get you going. What you may find is that you become more aware of the possibility of compassion. When you're at a bus stop, on a train or in the bath, or anywhere where your mind can run free, you might consider slowing your breathing down and then focusing on a compassionate exercise. Imagine what's happening in your brain each time you do this. Imagine that those areas of your brain that are conducive to well-being and recovering from depression are being stimulated. As you get more into that practice, you may want to spend more and more time on it. For example, you might put aside 20 minutes or even longer each day, or a few days a week to focus on mindfully developing the feelings of compassion, practising directing compassion to others and to various parts of yourself. It's useful to keep a journal so that you can see your practice developing over time. You may want to find other groups or retreats where you can take this further.

Keep in mind that we often *bring compassion into life through action*. For example, someone who is frightened of going out of the house will need to confront that fear at some point by going out. They are more likely to develop the courage to do this if they can attend to a kind, supportive and understanding voice in their head rather than the critical *or* panicking one. It is the same with depression. We are more likely to be able to develop alternative thinking, accept ourselves and our emotions, and act against our depression if we learn to attend to a kind and supportive voice in our heads rather than critical or pessimistic ones.

So it has been a long journey. Depression can indeed indeed be a dark night of the soul but with practice and compassion we can begin to light a few candles. May your compassion grow with you. We wish you well.

WORKSHEET 1: COMPASSIONATE IDEAS TO COPE WITH LIFE DIFFICULTIES AND UPSETTING EMOTIONS

Record your regular practice, choosing an activity	Reflections on what helped, what was difficult and what requires practice
Compassionate attention Compassionate attention is about our focus and how we create images and recall helpful memories: Engage and attend to your soothing breathing rhythm (see Chapter 3) Adopt a compassionate body posture and facial expression. Become mindful – hold your attention 'in this moment' rather than becoming distracted by 'what ifs?' and ruminations (see Chapter 7). Recall times when you've coped. Recall times when you were happy. Focus on your compassionate image. Keep in mind that things and feelings change. Create an image of yourself coping or of you at your best. Imagine yourself having got through this difficulty – and really focus on that. Observe thoughts and feelings as patterns created in you – and realize that you can experience many different patterns. **Compassionate thinking/reasoning** Compassionate thinking/reasoning is about how we think things through – the kinds of self-talk and conversations that go through our minds: Notice if you're ruminating and decide to move out of it. Notice if your feelings or thoughts are self-critical and decide to switch to a kinder and compassionate focus (see Chapter 13). Imagine yourself as a compassionate person speaking to a friend. Actually speak out loud with a warm voice tone. Listen to yourself offer coping and helpful ideas (see Chapter 8). Put yourself in compassionate self mode and feel compassion for your upset self. Stay in that compassion mode. Compassionately speak to your upset self. If it helps, place a hand just over your heart area. Bring as much wisdom, strength, warmth and non-condemning to this as you can.	

WORKSHEET 1 (continued)

Record your regular practice, choosing an activity	Reflections on what helped, what was difficult and what requires practice
Bring to mind your common humanity and become aware that many humans can struggle with difficult feelings.	
Feel at one with them rather than alone or different.	
Recognize how often some of what you feel and especially depression isn't your fault. Focus on the reasons why it isn't (e.g. we did not design our brains or backgrounds).	
Assume that others will be helpful until you get evidence that they won't.	
Keep in mind the motto: 'The secret of success is the ability to fail.'	
Focus on your efforts rather than on results.	
Compassionate behavior	
Compassionate behavior is behavior that will help you cope with your difficulty.	
Make a commitment to behave in ways that help you move forward in life, even if this means short-term difficulty.	
Practise trying out different behaviors and see which ones work for you.	
Decide to act against your depressive feelings and try to do more.	
Commit yourself to trying or (even for a short while) some anti-depressant behaviors (see Chapter 12).	
Do a little (more if your can) thing you will be pleased with.	
Reach out to others and see if help is available for you.	
Keep in mind that confidence develops from engaging with the difficulty, and that this trying time you are going through now may, in the long term, build your confidence.	
Recognize your limits, and when you need to, rest, slow down or take time out.	
If problems seem large, try to break them down into smaller elements.	
Compassionate feeling	
Whatever you attempt to do, always try your best to do it with kindness so that you feel your efforts to be ones of support and encouragement, in the service of helping yourself cope and flourish.	
Remember that coping can be hard and can take practice. There are no oughts or shoulds here, no perfect ways to cope, no freeing or ridding oneself of difficult feelings – just basic kindness for life difficulties that many of us find ourselves in. This won't remove those difficulties but it might ease your path through them – good luck!	

WORKSHEET 2: COMPASSIONATE PRACTICES

Record your regular practice, choosing an activity	Personal comments and reflections on your practice
Soothing breathing rhythm and mindfulness: being 'in-the-moment'. Practise looking at things in new ways, noting the things you enjoy and can savour, no matter how small – e.g. the first cup of tea of the day, the warmth of a bath. Consider things you are grateful for in joyous, fun ways, no matter how small. Even noting the first cup of tea of the day or the smell of coffee.	
When in a place of quiet, focus on your **ideal compassionate/caring image**. It has the qualities of wisdom, strength, warmth and non-judging/condemning and gives these unconditionally to you, with the deep desire for you to flourish and be free from suffering. Practise feeling that flowing into you from your image. Remember that images can be fleeting and more felt than seen. Your image is well aware of how difficult our evolved brains/minds can be for us.	
When in a place of quiet, focus on **feeling yourself to be a compassionate person** with the qualities of wisdom, strength, warmth and non-judging /condemning – which you direct unconditionally towards yourself. Also practise directing compassionate feelings towards others. In both cases (directing towards yourself and towards others), focus on the deep desire for you and others to flourish, be happy and free from suffering.	
Compassionate behavior: choose and enact compassionate behavior that has the intention and deep desire for you and others to flourish and be free from suffering. This may include letter writing or acts of appreciation or gratitude or courageously doing something you are fearful of but would like to overcome. Make a commitment to look after and take care of yourself, as you would a dear friend. Seek out ways to learn assertiveness if you feel this would help you. Express your appreciation to others. Make a point of trying to be kind to others and see how you feel when doing that. Pay attention to how different things you do affect your feelings. If you're in conflict with someone or something, work on the most compassionate and helpful (non-submissive) way forward.Note any novel ways you have found to develop your compassion-focused lifestyle.	

Appendix 1

Monitoring and balancing your thoughts

These forms and how to use them are explained in Chapter 11.

Using Thought Forms

Chapter 11 introduced the idea of thought forms to help you monitor and record your key thoughts and to practise generating a helpful alternative. At the end of the book you will find some blank forms for your own use (and you can photocopy them). You will also find some worked examples. Although the forms may look somewhat complicated, they are fairly straightforward when you get the hang of them. Remember, as we said in Chapter 11, you can use a form that simply has two columns, one to record your negative thoughts and one to record your helpful alternative. The thought forms here have five columns, which are used as follows.

- **Column 1**. In this column write down any situation(s), event, memory, feeling or image that has sparked off feelings of anger, despair or depression, etc.
- **Column 2**. Where it says 'Beliefs and key thoughts', ask yourself some questions, such as how are you seeing this event? What is going through your mind? What are you thinking about yourself? (For example, are you telling yourself you are no good?) How do you think this event affects your future?

What do you think other people are thinking about you? All these questions are designed to explore your key beliefs, those thoughts that can make you feel sad, down and upset, etc.

- **Column 3**. In this column (the 'Feelings' column), write down what your feelings are/were and how intense they were. The reason we put the feelings in the third column is so you can see how your thoughts link the situation with your feelings – like a bridge between the two. (You may want to fill in this column before column 2.)

- **Column 4**. In this column, labelled 'Compassionate alternatives to depressive thoughts', stand back and think what you might say to a friend who had these negative ideas. Can you think of evidence of why your depressing thoughts may be a bit distorted? Can you think of evidence against your negative thoughts and beliefs? What alternatives might there be? How might you best cope with this? What kinds of ideas would be helpful here? Again, it is helpful to get the idea that you are not going to accept your depressing thoughts simply because your feelings of depression tell you to.

- **Column 5**. When you have taken some time to compassionately refocus your thinking, look at what you have written down and see if this has changed your feelings. If so, write down how much your feelings might have changed about that event now. Focusing on this possible change may give you an opportunity to see that by stepping back from your thoughts, you can change your perspective and feel better.

Some people like to read what others have written and ways they have challenged their thoughts, but don't just write out *their thoughts*. Do it yourself – with your own thoughts. Try it out – after all what have you got to lose?

Compassionate working

Remember that one of the main reasons for working on your thoughts is to help you *feel* differently about things and, in particular, not add to your stress. It is important to approach this with as much warmth and understanding as you can manage. Your alternatives should not be cold, bullying or irritable in their emotional tone. The more you learn to have sympathy with yourself, while at the same time looking at the helpful alternatives, the easier you may find it to change your feelings.

So, let's look at the forms now. The first form will provide you with some single (one-line) or basic example. Get the hang of this first and then you may wish to have more of a dialogue with yourself. Forms 2, 3 and 4 offer more complex examples for generating compassionate alternatives. I have also put in possible ratings for degrees of beliefs and feelings, which you may find useful.

THOUGHT MONITORING AND CREATING HELPFUL ALTERNATIVES: EXAMPLE 1

Triggering events, feelings or images	Beliefs and key thoughts	Feelings	Compassionate alternatives to depression thoughts	Degree of feeling change
Key Questions to help you identify your thoughts. What actually happened?	What went through your mind? What are you thinking about yourself, and your future? What are you thinking about others?	What are your main feelings and emotions? Rate degree of feelings 0–100	What would you say to a friend? What is the evidence against this view? How would you see this if you were not depressed? What would your compassionate friend say? Rate degree of belief in alternatives.	Write down any degree of change in your feelings.
Example 1 Friend at work snubbed me.	Rate degree of belief 0–100 He/she doesn't like me. Sees me as inadequate. 70%	Upset, hurt, angry. 60%	Probably nothing to do with me at all. My friend can be quite moody and I have seen him/her do this to others. 50%	20%
Example 2 Forgot to take important file to work.	This is typical me. I am useless and a failure. 80%	Frustrated. Angry. 90%	It is understandable to feel frustrated because it will hold up my work today. However, this does not make me useless. I won't even remember this event in three months' time. Accept my frustrations, practise compassionate self-forgiveness and focus on what I need to do now – what is helpful in this moment. 70%	40%
Example 3 Just feeling down today.	I am always going to be depressed. Nothing will ever work for me. 70%	Depressed. Fed up. 80%	Moods do go up and down. This is typical and is not my fault. I have better days than today. I am disappointed but I can see the sense of working with my thoughts, and in my heart I know if I keep going I'll feel better. 30%	20%
			Compassionate focusing Now read all the above through slowly but this time just focus on creating as much warmth, kindness and support rather than trying to convince yourself of the alternative. See what happens when you do this.	

THOUGHT MONITORING AND CREATING HELPFUL ALTERNATIVES: EXAMPLE 2

Triggering events, feelings or images	Beliefs and key thoughts	Feelings	Compassionate alternatives to depression thoughts	Degree of feeling change
Key questions to help you identify your thoughts. What actually happened?	What went through your mind? What are you thinking about yourself, and your future? What are you thinking about others? Rate degree of belief 0–100	What are your main feelings and emotions? Rate degree of feelings 0–100	What would you say to a friend? What is the evidence against this view? What would your compassionate mind say? How would you see this if you were not depressed? Rate degree of belief in alternatives.	Write down any degree of change in your feelings.
Too much work to do.	I can't get it all done. I will never succeed. Others can do more than me. I am incompetent and a failure. 80%	Depressed. Fed up. 80%	Depression often makes us feel like this, which is very hard. Let me just slow down a moment and take a breath for moment or two and focus my mind. Key thing is to focus on one thing at a time rather than 'everything' to do. Kind of like don't down look if you're climbing a ladder — just go step at a time. I have actually managed to do things when I have taken this approach My problem is my depression, which turns off my energy making it hard to engage. It is absolutely not about being a failure — many millions feel like I do. It is important to also try to see if I can do something I would enjoy no matter how small — even having a cup of tea — and focus on the pleasure of that. Just steady as we go. Noticing but, to the best of my ability not reacting to my critical or pessimistic thoughts. **Compassionate focusing** Now read all the above through slowly but this time just focus on creating as much warmth, kindness and support rather than trying to convince yourself of the alternative. See what happens when you do this	20%

THOUGHT MONITORING AND CREATING HELPFUL ALTERNATIVES: EXAMPLE 3

Triggering events, feelings or images	Beliefs and key thoughts	Feelings	Compassionate alternatives to depression thoughts	Degree of feeling change
Key Questions to help you identify your thoughts. What actually happened?	What went through your mind? What are you thinking about yourself, and your future? What are you thinking about others? Rate degree of belief 0–100	What are your main feelings and emotions? Rate degree of feelings 0–100	What would you say to a friend? What is the evidence against this view? What would your compassionate mind say? How would you see this if you were not depressed? Rate degree of belief in alternatives.	Write down any change in your feelings.
Argument with partner.	I am going to end up rejected. It's all my fault. I must be very unlovable.	Depressed 75%.	That is distressing isn't it. However let's take a soothing breath here and refocus. My fear of rejection is probably what is behind this thinking, so hold on. There are problems in the relationship but I can't take all the blame (see pages 284–6). There are things that we are both unhappy with and need to sort out. If I take the blame then we can't work together. Self-blaming makes me depressed which actually stops me from trying to make the relationship work. It is upsetting to have arguments, but if I avoid all-or-nothing thinking about my lovability I am more likely to see them through. Anyhow, I have friends who like me, and we have had good times together in the past, so I can't be as bad as I am painting myself. 60% **Compassionate focusing** Now read all the above through slowly but this time just focus on creating as much warmth, kindness and support rather than trying to convince yourself of the alternative. See what happens when you do this.	30%

THOUGHT MONITORING AND CREATING HELPFUL ALTERNATIVES: EXAMPLE 4

Triggering events, feelings or images	Beliefs and key thoughts	Feelings	Compassionate alternatives to depression thoughts	Degree of feeling change
Key questions to help you identify your thoughts. What actually happened?	What went through your mind? What are you thinking about yourself, and your future? What are you thinking about others? Rate degree of belief 0–100	What are your main feelings and emotions? Rate degree of feelings 0–100	What would you say to a friend? What alternatives might there be? What is the evidence against this view? How would you see this if you were not depressed? Rate degree of belief in alternatives.	Write down any degree of change in your feelings.
Children need clean clothes, ironing not done, just too many demands on me.	I can't cope with the needs of my family. I just want to run away and leave it all behind. Can't be bothered with them. I must be a selfish, cold person for feeling this way. If I was a better mother I wouldn't feel like this and would do more. 80%	Overwhelmed. Guilty. Depressed. 80%	To be honest, I am feeling exhausted right now which is understandable given the demands on me. I need to create more space for myself, take some time out for myself if I can, and ask my family to help out more. I can break my problems down and just focus on things I can cope with. I can prioritize and see how I can focus on the key things. The desire to escape is a natural and normal feeling when one is exhausted and is not evidence of being a poor mother, indeed many mothers feel like I do from time to time. Okay let's go step at a time and see how we do. 60%	20%
			Compassionate focusing Now read all the above through slowly but this time just focus on creating as much warmth, kindness and support rather than trying to convince yourself of the alternative. See what happens when you do this.	

Appendix 2

Quick guides

Identifying your thinking style

To *identify* your threat- and loss-focused thinking style, pay attention to your feelings (see Chapters 9 and 10). Then ask yourself:

- What is / was going through my mind?
- What is / might be my underlying threat – may there be fear or sense of loss here?
- What am I thinking about me?
- What kind of judgements am I making about myself?
- What judgements or assumptions am I making about other people?
- What am I thinking about my future?

The way you think about things can affect the way you feel. Below is a summary of some typical ways of thinking that can worsen depression. This is a brief summary of what was discussed in Chapter 10. If you can learn to spot these styles of thinking in yourself, it can be a helpful first step to pulling back from them, taking the view from the balcony, and trying to bring balance to one's thinking We all use these styles of thinking from time to time; no one is 100 per cent logical or compassionate all the time. But in depression they are taken to extremes.

- **Jumping to conclusions**. This involves the tendency to make decisions rapidly, especially when under stress. For example, you might jump to the conclusion that someone does not like you because they ignore you. You may predict the future, e.g., that nothing you do will work out. Jumping to conclusions means that you don't look at the evidence. Instead, you go for immediate gut reactions and assume these to be true.

- **Emotional reasoning**. This involves an over-reliance on feeling to guide judgements, for example, 'I feel this is dangerous, therefore it is', or 'I feel I am stupid therefore I am', or 'I feel unlovable or unattractive therefore I am'. You assume that negative feelings reflect the way things actually are: 'I feel it, so it must be true'. Feelings are often poor guides to reality. The 'power' of feelings comes from our more primitive brains having more control than is often good for us. Remember to test out feelings: look for alternatives and explore the evidence for and the evidence against. Does it pass the friend test – is it something you'd be happy to say to a friend?

- **All-or-nothing thinking**. This is also called 'black-and-white' or 'polarized' thinking. We see things in 'either/or' categories. If our performance falls short of what we wanted, we see it or even ourselves as a total failure. We may think: 'Either X loves me or s/he doesn't', or 'Either I succeed or I fail'. However, life is full of indeterminate areas. Love is not either/or; there are degrees of love. Success is not either/or; there are degrees of success. It is more useful to think of the degree of success rather than the degree of failure. It is always worth thinking if there is a sense of threat, fear or loss that might be driving this all-or-nothing thinking. If so, consider some of the ideas I have offered to become compassionate to your fears and balanced in your thinking.

- **Overgeneralizing**. This is when we take a single negative event and see it as a never-ending pattern of defeat. Here, one swallow does make a summer. We may think that things can never change, or that one failure means that everything one has done was a failure or faked. Think back and ponder if you tend to think like this and it turns out to be wrong. Is this style of thinking linked to your frustration or fear? If so, consider some of the ideas I have offered to become compassionate to your fears and balanced in your thinking.

- **'I must'**. These thoughts involve feelings of being compelled to do something. 'I must be in a relationship to be happy; I must achieve things to be a worthwhile person; I must never be criticized; I must never fail.' Turn musts into preferences, for example, 'I would like to do this, but if I can't then it does not mean that I am a no-good person or that I can't be happy.' The typical helpful thing here is to learn to accept feelings as they are. We can turn 'musts' into preferences. It's not quite as good as turning water into wine, but it helps.

- **Emotional tolerance**. Telling ourselves that our emotions are intolerable and we must get rid of them is usually a recipe for problems. We have emotions because our brain is designed to create them in us – and pretty powerful they can be, too. The key here is to be mindful and to observe them (watch your evolved brain at work) then engage in compassion for them and for you going through them. Consider how you can be like the rock when the wind blows, you are solid – how might you develop this ability? Look out for threat-focused thinking related to your emotions; desire to be able to tolerate emotions (see pages 208–13).

- **Discounting and disbelieving the positives**. This involves the tendency to ignore or dismiss positive attributes, events or achievements. You either take them for granted or think 'anyone could do that'. When you disqualify the positives it is difficult to get started on the way up. Focus on what you can do rather than on what you can't. Usually we are frightened to trust in the positives, so it is worth thinking about your fear of the positives and then practise compassion for the fear – see your 'fear of the positives' self in front of you and be compassionate to it – balance your 'thoughts' – try allowing a bit of positive, and build up.

- **Discounting and disbelieving others**. This involves things like thinking that other people's (good) opinions of you don't count. You think that either they don't really know you or you have kept things hidden and deceived them. At other times you may think that others only say positive things to be nice; they don't, in their hearts, really mean it. This often involves a loss of trust. Think about if this is a bit of black-and-white thinking – maybe they know you a bit and like that bit?

- **Amplifying the negatives**. When we're depressed it is all too easy to dwell on negatives and difficulties. They take on more importance and we are very attentive to possible rejections, put-downs or failures. We can easily lose perspective by amplifying negatives and dwelling on them. Regain perspective by generating alternatives. Keep in mind this is not your fault because it is how your evolved brain and threat self-protection systems are designed to think in terms of 'better safe than sorry' and 'assume the worse'. Therefore we need the balance of our rational and compassionate self.

Recognizing your self-attacking thoughts and styles

- **Self-criticism**. This is when part of us becomes like an observer and a judge. We're constantly passing negative judgements on ourselves, as if a critical parent were sitting on our shoulder. We're more focused on what we do wrong or badly, rather than on what we do well. Practise the art of compassionate self-correction (see Chapter 13).

- **Personalization and self-blaming**. This involves the automatic tendency to assume that we are in the wrong or are responsible for negative events. We may not look at the evidence or consider alternatives, or reflect that most things are caused by a number of different factors (see Chapter 13).

- **Self-labelling**. This involves 'all-or-nothing' thinking about yourself as a person. If your behavior fails, you think you are a failure, unlovable or inadequate, etc. In depression this type of thinking involves blaming and name-calling (e.g., I am useless, inadequate, weak, a nuisance, a fake, worthless, bad, etc.). Refocus on taking a broad perspective and compassionate alternatives.

- **It–me**. This involves the tendency to judge ourselves rather than our behavior. We think that only our behavior matters; if that is not good, then we are no good. But behavior and self are quite different. A self is a conscious, feeling being, with hopes, desires and wishes. A behavior is just a behavior, that may or may not be disappointing. The trick here is learn to see that the emotions of frustration might confuse you into believing you are the label.

- **Self-attacking**. This involves a degree of anger and hostility directed at yourself. It is more than being critical – after all, not all criticism involves hostility, but in self-attacking one is hostile with oneself. Sometimes this part is frightened that if it doesn't criticize then you won't achieve anything. It is really fear-based. If we see that, then we can change our feelings about it. We can be compassionate to the fear. You can teach it compassionate self-improvement (see Chapter 13). Rather than dispute or argue with your self-criticism (although you can if it helps you, of course), engage your compassionate self and feel it expanding in you – in a way you are becoming bigger than the self-critical part (because it is only a part of you). Then feel compassion for it. If it shrinks, note that it's grateful to be released from critiquing. If nothing happens, or it seems to grow too much for you, then let the image fade and pull back to compassionate self-focusing, until you have stabilized again and are ready to have another go.

- **Self-hatred**. This is an extreme form of self-attacking. It is more than just anger with the self and often involves judgements and feelings of being bad, evil or disgusting. Unlike self-criticism, which aims to improve through punishment, self-hatred can be about wanting to destroy and get rid of the self. Rather than dispute or argue with your self-hatred (although you can if it helps you, of course), engage your compassionate self and feel it expanding in you – in a way, you are becoming bigger than the self-hatred part (because it is only a part of you). Feel compassion for it. If it shrinks, note that it's grateful to be released from hatred. If nothing happens or it seems to grow too much for you, then just let the image fade and pull back to just compassionate self-focusing – until you have stabilized again and are ready to have another go. In this was you are slowly desensitizing yourself to your self-hatred.

- **Social comparison**. Although we all compare ourselves to other people, try to become more aware of when you do it. Check out how your mood changes and ask yourself if the social comparison is valid. Does it help you? Are you engaging in envious thoughts? Do such thoughts help you? Explore some compassionate ways to balance it.

Once you have identified your depressing thoughts, consider that you are now going to come at them with compassionate attention, thinking, behavior and feelings. Have a look at some of the worked examples in Chapter 9. Remember, too, they have to pass the friend test: would you recommend them to someone you care for or a child you love?

Appendix 3

Making your own flash cards

Throughout this book I have offered ways to generate compassionate alternatives for some of our depressing thoughts. Here are some ideas you could write down on flash cards (see Chapter 15) to deal with common depressing ideas and feelings. You might want to choose a card with a soothing picture.

I am weak to be depressed

- Depression is a horrible state to be in, but it is not evidence of weakness.
- Depression affects animals and humans because it is brain state made possible by the way our brains have evolved, therefore it is not my fault.
- Depression is a state of mind. Just as I can have other states of mind (e.g. happy, relaxed, angry, anxious), I can be depressed.
- Depression is unpleasant, but sadly many millions suffer from it because to the brain this is just one of its patterns for feeling.
- Depression can affect anyone – even people who are often regarded as strong (e.g. Winston Churchill).
- Depression is most often about becoming exhausted, trying too hard, feeling defeated, losing hope. Often there is something threatening us in our depression.
- By understanding it more, I can try to bring my rational/compassionate mind to help tackle it.

- There may be very real problems in my life that have exhausted me and made me vulnerable to being depressed.

If I need an antidepressant drug it means I am weak

- Depression is not about weakness, but can be about being exhausted.
- I need to get the evidence of whether an antidepressant would help me. If it can help me sleep better and boost my mood and confidence, then that might help me to get on top of my depression.
- Millions of people take antidepressant drugs.
- Whether I choose to take an antidepressant drug or not is my own decision. I don't need to prove that I can cope without one as some kind of test of my strength.

If I need some therapy I might have to reveal my anger or shame

- It is understandable to be anxious about revealing personal things to someone else, like a therapist.
- Properly qualified therapists are well aware that it is the things we are ashamed of that cause us problems.
- I have no evidence that a therapist will look down on me if I talk about the things that I am ashamed about. Indeed, just as a surgeon expects to deal with blood and guts, so therapists expect to deal with the less pleasant sides of life.
- The more I am prepared to face up to what I feel ashamed about, the more I may get to know myself and learn how to let things go, or see them in a different way.
- A therapist can't force me to talk, so I can go at my own pace and decide whether the therapy is helpful.

I can't do what I used to do, therefore I am a failure

- I am depressed right now, so it's natural not to have my normal drive.
- Even though I can't do what I used to, I can still do some things.
- I can praise myself for what I do do, rather than attacking myself for what I don't do.
- There is no way I am going to bully myself out of depression.
- I can go step by step.
- By praising my steps, no matter how small they may be, I am moving forward.
- My task now is to try to develop a kind and compassionate approach to tackling this depression.

I am worthless

- To sum up a person (e.g. myself) in simple terms of good–bad, worthwhile–worthless, is all-or-nothing thinking. 'Kind of' unkind too.
- Just because I feel stupid and worthless this does not mean that I am.
- If I over-identify with feelings of worthlessness then I am more likely to get depressed.
- The idea of worth can be applied to objects like cars or soap powder, but not to people.
- If I say 'worthless' is just one of a number of possible feelings that I, as a human being, can have about myself, then I can keep a perspective on these negative feelings.

I am so filled with anger I must be bad

- Anger is, like other feelings, something we are all capable of.
- High levels of anger usually point to high levels of hurt or vulnerability.
- My anger tells me that there is something I want to change and push against.
- True, flying into rages is not helpful, but I can learn to be more honest with my own needs and put them assertively.
- I can learn to understand my anger rather than just labelling myself as bad and trying to push my anger away.
- Maybe I can learn compassionate acceptance of my feelings and then slowly work to see how I want to act on them.

I am not as competent as other people, therefore I am a failure

- It is natural to want to compete in the world and feel that we are up there with others.
- All human beings are unique and need to go at their own pace. Just because some people seem more able than me does not make me a failure. I dare to be average or even less. Just 'doin' me best'.
- I can focus on what I can do and what is important to me, in my own unique life, rather than on what others are doing.

Nothing ever seems as good as I want it to be, therefore there is no point in trying

- Disappointment is part of life and I can learn to cope with it if I keep it in perspective.
- I can learn to focus on what I do get out of doing things rather than how far short they fall of my expectations.
- I can practise the appreciation exercises and see how I go.
- I can check out whether I attack myself when I am disappointed and learn how to be kinder with myself.
- This type of thinking is rather all-or-nothing. Therefore I can learn to focus on what I enjoy rather than on what I don't. It's the old story of the glass as half empty or half full – happiness lies in seeing the half-full bits of life.

I will never get better

- After reading this book, I realize that there are many ways to tackle depression and these work for many people (e.g. drugs, psychotherapy, family therapy, and various forms of self-help etc.).
- I don't have to suffer in silence.
- If I need extra help, I can talk to my family doctor and see what is available.
- I haven't always been depressed, so depression is a state of mind that I am in right now, but this does not mean that I'll always be depressed.
- I may have been trying to deal with my depression but, as this book points out, maybe I have been enduring it, trying to soldier on, rather than really tackling it.

Appendix 4

Useful resources

Books and CDs

DEPRESSION

Brantley, J. (2003). *Calming Your Anxious Mind: How Mindfulness and Compassion can Free You From Anxiety, Fear and Panic.* New York: Harbinger. Comes with a very useful CD.

Foreman, E.I., Elliott, C. and Smith, L. (2008). *Overcoming Depression for Dummies.* Chichester: Wiley. This recently published self-help book for depression is full of helpful pointers and tips. Don't be put off by the title!

Lazarus, R. (1999). *Stress and Emotions: a New Synthesis.* New York: Free Association Press.

Leahy, R. (2006). *The Worry Cure.* New York: Piatkus Books. Useful if you tend to ruminate and fret about things (don't we all!). There is also a CD that goes with this.

Lyubomirsky, S. (2007). *The How of Happiness.* New York: Sphere. Useful for finding out how to develop happiness.

Marra, T. (2003). *The Dialectical Behavior Therapy Workbook for Overcoming Depression and Anxiety.* Oakland, CA: New Harbinger Publications. A helpful guide from a slightly different approach.

Nesse, R. and Williams, G. (1996). *Evolution and Healing. The New Science of Darwinian Medicine,* London: Phoenix.

Stewart, A. (1993). *Tired All the Time.* London, Optima. Explores common causes of tiredness, including things like allergy and diet.

Stone, H. and Stone, S. (1993). *Embracing Your Inner Critic: Turning Self-criticism into a Creative Asset.* New York: HarperCollins. Explores in detail some origins and consequences of self-criticism. Not specific to depression.

Veal, D. and Willson, R. (2008). *Manage Your Mood*. London: Constable & Robinson.

Williams, C.J. (2001). *Overcoming Depression: A Five Areas Approach*. London: Arnold.

Williams, M., Teasdale, J., Segal, Z. and Kabat-Zinn, J. (2007). *The Mindful Way Through Depression: Freeing Yourself From Chronic Unhappiness*. New York: Guilford. This is the first book on mindfulness dedicated to depression and comes with a CD to guide your practice. These authors are well-respected international researchers in depression and mindfulness.

Other self-help books in the same series as this one are also available: *Overcoming Low Self-Esteem, Stress, Anxiety, Childhood Trauma, Grief, Insomnia, Obsessive Compulsive Disorder, Panic and Agoraphobia, Traumatic Stress, Social Anxiety and Shyness, Worry, Mood Swings* (see www.overcoming.co.uk).

MEDITATION

Two useful book/CD combinations:

Dagsay Tulku Rinpoche (2002). *The Practice of Tibetan Meditation: Exercises, visualisations, and mantras for health and well being*. Rochester, VT: Inner Traditions. This book offers a very useful set of postures and exercises, along with a CD of mantras and instructions.

Kornfield, J. (2004). *Meditation for Beginners*. New York: Bantam Books. A good introduction.

MINDFULNESS

The Dalai Lama is the spiritual head of Buddhism, which can be seen as both a spiritual approach and a basic psychology. It's particularly useful for its psychology and insights built up over thousands of years of meditation and introspective observation.

Dalai Lama (1995). *The Power of Compassion*. London: Thorsons.

Dalai Lama (ed. N. Vreeland) (2001). *An Open Heart: Practising Compassion in Everyday Life*. London: Hodder & Stoughton.

Two classics:

Kabit-Zinn, J. (2005). *Coming to Our Senses: Healing ourselves and the world through mindfulness*. New York: Piatkus.

Thich Nhat Hanh (1991). *The Miracle of Mindfulness*. London: Rider.

Other books:

Bikshu Sangharakshita (2008). *Living with Kindness: The Buddha's Teaching on Metta*. London: Windhorse Publications.

Hopkins, J. (2001). *Cultivating Compassion: A Buddhist perspective*. New York: Doubleday.

Ricard, M. (2007) *Happiness: A Guide to Developing Life's Most Important Skill*. New York: Atlantic Books.

If you want a more technical approach, have a look at:

Davidson, R.J. and Harrington, A. (eds) (2002). *Visions of Compassion: Western Scientists and Tibetan Buddhists Examine Human Nature*. New York: Oxford University Press.

Gilbert, P. (2005). *Compassion: Conceptualisations, Research and Use in Psychotherapy*. London: Routledge (pages 148–67).

Leighton, T.D. (2003). *Faces of Compassion: Classic Bodhisattva Archetypes and their Modern Expression*. Boston: Wisdom Publications.

Vessantara (1993). *Meeting the Buddhas: A Guide to Buddha, Bodhisattvas, and Tantric Deities*. London: Wisdom Books.

CDs

Some useful CDs that will guide you:

Brantley, J. (2003). *Calming Your Anxious Mind: How Mindfulness and Compassion Can Free You from Anxiety, Fear and Panic*. New York: Harbinger.

Chodron, P. (2007). *How to Meditate: A Practical Guide To Making Friends With Your Mind*. Boulder, CO: Sounds True.

Kabat-Zinn, J. (2005). *Guided Mindfulness Meditation*. Boulder, CO: Sounds True.

Williams, M., Teasdale, J., Segal, Z., and Kabat-Zinn, J. (2007). *The

Mindful Way through Depression: Freeing yourself from chronic unhappiness. Boulder, CO: Sounds True.

Finding help

Useful websites

FOR DEPRESSION

Beyondblue
www.beyondblue.org.au
This is thought to be one of the best self-help and information depression-focused websites in the world. It is full of helpful ideas and advice.

Living life to the full
www.livinglifetothefull.com
This website has been sponsored by the UK government and is another very helpful and important website for depressed people.

Derbyshire depression website
www.derbysmhnice.co.uk
The Derbyshire Mental Health Services NHS Trust has developed its own website which has general as well as local interest.

NICE Guidelines
www.nice.org.uk/Guidance/CG23
NICE is the British government's guideline body that offers advice on the treatments of various conditions. It brings a range of clinicians together to develop that advice. You can find out the guidelines for depression at the address given here.

FOR COMPASSION-FOCUSED WORK

Compassionate Mind Foundation
www.compassionatemind.co.uk
In 2007, a number of colleagues and I set up a charity called the Compassionate Mind Foundation. On this website, you'll find various essays and details of other sites that look at different aspects of compassion. You'll also find a lot of material that you can use for meditation.

Mind and Life Institute
www.mindandlife.org
The Dalai Lama has formed relationships with Western scientists to develop a more compassionate way of living. More information on this can be found on this website.

Self-Compassion
www.self-compassion.org
The website of Dr Kristin Neff, one of the leading researchers into self-compassion.

Useful organizations

UK

MIND, The National Association for Mental Health
Granta House
15–19 Broadway
Stratford
London E15 4BQ
Tel.: 020 8519 2122
www.mind.org.uk
A very helpful organization that can offer advice on services for a wide range of psychological difficulties. It also has a wide range of literature.

Association for Post Natal Illness
145 Dawes Road
Fulham
London SW6 7EB
Tel: 0207 386 0868
http://apni.org

MDF The Bipolar Organisation
Castle Works
21 St. George's Road
London SE1 6ES
Tel.: 08456 340 540 (UK only)
Tel: 0044 207 793 2600 (Rest of world)
www.mdf.org.uk

Depression Alliance
212 Spitfire Studios
63–71 Collier Street
London N1 9BE
www.depressionalliance.org/
Email: *information@depressionalliance.org*
Tel.: 0845 123 23 20

Seasonal Affective Disorder (SAD) Association
PO Box 989
Steyning
BN44 3HG
www.sada.org.uk

SANE
A general website for mental health problems.
www.sane.org.uk

Samaritans
An outline of the work of the Samaritans and also how to contact them
if you want to contact somebody confidentially.
www.samaritans.org
Email: *jo@samaritans.org*

Befrienders Worldwide
This is a worldwide support website for people who are distressed and suicidal with various contacts.
www.befrienders.org

British Association for Behavioral and Cognitive Psychotherapies
www.babcp.com

NORTH AMERICA

American Psychological Association
www.apa.org
A useful website carrying various articles on mental health issues.

National Alliance on Mental Illness
www.nami.org

Depression and Bipolar Support Alliance (DBSA)
730 N. Franklin Street, Suite 501
Chicago, Illinois 60654–7225
Toll free: (800) 826–3632
www.dbsalliance.org

Association for Behavioral and Cognitive Therapies
305 7th Avenue, 16th Fl.
New York, NY 10001
Phone (212) 647–1890

Behavior Therapy of New York
51 East 42nd Street, Suite 1400
New York, NY 10017
Tel.: (646) 522–7795

Center for Cognitive-Behavioral Psychotherapy
137 East 36th Street
New York
NY 10016
Tel.: (212) 686–6886

The American Institute for Cognitive Therapy
136 East 57th Street, Suite 1101
New York
NY 10022
www.cognitivetherapynyc.com/

HELPLINES FOR SEXUAL ABUSE (UK BASED)

Careline
For all adult survivors of childhood sexual abuse.
0845 122 8622
www.carelineuk.org

Rape and Sexual Abuse Support Centre
Offers support and information for women and girls who have been
raped or sexually abused, however long ago.
08451 221 331
http://rasasc.bizview.co.uk/

Survivors UK
For survivors of male rape and sexual abuse.
0845 122 1201
www.survivorsuk.org

National Association for People Abused in Childhood
Does not offer counselling or ongoing support but will listen, validate
and do whatever is most helpful to the caller.
Support Line 0800 085 3330
www.napac.org.uk

Notes and references

These notes are intended for readers who would like more technical information or ideas to follow up.

Chapter 1: What is depression?

There is now much information on the Internet about depression. Websites such as beyondblue *(www.beyondblue.org.au)* and Living Life to the Full *(www.livinglifetothefull.com)* are excellent sources for further reading.

A good basic book is Power, M. (ed.) (2004). *Mood Disorders: A Handbook of Science and Practice.* Chichester: Wiley. For my own technical work on depression, see Gilbert, P. (2007) *Psychotherapy and Counselling for Depression* (3rd edition). London: Sage.

Chapter 2: Causes of depression: How and why it happens

I go into more detail on these themes in a recent book: Gilbert, P. (2009). *The Compassionate Mind: A New Approach to Life Challenges.* London: Constable & Robinson. I am also just completing a technical book (*Compassion-Focused Therapy: An Introduction to the Theory and Practice*) for Routledge.

1   Depue, R.A. and Morrone-Strupinsky, J.V. (2005). A neurobehavioral model of affiliative bonding. *Behavioral and Brain Sciences* 28, 313–395.

2   LeDoux, J. (1998). *The Emotional Brain.* London: Weidenfeld & Nicolson.

3   For a good, accessible account of the evolutionary approach to depression see Keedwell, P. (2007). *How Sadness Survived: The Evolutionary Basis of Depression.* Oxford: Radcliffe Publishing. I have also discussed this in more detail in Gilbert, P. (2007). *Psychotherapy and Counselling for Depression* (3rd edition). London: Sage.

4   Siegle, G., Carter, C.S. and Thase, M.E. (2006). Use of fMRI to predict

recovery from unipolar depression with cognitive behavior therapy. *American Journal of Psychiatry*, 163, 735–738.

5   Carter, C.S. (1998). Neuroendocrine perspectives on social attachment and love. *Psychoneuroendocrinlogy*, 23, 779–818. See also Wang, S. (2005). A conceptual framework for integrating research related to the physiology of compassion and the wisdom of Buddhist teachings. In Gilbert, P. (ed.) *Compassion: Conceptualisations, Research and Use in Psychotherapy* (pp. 75–120). London: Brunner-Routledge.

Chapter 3: How evolution may have shaped our minds for depression

1   Perhaps one of the most comprehensive books on emotions and their functions is by Oatley, K., Keltner, D. and Jenkins, J. (2006). *Understanding Emotions* (2nd revd edition). Oxford: Blackwell.

2   Fredrickson, B.L. (1998). What good are positive emotions? *Review of General Psychology*, 2, 300–319. See also our work: Gilbert, P., McEwan, K., Mitra, R., Franks, L., Richter, A. and Rockliff, H. (2008) Feeling safe and content: A specific affect regulation system? Relationship to depression, anxiety, stress and self-criticism. *Journal of Positive Psychology*, 3,182–191.

3   As noted in the last chapter, a good accessible account of the evolutionary approach to depression is the book by Keedwell (2007). I have also discussed this in more detail in Gilbert, P. (2007) *Psychotherapy and Counselling for Depression* (3rd edition). London: Sage.

4   This view was popularized by Nesse, R.M. (2000). Is depression an adaptation? *Archives of General Psychiatry*, 57, 14–20. I have discussed this in Gilbert, P. (2007) *Psychotherapy and Counselling for Depression* (3rd edition). London: Sage.

5   My recent book (Gilbert 2009) covers some of these ideas. A very readable book is by Smith, E.O. (2002). *When Culture and Biology Collide: Why we are Stressed, Depressed and Self-Obsessed*. Piscataway, NJ: Rutgers University Press.

Chapter 4: Bodies, genes, stress and coping: More on the mind–body link

1   A good overview and guide to this work can be found in Caspi, A., Sugden, K., Moffitt, T.E. et al. (2003). Influence of life stress on depression: Moderation by a polymorphism in the 5-HTT gene. *Science* 301, 386–398. For a more general discussion see Caspi, A. and Moffitt, T.E. (2006). Gene-environment interactions in psychiatry: Joining forces with neuroscience. *Nature Reviews: Neuroscience* 7, 583–590.

2   Panskepp, J. (1998). *Affective Neuroscience*. New York: Oxford University Press.

3   Cozolino, L. (2007). *The Neuroscience of Human Relationships: Attachment and the Developing Brain*. New York: Norton. See also Gerhardt, S. (2004). *Why Love Matters. How Affection Shapes a Baby's Brain*. London: Routledge.

4   Lazarus, R.S. (1999). *Stress and Emotions: A New Synthesis*. London: Free Association Press. An accessible book, offering an excellent overview of his work for those who would like to read more on the subject.

Chapter 5: Early life and the psychological and social aspects of depression

1   Beck, A.T. (1976). *Cognitive Therapy and the Emotional Disorders*. New York: International Universities Press. Leahy, R. L and Holland, S.J. (2000). *Treatment Plans and Interventions for Depression and Anxiety Disorders*: New York: Guilford Press.

2   Perry, B.D., Pollard, R.A., Blakley, T.L., Baker, W.L. and Vigilante, D. (1995). Childhood trauma, the neurobiology of adaptation and 'use-dependent' development of the brain: How 'states' become 'traits'. *Infant Mental Health Journal* 16, 271–291.

3   Gerhardt, S. (2004). *Why Love Matters. How Affection Shapes a Baby's Brain*. London: Routledge. Cozolino, L. (2007). *The Neuroscience of Human Relationships: Attachment and the Developing Brain*. New York: Norton.

4   Caspi, A. and Moffitt, T.E. (2006). Gene-environment interactions in psychiatry: Joining forces with neuroscience. *Nature Reviews: Neuroscience* 7, 583–590.

5   There are many books now on childhood sexual abuse, because sadly it is common in depressed people. The present book does not go into detail on this but you might like to look, for example, at Ainscough, C. and Toon, K. (2000). *Breaking Free Workbook: Practical Help for Survivors of Child Sexual Abuse*. London: Sheldon Press. We also know that various forms of abuse, emotional neglect and hurting can leave people vulnerable (not just sexual abuse). See for example Bifulco, A. and Moran, P. (1998). *Wednesday's Child: Research into Women's Experiences of Neglect and Abuse in Childhood, and Adult Depression*. London: Routledge. For some more recent research see Teicher, M.H., Samson, J.A., Polcari, A. and McGreenery, C.E. (2006). Sticks and stones and hurtful words: Relative effects of various forms of childhood maltreatment. *American Journal of Psychiatry*, 163, 993–1000.

6   There is now considerable evidence of these parenting styles and their impact on people. This research has been pioneered by attachment theorists. An excellent review of this work, written by the leading researchers in this area can be found in Mikulincer, M. and Shaver, P.R. (2007). *Attachment in Adulthood: Structure, Dynamics, and Change*. New York: Guilford.

7   Brown, G.W. and Harris, T.O. (1978). *The Social Origins of Depression*. London: Tavistock. Brown, G.W., Harris, T.O. and Hepworth, C. (1995). Loss, humiliation and entrapment among women developing depression: A patient and non-patient comparison. *Psychological Medicine* 25, 7–21.

8   Champion, L. and Power, M. (1995). Social and cognitive approaches to depression: Towards a new synthesis. *British Journal of Clinical Psychology* 34, 485–503.

Chapter 6: The relationship between our thoughts and feelings in depression

1   The idea that automatic thoughts arise from our core beliefs and attitudes and underpin and maintain depression was developed by the psychiatrist Aaron Beck: see Beck, A.T., Rush, A.J., Shaw, B.F. and Emery, G. (1979). *Cognitive Therapy of Depression*. New York: Wiley. The British government's assessment committee (called NICE) that

looked into the value of different therapies for depression found that there is good evidence to suggest cognitive behavior therapy helps a number of people with depression, but not all. Beck also understood the importance of understanding how our minds have evolved as being central to understanding depression: see Beck, A.T. (1987). Cognitive models of depression. *Journal of Cognitive Psychotherapy: An International Quarterly*, 1, 5–38.

2   Haidt, J. (2001). The emotional dog and its rational tail: A social intuitionist approach to moral judgement. *Psychological Review*, 108, 814–834. Baldwin, M.W. and Dandeneau, S.D. (2005). Understanding and modifying the relational schemas underlying insecurity. In Baldwin, M.W. (ed.) *Interpersonal Cognition* (pp.33–61). New York: Guilford. Mark Baldwin is at the forefront of research on how faces affect our feelings and his book on interpersonal cognition is well worth a look. To find out more about his research on games and emotion visit his websites, *www.selfesteemgames.mcgill.ca* and *www.mindhabits.com*

3   Leahy, R.L. (2002). A model of emotional schemas. *Cognitive and Behavioral Practice*, 9, 177–171.

Chapter 7: Mindful preparations for working with depression

1   This account is a modified version of the chapter that appears in my book *The Compassionate Mind: A New Approach to Life Challenges*, mentioned earlier, but here we will be more focused on depression.

2   Williams, M., Teasdale, J., Segal, Z. and Kabat-Zinn, J. (2007). *The Mindful Way Through Depression: Freeing Yourself From Chronic Unhappiness*. New York: Guilford. This is the first book on mindfulness dedicated to depression and comes with a CD to guide your practice. These authors are well respected international researchers in depression and mindfulness.

3   Keep in mind that if you would like to know more about this and get more into the deep aspects of practice then you would benefit from guided practice by a trained teacher or trainer. However, to get you started there are many good books that outline the basic practice of mindfulness. Some I have found helpful are Gunaratana,

B.H. (2002). *Mindfulness in Plain English.* Boston: Wisdom Publications; Kabat-Zinn, J. (2005). *Coming to our Senses: Healing Ourselves and the World Through Mindfulness.* New York: Piatkus; Brantley, J. (2003). *Calming Your Anxious Mind: How Mindfulness and Compassion Can Free You from Anxiety, Fear and Panic.* New York: Harbinger.

4   Gilbert, P. (2007). *Overcoming Depression: Talks with your Therapist CD.* London: Constable & Robinson.

5   Gilbert, P. and Procter, S. (2006). Compassionate mind training for people with high shame and self-criticism: A pilot study of a group therapy approach. *Clinical Psychology and Psychotherapy* 13, 353–379. If you would like to try some CDs that take you through various mindful exercises then Chodron, P. (2007). *How to Meditate: A Practical Guide to Making Friends with Your Mind* offers an extensive course, or if you want something shorter you might like Bodhipaksa (2005) *Guided Meditations for Busy People.* For videos and websites on mindfulness and compassion, see the Compassionate Mind Foundation website, *www.compassionatemind.co.uk.*

Chapter 8: Switching our minds to kindness and compassion

1   You can read more about self-compassion on Kristen Neff's website at *www.self-compassion.org.* Neff is a major international researcher in self-compassion. Look at our own Compassionate Mind Foundation website at *www.compassioantemind.co.uk.*

2   Lutz, A., Brefczynski-Lewis, J., Johnstone, T. and Davidson, R.J. (2008). Regulation of the neural circuitry of emotion by compassion meditation: Effects of meditative expertise. *Public Library of Science* 3, 1–5. Rein, G., Atkinson, M. and McCraty, R. (1995). The physiological and psychological effects of compassion and anger. *Journal for the Advancement of Medicine* 8, 87–105. These researchers found that anger images and fantasies had a detrimental effect on the functioning of the immune system, whereas compassion-focused fantasies and images had a very positive effect. You'll also find a review of lots of studies of how mind training affects the body in Begley, S. (2007). *Train Your Mind, Change Your Brain.* New York:

Ballantine Books. Another book you may want to look at is Doidge, N. (2007). *The Brain that Changes Itself: Stories of Personal Triumph from the Frontiers of Brain Science*. New York: Penguin.

3   The creation of compassionate imagery for the purposes of self-development has a long history. A good but very technical book is Leighton, T.D. (2003). *Faces of Compassion: Classic Bodhisattva Archetypes and their Modern Expression*. Boston: Wisdom Publications. Another good book that covers these imagery exercises is Vessantara (1993). *Meeting the Buddhas: A guide to Buddha, Bodhisattvas, and Tantric Deities*. London: Wisdom Books.

4   Frederick, C. and McNeal, S. (1999). *Inner Strengths: Contemporary Psychotherapy and Hypnosis for Ego Strengthening*. Mahwah, NJ: Lawrence Erlbaum Associates. An interesting study is Wheatley, J., Brewin, C.R., Patel, T. et al. (2007). 'I'll believe it when I see it': Imagery re-scripting of intrusive sensory memories. *Journal of Behavior Therapy and Experimental Psychiatry* 39, 371–385.

5   Dandeneau, S.D., Baldwin, M.R., Baccus, J.R., Sakellaropoulo, M.P. and Pruessner J.C. (2007). Cutting stress off at the pass: Reducing vigilance and responsiveness to social threat by manipulating attention. *Journal of Personality and Social Psychology* 93, 651–666.

6   Childre, D. and Martin, H. (2000). *The HeartMath Solution*. San Francisco: Harper Collins.

Chapter 9: Changing unhelpful thoughts and feelings: Balance and compassion

1   Beck was one of the first to point out that the state of depression influences how we attend, think and reason about things in our lives – depression gives us negative biases. See Beck, A.T., Rush, A.J., Shaw, B.F. and Emery, G. (1979). *Cognitive Therapy of Depression*. New York: Wiley. There are now many self-help books that help people work on these biases. For example Williams, C.J. (2001). *Overcoming Depression: A Five Areas Approach*. London: Arnold. Leahy, R. (2006). *The Worry Cure*. New York: Piatkus Books is useful if you tend to ruminate and fret about things (don't we all!). There is also a CD that goes with this. A helpful guide from a slightly different approach

is Marra, T. (2003). *The Dialectical Behavior Therapy Workbook for Overcoming Depression and Anxiety*. Oakland, CA: New Harbinger Publications.

A recently published self-help book for depression is Foreman, E.I., Elliott, C. and Smith, L. (2008). *Overcoming Depression for Dummies*. Chichester: Wiley.

The CD that goes with this book, *Overcoming Depression: Talks with Your Therapist*, contains various talks and exercises.

Chapter 10: Styles of depressive thinking: How to develop helpful styles

1   The books listed in the notes for Chapter 9 are also relevant here.
2   Gilbert, P. (1998). The evolved basis and adaptive functions of cognitive distortions. *British Journal of Medical Psychology*, 71 447–463 gives a technical and evolutionary approach to how cognitive biases work, while Tobena, A., Marks, I. and Dar, R. (1999). Advantages of bias and prejudice: An exploration of their neurocognitive templates. *Neuroscience and Behavioral Reviews*,23, 1047–1058 offers a very good, detailed approach to how and why so much of our thinking is biased.

Chapter 11: Writing things down: How to do it and why it can be helpful for us

1   Pennebaker, J.W. (1997). *Opening Up: The Healing Power of Expressing Emotions*. New York: Guilford. More technical is Smyth, J.M. and Pennebaker, J.W. (eds) (2008). Boundary conditions of expressive writing. *Health Psychology (Special Section). British Journal of Health Psychology* 13, 1–95.
2   Forgiveness research has taken off recently: see Worthington, E.L., O'Connor, L. E., Berry, J.W., Sharp, C., Murray, R. and Yi, E. (2005). Compassion and forgiveness: Implications for psychotherapy. In Gilbert, P. (ed). *Compassion: Conceptualisations, Research and Use in Psychotherapy* (pp. 168–192). London: Routledge. Worthington's website (*www.forgiving.org*) provides a lot more information on how forgiveness can help us in many ways but is not submissive acceptance.

3   Lyubomirsky, S. (2007). *The How of Happiness*. New York: Sphere. A
    very readable book that makes accessible a lot of the research on grat-
    itude and appreciation and how and why they can help us develop
    feelings of well-being and counteract depression.

Chapter 12: Changing your behavior: A compassionate approach

1   Martell, C.R., Addis, M.E., and Jacobson, N.S. (2001). *Depression in
    Context: Strategies for Guided Action.* New York: Norton. A technical
    study on this approach is by Dimidjian, S., Hollon, S.D., Dobson, K.S.
    et al. (2006). Randomized trail of behavioral activation, cognitive
    therapy, and anti-depressant medication in the acute treatment of
    adults with major depression. *Journal of Consulting and Clinical
    Psychology* 74, 658–670.
2   Veal, D. and Willson, R. (2008). *Manage You Mood*. London: Constable
    & Robinson.
3   Ross, J. (2003). *The Mood Cure.* London: Thorsons. Although it is a
    bit hyped it seems good to me on the issues of diet and supple-
    ments – I found it interesting and well written, although the evidence
    is still developing so I can't vouch for that.
4   A good book is Dr Alan Stewart's *Tired All the Time.*

Chapter 13: Stop criticizing and bullying yourself: How to treat yourself with compassion

1   Self-criticism has been associated with a lot of mental health diffi-
    culties including eating disorders, alcohol problems, anxiety and
    of course depression. For a technical account of this, see Gilbert,
    P. and Irons, C. (2005). Focused therapies and compassionate mind
    training for shame and self attacking. In Gilbert, P. (ed.) *Compassion:
    Conceptualisations, Research and Use in Psychotherapy* (pp. 263–325).
    London: Routledge. We also know that self-criticism is not just about
    negative thoughts but it is people's feelings about themselves that
    is crucial. See Whelton, W.J. and Greenberg, L.S. (2005). Emotion
    in self-criticism. *Personality and Individual Differences*, 38, 1583–1595.
    There are now many self-help books on self-criticism and how to
    heal it.

2   A classic text in this regard is Lasch, C. (1979). *Culture of Narcissism: American Life in an Age of Diminishing Expectations*. New York: Norton. See also McKinley, N.M. (1999). Women and objectified body consciousness: Mothers' and daughters' body experience in cultural, developmental and familial context. *Developmental Psychology* 35, 760–769.

    There have been many studies showing the negative effect of the media on self-esteem. See for example Mazzeo, S.E., Trace, S.E., Mitchell, K.S. and Walker Gow, R. (2007). Effects of a reality TV cosmetic surgery makeover program on eating disordered attitudes and behaviors. *Eating Behaviors* 8, 390–397. Basically these programmes can lead people to compare themselves unfavourably with others. James, O. (1997) *Britain on the Couch*. London: Arrow Books also goes into this in excellent detail and you can watch the videos of two documentaries on his website (*www.selfishcapitalist. com*).

3   Gilbert, P., Broomhead, C., Irons, C. et al. (2007). Striving to avoid inferiority: Scale development and its relationship to depression, anxiety and stress. *British Journal of Social Psychology* 46, 633–648.

4   Work by Cory Gelsma found that feeling less favoured as a child was highly linked to depression. Gilbert, P. and Gelsma, C. (1999). Recall of favouritism in relation to psychopathology. *British Journal of Clinical Psychology* 38, 357–373.

5   Bernice Andrews has looked at the relationship between child sexual abuse and chronic depression. See for example Andrews, B. (1998). Shame and childhood abuse. In Gilbert, P. and Andrews, B. (eds) *Shame: Interpersonal Behavior, Psychopathology and Culture* (pp. 176–190). New York: Oxford University Press.

6   There are now many reports and self-help books on the theme of childhood sexual abuse. One that gives a number of exercises to work through is Ainscough, C. and Toon, K. (2000). *Breaking Free Workbook: Practical Help for Survivors of Child Sexual Abuse*. London: Sheldon.

7   Gilbert, P., Clarke, M., Kempel, S., Miles, J.N.V. and Irons, C. (2004).

Criticizing and reassuring oneself: An exploration of forms, style and reasons in female students. *British Journal of Clinical Psychology* 43, 31–50. For a review see Gilbert and Irons (2005), mentioned earlier.

Chapter 14: Depressed ways of experiencing ourselves: How compassionate re-focusing can change our experience
See the notes for Chapter 13.

Chapter 15: Further ways of helping ourselves change
See the notes for Chapters 9–13.

Chapter 16: Approval, subordination and bullying: Key issues in relationships

1 This chapter follows a clinical and evolutionary approach to the importance of relationships: see Gilbert, P. (2007). *Psychotherapy and Counselling for Depression*. London: Sage. There is much research now showing how relationships are important in depression. One well-researched approach to depression is McCullough, J.P.Jr (2000). *Treatment for Chronic Depression: Cognitive Behavioral Analysis System of Psychotherapy.* New York: Guilford. This teaches people what to think about and how to act in relationships in order to feel more in control and build helpful relationships. There is a good review of evidence of the importance of relationships to our well-being in Gurman, A.S. and Jacobson, N.S. (eds.) (2002). *Clinical Handbook of Couple Therapy* (3rd edition). New York: Guilford Press. It is also the case that many of our emotions are evolved to operate in and through social relationships. See for example Tracy, J.L., Robins, R.W. and Tangney, J.P. (eds) (2007). *The Self-Conscious Emotions: Theory and Research* (pp. 283–309). New York: Guilford.

Social neuroscience is a new branch of neuroscience that focuses on the importance of relationships to the way our brain works and our mental health. A good introduction to this is Cacioppo, J.T., Berston, G.G., Sheridan, J.F. and McClintock, M.K. (2000). Multilevel integrative analysis of human behavior: Social neuroscience and the complementing nature of social and biological approaches. *Psychological Bulletin* 126, 829–843. You might also enjoy Cozolino, L.

(2007). *The Neuroscience of Human Relationships: Attachment and the Developing Brain*. New York: Norton. You might also want to revisit Chapter 2. This chapter just touches the tip of a large and growing iceberg of knowledge about the importance of how we respond to and think about social relationships.

2   A very readable introduction to mind reading for the general reader is O'Connell, S. (1998). *Mindreading: How We Learn to Love and Lie*. New York: Arrow Books. There is also a new therapy approach called mentalizing which helps people to develop their abilities for empathy and to work out why and what others are thinking and feeling. For example, people can be unkind if they are tired or stressed, and it may have nothing to do with oneself. Some people really struggle to consider what might be going on in the minds of other people: see Allen, J.G. and Fonagy, P. (eds.) (2007). *Handbook of Mentalization-Based Treatment*. Chichester: Wiley. If you want to explore the neuroscience and some of the new work on mirror neurons try Decety, J. and Jackson, P.L. (2004). The functional architecture of human empathy. *Behavioral and Cognitive Neuroscience Reviews* 3, 71–100. All these are really important to how we think about the minds of others and cannot be understood only in cognitive terms.

3   A key researcher in this area is John Gottman who studied various physiological responses when couples interact as ways of seeing which couples would stay together and which break up. See Gottman, J.M., Driver, J. and Tabares, A. (2002). Building the sound marital house: An empirically derived couple therapy. In Gurman A.S. and Jacobson, N.S. (eds). *Clinical Handbook of Couple Therapy* (3rd edition, pp.373–399). New York: Guilford.

4   There is increasing evidence that feeling trapped is a common experience in depression (including feeling trapped by the illness). Gilbert, P. and Gilbert, J. (2003). Entrapment and arrested fight and flight in depression: An exploration using focus groups. *Psychology and Psychotherapy: Theory Research and Practice* 76, 173–188. Feelings of entrapment are now strongly linked to depression as both cause and consequence. See Brown, G.W., Harris, T.O. and Hepworth, C. (1995). Loss, humiliation and entrapment among women developing

depression: A patient and non-patient comparison. *Psychological Medicine* 25, 7–21. See also our own research: Gilbert, P., Gilbert, J. and Irons, C. (2004). Life events, entrapments and arrested anger in depression. *Journal of Affective Disorders* 79, 149–160.

5   Wearden, A.J., Tarrier, N., Barrowclough, C., Zastowny, T.R. and Rahil, A.A. (2000). A review of expressed emotion research in health care. *Clinical Psychology Review* 5, 633–666.

Chapter 17: Understanding and healing shame in depression

1   There has recently been a major research interest in shame. There is a very good overview in Tracy, Robins and Tangney (2007), mentioned earlier. You might also be interested in Gilbert, P. and Andrews, B. (eds) (1998). *Shame: Interpersonal Behavior, Psychopathology and Culture.* New York: Oxford University Press and Gilbert, P. and Miles, J. (2002). *Body Shame.* London: Routledge.

2   Gilbert, P. (2009). *The Compassionate Mind: A New Approach to Life's Challenges.* London: Constable & Robinson.

3   Kaufman, G. (1989). *The Psychology of Shame.* New York: Springer.

4   Bernice Andrews has looked at the relationship between child sexual abuse and chronic depression. See for example Andrews, B. (1998). Shame and childhood abuse. In Gilbert, P. and Andrews, B. (eds) *Shame: Interpersonal Behavior, Psychopathology and Culture* (pp. 176–190). New York: Oxford University Press.

5   There are now many reports and self-help books on the theme of childhood sexual abuse. One that gives a number of exercises to work through is Ainscough, C. and Toon, K. (2000). *Breaking Free Workbook: Practical Help for Survivors of Child Sexual Abuse.* London: Sheldon.

Chapter 18: Understanding and coping with guilt

1   Tangney, J.P. and Dearing, R.L. (2002). *Shame and Guilt.* New York: Guilford Press. This is a very well written and accessible book that brings the reader up to date with a lot of research. See also Baumeister, R.F., Stillwell, A.M. and Heatherton, T.F. (1994). Guilt: an interpersonal approach. *Psychological Bulletin* 115, 243–267. A very interesting approach to guilt can be found in O'Connor, L.E. (2000). Pathogenic

beliefs and guilt in human evolution: Implications for psychotherapy. In Gilbert, P. and Bailey, K.G. (eds.) *Genes on the Couch: Explorations in Evolutionary Psychotherapy* (pp. 276–303). Hove: Brunner-Routledge. You may also be interested in Gilbert, P. (1997). The evolution of social attractiveness and its role in shame, humiliation, guilt and therapy. *British Journal of Medical Psychology* 70, 113–147. A review can be found in Gilbert, P. (2003). Evolution, social roles, and differences in shame and guilt. *Social Research*, 70, 1205–1230.

2   Hoffman, M.L. (1991). Empathy, social cognition and moral action. In Kurtines, W.M. and Gewirtz, J.L. (eds.) *Handbook of Moral Behavior and Development. Vol 1: Theory* (pp. 275–301) Hillsdale, NJ: Lawrence Erlbaum Associates.

3   Gilbert, P. (2007). *Psychotherapy and Counselling for Depression* (3rd edition). London: Sage.

4   Gilbert, P. (2009). *The Compassionate Mind: A New Approach to Facing the Challenges of Life.* London: Constable & Robinson.

5   O'Connor, L.E. (2000). Pathogenic beliefs and guilt in human evolution: Implications for psychotherapy, In Gilbert, P. and Bailey, K.G. (eds.) *Genes on the Couch: Explorations in Evolutionary Psychotherapy* (pp. 276–303). Hove: Brunner-Routledge.

6   Yalom, I.D. (1980). *Existential Psychotherapy.* New York:Basic Books.

7   Baumeister, R.F., Stillwell, A.M. and Heatherton, T.F. (1994). Guilt: an interpersonal approach. *Psychological Bulletin,* 115, 243–267.

Chapter 19: Coping with anger

1   Gilbert, P., Irons, C., Olsen, K., Gilbert, J. and McEwan, K. (2006). Interpersonal sensitivities: Their link to mood, anger and gender. *Psychology and Psychotherapy: Theory Research and Practice* 79, 37–51. We have also found that if one broods on one's resentment this is linked to depressed mood too: Gilbert, P., Cheung, M., Irons, C., and McEwan, K. (2005). An exploration into depression focused and anger focused rumination in relation to depression in a student population. *Behavioral and Cognitive Psychotherapy* 33, 273–283.

2   Some important work has looked at how we express anger to those above and those below us in the pecking order. Fournier, M.A.,

Moskowitz, D.S. and Zuroff, D.C. (2002). Social rank strategies in hierarchical relationships. *Journal of Personality and Social Psychology* 83, 425–433.

3   Our own and other people's research has also shown that depressed people can feel angry but can be frightened of it and try to suppress it. See Gilbert, P., Gilbert, J. and Irons, C. (2004). Life events, entrapments and arrested anger in depression. *Journal of Affective Disorders* 79, 149–160. Dana Jack has also outlined some fascinating and important issues about the fear of anger in her work on silencing the self. See for example Jack, D.C. (1992). *Silencing The Self: Women and Depression.* New York: HarperCollins (Paperback).

There are many books on learning to recognize and cope with anger.

Chapter 20: From anger to assertiveness and forgiveness

1   You can read more on the work of Arrindell and his colleagues on assertiveness in a number of papers stretching back to the 1980s. Here are a couple to follow up: Arrindell, W.A., Bridges, K.R., van der Ende, J. et al. (2001).Normative studies with the Scale for Interpersonal Behavior (SIB): II. US students. A cross-cultural comparison with Dutch data. *Behavior Research and Therapy* 39, 1461–1479; Arrindell, W. A., van der Ende, J., Sanderman, R., Oosterhof, L., Stewart, R., and Lingsma, M.M. (1999). Normative studies with the Scale for Interpersonal Behavior (SIB): I. Nonpsychiatric social skills trainees. *Personality and Individual Differences* 27, 417–431. See also *http://share.eldoc.ub.rug.nl/FILES/root2/2005/Normstwit/Arrindell_ 2005_Personal_Indiv_Differen.pdf.*

2   Bono, G. and McCullough M.E. (2006). Positive responses to benefit and harm: Bringing forgiveness and gratitude into cognitive psychotherapy. *Journal of Cognitive Psychotherapy: An International Quarterly.* 20, 147–158. A helpful review chapter is Worthington, E.L., O'Connor, L.E., Berry, J.W., Sharp, C., Murray, R. and Yi, E. (2005). Compassion and forgiveness: Implications for psychotherapy. In Gilbert, P. (ed). *Compassion: Conceptualisations, Research and Use in Psychotherapy* (pp. 168–192). London: Routledge.

You will also find a lot on the Internet on forgiveness.

Chapter 21: Dealing with frustrations, disappointments and lost ideals

1 Many of the books by the Dalai Lama address these issues from a Buddhist point of view. Craib, I.(1994). *Importance of Disappointment*. London: Routledge is an interesting book outlining how and why disappointment and frustrations are actually key to our personal development; we should not see them as just bad things to be dealt with as they can give insight into our values and self. The late Dr Albert Ellis, a famous New York therapist, also wrote much on the issue of how we impose conditions on life with our insistence on 'must' and 'have to' and telling ourselves things are unbearable. He wrote many books. Dr Windy Dryden, a UK-based therapist, is also a prolific writer on this form of therapy and you will find many outlines of their work on the Internet.

Chapter 22: Summing up

1 Morgan, A.J. and Jorm, A. (2008). Self-help strategies that are help-ful for the subthreshold depression: A Delphi consensus. *Journal of Affective Disorders*. doi 10.1016.

2 Begley, S. (2007). *Train Your Mind, Change Your Brain*. New York: Ballantine Books. I discussed some of this information in Chapter 8. Another book you may want to look at is Doidge, N. (2007). *The Brain that Changes Itself; Stories of Personal Triumph from the Frontiers of Brain Science*. New York: Penguin.

Index

Note: page numbers in *italic* refer to illustrations or examples. The letter 't' after a page number refers to a table. Where more than one page number is listed against a heading, page numbers in **bold** indicate significant treatment of a subject